Gender and
Second-Temple Judaism

Gender and Second-Temple Judaism

Edited by Kathy Ehrensperger
and Shayna Sheinfeld

LEXINGTON BOOKS/FORTRESS ACADEMIC
Lanham • Boulder • New York • London

Published by Lexington Books/Fortress Academic
Lexington Books is an imprint of The Rowman & Littlefield Publishing Group, Inc.
4501 Forbes Boulevard, Suite 200, Lanham, Maryland 20706
www.rowman.com

6 Tinworth Street, London SE11 5AL, United Kingdom

Copyright © 2020 by The Rowman & Littlefield Publishing Group, Inc.

All rights reserved. No part of this book may be reproduced in any form or by any electronic or mechanical means, including information storage and retrieval systems, without written permission from the publisher, except by a reviewer who may quote passages in a review.

British Library Cataloguing in Publication Information Available

Library of Congress Cataloging-in-Publication Data Available

ISBN 978-1-9787-0786-3 (cloth)
ISBN 978-1-9787-0788-7 (pbk)
ISBN 978-1-9787-0787-0 (electronic)

For the Jewish matriarchs in my family
Great Grandma Rita - רבקה בת שרה - ז״ל
Grandma Mickey - מושקה בת רבקה - ז״ל
And my mother, Beverly - ברכה בת מושקה

~Shayna

To all my teachers who encouraged
and inspired me along the way.

~Kathy

Contents

Acknowledgments ix

Introduction
   Gender and Second-Temple Judaism: Challenges and Possibilities   1
   Shayna Sheinfeld

1 "The Brooten Phenomenon": Moving Women from the Margins in Second-Temple and New Testament Scholarship   23
   Sara Parks

2 Women Itinerants, Jesus of Nazareth, and Historical-Critical Approaches: Reevaluating the Consensus   45
   Amy-Jill Levine

3 Paul, the Man: Enigmatic Images   65
   Kathy Ehrensperger

4 From Pain to Redemption: 1 Timothy 2:15 in its Jewish Context   85
   Sarah E. G. Fein

5 Traversing the Boundaries of Gender: Rebekah's Usurpation of the Patriarchal Role in the Book of *Jubilees*   101
   Chontel Syfox

6 The Reinforcement of Patriarchy and the (De)Construction of Gender Roles in *Jubilees*' Reception of the Jacob-Esau-Narrative   119
   Daniel Vorpahl

7 Women and Gender in the Gospel of John   137
   Adele Reinhartz

8	The Framing of Female Knowledge in the Prologue of the Sibylline Oracles *Francis Borchardt*	155
9	Female Authorship in Jewish Antiquity? *Gerbern S. Oegema*	171
10	Pheroras' Wife: A Pharisee Woman *Tal Ilan*	185
11	Cross-dressing Zealots in Josephus's War Account *Gabriella Gelardini*	197
12	Female Officiants in Second-Temple Judaism *Angela Standhartinger*	219

| Index | 241 |
| About the Contributors | 247 |

Acknowledgments

The contributions contained in this volume were first offered at the Tenth Nangeroni Meeting of the Enoch Seminar, "Gender and Second Temple Judaism." We would like to warmly thank all the scholars who contributed to this meeting, including: Matthew Anderson, Gabriele Boccaccini, Catherine Bonesho, Francis Borchardt, Daniel Boyarin, William S. Campbell, Anna Cwikla, Sari Fein, Gabriella Gelardini, R. Gillian Glass, Betsy Halpern-Amaru, Andrew Higginbotham, Walter Homolka, Juni Hoppe, Tal Ilan, Anders Klostergaard Petersen, A.-J. Levine, Gerbern Oegema, Sara Parks, Annette Yoshiko Reed, Adele Reinhards, Bettina Schwarz, Joshua Scott, Angela Standhartinger, Ekkehard Stegemann, Chontel Syfox, Moshe Taube, Hanna Tervanotko, Jacqueline Vayntrub, Daniel Vorpahl, and Meredith Warren.

The meeting took place 17–21 June 2018 in Rome and was graciously hosted by Professor Bettina Schwarz at Casa Schwarz whose hospitality was beyond compare and who contributed significantly to the constructive and stimulating atmosphere in which the discussions were conducted. We are grateful for the support of the Enoch Seminar, the Encyclopedia of Early Jewish-Christian Relations, Thyssen Stiftung, the Alessandro Nangeroni International Endowment, and Pontificio Istituto Biblico, all of whom made the meeting possible. We also appreciate the support of the Michigan Center for Early Christian Studies. Special thanks goes to Gabriele Boccaccini for recognizing the importance of this topic and supporting our vision to support this seminar and our subsequent meeting on Gender and Late Antiquity (Berlin, July 2021) as Nangeroni Meetings of the Enoch Seminar.

It would be difficult to fully express our appreciation to Joshua Scott and Juni Hoppe, who worked hard to keep us on track and to keep things running smoothly before and during the seminar, and to handle many of the essential tasks that came up during the meeting—we could not have done this without your support. Juni Hoppe was an invaluable help in the process of getting this volume into shape, by formatting and indexing it. Joshua Scott also supported us during the publication process. We are incredibly grateful to both of them. Thanks also goes to Neil Elliott at Lexington/Fortress Academic for accepting this volume for publication.

Introduction

Gender and Second-Temple Judaism
Challenges & Possibilities[1]
Shayna Sheinfeld

INTRODUCTION

It was at the third Nangeroni meeting of the Enoch Seminar in June 2014 that Kathy Ehrensperger and I first talked about the idea of a Nangeroni meeting with a focus on gender. Initially we were hesitant as to whether this would be a good idea—after all, each Enoch seminar should already address gender in some form or fashion, as a matter of course. After some discussion, however, we agreed that the topic needed to be addressed outright; otherwise any discussion of gender ends up relegated *just* to a paper, an aside, or viewed as a niche topic.[2] Kathy and I decided to co-chair the seminar on Gender and Second-Temple Judaism with the hope and intention of moving the scholarly discussion of gender in antiquity forward, in its myriad conceptions and portrayals. Our hope, of course, was not that gender is *only* discussed at this seminar or among our colleagues who attended. Our hope was that while we moved the scholarly conversation forward at this seminar, it would follow into other Enoch Seminars and wider scholarly discussions.

Setting a title and focus for our meeting was more challenging than we expected. It was important that we encouraged a wide range of approaches to texts and that this should not only be a place for scholars interested in questions of women's history or feminist scholars—although both were quite welcome. Our interest was to focus on the variety of gendered experience and evidence (e.g., literary, inscriptional, material) in the ancient world. Surprisingly, deciding how to delimit the time period was nearly as challenging as deciding how to title the meeting. We recognize that the timelines we draw in our fields are useful to limit the evidence we work with, but also that they are arbitrary. Should we exclude second-century CE evidence because the temple was destroyed in the first century? Do we exclude Christianity when we know that the earliest Jesus followers were Jews? We decided that a simple title was best, with the hopes of being as open and inclusive as possible with what we mean when we say "Second-Temple Judaism." Below I address some of the issues with the terminology of the chosen title.

TERMINOLOGY

My goal in addressing terminology (e.g., "canon," "Judaism") here is to establish that these categories are not foregone conclusions but are themselves subjective constructions. Likewise, analyzing the category of "gender" is an attempt to normalize it as a topic that is well within mainstream Second-Temple and New Testament studies: Gender is not—and should not be treated as a niche category, but as with the other terms explored here, it is a necessary area of critical examination by scholars (regardless of their own gender identities) within our discipline.

"Gender"

Gender is a cultural construct.[3] Applying the terminology of "gender" to our ancient evidence presents challenges on the most basic level. Are we attempting to reconstruct gender as it might have been constructed in the ancient world? Are we applying our contemporary constructions of gender to the ancient evidence, with the caveat that we are aware of the anachronism if we do so? Normative gender is often presented as a binary, a discursive production of the masculine and the feminine; but in lived experience, gender is clearly *not* binary, but a spectrum. In antiquity, as today, there may be feminine-presenting men or masculine-presenting women. There may be someone whose gender is not easily defined: e.g., trans, nonbinary, gender queer, etc., and we need to be aware of gender constructs in antiquity, as well as breaks from normative portrayals of gender. Our challenge is not just in methodology, which I will address shortly, but also in acknowledging our approach, our lenses, and attempting to own our blind spots in the analysis. "Gender" is deeply ambiguous as a signifier.[4]

Beyond the challenges of attempting to define, analyze, and deconstruct gender and related discourses is the intersectionality of our project at this seminar. If the ancient evidence is primarily written by and for men in a worldview that is not only inherently patriarchal, but intersectionally kyriarchal,[5] how do we "get at" the historical reality of the ancient figures? Privilege, whether in the form of gender identity, citizenship, socio-economic status, imperialism, etc., plays an active role in the material we examine and in those who are examining it. Take, for example, Paul's famous statement in Galatians 3:28, "There is no longer Jew or Greek, there is no longer slave or free, there is no longer male and female; for all of you are one in Christ Jesus."[6] Paul's statement seems to be describing a type of equality regardless of gender, status, or ethnicity. Contextually Paul is removing these identity markers only while the assembly is gathered *in Christ*; Paul does not expect these societal markers to be erased permanently in his contemporaneous world.[7] At play here, then, is not just an equalizing *in Christ* according to Paul, but also an acknowledgement of the intersectionality of gender, ethnicity, socio-economic class, etc., which existed in the Roman world in the first century CE.[8]

"Second-Temple Judaism"

The delineation of our meeting as considering gender within the category called "Second-Temple Judaism" is problematic on at least two counts. First, presenting our discussion as being about "Judaism" suggests that Judaism is a thing that can be defined, described, and analyzed separately from other things, for instance other categories such as "Christianity" or "Paganism."[9] However, the members of the Enoch Seminar have long acknowledged that one cannot and should not attempt to identify Judaism as if it is not part and parcel of the Hellenistic and Roman worlds in which it actively engaged, just as the early Jesus movement was a part of Judaism and the larger cultural milieu in which it arose.[10]

Second, we must describe what we mean when we talk specifically about the period of the Second Temple. The end of the Babylonian Exile and the rebuilding of the temple in Jerusalem, finished circa 515 BCE, serve as the beginning of what is officially labeled the Second-Temple Period. However, the Persian period (~539–333 BCE) itself offers even less to scholars than usual in extant evidence, and most discussions of "Second-Temple Judaism" focus on the Hellenistic period, marked by Alexander the Great's conquest of much of the Mediterranean, circa 333 BCE. The end of the Second Temple period is sometimes said to end no later than the end of the first Jewish revolt against Rome (73 CE), but usually dated a few years earlier with the destruction of the temple by Titus and his armies in 70 CE; the majority of the work examined in this volume falls between these dates of 333 BCE–70 CE. However, these are indeed arbitrary dates. As historians we can see that these dates mark major events in history, which affect the type of evidence we have, but while Alexander the Great's conquests had wide-reaching consequences for some peoples, it was the drawn-out process of Hellenization which followed that created the major cultural shifts we see in this earlier period. For instance, 2 Maccabees, a piece of propaganda supporting the Hasmonean dynasty, highlights how those Jews who keep God's laws fight with God's support. While clearly depicting the piety of Judah Maccabee and his supporters, the text, written in the late second century BCE, is also written in florid Greek and emphasizes Greek philosophical ideals to support the Jewish commitment to God's commandments.[11] The Jewish piety represented in 2 Maccabees was shaped by the Greek-influenced culture of which Judaism of the second century BCE was a part.

Likewise, while the destruction of the second temple was certainly cataclysmic for many Jews, it did not end Judaism "as it was known"; for example, the apocalypse of 4 Ezra and the Bar Kokhba revolt (132–135 CE) both highlight Jewish continuity post-destruction.[12] While rabbinic texts attempt to paint a picture of continuity from Moses to the rabbis, suggesting that there was a seamless transition from the Second Temple into the Rabbinic period, recent scholarship in the discipline of Rabbinics suggests that the rabbis were one of multiple competing types of Judaism, and did not develop as the Jewish authority until very late.[13] Instead, the evidence from the period between the first Jewish revolt against Rome and the Rabbinic and Patristic periods highlights that while the destruction of the second temple did indeed affect many Jews, many elements of Jewishness existed in continuity with the period before the destruction—including continuity of certain problems, such as leadership.[14] Thus the title of our seminar and this volume as "Gender and Second-Temple Judaism," while meant to be broadly conceived, is in itself an arbitrary line in the sand that we expect to be crossed at times.

These artificial boundaries, while perceived as necessary for logistics and communication, can lead to additional artificial categories, such as the dichotomy of "Judaism" and "Hellenism" that I mentioned above, or the idea that somehow Judaism, and later Christianity, have "pure" versions that are separate from the Hellenistic and Roman worlds in which they existed. We must do our best to acknowledge the arbitrary boundaries and anachronistic categories that we insert on our ancient evidence as scholars in the twenty-first century, and that shape our scholarship on this material.

"Judaism"

I will not review the numerous articles and books that have been written on the discussion of how we can or cannot define "Jew," "Judaean," and "Judaism" here.[15] I would like to point instead to several more recent critiques of the easy way we use these categories as if they are stable. Cynthia Baker, for instance, notes that many of the recent discussions of Judaean versus Jew or of ethnicity versus religion in antiquity are actually reflected through a Pauline dichotomy of law versus faith—and that the discussion itself is really a reading of ancient Judaism through a post-Pauline Christian lens.[16] This is not surprising, as *Wissenschaft des Judentums* is tied very closely with the larger study of religion, which itself originated in Christian spheres.[17]

Instead of getting tied up in a discussion of what/who is a Jew, which could easily be a seminar in and of itself, I would urge the resistance of defined categories and acknowledge, at a minimum, that there is something that can be identified as Judaism, people who can be identified as Jews—in both the religious and the ethnic sense—and it is to these people, this category, again broadly construed, and the evidence they left behind that we seek to analyze in our seminar.

Canon

The canon is another area where we must be wary of how we step. Outdated terms like "intertestamental," referring usually to apocryphal and pseudepigraphic texts, suggest that somehow the material was written as if the Hebrew Bible and Christian testament were already canon, although there is plenty of evidence to suggest that, especially for the various parts of the Hebrew Bible, we are dealing with a much later process of canonization, not to mention that most of the texts in the New Testament had not been written by 70. Most scholars now agree that the Torah was canonized no earlier than the Babylonian Exile, but the process likely continued even into the Persian period.[18] One early (indirect) reference to the beginnings of the concept of Tanakh (but not to its boundaries) is Ben Sira, dated to the early second century BCE, who makes several mentions of the law and prophets and "other books" in his prologue:

> Many great teachings have been given to us through *the law and the prophets and the others that followed them,* and for these we should praise Israel for instruction and wisdom. Now, those who read the scriptures must not only themselves understand them, but must also as lovers of learning be able through the spoken and written word to help the outsiders. So my grandfather Jesus, who had devoted himself especially to the reading of *the law and the prophets and the other books of our ancestors,* and had acquired considerable proficiency in them, was himself also *led to write something pertaining to instruction and wisdom,* so that by becoming familiar also with his book those who love learning might make even greater progress in living according to the law. You are invited therefore to read it with goodwill and attention, and to be indulgent in cases where, despite our diligent labor in translating, we may seem to have rendered some phrases imperfectly. For what was originally expressed in Hebrew does not have exactly the same sense when translated into another language. Not only this book, but even *the law itself, the prophecies, and the rest of the books* differ not a little when read in the original. (Sirach, Prologue. Emphasis added)

Ben Sira mentions the law, which most likely refers to the books of the Torah, but he also mentions the "prophets"/ "prophecies" and "the rest of the books," as well as further writings by his grandfather. Some scholars have understood this mention of three distinct types of books to reflect the tripartite classification of Torah—Prophets—Writings.[19] However, it is more likely that beyond the law, Ben Sira's mention of the prophets/prophecies and other books are in references to unspecified prophetic texts and other scripture—scripture being broadly understood as texts that a particular community holds as sacred. There is no reason to assume that he is speaking of a canon of texts. Similarly, in late first-century texts found in what we now call the New Testament, there is mention of the law and the prophets (e.g., John 1:45, Acts 28:23, etc.). As with Ben Sira, the reference to the prophets is likely dealing not with a canon, but again, to a flexible body of texts that are considered sacred by various communities in varying degrees—in other words, scripture, not canon. Thus, we must be careful with our terminology and our assumptions of canonical versus noncanonical texts, and the inherent prioritizing of canonical texts that our discipline has inherited.[20]

Our volume, then, begins with a conscientious look at some of the problems of terminology that we have inherited and with which we must contend. From terms such as "gender" and "Judaism" to the dating of the Second-Temple period, and the highly problematic category of canon, before we even begin our analyses of literary and material evidence, we must be aware of the hermeneutical presuppositions that our disciplines bring to our work.[21] I will now turn to a consideration of some of the methodological issues we face as we consider gender in Second-Temple Judaism.

METHODOLOGY

Beyond the issues of terminology, discussions of methodology are of utmost importance to this project. When the majority of the sources—literary or material—were likely produced by and for men, examining them with an eye toward questions of gender is challenging.[22] How does one reconstruct ancient ideas around gender, or the historical lived experiences of women, in a situation where our evidence is already so biased as to border at times on non-existent?

Literary Analysis

One methodological approach is to keep the analysis at the literary level. One can examine a text and determine the role that women or gender plays *in the text*. For instance, we could examine the portrayal of the transformation of the woman in the late first/early second-century Jewish apocalypse 4 Ezra. In 4 Ezra 9:26–10:59, the prophetic figure of Ezra is eating the plants of a field untouched by humans as commanded by the angel.[23] He is then joined by a woman who tells him that she is in mourning because of the death of her son in his wedding chamber. Ezra chastises the woman, reminding her of the grand scale of the destruction of Zion which affects all Israel, as compared to her individual experience. Suddenly she is transformed into a city. The angel Uriel arrives to act as the *angelus interpres*, explaining the woman's story to Ezra as an analogy for the history of Zion and Israel, with her final transformation being equivalent to the eschatological Zion. In an example narrative such as this, attempting to reconstruct the lives of real women will not lead to fruitful results. Instead, comparative investigations of literary and material evidence where cities are portrayed as women will yield more rewarding analyses.[24]

Applying literary criticism to our texts is not only useful for comparative literary purposes, however. Examining ideas such as the personified Zion (or Sophia/Wisdom) takes seriously the idea that ancient peoples were capable of creating and enjoying—or savvily wielding—complex metaphors and symbolic ideas, and that this language expresses broader cultural conceptions of women. Likewise, literary criticism may be useful for uncovering the aims of the author(s), the (perceived) concerns of ancient communities, and for discovering and exploring intertextuality among myriad texts. Therefore, while this type of analysis does not assist directly with reconstructing the lives of ancient people, it does assist in providing cultural context for how individuals are portrayed and perceived as symbols, what those symbols might mean, defining gender norms, and for reconstructing the author's agenda and/or the intended audience.

Moving from Literary to Socio-Historical

Not all texts related to gender are clearly symbolic, however. Another methodological challenge is moving from a literary analysis to the realm of the historical. Shifting from the written words of literary evidence regarding women and gender to the goal of the historical reconstruction of women and of ancient gender dynamics is fraught with challenges and caveats. We cannot simply take what is written about women or femininity and masculinity and derive direct historical conclusions from the sources; the author(s), the production of the evidence, its genre, provenance, dating, language, intended audience, and more all affect the potential conclusions we can draw from the evidence itself. For instance, take Juvenal's sixth *Satire*, which represents a critique of Roman women.[25] In his description of their celebration of the *Bona Dea* festival, Juvenal depicts women of all classes participating in indiscriminate lust and copious sexual activity. Of particular interest is a passage near the end where he describes a Jewish woman:

> A palsied Jewess puts down her hay-box and comes a-begging, whispering secretly into her ear. She interprets the laws of Jerusalem, she is the priestess of the tree, who truly conveys the will of highest heaven. She too gets something, but less, for the Jews will sell you whatever view of a dream you like for a couple of coppers.[26]

If we were to take Juvenal's depiction of this Jewish woman at face value, we would note some rather interesting "facts": that she is attending the *Bona Dea* festival—a ritual dedicated to a deity other than the Jewish God, that she will read fortunes for money, although her fortune reading is made up to suit the customer, that she is a priestess and an interpreter of the laws of the Jews. While there may be truths hidden within this depiction (e.g., perhaps there were women who interpreted Torah; perhaps some people who told fortunes for money were Jews/Jewish women; perhaps some Jews participated in Roman religious celebrations, etc.), it is clear even beyond the name of the poems as *Satires* that Juvenal is using the "Jewess" to play on stereotypes and tell a story about the supposed insatiability of all women—his goal is entertainment for men, not to offer a historical report of the *Bona Dea* festivities or report on Jewish women.

Even with this caveat that the majority of our texts were written by men, for men, we can, however, draw careful if limited conclusions about women and about gender norms in the Second-Temple period. One possible approach is to employ numerous hermeneutical lenses to the text. Any lens through which we approach a text should be acknowledged, since there is the strong possibility of bringing anachronism to the reading. Within the academy, the historical-critical model is perhaps the most common, although it has not been without its recent critics.[27] This often-unacknowledged lens allows for a critical literary analysis combined with an effort to understand the text's *Sitz im Leben*. For example, one can apply the historical-critical lens to an examination of Paul's authentic letters, where he greets numerous named women as leaders and apostles within his assemblies. In Paul's letter to the Romans (~57–58 CE), Paul notes Phoebe, a *diakonos* (16:1), Priscilla, who together with her husband Aquila is a co-worker of Paul (16:3),[28] Mary (16:6), Junia (16:7) with her male companion Andronicus who are apostles and have been in prison with Paul, Tryphena and Tryphosa, and Persis (16:12), etc. These numerous mentions suggest that Paul accepted and expected women's active participation and leadership at all levels in his understanding of the early

Jesus movement. Applying the same lens to the later Pastoral Epistles allows us to see how certain authors were working hard to counteract women's leadership within certain communities. First Timothy discusses leadership roles and their qualifications, such as the *episkopos*, who must be

> above reproach, married only once, temperate, sensible, respectable, hospitable, an apt teacher, not a drunkard, not violent but gentle, not quarrelsome, and not a lover of money. He must manage his own household well, keeping his children submissive and respectful in every way." (1 Tim 3:2–4)

and that of the position of *diakonos* which must be

> serious, not double-tongued, not indulging in much wine, not greedy for money; they must hold fast to the mystery of the faith with a clear conscience. And let them first be tested; then, if they prove themselves blameless, let them serve as deacons. (1 Tim 3:8–10)

Following these job requirements, the author of 1 Timothy proceeds to mention how "women likewise must be serious, not slanderers, but temperate, faithful in all things" (1 Tim 3:11).

While scholars disagree on whether this depiction of women describes women as *diakonoi* since it follows the job description, most scholars think that it does not, in fact, support women in this leadership role.[29] Scholars using the historical-critical lens, then, are able to examine 1 Timothy in its context; this helps us see that it could not have been written by Paul but that it fits very well among second-century writings.

The gender-critical lens allows us to focus both on women as well as the patriarchal structures that are explicit and/or implicit in the evidence. The book of Judith, for example, was likely written during the Hasmonean period.[30] Judith, a pious and wealthy Jewish widow, lives in Bethulia, a city besieged by the general Holofernes (7:1). The town elders decide that since the water supply is cut off because of the siege, they will surrender in five days if divine help does not come (7:29–31). Judith chastises the elders for their lack of faith in God and for putting a human time limit on divine intervention (8:9–27). Judith instead takes matters into her own hands, getting dressed up and taking her enslaved woman—often translated as maid[31]—out of the city and into the camp of the enemy, where she seduces the general into drinking so much that he passes out (10:1–12:16). Judith then beheads Holofernes, hides his head in a basket, and returns to Bethulia (13:1–11). In the morning when her act is discovered, the armies are in disarray and flee, freeing Bethulia of its besiegement (14:11–15:7). Judith then returns to her home with her maid, taking no other husband and dying with great honor (16:21–25).

Through a gender critical lens of generosity, Judith can be seen as a woman who takes matters into her own hands when the men responsible for the well-being of the people are too afraid. Judith's actions show agency in her decision to go find and kill Holofernes despite the dangers, as well as her cleverness at managing to seduce him into inebriation without putting herself in a position where her own piety and chastity as a widow could be questioned. Judith here can be seen as a representation for what a woman in this situation might do, and also as a representation for what Israel as a collective might be capable of—after all, the name Judith does in fact mean Judah or Judea/Israel.

A gender-critical lens of suspicion, however, critiques the author's use of the character of Judith. While she does step outside the gender norms for women in that period, she both comes from and returns to those norms in the house of her late husband; for instance, she never sexually engages with another man—including Holofernes. On the part of the author, using a widow's sexuality to entice Holofernes is not as problematic as it would have been had she been a virgin or a married woman whose husband was alive. Through this lens Judith is seen as someone who briefly breaks out of approved Second-Temple gender norms but in doing so only reinforces them by returning to them willingly at the end: she only has agency as a matter of desperation and as an aberration,[32] and to point out the cowardice of the men. Her womanhood shames them.

Broadening beyond feminist interpretive lenses, which seek to uncover the histories and analyze the fictional representations of women, the gender-critical lens also includes the analysis of the construction of masculinity. Contemporary notions of gender affect the often-unconscious hermeneutics scholars apply to their analyses of not only female figures but also male ones. Ancient masculinity, very much like ancient ethnic identity, should be viewed, in the words of Caroline Johnson Hodge, as "a process [and] a perspective on the world, rather than a thing that exists independent of human arguments."[33] In addition to expanding our knowledge of the ancient world, masculinity studies move the study of gender beyond the study of women and show us that ancient men were as embedded within kyriarchal structures of oppression and domination as were ancient women. By analyzing the male figures through a gender-critical lens, scholars are able to better understand ancient texts and contexts; for instance, through considering Stoic constructions of masculinity, scholars are able to see that writers like Paul are, at times explicitly, contesting imperial definitions of manliness, and that alternative masculinities compete within our texts.[34] These studies push scholars who might otherwise be reticent to consider gender (or only consider it as an optional topic) to begin to internalize the concept that gender is not a concept that only applies to women, but that constructions of gender are at play among all of our ancient subjects and indeed all of our modern researchers, and that gender studies and/or feminist and other intersectional hermeneutics (e.g., post-colonial, marxist, queer, etc.) inevitably contribute to a better understanding of the ancient world.

Another methodological tool is the location of slippages, which can be found through close, careful reading. A "slippage" is a word used by Elisabeth Schüssler Fiorenza to indicate "small kernels of reality indicating the real-life struggle of women that are embedded in an androcentric text."[35] Of course slippages are useful for historical reconstruction beyond questions of gender, but they are particularly useful in attempts to glean information about women and gender in the ancient world. For example, in *Amores* 1.14, the Roman poet Ovid (43 BCE –17/18 CE) is describing the disastrous situation with Corinna's (his mistress in this poem) hair:

> How many times did I tell you—"Stop dyeing your hair!"
> Now there's nothing left to color.
> If only you'd left it alone. No one had hair like yours.
> It tumbled down full to your hips.
>
> [. . .]
>
> Now patiently they endured the rack of hot curling irons as you twisted them into ringlets.
> Again and again I cried—"It's a crime, a crime to singe them!"
> Is your heart cast-iron? Have mercy on your own head.
> Don't force the beauty nature gave you.
> What a perm couldn't learn from your natural wave.
>
> [. . .]
>
> Now the spoils of our triumphant armies will save you;
> You'll wear braids captured in Germany.
> But you'll blush every time someone raves about your new look:
> "I'm upstaged by a wig!" you'll cry.[36]

What Ovid also tells us as readers—an example of these slippages—is that at least some women, probably elite women, in ~first BCE–first CE might dye and/or curl their hair, and might wear wigs. Combined with information we might glean from material evidence, such as hair pins, hair nets, statues, frescoes, and mosaics, as well as other descriptions of women in literature from the same time period, we can begin to reconstruct an entire industry related to women and their hair. This example highlights the nuggets of information about the lived experience of women (and others on the gender spectrum) that can be found in the most unlikely of places, which may contribute to our reconstruction of life in the ancient world.

Material Evidence

I have already cited some examples of the use of material evidence above in my discussion about ancient hair styling. Here I would like to address this type of evidence directly. Material evidence can provide its own problems, such as one of provenance. For instance, Ross Kraemer breaks down the easy dichotomy between so-called Jewish and Christian depictions on epigraphs in her article "Jewish Tuna and Christian Fish."[37] She notes that while there are some symbols that seem to belong to one tradition (e.g., the chi rho as Christian, the menorah as Jewish, etc.), most images found on epigraphs are not of clear provenance and could be attributed to multiple religious categories. The same can be said of many of the names found on epigraphs.[38]

On the other hand, material evidence can work hand-in-hand with textual evidence to reinforce or challenge conclusion based on texts alone. For example, Davina C. Lopez discusses the gendered reading of Roman coins, focusing on how these coins communicate Roman imperial ideology using gendered images. Lopez notes that the

> Roman imperial emphasis on visual communication [. . .] makes the naturalization of ideas about institutions, cultural configurations and hierarchies intelligible to a wider range of people than just literate elites: all who could see and walk past a victory monument would probably be able to "read" it.[39]

Falling under these hierarchies would be constructions of gender and power, an example of which can be seen through the *Judaea Capta* coins. Lopez discusses this coin which depicts Roman domination over Judaea.

The man on the left side of the coin represents Roman imperial might, including the phallic positioning of the sword in scabbard at his left hip. He is in a position of domination, standing almost as tall as the palm tree, his left foot resting on his helmet. The palm tree is a common representation of the deserts in the Middle East, and the sitting woman is a personified Judaea. She is portrayed as subordinate, conquered, and Lopez argues, *feminized*.[40] Unlike with the discussion of Ovid's poem, hair pins, and statues above, the portrayal of the woman in this coin is an ideological representation, but one that can provide, with careful analysis, an understanding of the types of ideological gendering present in the late first century CE.

Just as Ovid's poem combined with our material evidence contributes a fuller understanding of women in the first centuries BCE/CE, Lopez's analysis of the *Judea Capta* coin offers an analysis of the feminized and

"IUDAEA CAPTA" by Patrick Rasenberg.

the conquered in the late first-century Roman empire. While much of our evidence is literary, and it is important to acknowledge and utilize a variety of methodological approaches to develop the most robust reconstruction of gender possible, it is essential that we do not neglect the material evidence in our reconstruction. It is only through close, careful analysis of *all* the available evidence that we will even begin to scratch the surface of gender within Second-Temple Judaism.

SUMMARY OF CONTRIBUTIONS

Our goal in putting together this collection of essays emerging from the 10th Nangeroni Meeting of the Enoch Seminar is to provide a snapshot of the state of the field of gender studies in relation to Second-Temple Judaism, and to highlight the importance of explicit methodology, while challenging anachronistic categories that we have inherited from our disciplines.

We begin the volume with an article by Sara Parks examining how the study of women and gender within early Judaism and Christian origins is considered "niche" and therefore not a part of mainstream scholarship. Parks nicknames this "The Brooten Phenomenon," after the ways in which Bernadette Brooten's work on women leaders in the ancient synagogue has been used (or not used) over the years.

In "Women Itinerants, Jesus of Nazareth, and Historical-Critical Approaches: Reevaluating the Consensus," Amy-Jill Levine reexamines the location of women in the ministry of Jesus, challenging scholars to refocus attention on women in the home rather than on the road where, she argues, many of the Galilean women followers of Jesus can be found.

Kathy Ehrensperger turns to masculinity studies in "Paul, the Man: Enigmatic Images." Here she focuses on the intersection of Paul's Jewish identity and Roman the perception of manliness, focusing in on evidence from Paul's letter to the Philippians. In "From Pain to Redemption: 1 Timothy 2:15 in its Jewish Context," Sarah E. G. Fein explores how the author of 1 Timothy understood Genesis 3:16 through Jewish interpretation that understood childbirth to be a redemptive act.

Chontel Syfox examines the figure of Rebekah in the book of Jubilees. She argues that the matriarch Rebekah temporarily transverses gender boundaries in the new episodes created in Jubilees by performing traditional masculine functions. Continuing with a focus on the book of Jubilees, Daniel Vorpahl compares the Jacob-Esau narrative in Genesis to its retelling in Jubilees in order to explore the development of the social construction of patriarchy and its impact on gender roles in the later text.

In "Women and Gender in the Gospel of John," Adele Reinhartz addresses three interrelated questions about the Gospel of John: first, should contemporary concerns about women's roles in churches be affected by the ancient evidence, specifically the Gospel of John? Second, is John's portrayal of Jesus's interactions with women a representation of first-century Judaism? Third, does the use of female figures and imagery in the Gospel of John contribute to our understanding of the early Jesus movement? Reinhartz concludes that the answer to these three questions is negative.

Francis Borchardt, in "The Framing of Female Knowledge in the Prologue of the Sibylline Oracles," explores how the prologue transmitted in two manuscripts of the Sibylline Oracles deemphasizes the divinatory performance of the Sibyl by proffering legitimization through male curation. Based on an examination of what is known about female authorship in the Hellenistic period, Gerbern Oegema examines whether 2 Maccabees 7 could have been written by a woman and concludes that the answer is yes.

In "Pheroras' Wife: A Pharisee Woman," Tal Ilan takes an in-depth look at the figure of Pheroras' wife, who, she argues, is a Pharisee. That this woman is never named is an intentional decision by Nicolaus of Damascus that serves as a sort of *damnatio memoriae* because of her actions against Herod, which is then carried over into Josephus's histories. In "Cross-dressing Zealots in Josephus's War Account," Gabriella Gelardini explores the gender dynamics present in the account of the cross-dressing Galilean Zealots found in Josephus's *Jewish War* 4.561–563. Finally, Angela Standhartinger explores how women, including Jewish women, acted as public liturgical officiants in ancient cultic settings.

This volume is intended to push the disciplinary boundaries of gender in the Second-Temple period. Beyond an incorporation of the examination of gender as it is portrayed in the literary and material evidence produced during this period, scholars in our disciplines must own our lenses and methodologies, and acknowledge that, while problematic, anachronisms and terminology can still be helpful at times in our attempt at reconstructing the ancient world through as many lenses as possible, including the lens of gender as an essential scholarly tool.

NOTES

1. I would like to thank Dr. Matthew Anderson for his excellent response of my paper at the 10th Enoch Nangeroni Meeting. I have incorporated many of Dr. Anderson's thoughtful comments into this introduction.
2. See Sara Parks, "The Brooten Phenomenon," in this volume.
3. See Judith Butler, *Gender Trouble: Feminism and the Subversion of Identity* (New York: Routledge, 2010), 8–10.
4. Virginia Burrus, "Mapping as Metamorphosis: Initial Reflections on Gender and Ancient Religious Discourse," in *Mapping Gender in Ancient Religious Discourse*, eds. T. Penner and C. Vander Stichele (Leiden: Brill, 2007), 1–2.
5. Kyriarchy is a neologism coined by Elisabeth Schüssler Fiorenza to recognize the complex intersectionality of dominion and submission within systems of power; *But She Said: Feminist Practices of Biblical Interpretation* (Boston: Beacon Press, 1992), 123.
6. All biblical and apocryphal translations are from the NRSV unless otherwise noted.
7. See Sara Parks, *Women in Q: Gender in the Rhetoric of Jesus* (Lanham, MD: Lexington Books/Fortress Academic, 2019), 165–66. I thank Dr. Parks for allowing me early access to this book. See also Karin B. Neutel, *A Cosmopolitan Ideal: Paul's Declaration "Neither Jew Nor Greek, Neither Slave Nor Free, Nor Male*

and Female" in the Context of First Century Thought (London: Bloomsbury T&T Clark, 2015).

8. While anachronistic, intersectionality is also a useful category for exploring the intersection of identities in the ancient world. The term was coined by Kimberlé Crenshaw, "Demarginalizing the Intersection of Race and Sex: A Black Feminist Critique of Antidiscrimination Doctrine, Feminist Theory and Antiracist Politics," *University of Chicago Legal Forum*: 1.8 (1989).

9. Daniel Boyarin is one scholar who discusses the problematic usage of the term "Judaism." See Daniel Boyarin, "Semantic Differences: or, 'Judaism'/'Christianity,'" in *The Ways that Never Parted: Jews and Christians in Late Antiquity and the Early Middle Ages*, eds. Adam H. Becker and Annette Yoshiko Reed (Minneapolis: Fortress Press, 2007), 65–87; Daniel Boyarin, *Judaism: The Genealogy of a Modern Notion* (New Brunswick: Rutgers University Press, 2018).

10. There is disagreement among scholars as to the best way to reference the earliest believers in Jesus. I use "Jesus movement" to signify this group whose beliefs and/or practices centered in some way on the figure who became known as Jesus Christ. I avoid "christ" language—christ or *christos* meaning anointed or messiah—in reference to this movement within the first century, as there is evidence that during this time period in Judaism there were multiple conceptions and claims of messianic status. Meredith J. C. Warren, "'When the Christ appears, will he do more signs than this man has done?' (John 7:31): Signs and the Messiah in the Gospel of John," in *Reading the Gospel of John's Christology as a Form of Jewish Messianism: Royal, Prophetic, and Divine Messiahs*, eds. Benjamin Reynolds and Gabriele Boccaccini (Leiden: Brill, 2018) 229–47. For a collection of primary sources on a messiah, see Gerbern S. Oegema, *The Anointed and His People: Messianic Expectations from Maccabees to Bar Kochba* (Sheffield: Sheffield Academic Press, 1998).

11. See Malka Z. Simkovich, "Greek Influence on the Composition of 2 Maccabees," *JSJ* 42 (2011): 293–310.

12. See, for instance, Hindy Najman's recent monograph, *Losing the Temple and Recovering the Future: An Analysis of 4 Ezra* (Cambridge: Cambridge University Press, 2014). On Bar Kokhba see, for instance, Menahem Mor, *The Second Jewish Revolt Against Rome: The Bar Kokhba Revolt 132–136 CE* (Boston: Brill, 2016).

13. Jeffrey L. Rubenstein, "Social and Institutional Settings of Rabbinic Literature," in *The Cambridge Companion to the Talmud and Rabbinic Literature*, eds. Charlotte E. Fonrobert and Martin S. Jaffee (Cambridge: Cambridge University Press, 2007), 70; Shayna Sheinfeld, "Crises of Leadership in the Post-Destruction Apocalypses of 4 Ezra and 2 Baruch" (PhD diss., McGill University, 2015).

14. Sheinfeld, "Crises of Leadership."

15. For example, see Shaye J.D. Cohen, *The Beginnings of Jewishness: Boundaries, Varieties, Uncertainties* (Berkeley: University of California Press, 1999); Daniel R. Schwartz, *Judeans and Jews: Four Faces of Dichotomy in Ancient Jewish History* (Toronto: University of Toronto Press, 2014); "Jew and Judean: A Forum on Politics and Historiography in the Translation of Ancient Texts," *Marginalia*, 26 August, 2014, https://marginalia.lareviewofbooks.org/jew-judean-forum/; Boyarin, *Judaism*.

16. Cynthia Baker, *Jew* (New Brunswick: Rutgers University Press, 2016), 33–46. While not the focus of this chapter, or the book, Baker also shares Daniel Schwartz's comment that in relation to women and Jews in antiquity, "there is a problem about women" (*Jew*, 27–33). For related discussions on the ever-changing category of "Jew" and "Judaism," see Leora Batnizky, *How Judaism Became a Religion: An Introduction to Modern Jewish Thought* (Princeton: Princeton University Press, 2013) and Steven Weitzman, *The Origins of the Jews: The Quest for Roots in a Rootless Age* (Princeton: Princeton University Press, 2017).

17. Kerstin von der Krone and Mirjam Thulin, "Wissenschaft in Context: A Research Essay on the Wissenschaft Des Judentums," *The Leo Baeck Institute Yearbook* 58.1 (2013): 249–80. doi:10.1093/leobaeck/ybt010.

18. See, for instance, Lee Martin McDonald and James A. Sanders (eds.), *The Canon Debate* (Peabody: Hendrickson Publishers, 2002).

19. See, for instance, the article by Julio C. Trebolle Barrera, "Origins of the Tripartite Old Testament Canon," in *The Canon Debate*, eds. Lee Martin McDonald and James A. Sanders (Peabody, MA: Hendrickson Publishers, 2002) 128–45.

20. In her recent book, Eva Mroczek notes that not only does "Bible," understood as canon, provide an anachronism that informs the scholarship in our discipline, but so does the idea of "book." See Mroczek, *The Literary Imagination in Jewish Antiquity* (Oxford: Oxford University Press, 2016), 3–6.

21. This list of terms is not comprehensive. I could easily add in others such as pagan, Greco-Roman, monotheism, Diaspora, etc.

22. For instance, Elisabeth Schüssler Fiorenza notes that "Ideas of men about women [. . .] do not reflect women's historical reality, since ideological polemics about women's place, role, or nature increase whenever women's actual emancipation and active participations in history become stronger," *Bread Not Stone: The Challenge of Feminist Biblical Interpretation* (Boston: Beacon Press, 1995), 109. Others, including Bernadette Brooten, note this challenge as well ("Early Christian Women and their Cultural Context: Issues of Method in Historical Reconstruction," in *Feminist Perspectives on Biblical Scholarship*, ed. Adela Yarbro Collins [Chico: Scholars, 1985], 67).

23. On the angel in 4 Ezra, see Benjamin E. Reynolds, "The Otherworldly Mediators in *4 Ezra* and *2 Baruch*: A Comparison with Angelic Mediators in Ascent Apocalypses and in Daniel, Ezekiel, and Zechariah," in *Fourth Ezra and Second Baruch: Reconstructions after the Fall*, eds. Matthias Henze and Gabriele Boccaccini (Leiden: Brill, 2013), 175–94.

24. See, for instance, Edith McEwan Humphrey, *The Ladies and the Cities: Transformation and Apocalyptic Identity in Joseph and Aseneth, 4 Ezra, the Apocalypse, and The Shepherd of Hermas* (Sheffield: Sheffield Academic Press, 1995); Loren T. Stuckenbruck, "Ezra's Vision of the Lady: The Form and Function of a Turning Point," in *Fourth Ezra and Second Baruch: Reconstructions after the Fall*, eds. Matthias Henze and Gabriele Boccaccini (Leiden: Brill, 2013), 137–50.

25. Juvenal wrote in the late first and early second centuries CE.

26. Translation from Niall Rudd, *Juvenal, "The Satires,"* with notes by William Barr (New York: Oxford University Press, 1999).

27. See Francis Borchardt, "CSTT and Gender #2: A Gender Theory Critique of the Historical-Critical Method," *Changes in Sacred Texts and Traditions*, 6 July 2017, https://blogs.helsinki.fi/sacredtexts/2017/07/06/cstt-and-gender-a-gender-theory-critique-of-the-historical-critical-method/, and Elisabeth Schüssler Fiorenza's critique of this methodology as used in historical Jesus scholarship in *Jesus and the Politics of Interpretation* (New York: Continuum, 2000), 1–29.

28. Cf. Acts 18:1–3; 1 Cor 16:19.

29. The construction likely implies that women are a new subject and drives home the fact that for this author *diakonoi* are not to be women; the construction is unclear, however. See Benjamin Fiore and Daniel Harrington, *The Pastoral Epistles: First Timothy, Second Timothy, Titus* (Collegeville: Liturgical Press, 2007), 81.

30. Carey A. Moore, *The Anchor Bible Judith: A New Translation with Introduction and Commentary* (Garden City: Doubleday, 1985), 67–71.

31. Jennifer A. Glancy, "Judith the Slaveholder," in *A Feminist Companion to Tobit and Judith*, eds. Athalya Brenner-Idan and Helen Efthimiadis-Keith (London: Bloomsbury, 2015), 200–11.

32. Amy-Jill Levine, "Sacrifice and Salvation: Otherness and Domestication in the Book of Judith," in *Women in the Hebrew Bible: A Reader* (New York: Routledge, 1999), 367–76. See also in this volume Chontel Syfox, "Traversing the Boundaries of Gender," who comes to similar conclusions for the portrayal of Rebekah in the book of Jubilees.

33. Caroline Johnson Hodge, "The Question of Identity: Gentiles as Gentiles—but also Not—in Pauline Communities," in *Paul Within Judaism*, eds. Mark D. Nanos and Magnus Zetterholm (Minneapolis: Fortress, 2015), 153–73.

34. See, for instance, Kathy Ehrensperger, "The Question(s) of Gender: Relocating Paul in Relation to Judaism," in *Paul Within Judaism*, 245–76, and in this volume, K. Ehrensperger, "Paul, the Man: Enigmatic Images."

35. "Among many hermeneutical strategies, Schussler Fiorenza identifies 'slippages,' which are small kernels of reality indicating the real-life struggle of women that are embedded in an androcentric text." Joan E. Taylor, "The Women 'Priests' of Philo's *De Vita Contemplativa*: Reconstructing the Therapeutae," in *On the Cutting Edge: The Study of Women in Biblical Worlds: Essays in Honor of Elizabeth Schussler Fiorenza*, eds. Jane Schaberg, Alice Bach, and Esther Fuchs: (New York: Continuum, 2003), 102. This use of slippage is different from Derrida's usage in his discussion of the signifier and the signified. See Jacques Derrida, *Of Grammatology* (Baltimore: Johns Hopkins Press, 1976), 144 ff.

36. "Ovid, *Amores* 1.14," translation by J. Svarlien, 2000, http://www.stoa.org/diotima/anthology/amores1.14.shtml

37. For instance, see the article by Ross Kraemer that shows just how difficult it is to distinguish between Jewish and Christian provenances on epigraphic evidence: "Jewish Tuna and Christian Fish: Identifying Religious Affiliation in Epigraphic Sources," *Harvard Theological Review* 84.2 (1991): 141–62.

38. Kraemer, "Jewish Tuna," 152. See also the extensive lexicon of Jewish names by Tal Ilan et al., *Lexicon of Jewish Names in Late Antiquity* 4 vol. (Tübingen: Mohr Siebeck, 2002–2012).

39. Davina C. Lopez, "Before Your Very Eyes: Roman Imperial Ideology, Gender Constructs, and Paul's Internationalism," in *Mapping Gender in Ancient Religious Discourse*, eds. Todd Penner and Caroline Vander Stichele; Leiden: Brill, 2007), 115–62, here 117.

40. For Lopez's excellent analysis of this coin in detail, see Lopez, "Before Your Very Eyes," 119–23.

BIBLIOGRAPHY

Baker, Cynthia. *Jew*. New Brunswick: Rutgers University Press, 2016.

Borchardt, Francis. "CSTT and Gender #2: A Gender Theory Critique of the Historical-Critical Method." *Changes in Sacred Texts and Traditions*, 6 July 2017, https://blogs.helsinki.fi/sacredtexts/2017/07/06/cstt-and-gender-a-gender-theory-critique-of-the-historical-critical-method/.

Boyarin, Daniel. *Judaism: The Genealogy of a Modern Notion*. New Brunswick: Rutgers University Press, 2018.

———. "Semantic Differences: or, 'Judaism'/'Christianity.'" In *The Ways that Never Parted: Jews and Christians in Late Antiquity and the Early Middle Ages*, edited by Adam H. Becker and Annette Yoshiko Reed, 65–87. Minneapolis: Fortress Press, 2007.

Brooten, Bernadette. "Early Christian Women and their Cultural Context: Issues of Method in Historical Reconstruction." In *Feminist Perspectives on Biblical Scholarship*, edited by Adela Yarbro Collins, 65–91. Chico: Scholars, 1985.

Burrus, Virginia. "Mapping as Metamorphosis: Initial Reflections on Gender and Ancient Religious Discourse." In *Mapping Gender in Ancient Religious Discourse*, edited by Todd Penner and Caroline Vander Stichele, 1–10. Leiden: Brill 2007.

Butler, Judith. *Gender Trouble: Feminism and the Subversion of Identity*. New York: Routledge, 2010.

Cohen, Shaye J. D. *The Beginnings of Jewishness: Boundaries, Varieties, Uncertainties*. Berkeley: University of California Press, 1999.

Crenshaw, Kimberle. "Demarginalizing the Intersection of Race and Sex: A Black Feminist Critique of Antidiscrimination Doctrine, Feminist Theory and Antiracist Politics." University of Chicago Legal Forum 1, no. 8 (1989).

Ehrensperger, Kathy. "The Question(s) of Gender: Relocating Paul in Relation to Judaism." In *Paul Within Judaism: Restoring the First-Century Context to the Apostle*, edited by Mark D. Nanos and Magnus Zetterholm, 245–76. Minneapolis: Fortress, 2015.

Fiore, Benjamin, and Daniel J. Harrington. *The Pastoral Epistles: First Timothy, Second Timothy, Titus*. Collegeville: Liturgical Press, 2007.

Glancy, Jennifer A. "Judith the Slaveholder." In *A Feminist Companion to Tobit and Judith*, edited by Athalya Brenner-Idan and Helen Efthimiadis-Keith, 200–11. London: Bloomsbury, 2015.

Humphrey, Edith McEwan. *The Ladies and the Cities: Transformation and Apocalyptic Identity in Joseph and Aseneth, 4 Ezra, the Apocalypse, and The Shepherd of Hermas*. Sheffield: Sheffield Academic Press, 1995.

Ilan, Tal et al. *Lexicon of Jewish Names in Late Antiquity* 4 vol. Tübingen: Mohr Siebeck, 2000–2012.

"Jew and Judean: A Forum on Politics and Historiography in the Translation of Ancient Texts," *Marginalia*. 26 August, 2014, https://marginalia.lareviewofbooks.org/jew-judean-forum/.

Johnson Hodge, Caroline. "The Question of Identity: Gentiles as Gentiles—but also Not—in Pauline Communities." In *Paul Within Judaism: Restoring the First-Century Context to the Apostle*, edited by Mark D. Nanos and Magnus Zetterholm, 153–73. Minneapolis: Fortress, 2015.

Kraemer, Ross. "Jewish Tuna and Christian Fish: Identifying Religious Affiliation in Epigraphic Sources," *Harvard Theological Review* 84.2 (1991): 141–62.

Krone, Kerstin v. d., and M. Thulin. "Wissenschaft in Context: A Research Essay on the Wissenschaft Des Judentums." *The Leo Baeck Institute Yearbook* 58, no. 1 (2013): 249-80. doi:10.1093/leobaeck/ybt010.

Levine, Amy-Jill. "Sacrifice and Salvation: Otherness and Domestication in the Book of Judith." In *Women in the Hebrew Bible: A Reader*, edited by Alice Bach, 367–76. New York: Routledge, 1999.

Lopez, Davina C. "Before Your Very Eyes: Roman Imperial Ideology, Gender Constructs, and Paul's Internationalism." In *Mapping Gender in Ancient Religious Discourse*, edited by Todd Penner and Caroline Vander Stichele, 115–62. Leiden: Brill, 2007.

McDonald, Lee M. and James A. Sanders, eds. *The Canon Debate*. Peabody: Hendrickson Publishers, 2002.

Moore, Carey A. *The Anchor Bible Judith: A New Translation with Introduction and Commentary*. Garden City: Doubleday, 1985.

Mor, Menahem. *The Second Jewish Revolt Against Rome: The Bar Kokhba Revolt 132–136 CE*. Boston: Brill, 2016.

Mroczek, Eva. *The Literary Imagination in Jewish Antiquity*. Oxford: Oxford University Press, 2016.

Najman, Hindy. *Losing the Temple and Recovering the Future: An Analysis of 4 Ezra*. Cambridge: Cambridge University Press, 2014.

Neutel, Karin B. *A Cosmopolitan Ideal: Paul's Declaration "Neither Jew Nor Greek, Neither Slave Nor Free, Nor Male and Female" in the Context of First Century Thought*. London: Bloomsbury T & T Clark, 2015.

Oegema, Gerbern S. *The Anointed and His People: Messianic Expectations from Maccabees to Bar Kochba*. Journal for the Study of the Pseudepigrapha. Supplement Series, 27. Sheffield: Sheffield Academic Press, 1998.

Parks, Sara. *Women in Q: Gender in the Rhetoric of Jesus*. Lanham, MD: Lexington Books/Fortress Academic, 2019.

Reynolds, Benjamin E. "The Otherworldly Mediators in *4 Ezra* and *2 Baruch*: A Comparison with Angelic Mediators in Ascent Apocalypses and in Daniel, Ezekiel, and Zechariah." In *Fourth Ezra and Second Baruch: Reconstructions after the Fall*, edited by Matthias Henze and Gabriele Boccaccini, 175–94. Leiden: Brill, 2013.

Rubenstein, Jeffrey L. "Social and Institutional Settings of Rabbinic Literature." In *The Cambridge Companion to the Talmud and Rabbinic Literature*, edited by Charlotte E. Fonrobert and Martin S. Jaffee, 58–74. Cambridge: Cambridge University Press, 2007.

Rudd, Niall, translator. Notes by William Barr. *Juvenal, "The Satires."* New York: Oxford University Press, 1999.

Schüssler Fiorenza, Elisabeth. *But She Said: Feminist Practices of Biblical Interpretation*. Boston: Beacon Press, 1992.

———. *Bread Not Stone: The Challenge of Feminist Biblical Interpretation*. Boston: Beacon Press, 1995.

———. *Jesus and the Politics of Interpretation*. New York: Continuum, 2000.

Schwartz, Daniel R. *Judeans and Jews: Four Faces of Dichotomy in Ancient Jewish History*. Toronto: University of Toronto Press, 2014.

Sheinfeld, Shayna. "Crises in Leadership in the Post-Destruction Apocalypses of 4 Ezra and 2 Baruch." PhD diss., McGill University, 2015.

Simkovich, Malka Z. "Greek Influence on the Composition of 2 Maccabees." *JSJ* 42 (2011): 293–310.

Stuckenbruck, Loren T. Stuckenbruck. "Ezra's Vision of the Lady: The Form and Function of a Turning Point." In *Fourth Ezra and Second Baruch: Reconstructions after the Fall*, edited by Matthias Henze and Gabriele Boccaccini, 137–50. Leiden: Brill, 2013.

Svarlien, John. Translator. "Ovid, *Amores* 1.14." 2000. http://www.stoa.org/diotima/anthology/amores1.14.shtml.

Taylor, Joan E. "The Women 'Priests' of Philo's *De Vita Contemplativa*: Reconstructing the Therapeutae." In *On the Cutting Edge: The Study of Women in Biblical Worlds: Essays in Honor of Elizabeth Schussler Fiorenza*, edited by Jane Schaberg, Alice Bach, and Esther Fuchs, 102–22. New York: Continuum, 2003.

Trebolle Barrera, Julio C. "Origins of the Tripartite Old Testament Canon." In *The Canon Debate*, edited by Lee Martin McDonald and James A. Sanders, 128–45. Peabody: Hendrickson Publishers, 2002.

Warren, Meredith J. C. "'When the Christ appears, will he do more signs than this man has done?' (John 7:31): Signs and the Messiah in the Gospel of John." In *Reading the Gospel of John's Christology as a Form of Jewish Messianism: Royal, Prophetic, and Divine Messiahs*, edited by Benjamin Reynolds and Gabriele Boccaccini, 229–47. Leiden: Brill, 2018.

Weitzman, Steven. *The Origins of the Jews: The Quest for Roots in a Rootless Age*. Princeton: Princeton University Press, 2017.

Chapter One

"The Brooten Phenomenon"

Moving Women from the Margins in Second-Temple and New Testament Scholarship[1]

Sara Parks

There is no question that scholarship in early Judaism[2] and nascent Christianity that is done either *by* or *about* women and gender is by no means the rare exception it would have been just fifty years ago. And yet, although at least half of the scholars entering the field may now be women, and although scholarship on ancient women, on biblical and apocryphal female characters, and on the construction of femininity and masculinity in antiquity is now thriving, there remains, I argue, an impermeable conceptual wall between them and what is perceived as "regular" scholarship. On the one side of the wall is "mainstream" scholarship, what Elisabeth Schüssler Fiorenza (1999) has dubbed "malestream" scholarship due to its unspoken patriarchal or kyriarchal assumptions around what constitutes appropriate method and subject matter. On the other side of the wall are scholars and subjects that, whether or not we admit it, are envisioned as nonmainstream or "niche." This is a largely unwritten rule, which nevertheless conceptually limits investigations into ancient women, into ancient female literary characters, and into the construction of gender in the Second-Temple Period and early Christianity as "ancillary" rather than of general relevance. Scholars feel they can safely ignore these people and these fields and not be missing anything that will affect their ability to remain well-read and current. In video-game or *Dungeons & Dragons* terms, gender investigations are "side quests." They can be fun, and they are interesting for the quester, but they are easily compartmentalized and do not fundamentally affect the real game or the other characters in the main quest.

I cannot pretend to be able to solve this problem in my lifetime, let alone in a brief article. However, I *will* do two things. I will at least give the problem a name: I have nicknamed it the "Brooten Phenomenon" for reasons explained below. I will also demonstrate, using two brief case studies from Q and from the gospels, that it is, indeed, a problem. Further, I do not mean to say that it is a problem only from the perspective of women or feminists. I mean rather to say that it is a methodological error that threatens to reduce the quality of *all* scholarship, most definitely including scholarship that is ostensibly by, about, and for men. I propose that getting rid of the view that feminist scholarship or scholarship about gender is a "niche" is the only advisable way forward.

WHAT IS "THE BROOTEN PHENOMENON"?

In short, "The Brooten Phenomenon" refers to the way in which women's scholarship, and scholarship on women, doesn't cross the bridge into what is considered to be "real" (i.e., male-centered) scholarship. I have chosen this term because of a crowning example: Brooten's masterful *Women Leaders in the Ancient Synagogue*, published in 1982, has yet to pass through the barrier to change the classroom or the field outside of what is incorrectly perceived as the realm of "women's" scholarship.

One of the first things I read by Bernadette Brooten, as a young Master's student, was her revised dissertation, *Women Leaders in the Ancient Synagogue: Inscriptional Evidence and Background Issues* (1982). As a new scholar, I so admired its caution and breadth; it was everything I hoped to achieve one day—as close as a scholar could come to a "final word on the subject." In it, Brooten refuted—roundly—the argument (or, rather, the unargued assumption) that, unlike other religions in Greco-Roman antiquity, ancient Judaism had no female religious leadership in the form of priestesses or synagogue heads. In a style that has turned out to be typical for Brooten, at the core of the book is a thorough catalogue of ancient primary material, in this case mainly inscriptions. Each inscription in the book provides evidence for women leaders in Jewish antiquity. The effect is all the stronger when the totality of the evidence is considered.

The subtitle of Brooten's book, "Inscriptional Evidence and Background Issues," refers to: a) the collection of inscriptions Brooten gathered, and; b) the history of their analysis. This second aspect of the book has some unexpected entertainment value. When Brooten lays before the reader the lengths to which commentators through the centuries have gone in order to avoid the plain sense of the readings, the effect is almost hilarious. Each inscription had previously been read blatantly unnaturally, including by revered specialists of Jewish and Christian antiquity. Brooten reanalyzed (or perhaps *actually* analyzed for the first time) this previously-misread inscriptional data using the same methods that one might use for other religions of ancient Greece and Rome, such as the cult of Isis or Rome's Vestals, and piled up a veritable avalanche of evidence for ancient Jewish women in leadership of various kinds.

The scholars before Brooten who had treated these inscriptions—which we now know to provide evidence for ancient Jewish women who were heads of synagogues, elders, or even priests—may have been cautious enough in their other work. But in the case of the evidence for women in positions of power within Jewish antiquity, each scholar, to a man, had dismissed the plain sense of each inscription as being impossible. *A priori* they had collectively said, "we know that women were not leaders in ancient Judaism, so this inscription must have a meaning other than what it says." But, as Brooten notes, if it had been newly-discovered evidence for a mystery cult, no one would have thought that it made any methodological sense to doubt the inscription (1982, 99). Carrie Duncan neatly summarizes this remarkable situation: "Although synagogue title inscriptions have been a topic of study since the nineteenth century, early scholars gave only passing interest to the fact that on rare occasions these titles were bestowed upon women. Whereas these scholars assumed practical responsibilities and obligations were incumbent upon male title bearers, they also assumed a complete male dominance of Judaism that would preclude the possibility of female leadership. [. . .] As a result of these assumptions, early scholarship typically explained away the significance of female title bearers in a variety of ways." (2012, 39)

I will here discuss but a few of the acrobatic antics performed in order for interpreters to maintain these assumptions in the face of clear evidence to the contrary. In three Greek inscriptions in particular, women are accorded the specific title "head of synagogue" (*archisynagogos*). The inscriptions are not ambiguous. One, found on a tomb, reads:

> Rufina, a Jewess, head of the synagogue, built this tomb for her freed slaves and the slaves raised in her house. No one else has the right to bury anyone (here). (Brooten 1982, 5)

Brooten traced the history of scholarship on this cautionary epitaph and found the following: Salomon Reinach first published the inscription; he declares that the title *archisynagogos* must be merely *honorary* rather than *functional*. To get over the fact that *archisynagogos* had already been established as a functional title, he decides, when faced with female *archisynagogoi*, that there must have been two stages in the history of the word's usage—an early functional stage, and a later honorific stage (Reinach 1883, in Brooten 1982, 5). His reasoning is that, *a priori*, the word cannot have meant what it usually means because in this case it is referring to a woman. Next, M. Weinberg solves the dilemma of a Jewish woman in a position of power by explaining that Rufina was clearly the *wife* of an *archisynagogos*. His reasoning for this little linguistic minuet is simple: "for women have never held an office in a Jewish community, and certainly not a synagogue office" (Weinberg 1897,

658, cited in Brooten 1982, 6). Brooten reveals that Emil Schürer has been equally dismissive: "Rufina herself bears the title *archisynagogos*, which in the case of a woman is, of course, just a title" (Schürer 1973–1979, 2.435, cited in ibid.).

Brooten collects example after example of this sort of sidestepping of the not one but three clear inscriptions assigning the term "head of synagogue" to a woman. She cites another scholar, who writes that Rufina "was very likely a lady whom the congregation wished to honour, but to whom it could hardly have entrusted the actual charge of an office" (Baron, 1942, 1.97, cited in Brooten 1982, 6). Another has concluded that, "concerning the women, it can certainly not mean that they were bestowed with the dignity of a head of the synagogue, for the synagogue did not allow women such honours; it is rather the wives of presidents of synagogues who are meant" (Krauss, 1922, 118, cited in ibid.). Brooten's catalogue of previous scholarship highlights the stunning fact that not one of these scholars bothers to *argue* these positions which represent awkward readings of the evidence; they are mentioned in passing as obvious.

Brooten's book covers numerous additional assignments of titles to women, ranging from "elder" to "synagogue mother" to "synagogue head" to "priest," again and again exposing the gymnastic contortions to which male scholars would subject the inscriptions in order to avoid taking them at face value. In every case where an inscription which suggested female leadership had been unearthed, scholars had posited bizarre explanations for what they clearly perceived as a problem. The term "priest" (*hiereia/hierissa*) had to be a proper name. Had to be the title of the woman's father. Had to be a misspelling. Or the priest had to be male, but—for reasons unknown—had a female name! Granted, some of the inscriptions are fragmentary or ambiguous, but, as Brooten points out, "if these inscriptions had come from another Graeco-Roman religion, no scholar would have thought of arguing that 'priest' does not really mean 'priest'" (1982, 99). Yes, these cases are mainly evidenced in diasporic Judaism, and no, they do not seem to have survived after the coalescence of Rabbinic Judaism and the so-called Parting of the Ways, but they should at the very least complicate the question of Jewish leadership in antiquity. The too-easy dichotomy that exists between Judaism and Hellenism should not be allowed to serve as a reason why we can ignore Brooten's findings.

Yet despite the publication of Brooten's exhaustive collection of clear examples, it has been my experience on both sides of the Atlantic that the old assumption *still* reigns in both classrooms and publications: ancient Judaism had no women leaders. I posit that the case of Brooten's still-unincorporated yet completely convincing and exhaustive work of over thirty years ago indicates that the question of women in antiquity is not one that is gaining traction beyond what is perceived as its own niche, precisely because, in general, the study of women is treated as an accessory, at best ancillary to what are considered primary fields.

Although *Women Leaders in the Ancient Synagogue* is incorporated into, say, *A Companion to Women in the Ancient World* (James and Dillon 2012), or *Daughters of the King: Women and the Synagogue* (Grossman and Haut 1993), it is not incorporated into general scholarship on synagogues or on the Jewish priesthood. If it is, it is in the manner of the recent volume *The Ancient Synagogue: The First Thousand Years* (Levine 2000). That is, it has a chapter on women in which Brooten's work, along with the work of others—such as Kraemer, who analyzed a similar inscription with a diasporic Jewish woman elder (1985)—is discussed. Yet the contents of the one chapter called "Women in the Synagogue" remain almost completely compartmentalized. While Brooten's and others' evidence of the active participation of Jewish women in a variety of administrative and religious capacities is treated in this chapter, the material is kept largely hermetically separate from influencing the rest of the book.

Despite the book's treatment (in the chapter on women) of a number of instances where Jewish women are referred to as *hiereia or hierissa* (priestess), the very next chapter, called "Priests," makes no mention of any such complication. Furthermore, the treatment of Brooten's work on these inscriptions is dismissive. It reads: "In sum, there is certainly a possibility that most, if not all the titles that appear in over a score of Diaspora inscriptions are those of functioning women officials. The challenge, however, is finding a way to substantiate this claim, and not merely assert it" (Levine 2000, 511). This, of course, misses the whole point of Brooten's work, which is that unsubstantiated claims and assumptions have marked the opposite view, that is, that Jewish women could not, *a priori*, have been leaders, and thus Brooten's challenge is that the burden of proof should fall on those who wish to read all of these inscriptions against their simplest reading.

The author goes on to spend some time to make sure that the reader knows that such cases of women's leadership were aberrations and "departures," and to form a narrative where Judaism had, in these cases, been "influenced by the surrounding culture" (Levine 2000, 515), as though such a thing were somehow not the case for every human group everywhere at all times. As though asking for *more* proof of Jewish women leaders, isolating the proof we have as aberrant, and then associating women's leadership with "other cultures" had closed the case, the book goes on to largely tell the history of men, and treat subjects topically without having to bother too much with women's history except as a separate category. The author even concludes, sweepingly:

Jewish society was quite different from its social environs. To the best of our knowledge, women did not play any kind of liturgical role in the synagogue
. . . Perhaps it was the Semitic, Near Eastern roots of Israelite tradition that might explain why Jews looked askance at women's cultic participation . . . or perhaps it was because of the monotheistic nature of Judaism: at the centre of Judaism is one God, of masculine gender. (518)

Although Brooten is now a distinguished and world-class senior scholar, this seminal work still languishes in many ways. People still say "unlike other religions of Greco-Roman antiquity, Judaism had strictly male religious leadership." Or, worse, they contrast this stereotype of Judaism with early Christianity using the trope that A.-J. Levine has pointed out within Christian scholarship, whereby "ancient Judaism was hopelessly patriarchal until Jesus came along and emancipated everyone."[3] This lack of integration of Brooten's work into "regular scholarship" is not because Brooten's work is lacking. It is because—dare I write the words—*work on or by women often struggles to cross the bridge into scholarship written by men or purportedly about general (rather than gender-specific) topics*. We have come a long way in the study of women in antiquity,[4] but not in an integrated manner. Advancements in our knowledge of ancient women which are not then incorporated into scholarly consensus and which never really "trickle down" are not changing the field, but remain contained in their own bubble, safely away from the "malestream" scholarship. This is what I mean by "The Brooten Phenomenon."

WHAT NEEDS TO CHANGE? EVERYTHING.

What needs to change? In my estimation, our whole paradigm does. I am calling for honed methods, an ethics of interpretation, and, most importantly, scholarship on women and gender *by men, for men*.

If more women than ever before in history are working in the fields of early Judaism, early Christianity, biblical studies, and theology, and more scholars in those fields have their eye on women and gender, but their conclusions are quite frequently remaining in closed feedback loops without dissemination and integration, something is not working correctly. If the problem is not the scholarship itself,[5] then the problem is the environment in which it is taking place. What is needed in order for women and gender to break through the wall so that they are no longer conceptualized as a niche but are integrated into all questions is nothing less than a paradigmatic overhaul. I propose a threefold transformation. We need methodological changes, as Brooten suggests in "Early Christian Women and their Cultural Context: Issues of

Method in Historical Reconstruction" (1985, 65–91); we need an ethical framework in which to work, as Schüssler Fiorenza suggests in *Rhetoric and Ethic: The Politics of Biblical Studies* (1999), and in both of these things, we need widespread participation from those who have somehow found themselves in the position of "default human beings"—otherwise known as "men." In particular, we need the participation of the privileged men at the top of all the intersectional hierarchies of our species.

1. HONED METHODS AND ETHICS OF INTERPRETATION

Ours has been a century of cutting-edge methodology. There have been myriad disruptions of the popular scholarly dichotomies and oversimplifications that were once the most common tools of the trade. In general, maybe because the field of early Judaism is newer and we have wrested it but recently from the clutches of the problematic "Intertestamental Studies," scholars who have moved away from canon-based study are constantly checking themselves against assumptions around words like "biblical," "Christian," "Hellenistic," "canonical," "orthodox," etc.[6] I think we are therefore also capable of forging a path out of the "malestream." Many before us have already undertaken deep methodological reflection on this matter.

a. Bernadette Brooten

Brooten, for instance, suggests that we cannot necessarily approach the study of ancient women using the same categories that we do for ancient men (1985, 65). She suggests that a "shift of emphasis" that places women "in the centre of the frame" (ibid.) may necessitate the delineation of new boundaries, and that "the categories developed to understand the history of man may no longer be adequate, that the traditional historical periods and canons of literature may not be the proper framework, and that we will need to ask new types of questions and consider hitherto overlooked sources" (ibid.). The categories of Judaism and Hellenism employed by Lee Levine, above, in order to dismiss Brooten's work, are one example. Brooten writes:

> The assumption is usually that the Hellenistic world was more progressive and the Jewish world more conservative with respect to women, so that when one discovers progressive elements in Judaism, the tendency is to attribute these to Hellenistic influence. (76)

Brooten suggests a combination of shifts in addition to redrawing scholarly categories, including widening typical pools of evidence (1985, 67), acknowledging radical differences in the amount of evidence available for studies of ancient women (ibid.), understanding that history has been and still is a men's endeavor, and accepting that *imagination* is a necessary part of reconstructing women's history. (ibid.)

b. Tal Ilan

As Tal Ilan has shown, not only by the example of her work, but also explicitly in discussions of method, most of our evidence for women is filtered through what ancient men thought about them; what was seen as evidence for women's behaviors may often instead represent the behavior of women in the fantasies of men. The important contribution of Ilan's *Mine and Yours are Hers: Retrieving Women's History from Rabbinic Literature* (1997), is not only to lay bare the problematic tendency of previous historians to use Rabbinic sources unquestioningly as face-value documents for women's realities, but also to reveal how, over time, we are able to see that women characters have been deliberately effaced or even maligned, when we pay attention to women comparatively across rabbinic collections. My own research affirms that these tendencies toward the erasure or even slander of women also play out in the time frame between the early Jesus movement and the patristic period.[7]

c. Elisabeth Schüssler Fiorenza

In addition to the above caveats, one of Elisabeth Schüssler Fiorenza's most important contributions is the identification of a central obstacle to the integration of women's scholarship and scholarship about gender: the stereotype that "malestream" scholarship is *objective*, whereas feminist scholarship is "engaged" and therefore somehow unscientific. She proposes an interdisciplinary "ethics of interpretation" which:

> means to overcome the assumed dichotomy between engaged scholarship (such as feminist, postcolonial, African American, queer, and other subdisciplines) and scientific (malestream) interpretation. Whereas the former is allegedly using ethical criteria, the latter is said to live up to a scientific ethos that gives precedence to cognitive criteria. Instead, I would argue that a scientific ethos demands both ethical and cognitive criteria. (1999, 195–96)

The claim that one can undertake historical work from a "neutral" or "unbiased" standpoint is problematic at best, and violent at worst. Scientific neutrality is not only impossible,[8] but also unethical. Contrary to what is typically assumed, it is not only the scholarship from or about marginalized voices that is "engaged" and has political and socio-historical consequences; rather, it is just that only some scholarship *admits* that it is situated from within gendered, ethnic, socio-economic, racialized, geographical, ideological, and cultural standpoints. Women's scholarship may have an engaged interest and an overt bias in its questions—but scholarship that systematically ignores women and nonbinary gender and operates from the presumption that being male, white, Western, and Christian or post- Christian is an acceptable neutral "default" is *also* engaged and biased, under false cover of objectivity.

d. A.-J. Levine

A number of scholars, most notably A.-J. Levine, have guided us away from a common peril of New Testament scholarship by helping to push work on women and gender in antiquity away from the edge of the precipice of anti-Judaism. Levine's "Second-Temple Judaism, Jesus, and Women" (1996, 303) and her "Matthew, Mark, and Luke: Good News or Bad?" (2002) remind us that we need to pay close methodological attention when we use feminist hermeneutics of generosity on biblical texts. There is a difference between the work of providing readings that seek overtly to redeem patriarchal texts by uncovering women's voices and agency, and the work of doing history.

Levine has cautioned that such conflation has resulted in early feminist scholarship on women in Christianity being disturbingly problematic in its inaccurate denigration of first-century Judaism on its way to find gender equality at the roots of the Christian tradition. Works like Judith Plaskow's "Anti-Judaism in Christian Feminist Interpretation" (1993), Schüssler Fiorenza's "The Power of Naming: Jesus, Women, and Christian Anti-Judaism" (1995), and Kathleen Corley's *Women and the Historical Jesus: Feminist Myths of Christian Origins* (2002) support Levine's critique of Christian feminist readings that treat Judaism as a flattened patriarchal foil against which to contrast gender in the early Jesus movement.

Alicia Batten's "More Queries for Q: Women and Christian Origins" (1994) shows that while Jesus's sayings material may contain gender-levelling rhetoric, it did not pop spontaneously from a vacuum, but was in keeping with a number of diverse shifts in gender dynamics in the surrounding Mediterranean, involving Jews and non-Jews alike. Batten, Levine, and others have sounded a clear, decades-long call against the inadvertent perpetuation of anti-Semitism caused by discussing New Testament texts in a way that divorces them from their early Jewish context. This is a call that more New Testament scholarship, not just on the question of gender, would do well to heed.

2. SCHOLARSHIP ON WOMEN BY MEN FOR MEN

Many of us are already aware of the need for shifts toward these kinds of methodological approaches. Virtually everyone who works on women and gender in early Judaism already incorporates the above-mentioned considerations. However, part of the point of this article is to suggest that the people who will need to carry the burden of integrating these methods so that they transform our wider fields are men.

This past year, many of us observed or even took part in a turning point in history: survivors of sexual harassment and sexual assault, the majority of whom were women, broke with social convention across the English-speaking world and shared publicly via social media that they had been victims of sexual harassment, assault, and rape. Typically disclosed only privately to trusted friends, and rarely officially reported, admissions that one had experienced sexual assault were now flying through newsfeeds alongside cute kittens and political memes, thanks to the #MeToo movement. Our professional guilds were not exempt from these disclosures; I noticed that a few days after the movement had "gone viral," one female colleague in the study of religion after another also decided to go public. The phenomenon was overwhelmingly driven and supported by women, including women scholars, but I noticed with admiration the handful—perhaps three or four—men in my social networks who joined in attempts to speak out against societal norms that work to make rape normal and leave the vast majority of people who commit rape unscathed, unashamed, or even unaware.

The societal frameworks that make sexual assault against women commonplace may have far more traumatizing results than those which make scholarship on ancient women remain ancillary, but they both fall along the same patriarchal—or kyriarchal—spectrum of silencing and domination. As women are the ones most frequently marginalized along the spectrum of silencing that is patriarchy, it should not fall exclusively to women to drive change toward the more integrated and ethical scholarship we want. We have now come, at least within Second-Temple scholarship, to be aware that canons, terminology, artificially-imposed time periods, and the elite nature of ancient textual evidence all work together to obscure our results, and we all work to adjust for these issues. I envision a day when constructions of masculinity and femininity, binary views of gender, patriarchal and kyriarchal worldviews, and male-privileging views of history are also acknowledged in all questions, by all scholars. What I hope to demonstrate now, is that, if such a change were to take place, the benefits would by no means be restricted to women and nonbinary individuals.

3. WHEN QUESTIONS ABOUT WOMEN'S HISTORY ANSWER "MAN QUESTIONS"

I would like to share just two recent examples of how, in my research on ancient women, I inadvertently uncovered useful information that answered "man questions." By "man" questions, I—only partially facetiously—mean what are considered to be "real" questions according to "malestream" scholarship. I hope that these two brief examples will demonstrate concretely how asking ancient texts to answer questions about women is by no means a fringe concern, nor are the results of such a study only of interest to one particular marginalized group.[9] Rather, it is only when asking questions from all possible angles and with diverse interests in mind that we do ancient texts—and the contemporary search for knowledge about them—any justice at all.

Example 1: Women in Q provide evidence against Kloppenborg's strata

In the first case, I was researching the role of women in Jesus's sayings material.[10] Specifically, I was dealing with what I call the Q "Gender Pairs"—what Jeremias first called the *Doppelgleichnisse*.[11] These are cases in the recorded teaching material of Jesus of Nazareth where he tells twin parables with nearly identical didactic content, except that one features a female protagonist or feminine activity and the other features a male protagonist or masculine activity, such as the parables of the man who loses a sheep (Mt 18:12–14; Lk 15:3–7) and the woman who loses a coin (Lk 15:8–10). While I was in the process of identifying all these gendered pairs in Q and classifying them into subcategories,[12] I remained aloof to Kloppenborg's popularization of Schulz's theory that Q comprises three redactional strata, with different social situations behind each stratum of development.[13] Q is already a hypothetical document cautiously reconstructed from the sayings material in Matthew and Luke. I was reticent to follow Kloppenborg when he further hypothesized Q to have three separate literary stages. Kloppenborg, Mack (1995 and 1993), and others (e.g., Cotter 2014; Hartin 1994; Howes 2015; Vaage 1994), imagine three distinct phases of community development, often positing that the sapiential material is from an earlier and less organized *formative* phase, directed more toward the group's own members (Q^1), whereas the apocalyptic material came on the scene later as the group experienced rejection and persecution, and is a major *redactional* phase directed more toward outsiders (Q^2) (Kloppenborg 2007; cf Piper 1989, 176–78).[14] Brief narrative additions (mainly the baptism in Q 3:21–22, and the temptation scene in Q 4:1–13) form the final smallest stratum (Q^3).[15]

I happened to be using a copy of Q that was color-coded according to the posited strata, when I noticed that the gendered parable pairs occur across both main strata of Q—the so-called formative or "wisdom" layer *and* the so-called redactional or apocalyptic layer.

There are six gendered parable pairs in the critical edition of Q (Robinson, Hoffman, Kloppenborg 2000). We find four of them in Q^1, as the earliest hypothetical layer is called: The Bread and the Fish (Q 11:11–12); The Ravens and the Lilies (Q 12:24, 27); The Mustard Seed and The Yeast (Q 13:18–21); and the Lost Sheep and the Lost Coin (Q 15:4–5, 7–9). And we find two of them in Q^2, as the so-called main redactional layer is called: the Queen of the South and the Ninevite Men (Q 11:31–32); and the Men in the Field and the Women at the Mill (Q 17:34–35).

In my estimation, this existence of gendered pairing across both layers calls into question the notion of a stratified Q. I am not saying that it *proves* that Q has no redactional strata, but I do think that the presence of the gender pairs across both main strata complicates the hypothesis and must be reckoned with. It is a text-critical discovery that I would certainly not have made had I not been researching the attitude toward women in the Q sayings.

Example 2: Women in the gospel resurrection scenes provide evidence for a literary relationship between John and the Synoptics.

A second recent example of how the investigation of women in our ancient sources can elucidate other questions about those sources came to me while I was teaching undergraduates at the University of Nottingham about women in the New Testament, and I had them do a side-by-side comparison of the four canonical resurrection accounts. I asked them to compare all the characters mentioned at the foot of the cross and in the empty tomb scenes, in the hopes that they would notice the striking consistency of Mary Magdalene's presence alongside the otherwise wide discrepancies. As I was looking at all four passages synoptically, focusing specifically on the women, I noticed something that had not previously occurred to me, at least not in a way I took seriously—a piece of evidence that suggests a literary relationship between John and Luke.

It is often taught to undergraduates without too much complication that John is probably literarily unrelated to the synoptic gospels. We typically call upon John in its capacity as a separate witness to kernels of historicity around Jesus of Nazareth, thanks to its role as an independent attestation.

A few people over the years—beginning, I think, with Eusebius (*Historia Ecclesiastica* 3.24.2)—have put forth a possible literary relationship between John and one or other of the Synoptics (e.g. Dowell 1992; Windisch 1926), but I have until now accepted the general consensus that the gospel of John is literarily independent, which of course makes a difference to internal interpretations of John, but also to historical Jesus research. However, an element of the resurrection accounts, which I only noticed when focusing closely on the women, complicates matters.

In the earliest gospel, Mark, the resurrection pericope goes like this:[16]

> When the Sabbath was over, Mary Magdalene, and Mary the mother of James, and Salome bought spices, so that they might go and anoint him. And very early on the first day of the week, when the sun had risen, they went to the tomb. They had been saying to one another, "Who will roll away the stone for us from the entrance to the tomb?" When they looked up, they saw that the stone, which was very large, had already been rolled back. As they entered the tomb, they saw a young man, dressed in a white robe, sitting on the right side; and they were alarmed. But he said to them, "Do not be alarmed; you are looking for Jesus of Nazareth, who was crucified. He has been raised; he is not here. Look, there is the place they laid him. But go, tell his disciples and Peter that he is going ahead of you to Galilee; there you will see him, just as he told you." So they went out and fled from the tomb, for terror and amazement had seized them; and they said nothing to anyone, for they were afraid. (Mark 16:1-8 NRSV)

Here, we have three named women (two Marys and Salome), an encounter with a shining young man, and no male disciples on the scene. The male disciples are mentioned in the instructions at the end, where the women are encouraged to tell "his disciples and Peter" to meet a resurrected Jesus in Galilee. Everyone leaves, terrified.

In the gospel that was probably written next, that of Matthew, the literary dependence, with a bit of embellishment and Matthean flair, is clear:

> After the Sabbath, as the first day of the week was dawning, Mary Magdalene and the other Mary went to see the tomb. And suddenly there was a great earthquake; for an angel of the Lord, descending from heaven, came and rolled back the stone and sat on it. His appearance was like lightning, and his clothing white as snow. For fear of him the guards shook and became like dead men. But the angel said to the women, "Do not be afraid; I know that you are looking for Jesus who was crucified. He is not here; for he has been raised, as he said. Come, see the place where he lay. Then go quickly and tell his disciples, 'He has been raised from the dead, and indeed he is going ahead of you to Galilee; there you will see him.' This is my message for you." So they left the tomb quickly with fear and great joy, and ran to tell his disciples.[9] Suddenly Jesus met them and said, "Greetings!" And they came to him, took hold of his feet, and worshiped

him. Then Jesus said to them, "Do not be afraid; go and tell my brothers to go to Galilee; there they will see me."

Here we have just two women—the Marys—and an angel with an almost verbatim message that Jesus has been raised and to tell the disciples to meet him in Galilee. Peter is not mentioned here. Note that we also have here a pre-Galilee appearance of Jesus to both Marys. Such an appearance (of Jesus to Mary Magdalene before everyone returned to Galilee) was eventually appended to Mark—relatively late in the tradition, as Eusebius, Jerome, and Origen do not know it (Metzger 2005).

The remaining two gospels are Luke and John. The order in which they were written is unclear as the dating is disputed. Markus Borg makes some good arguments for placing Luke last (2012, 424–5), but this is not (yet?) conventional (Shellard 1995). Regardless, both are later in comparison with Mark and Matthew.

In comparing the location of the women in all four accounts, two things stand out in Luke and John which might suggest a literary relationship between them, contrary to current thinking. The lesser of the two is the way all four pericopes begin. I have made a table of the four beginnings (Table 1.1) to illustrate the various overlaps. The translation is mine to reflect similar and different Greek construction. Across all four accounts there is an agreement of the "bones" of the content at the beginning of the pericope, along with many small differences. For example, all four mention that it is very early in the morning, but all four do so with a different wording: Mark says it is "very early" (λίαν πρωΐ), Matthew says it is "dawn" (ἐπιφωσκούσῃ), John says it was "early, still being dark" (πρωΐ, σκοτίας ἔτι οὔσης), and Luke says something like "deep daybreak," including the concepts of early and dawn, but with different words (ὄρθρου βαθέως). Thus, in some ways each author agrees on the setting, but describes it in a unique way.

There is, of note for our purposes, an interesting agreement of John and Luke against Mark and Matthew in these verses. Where Mark and Matthew mention that the Sabbath is over, and it is the first of the week, John and Luke drop the Sabbath being over and simply state that it is the first of the week. Alone, this can by no means be used to argue for literary dependence. It may simply reflect the fact that both John and Luke are of later date, and thus both drop the mention of the Sabbath because they have fewer Sabbath-observant Jews in their audiences.

However, a stronger, slightly bizarre addition to the empty tomb scenes by John and Luke against Mark and Matthew provide more interesting possibilities for literary interdependence. The two earlier gospels end the empty tomb scene with the women tasked with rallying the other disciples in Galilee. The male disciples are not involved in their empty tomb scenes. In contrast, the

Table 1.1.

The sabbath having been past, Mary Magdalene, and Mary the mother of James, and Salome bought spices, so that having come, they might anoint him. And **very early on the first of the week**, when the sun had risen, they come to the tomb.	After sabbath, it being dawn toward (the) first of (the) week, Mary Magdalene and the other Mary went to see the tomb.	First of the week, early, it yet being dark, Mary Magdalene comes to the tomb . . .	The first of the week, very early morning, they came to the tomb, taking the spices that they had prepared.
διαγενομένου τοῦ σαββάτου	Ὀψὲ . . . αββάτων	. . . no mention	. . . no mention
λίαν πρωΐ **τῇ μιᾷ τῶν σαββάτων**	τῇ ἐπιφωσκούσῃ εἰς **μίαν σαββάτων**	Τῇ . . . μιᾷ τῶν σαββάτων . . . πρωΐ, σκοτίας ἔτι οὔσης	τῇ . . . μιᾷ τῶν σαββάτων, ὄρθρου βαθέως
ἔρχονται ἐπὶ τὸ μνημεῖον	ἦλθεν . . . εωρῆσαι τὸν τάφον	ἔρχεται . . . εἰς τὸ μνημεῖον	ἐπὶ τὸ μνῆμα ἦλθον

two later gospels each seem to want to provide male witnesses, rather than leaving women as the only eyewitnesses to the empty tomb. Luke has the women go and relate the resurrection to the other disciples, where they are met with disbelief except by Peter, *who runs to the tomb to see for himself*: "But Peter got up and ran to the tomb; stooping and looking in, he saw the linen cloths by themselves; then he went home, amazed at what had happened" (Lk 24:12 NRSV). John also has Peter witnessing the empty tomb and the linen clothes, but not without a footrace between Peter and "the disciple Jesus loved":

> Then Peter and the other disciple set out and went toward the tomb. The two were running together, but the other disciple outran Peter and reached the tomb first. He bent down to look in and saw the linen wrappings lying there, but he did not go in. Then Simon Peter came, following him, and went into the tomb. He saw the linen wrappings lying there, and the cloth that had been on Jesus' head, not lying with the linen wrappings but rolled up in a place by itself. Then the other disciple, who reached the tomb first, also went in. (Jn 20:3–8 NRSV)

It looks to me as though these two texts are in conversation. Both want a male witness for the empty tomb, but they are not in agreement about *which* male should have this honor. For Luke, the honor goes to Peter, who runs to see the tomb for himself, but in the Johannine account there is a struggle between Peter and "the beloved disciple," who beats Peter in the race to the tomb, although he does not go inside first. Does whichever of these gospels was written last know of the other "race to the tomb" tradition and attempt to challenge it?

Upon investigation, I came to realize that a handful of scholars have already noticed this and have posited direct interaction between the two empty tomb accounts, although they have not been able to budge consensus. For instance, in 2016, Chris Keith suggested that the two narratives are in direct competition (2016). Udo Schnelle thought the same, positing in the 1990s that John reacts to Luke (Schnelle 2001, 299, 301).

The differing accounts of Peter and the empty tomb cannot by themselves prove a literary relationship between John and Luke/Acts. Others before me have also noticed and thought about direct literary dependence based on these scenes. What, then, is the point? The point is not that I, as a non-Johannine scholar, have definitively exploded the theory of John's literary independence all because I have an interest in Mary Magdalene. The point, so simple and yet not to be underestimated, is that *closer interaction with gender dynamics in our texts can provide additional vantage points toward questions that do not have to do with gender*. Until examining the place of the women at the resurrection scenes, I had not engaged with the discussion of relationships between John and the Synoptics because I had accepted consensus. Going forward, I will no longer simply tell my undergraduates that the consensus is that John is literarily independent, without putting these primary texts in front of them and mentioning other viewpoints.

In both above cases, paying attention to women and gender helped me think about longstanding text-critical and source-critical questions in different ways, and in the case of Q, in new ways.

4. WHO WILL BENEFIT FROM MOVING WOMEN FROM THE MARGINS? EVERYONE.

Attempting to reconstruct the history of women or to analyze ancient literature with an eye to gender is a nice, politically-correct, feminist, ethical thing to do. But it is more than that. *It is actually the only way to obtain accurate results as historians*. As Brooten has suggested, the typical time periods, categories, and canons created by men both ancient and modern "determine the very results of research" (1985, 70). In other words, the incorporation and structural integration of feminist scholarship, scholarship about women, and women's scholarship into "regular" scholarship simply *yields better results*.

The inclusion of ancient women in the scope of our work, rather than only providing answers to a "niche" set of questions, provides answers, in the end, to many important questions that don't just have to do with gender. Historical studies that include women, or highlight gender, in ways that haven't been done in the past, provide new pathways into old questions where the academy may be stuck. They break open the data from new angles. They help us to see the whole picture, so that we can answer *all* of our questions more accurately *and* more ethically.

I argue that if we want to find more nuanced and robust answers to questions of history, we *all* need to engage in a paradigm shift where the study of women is not compartmentalized. This will by no means only enlighten scholarship where women are concerned, but it will actually give us the fuller picture necessary to better understand men too. The study of women and gender has already given us the more recent line of inquiry into the ways in which masculinity is also constructed. Virginia Burrus reminds us that, "at a basic level, gender now signals interest in the social construction of men's roles as well as women's and/or in the discursive production of masculinity as well as femininity" (2007, 2). The two above case studies work to illustrate how the inclusion and integration of an interest in women and gender can elucidate questions far beyond the so-called niche of gender studies.

5. GOING FORWARD

Going forward, women's scholarship and scholarship on women should not be construed as optional "identity politics." Rather, they must be accepted as essential to so-called "regular" scholarship. Without them, our scholarship is incomplete, or even incorrect.

If all of us—all Second-Temple Judaism and New Testament scholars— would undertake the major methodological shift suggested here, I suspect that it would not just make us feel good for creating a more equitable environment. I suspect it would mean improved results for *all* of our questions: text-critical, literary, generic, rhetorical, and theological. We have had a methodological blind spot, and it has lowered the quality of our work for a thousand years. We need to move women and gender away from the margins, away from the model where women get one hermetically compartmentalized chapter per volume, or one book per series, and thus away from the notion that women study women for women, and men do not need to pay any attention. We need to do this because *all* of scholarship suffers from its patriarchal biases. This is not a new recommendation; it has been a desideratum since the 1960s. However, I do not believe the integration of scholarship on and by women into "malestream" scholarship will happen unless men choose to pick up the task. I conclude this article with a challenge to male scholars to do themselves a favor and make all scholarship feminist scholarship. Only when this happens can we claim to be conducting historical reconstruction in any meaningful way.

NOTES

1. This chapter was first published in *Bible & Critical Theory* 14/2 (2018): 46–64.

2. My field is early Judaism, by which I mean the study of Jewish history and literature within and around the period of the Second Temple, including early Jesus movements and the texts that came to be collected as the New Testament. Approaching the texts of early Christianity without attention to their early Jewish and Hellenistic context is unlikely to produce readings that are sensitive to the cultural repertoire of their authors and first hearers. That is why this article, whose case studies come from the canonical gospels and Q, is framed as a study within Second-Temple Judaism.

3. Amy-Jill Levine sounds an alarm about the dichotomy that much of the scholarship on women in early Christianity has set up between "women in early Judaism" *versus* "women in early Christianity," noting that both are extreme caricatures, with Judaism assumed (*a priori*) to be hopelessly patriarchal and restrictive for women, and Christianity depicted as unflaggingly emancipatory. See Levine (1996, 307).

4. According to Sidnie White Crawford, "interest in the role and status of women in Second Temple Judaism (and generally in Judaism and Christianity) has increased exponentially in the past twenty-five years" (2001, 330). Murphy writes, in *The Word According to Eve*, "until recently, [the Bible] was studied by female scholars hardly at all, let alone by female scholars who were interested specifically in what the Bible had to say about women. This has changed, to put it mildly" (1998, x). Volumes dedicated to uncovering the historical realities of women in antiquity are beginning to appear as well, as, for example, Harvard University's five-volume history of women from ancient goddesses to the twentieth century, *A History of Women in the West* (Duby and Perrot 1994–96). Other examples in the last thirty years that show the extent to which a serious interest is taking hold (but only among women) in the role of women in early Judaism, early Christianity, and in biblical studies include Yarbro Collins 1985; Fiorenza 2014; Eisen and Standhartinger 2013; Meyers 2000.

5. Spoiler alert: it is not.

6. A crowning example of this type of scholarship is Mroczek (2016).

7. See my *Gender in the Rhetoric of Jesus: Women in Q* (Lanham, MD: Lexington/Fortress Academic, 2019)

8. As Achtemeier puts it, "there is no such thing as a neutral, historical-critical, scientific, objective interpretation of the Scriptures" (1988, 50).

9. It may sound strange to categorize 50 percent of the world as marginalized, and yet, in practical terms, the term fits.

10. I thank my dear Doktorvater Gerbern Oegema for supervising this research with unfailing encouragement.

11. One of the first scholars to notice this phenomenon in the gospels was J. Jeremias, who named it *Doppelgleichnis* (1998).

12. The foundation for this work of classification had been laid by William Arnal (1997) and Denis Fricker (2004).

13. The idea of discerning a literary development within Q was first discussed by Schulz in 1964. Kloppenborg went on to develop this hypothesis, resulting in a quite widely-used three-tier stratification of the Q Document (2000; 2007).

14. Piper (1989) sees struggles with outsiders across both Q^1 and Q^2.

15. The third stage consists mainly of the temptation narrative and is "an example of a historicizing tendency" (Piper 1995, 11).

16. I include here only the undisputed section, vv. 1–8, rather than the shorter and longer endings added later, around which there is some conflicting manuscript evidence. On the various endings of Mark, see Moloney (2002, 339–62).

BIBLIOGRAPHY

Achtemeier, Elizabeth. "The Impossible Possibility: Evaluating the Feminist Approach to Bible and Theology." *Interpretation* 42 (1988): 45–57.

Arnal, William E. "Gendered Couplets in Q and Legal Formulations: From Rhetoric to Social History." *Journal of Biblical Literature* 116.1 (1997): 75–94.

Baron, Salo Wittmayer. *The Jewish Community*. 3 volumes. Philadelphia: The Jewish Publication Society of America, 1942.

Batten, Alicia. "More Queries for Q: Women and Christian Origins." *Biblical Theology Bulletin* 24.2 (1994): 44–51.

Borg, Marcus. *The Evolution of the Word: The New Testament in the Order the Books Were Written*. New York: HarperOne, 2012.

Brooten, Bernadette. "Early Christian Women and their Cultural Context: Issues of Method in Historical Reconstruction." In *Feminist Perspectives on Biblical Scholarship*, edited by Adela Yarbro Collins, 65–91. Chico: Scholars Press, 1985.

———. *Women Leaders in the Ancient Synagogue: Inscriptional Evidence and Background Issues*. Chico: Scholars, 1982.

Burrus, Virginia. "Mapping as Metamorphosis: Initial Reflections on Gender and Ancient Religious Discourse." In *Mapping Gender in Ancient Religious Discourses*, edited by Todd Penner and Caroline Vander Stichele, 1–10. Leiden: Brill, 2007.

Collins, Adela Yarbro, ed. *Feminist Perspectives on Biblical Scholarship*. Chico: Scholars Press, 1985.

Corley, Kathleen. *Women and the Historical Jesus: Feminist Myths of Christian Origins*. Santa Rosa: Polebridge, 2002.

Cotter, Wendy. "Prestige, Protection and Promise: A Proposal for the Apologetics of Q." In *The Gospel Behind the Gospels: Current Studies on Q*, edited by Ronald Allen Piper, 117–38. Leiden: Brill, 2014.

Crawford, Sidnie White. "Women: Second Temple Period." In *The Oxford Guide to People and Places of the Bible*, edited by Bruce M. Metzger, 330–34. Oxford: Oxford University Press, 2001.

Dowell, Thomas M. "Why John Rewrote the Synoptics." In *John and the Synoptics*, edited by Adelbert Denaux, 453–57. Leuven: Leuven University, 1992.

Duby, Georges, and M. Perrot, eds. A *History of Women in the West*. Cambridge: Harvard University Press, 1994–96.

Duncan, Carrie. "Inscribing Authority: Female Title Bearers in Jewish Inscriptions." *Religions* 3 (2012): 37–49.

Eisen, Ute E., Christine Gerber, and Angela Standhartinger, eds. *Doing Gender—Doing Religion. Fallstudien zur Intersektionalität im frühen Judentum, Christentum und Islam*. Tübingen: Mohr Siebeck, 2013.

Eusebius. *Ecclesiastical History, Volume I: Books 1–5.* Translated by Kirsopp Lake. Loeb Classical Library 153. Cambridge: Harvard University Press, 1926.

Fiorenza, Elisabeth Schüssler. *Jesus: Miriam's Child, Sophia's Prophet*. New York: Continuum, 1995.

———. *Rhetoric and Ethic: The Politics of Biblical Studies*. Minneapolis: Fortress, 1999.

———, ed. *Feminist Biblical Studies in the 20th Century*. Atlanta: Society of Biblical Literature, 2014.

Fricker, Denis. *Quand Jésus Parle au Masculin-Féminin: Étude Contextuelle et Exégétique d'une Forme Littéraire Originale*. Paris: Gabalda, 2004.

Grossman, Susan and Rivka Haut, eds. *Daughters of the King: Women and the Synagogue*. Philadelphia: Jewish Publication Society, 1993.

Hartin, Patrick John. "The Wisdom and Apocalyptic Layers of the Sayings Gospel Q: What is their significance?" *HTS Teologiese Studies / Theological Studies* 50.3 (1994): 556–82.

Howes, Llewellyn. "'Whomever You Find, Invite': The Parable of the Great Supper (Q 14:16–21, 23) and the Redaction of Q." *Neotestamentica* 49.2 (2015): 321–50.

Ilan, Tal. *Mine and Yours are Hers: Retrieving Women's History from Rabbinic Literature*. Leiden: Brill, 1997.

James, Sharon, and Sheila Dillon, eds. *A Companion to Women in the Ancient World*. Chichester: Wiley Blackwell, 2012.

Jeremias, Joachim. *Die Gleichnisse Jesu*. Göttingen: Vandenhoeck & Ruprecht, [1947] 1998.

Keith, Chris. "The Competitive Textualization of the Jesus Tradition in John 20:30-31 and 21:24-25." *Catholic Biblical Quarterly* 78.2 (2016): 321–37.

Kloppenborg, John S. *Excavating Q: The History and Setting of the Sayings Gospel*. Minneapolis: Fortress, 2000.

———. *The Formation of Q: Trajectories in Ancient Wisdom Collections*. Minneapolis: Fortress Press, 2007.

Kraemer, Ross Shepard. "A New Inscription from Malta and the Question of Women Elders in the Diaspora Jewish Communities." *Harvard Theological Review* 78 (3–4): 431–38, 1985.

Krauss, Samuel. *Synagogale Altertumer*. Berlin: Benjamin Harz, 1922.

Levine, Amy-Jill. "Matthew, Mark, and Luke: Good News or Bad?" In *Jesus, Judaism, and Christian Anti-Judaism*, edited by P. Fredriksen and A. Reinhartz, 77–98. Louisville: Westminster John Knox Press, 2002.

———. "Second-Temple Judaism, Jesus, and Women: Yeast of Eden." In *A Feminist Companion to the Hebrew Bible in the New Testament*, edited by Athalya Brenner, 302–31. Sheffield: Sheffield Academic Press, 1996.

Levine, Lee I. *The Ancient Synagogue: The First Thousand Years*. New Haven: Yale, 2000.

Mack, Burton. *The Lost Gospel: The Book of Q and Christian Origins*. San Francisco: HarperSanFrancisco, 1993.

———. *Who Wrote the New Testament: The Making of the Christian Myth*. New York: HarperCollins, 1995.

Metzger, Bruce. *A Textual Commentary on the Greek New Testament*. Peabody: Hendrickson, 2005.

Meyers, Carol, ed. *Women in Scripture: A Dictionary of Named and Unnamed Women in the Hebrew Bible, the Apocryphal/Deuterocanonical Books, and the New Testament*. Boston: Houghton Mifflin, 2000.

Moloney, Francis J. *The Gospel of Mark: A Commentary*. Grand Rapids: Baker Academic, 2002.

Mroczek, Eva. *The Literary Imagination in Jewish Antiquity*. Oxford: Oxford University Press, 2016.

Murphy, Cullen. *The Word According to Eve*. Boston: Houghton Mifflin, 1998.

Owen, Henry. *Observations on the Four Gospels: Tending Chiefly to Ascertain the Times of Their Publication and to Illustrate the Form and Manner of their Composition*. London: T. Payne, 1764.

Piper, Ronald A. "In Quest of Q: The Direction of Q Studies." In *The Gospel Behind the Gospels: Current Studies on Q*, edited by Ronald Allen Piper, 1–18. Leiden: Brill, 1995.

———. *Wisdom in the Q-Tradition: The Aphoristic Teaching of Jesus*. Cambridge: Cambridge University Press, 1989.

Plaskow, Judith. "Anti-Judaism in Christian Feminist Interpretation." In *Searching the Scriptures: A Feminist Introduction*, edited by Elisabeth Schüssler Fiorenza, 7–29. New York: Crossroad, 1993.

Reinach, Salomon. "Inscription grecque de Smyrne. La Juive Rufina." *Revue des Etudes Juives* 7 (14): 161–66, 1883.

Robinson, James, Paul Hoffmann, and John Kloppenborg, eds. *The Critical Edition of Q: Synopsis including the Gospels of Matthew and Luke, Mark and Thomas, with English, German, and French translations of Q and Thomas*. Minneapolis: Fortress, 2000.

Schnelle, Udo. *Das Evangelium nach Johannes*. Leipzig: Evangelische Verlagsanstalt, 1998.

Schulz, Siegfried. *Q: Die Spruchquelle der Evangelisten*. Zurich: Theologischer Verlag, 1964.

Schürer, Emil. *History of the Jewish People in the Age of Jesus Christ*. 2 volumes. Revised edition. Revised and edited by G. Vermes, F. Millar, M. Black, and P. Vermes. Edinburgh: T & T Clark, 1973–1979.

Shellard, Barbara. "The Relationship of Luke and John: A Fresh Look at an Old Problem." *Journal of Theological Studies* 46.1 (1995): 71–98.

Vaage, Lief. *Galilean Upstarts: Jesus' First Followers According to Q*. Valley Forge: Trinity Press International, 1994.

Weinberg, Magnus. "Die Organisation der judischen Ortsgemeinden in der talmudischen Zeit." *Monatsschrift für Geschichte und Wissenschaft des Judentums* 41.5 (1897): 658–59.

Windisch, Hans. *Johannes und die Synoptiker*. Leipzig: J.C. Hinrichs, 1926.

Chapter Two

Women Itinerants, Jesus of Nazareth, and Historical-Critical Approaches

Reevaluating the Consensus[1]

Amy-Jill Levine

In 1976, the Congregation for the Doctrine of the Faith claimed in its *Inter Insigniores: Declaration on the Question of Admission of Women to the Ministerial Priesthood*, "Jesus Christ did not call any women to become part of the Twelve. If he acted in this way, it was not in order to conform to the customs of his time, for his attitude towards women was quite different from that of his milieu, and he deliberately and courageously broke with it . . . In his itinerant ministry Jesus was accompanied not only by the Twelve but also by a group of women (Lk 8:2)."[2] In one of the first exegetical studies of women in the Gospel tradition, Ben Witherington III's "On the Road with Mary Magdalene, Joanna, Susanna, and Other Disciples–Luke 8:1–3"[3] located women as traveling with Jesus, proclaiming the Gospel, and attending to domestic duties. Luise Schottroff asserted, "There is a widely held notion, much taken for granted and rarely questioned, that itinerant prophets were men. Such a notion derives from the patriarchal assignment of women to the household; it fails to correspond, however, to the actual reality of patriarchy."[4]

Gerd Theissen together with Annette Merz writes, "There were women among the followers who went around with Jesus (their number and composition probably changed), some of whom accompanied him to Jerusalem and remained itinerant preachers even after his death. . . . The itinerant charismatics, *both men and women*, depended on the settled followers of Jesus for support (Mark 6:10; Matt 10:11–13; Luke 10:5–9)."[5]

Popular author Reza Aslan insists that the "seventy-two disciples in all (Luke 10:1–12) . . . undoubtedly included women, some of whom, in defiance of tradition, are actually named in the New Testament" and "obviously the sight of unaccompanied women following an itinerant preacher and his mostly male companions from town to town would have caused a scandal in Galilee, and in fact there are numerous passages in the gospels in which Jesus is accused of consorting with 'loose women.'"⁶ He cites no such passages; there is none to cite.

Azlan's trade publication echoes John Meier's scholarly works; Meier similarly concludes, "The sight of a group of women—apparently, at least in some cases, without benefit of husbands accompanying them—traveling around the Galilean countryside with an unmarried male who exorcised, healed, and taught them as he taught their male disciples could not help but raise pious eyebrows and provoke impious comments. . . . A traveling entourage of husbandless female supporters, some of whom were former demoniacs who were now giving Jesus money or food, would only have heightened the suspicion or scandal Jesus already faced in a traditional peasant society."⁷ Meier concludes: "even apart from Jesus' custom of issuing explicit calls to potential male disciples, it seems hardly likely that Palestinian-Jewish women could have undertaken the unusual, not to say scandalous, step of following Jesus and his male disciples around Galilee for a good amount of time without Jesus' summons beforehand or at least his clear assent after the fact."⁸

The presence of women in the itinerant entourage around Jesus, regarded if not named as disciples and engaging in some form of ministry (*diakonia*), has become both scholarly and popular gospel; equally part of the consensus is that such presence was not merely unusual but also scandalous.⁹

Lest the argument for women's participation in Jesus's itinerant mission be regarded as a feminist desideratum determined by the hermeneutics of imagination, its proponents adduce the criteria of authenticity to support their claims. They find the criterion of multiple attestation to show women's presence in Jesus's company across various Gospel sources of Mark, Q, special M and L, John. The criterion of embarrassment (or dissimilarity) finds frequent invocations: women accompanying men not their husbands would be shameful and scandalous. The criterion of coherence serves to show that the women could accompany Jesus because Jesus himself disregarded Jewish purity laws. The arguments, although ostensibly historical-critical, serve to buttress Christology: the conclusion is that Jesus was unique among his fellow Jews: he disregarded purity laws, he treated women in an egalitarian manner, and women found in his presence a social liberation from patriarchal Judaism.

Two decades ago, in detailing how some feminist readers constructed a negative image of Judaism in order to create a feminist Jesus and an egalitarian Jesus movement (an example of which can be found in the quotation that begins this essay), I noted, "Evidence for women's itinerant missionary work . . . may have been suppressed, to be sure, but such evidence may not have existed in the first place."¹⁰ I also argued that "accounts of women at the cross, such as Mk 15.40–4," do not "attest to their roles as itinerant missionaries."¹¹ I would like to believe the consensus view; my feminist sensibilities would like to provide women leverage against what is known in the United States as the "stained-glass ceiling," ecclesial structures that bar women from church-based leadership positions. Further, I would like to find these *Jewish* women exercising a prominent role in the circles around Jesus.[12] The best I can conclude is that women's accompanying Jesus and engaging in evangelical itineracy is a possibility, but it cannot be demonstrated on the basis of the Gospel evidence. As Carla Ricci correctly notes, "The first major problem encountered on undertaking research into the presence of women accompanying Jesus on his itinerant preaching ministry is the remarkable scarcity of sources from which to obtain information."[13] Even Schottroff observes, in speaking of *Wanderprophetinnen*, that in Q material, women "are never acknowledged as independently operative outside of the home."[14]

This paper first reconsiders the application of the criteria of authenticity with attention to embarrassment, multiple attestation, and coherence. Then, it looks at the texts typically cited to demonstrate women's roles in the movement. Finally, it suggests avenues for investigation on the broader topic of (the historical) Jesus and women by refocusing attention from women on the road to women in the homes, where the majority, if not all, of the Galilean women followers of Jesus can better be located, prior to his fatal final trip to Jerusalem.

THE CRITERIA OF AUTHENTICITY

John P. Meier makes the most extensive use of the criteria for arguing for the presence of women in the entourage around Jesus during the Galilean phase of his activity. For example, Meier asserts, "Various Jewish women who had come to believe in Jesus' mission had—perhaps gradually over the course of time—attached themselves to Jesus' itinerant band of disciples and followed him on his preaching tours of Galilee and up to Jerusalem for his final Passover."[15] He finds that the "criterion of embarrassment argues that various unchaperoned women did in fact travel with the celibate Jesus and his male disciples on various preaching tours in Galilee."[16]

The first problem is that no Gospel finds the presence of women supporters shocking, embarrassing, or even unusual. Meier notes that given "Luke's desire to present Christianity as a 'respectable' religion that does not threaten the Roman order, it hardly seems likely that he would have created the potentially shocking picture of women, some married, traveling around Galilee with Jesus and his twelve male disciples without benefit of husbands."[17] His argument is easily reversed: Luke does not present women "traveling with the male disciples" in the sense of camping out at night or bedding down with strangers. Lk 8:1–3 notes that Jesus "went through cities and villages" with an entourage; the Gospel does not state that they spent nights on rocky ground or even welcoming homes. To the contrary, when Luke does portray Jesus as receiving hospitality, such as at Martha's home (10:38), he is not accompanied by the entourage and he does not, as far as Luke records, spend the night. Luke finds nothing shocking, because there is nothing shocking to find.

Surprisingly (at least to me), Meier is more accepting of these women itinerants than is John Dominic Crossan, who proposes, "the only way the earliest kingdom movement could have had women as itinerant prophets in that cultural situation was they traveled with a male as his 'wife,'"[18] as 1 Corinthians 9:5 suggests (see also Mk 6:7; Lk 10:1; 24:13, 18). Despite Crossan's own early attachment to the criteria of authenticity, he also cannot secure his case on the basis of embarrassment. The appeal to Peter's being accompanied by a "sister wife" (1 Cor 9:5) does not tell us about the people around Jesus but only about the people whom Paul, *following Jesus's crucifixion*, encountered. There is no mention of Peter's wife in the Gospels, despite the note that Jesus healed Peter's mother-in-law. To the contrary, the Gospels' Peter consistently insists that he has "left everything" even as Jesus praises those who have left their kinship groups.

The only way to find embarrassment is to suggest something embarrassing is going on. Jesus is *not* stigmatized as a "friend of women," let alone as one who is sexually debauched or as sexually suspect in any way other than celibacy. Jesus is accused of being a drunk and a glutton; he's accused of being both in league with Satan and of being demon possessed; he's accused of being a Samaritan and (potentially) of being illegitimate; he's accused of being a liar and a blasphemer. He may even have been accused of being a eunuch (if Mt 19:12 is a response to a charge leveled against him). But no accusation questions his association with women.

Were the women an embarrassment, then Jesus, likely, would have been accused of associating with prostitutes, for that is how scandalous women following a man would have coded. Jesus is nowhere accused of associating with prostitutes. There are only three references to "prostitutes" in the Gospel tradition, and none bears direct association with the women followers.[19] Lk 15:30 locates prostitutes, in the Parable of the Two Sons, in the imagination of the older brother. Matthew has Jesus tell the "chief priests and the elders" that "the tax collectors and the prostitutes are going into the kingdom of God ahead of you" (21:31). Finally, Mt 21:32 locates the tax collectors and the prostitutes as believing in John the Baptist; there is still no direct association of prostitutes with Jesus. Not even Celsus, in his denunciation of Jesus, suggests he was engaging in some sort of untoward relationship with women.

One could bundle prostitutes into the "sinner" category and so see them as dining with Jesus, but since the tradition tends to make explicit particular forms of social sin, such as tax collecting, the silence on the presence of prostitutes can be read as indicating absence. The woman, from the city, who was a sinner (Lk 7:37) *could* be coded as a prostitute, but that is not a necessary reading. Women are quite capable of committing nonsocially sanctioned actions other than engaging in sex for money.

After asserting rather than demonstrating the applicability of the criterion of embarrassment to the question of women itinerants, Meier then applies a form of the criterion of coherence: since in his view Jesus disregarded some purity laws, he likely disregarded any problems women's periodic states of impurity would cause the entourage. "The picture of a celibate Jewish prophet, teacher, and healer traveling around the Galilean countryside with both male disciples (some of whom had left wives back home) and female supporters (some of whom had left husbands back home) may well have been more than a little disturbing for devout Jews. When we add to this mix the further problem that (a) the women would presumably be menstruating at various times in any given month and that (b) living in close contact on a journey with a group of males, these women would have almost unavoidably exposed the males to impurity on a regular basis, Jesus' total silence on the question of menstrual impurity is remarkable, if not astounding."[20] The footnote adds, "Even if we do not suppose the more detailed rules of the Mishnaic tractate *Niddah* were in force at the time of Jesus (or were observed by Jesus's disciples), the simple rules of Lev 15:19–24 would have created enough practical problems for a traveling group composed of both male and female Jews. For instance, according to Leviticus, the menstruating woman was in a state of ritual impurity for seven days; anyone touching her during that time was unclean until evening; anything on which she lay or sat was unclean; anyone who touched where she had slept had to wash his garments, bathe himself in water, and remain unclean until evening; anyone who touched anything on which she sat had to go through the same routine."[21]

THE CRITERION OF COHERENCE DOES NOT HOLD

First, the claim that "Jesus' total silence on the question of menstrual impurity is . . . astounding" misses the point of Jesus's engagement with purity.[22] Jesus interacts explicitly with people who are in *abnormal* states regarding impurity: people with leprosy; a woman with a hemorrhage. Menstruation—like giving birth or ejaculating—places one in a temporary, and regular, state of impurity. There is no reason for Jesus to address such matters. He need no more discuss menstruating that he need discuss childbirth or ejaculation (which, I suspect, occurred on occasion among the male in the group). Menstruation like ejaculation is not a "practical problem" that requires addressing. Second, Jesus makes no comment about the state of ritual purity of the householders his itinerant followers would have visited, and it would have been odd were he to do so. Surely some of those women householders would have menstruated at one time or another; that the men in the household would have ejaculated is even more likely. Fourth, Jesus does *not* dismiss ritual purity concerns. To the contrary, he upholds them. For example, he sends men cleansed from leprosy to the priests with the command to offer the appropriate sacrifice (Mk 1:40–45//Mt 8:2–4//Lk 5:12–16). More, he several times *restores* people to states of ritual purity: he "dries up" (Mk 5:29, ξηραίνω) the hemorrhaging woman;[23] he raises dead bodies. Since purity is not a problem, it is irrelevant to the question of women itinerants. Since Jesus does not dismiss matters of ritual purity but rather makes the impure pure, he did not "dismiss" concerns about menstruating itinerants in his entourage. The criterion of coherence, adduced for the argument concerning women itinerants, does not hold in regard to the matter of purity; the matter of purity is irrelevant.

The criterion of embarrassment does not find purchase in the Gospel accounts, and the criterion of coherence, applied to the matter of purity laws, proves irrelevant. The criterion of multiple attestation, the third prong of the classical historical critical approach, also fails to deliver. As scholarship is both increasingly questioning the existence of a Q source and increasingly arguing for John's knowledge of the Synoptic Gospels, the possibility of determining independent sources is reduced if not eliminated. Meier's warning, "I cannot help thinking that biblical scholarship would be greatly advanced if every morning all exegetes would repeat as a mantra, 'Q is a hypothetical document,'" is well taken.[24]

Many years ago, when I was more sanguine both about the existence of Q and therefore about the existence of a community for which Q, in whatever form, served as its ethical guide, I attempted to imagine the life of women in the Q communities.[25] The approach had to remain hypothetical: A text is not a community, and a text may be ideal or prescriptive rather than descriptive.

Q appears to be falling by the wayside, as alternative constructions of the Synoptic problem, with a focus on the Farrar solution, are gaining ground.[26] The consensus appears to be moving in the direction of arguing that John had access to Mark, with access to Luke not far behind. James Barker has cogently argued that John has familiarity with Matthean redaction.[27]

Yet even were the Q hypothesis secure, and even were we to conclude that the Johannine tradition suffered no Synoptic influence, we still would lack evidence for women's itinerancy according to the criterion of multiple attestation.

For example, Meier claims, "The presence of the women at the crucifixion of Jesus is supported by multiple attestation."[28] Since I am not convinced that John is an independent account, the claim of multiple attestation does not hold. Even if it does, the presence of the women at the cross cannot be adduced to argue that the women traveled throughout Galilee with Jesus.

Mark first spots the women at Jesus's death: "There were also women looking on from a distance; among them were Mary Magdalene, and Mary the mother of James the younger and of Joses, and Salome. These, when he was in Galilee, were following him (ἠκολούθουν αὐτῷ) and were serving him (διηκόνουν αὐτῷ); and there were many other (women) who had come up with him to Jerusalem" (15:40–41). Calling into question the itineracy reading are (1) Mark's need for the women to provide the narrative thread from the cross to the burial to the tomb and (2) alternative ways of understanding the technical terms "follow" and "serve."

Mark depicts women as following Jesus in the Galilee to secure their witness that the body that died on the cross was the same body that was entombed. The women also serve a narrative purpose: Mark's three named women followers, who seek to anoint Jesus but who flee silently from the tomb, match the three named disciples who sleep in Gethsemane and flee from the arrest. The anointing woman (Mk 14:8), who is not an itinerant, takes her place alongside the unnamed centurion at the cross (Mk 15:39): both figures realize who Jesus is and act upon that realization when the male disciples and the women from Galilee do not.

Matthew and Luke follow Mark in locating women at the cross and the tomb. The names change, but such shifts do not indicate independent accounts. Matthew 27:55a records, "Many women were also there" and thus rephrases Mark's "among them." That Matthew would increase the number to "many" is consistent with redactional concerns: Matthew upgrades the participants at the feeding of the four and five thousand by indicating that the total was "not including the women and the children" (Mt 14:21; 15:38). Matthew also suggests that the women did not itinerate with Jesus during the Galilean phase: "They had followed Jesus from Galilee and had served him" (Mt 27:55b) does not clearly indicate itineracy in the Galilee. "Served him" or, as the NRSV reads, "provided for" (διακονοῦσαι αὐτῷ) could easily mean "offered hospitality in the home" as do Peter's mother-in-law (Mt 8:15//Mk 1:31) and Mary and Martha (Lk 10:38–42).

Lk 23:49 bundles the "women who had followed him from Galilee" along with "all his acquaintances." Nothing new here.

John locates at the cross Jesus's "mother, and his mother's sister, Mary the wife of Clopas, and Mary Magdalene" (19:25). The mother completes the role she began at Cana: there Jesus had told her that his "hour had not yet come" (John 2:4b), and there he suggested his distance from her: "What to you and to me, woman?" (2:4a). At the cross, his hour has come, and at the cross, Jesus tells this "woman" that she has a new kinship structure (19:26), a point reinforced by the presence of "his mother's sister." The mother goes with the unrelated Beloved Disciple and not with her other biological relatives. There is no multiple attestation here: there is the same story with variants, each serving the narrative purposes of the Evangelists. In no case is women's itineracy demonstrated.

Mark next locates the women at the tomb, and the other Gospels follow Mark, although changing who the women are and what the women do: come to anoint (Mk 16:1); see the tomb (Mt 28:1); bring spices and ointment (Lk 24:1); or visit (Jn 20:1).

According to various Gospel accounts, the women both "followed" and "ministered" to Jesus. However, the verbs "follow" and "serve/minister" need not suggest itineracy. "Follow," ἀκολουθέω, appears approximately ninety times in the New Testament, where in most cases it does not suggest wandering from place to place in terms of itineracy.[29] Connotations of itineracy or, more narrowly, of leaving one's home permanently, depend on context. For example, Matthew 4:25 states that "Great crowds followed [Jesus] from Galilee, the Decapolis, Jerusalem, Judea, and from beyond the Jordan" (Matthew is happy to mention, multiple times, that "Great crowds followed him": 4:25; 8:1; 12:15; 14:13; 19:2; 20:29; 21:9 . . .), but there is no indication either of itineracy or of scandalous activities among the entourage. Great crowds follow presidential candidates and movie stars, but most go home at night. In Mt 9:27, "two blind men followed [Jesus]," but they do not become part of the entourage (cf. Mt 9:31).

John uses the language of "follow" to indicate belief in Jesus (e.g., 8:12), where the road traveled is from darkness to light rather than from Capernaum to Jerusalem. Thus, the use of "follow" language does not lead directly to the idea that the women were consistently on the roads in Galilee. John gives no indication that women traveled with Jesus as he moved back and forth from Galilee to Judea. The mother of Jesus does not, as far as we know, "follow" her son to Cana for the wedding. Jesus goes to Capernaum "with his mother" (Jn 2:12), but this notice is not in an itineracy setting.

Had the women "left everything" to follow Jesus (e.g., Mt 19:27//Mk 10:28; Lk 5:11, 28), they could more easily be seen as itinerants. But they do not do so, explicitly, in any text. Nor does any Gospel text explicitly indicate that women traveling with Jesus in an itineracy capacity entered a house or a synagogue with him, distributing bread, engaging in a mission (unless they are among the 70 or 72), or even asked a question. If they did, one might wonder who was left at home to care for the children.[30] Only the hermeneutics of imagination has them on the road with Jesus, day after day and night after night, after having fully divested of their homes, goods, and biological and marital relations.

To provide for, or minister to, Jesus in the Galilee need not require that the women leave their homes for any extended period. The only relocation that may have some security is the final trip to Jerusalem: the prompt is not itinerant mission but pilgrimage festival.

As for the ministerial or serving or, best, diaconal work that the women from Galilee did: again, there is no necessity for their being on the road and engaging in evangelism, let alone being together with Jesus's male followers at night. Martha "ministers" to Jesus in her own home (Lk 10:38–42), and Luke marks no scandal here either. Should the followers of Jesus need funding or food, the women as part of the support network, like the male householders, were there to provide it. As we have seen, Peter's mother-in-law "serves" Jesus, but from within the home (Mk 1:31//Mt 8:15//Lk 4:39). The NRSV's translation for Mk 15:41b, "and provided for him when he was in Galilee," is apt, for "to provide for" is not the same thing as "to travel with." Matthew's wording also suggests that these women were not itinerating in the Galilee. Literally, Mt 27:55b reads, "these had followed Jesus from the Galilee, serving him" (αἵτινες ἠκολούθησαν τῷ Ἰησοῦ ἀπὸ τῆς Γαλιλαίας διακονοῦσαι αὐτῷ). "Followed *from*" (i.e., left Galilee with Jesus to go to Jerusalem) is not the same thing as "followed *in*" (i.e., were on the road with him in Galilee). Journeying with Jesus, likely among other Galileans heading to Jerusalem for Passover, would not be scandalous.

Only Lk (8:1–3) has the reference to women in Jesus's entourage prior to the cross. The statement need not be read as indicating women on the road, entering other people's homes, delivering the Gospel message. While Meier finds that "Luke's picture in 8:1–3 of unchaperoned women sharing the preaching tours of a celibate male teacher is discontinuous with both the Judaism of the time and with what Luke presents—and with what we know—of the first-generation Christian mission,"[31] more likely Luke imagines no discontinuity, because Luke does not imagine women on the road.

One could even read Luke's Greek as indicating that the twelve were with Jesus as he traveled while the women, cured of evil spirits, provided for him in a patronage capacity. Most English translations suggest that the women were on the road with Jesus. For example, the NRSV offers, ". . . he went on through cities and villages, proclaiming and bringing the good news of the kingdom of God. The twelve were with him, as well as some women who had been cured of evil spirits and infirmities: Mary, called Magdalene, from whom seven demons had gone out, and Joanna, the wife of Herod's steward Chuza, and Susanna, and many others, who provided for them out of their resources." The

NABRE is even more secure in the women's participation: "... he journeyed from one town and village to another, preaching and proclaiming the good news of the kingdom of God. Accompanying him were the Twelve and some women who had been cured of evil spirits and infirmities...."

Luke need not be understood as depicting women on the road. The text (Καὶ ἐγένετο ἐν τῷ καθεξῆς καὶ αὐτὸς διώδευεν κατὰ πόλιν καὶ κώμην κηρύσσων καὶ εὐαγγελιζόμενος τὴν βασιλείαν τοῦ Θεοῦ καὶ οἱ δώδεκα σὺν αὐτῷ καὶ γυναῖκές τινες αἳ ἦσαν τεθεραπευμέναι ἀπὸ πνευμάτων πονηρῶν καὶ ἀσθενειῶν Μαρία ἡ καλουμένη Μαγδαληνή ἀφ' ἧς δαιμόνια ἑπτὰ ἐξεληλύθει, καὶ Ἰωάννα γυνὴ Χουζᾶ ἐπιτρόπου Ἡρῴδου καὶ Σουσάννα καὶ ἕτεραι πολλαί αἵτινες διηκόνουν αὐτοῖς ἐκ τῶν ὑπαρχόντων αὐταῖς) could be translated, "And it was when he himself was passing through city and village, proclaiming and bringing the good news of the kingdom of God, and the Twelve with him. And some women who had been cured of evil spirits and infirmities . . . these were providing for them out of their resources." In this reading, the men traveled with Jesus, and the women provided the support needed for their travels. Luke offers no scandalous itinerary; instead, Luke depicts the women in the customary role of patrons. To serve as a patron is not the same thing as to travel with the beneficiaries from Capernaum to Bethsaida (wherever that is) back to Capernaum and on to Nazareth. Following Jesus from a home to the seashore does not make one an itinerant.

From her study of women's roles and the category of "disciple" in Mark's Gospel, Mercedes Navarro Puerto summarizes, "If ἀκολουθέω and διακονέω form a binomial of actions that define the trajectory of discipleship from its beginnings in Galilee through its end at the cross, we can confirm that women are the true followers."[32] What we cannot confirm, however, is that the following included itinerancy.

Given what the Gospels say coupled with Meier's reconstruction of both Roman family values and the definitions of being a disciple, there is no surprise that the Gospels do not label the women "disciples." For the Gospel text, the "disciple" is the one called or explicitly granted permission by Jesus to join the entourage. After Jesus's death, the term broadens to include people who dedicate their life to him, such as the female disciple Tabitha/Dorcas (μαθήτρια, Acts 9:36). The term "apostle" similarly broadens in Luke's corpus to include those who were not eyewitnesses to Jesus' activities in the Galilee, such as Barnabas and Paul (Acts 14:14; cf. Rom 1:1).

Even were we to grant, despite Paul's silence, the presence of the women at the cross and the tomb, we still have no secure indication of itinerancy in the Galilee. Women from Galilee may have accompanied Jesus on that final trip to Jerusalem, but we do not know if they went *only* with him, went with others and met him there, or were already in Jerusalem when he arrived. If we locate the women "followers" as home-based, then we can read their presence at the cross as not indicative of a one- or three-year journey outside of their homes but as a one-time trip to Jerusalem, at Passover, when many others were also making the journey, and women could easily travel together in groups. Thus, the presence of the Galilean women at the cross cannot be backtracked to an itineracy prior to the final trip to Jerusalem. Rather, with the exception of Mary the mother of Jesus, whom Luke locates in the Jerusalem community following the crucifixion, these other women may have returned to their homes.

Just as it took centuries for scholars to recognize that women were among Jesus' close followers (it takes Mark close to sixteen chapters to make this point), so it may have been the case that Luke's earliest readers did not see the women as itinerating with Jesus. That Roman audience would not have been surprised that women served as patrons of the Jesus movement. They may have seen Joanna, the wife of Herod's administrator, as based in Tiberias. Because "to follow" can mean "to agree with the teachings of," and because "to serve/to minister" does not require being on the road, there was no reason for Luke's readers to be scandalized. The women in Lk 8:1–3 can be seen as aligned with Mary and Martha as well as the numerous women in Acts: secondary or second-circle adherents, home-based, with resources expended for Jesus and his needs. These "sedentary supporters"[33] appear to be the right category for the women in the movement, epitomized by Mary and Martha and eventually imitated by women directing what have come to be called "house churches."

This patronage role fits women's antecedent and contemporaneous patronage roles: the widow of Zarephath served, in a mutually beneficial relationship, as Elijah's patron (1 Kings 17:10–24), as the Great Woman of Shunem (2 Kings 4:8–37) did for Elisha. Continuing in patronage capacity, Queen Salome Alexandra (76–67 BCE) supported the Pharisees but did not, as far as we know, travel with them: Josephus states, "Now, Alexandra hearkened to them to an extraordinary degree, as being herself a woman of great piety towards God" (*War* 1.111; see also *Ant.* 13.401–23). The (unnamed) wife of Pheroras, the youngest brother of Herod the Great, similarly served the Pharisees in a patronage capacity (*Ant.* 17.42–43).

SUPPORTING TEXTS

Schottroff, among others, argues that repeated material on intrafamilial conflict as well as the additional material in the Synoptic tradition, presupposes that "women were independently operative—whether sedentary or itinerant,"[34] within the Jesus movement. She then finds evidence for women's itineracy in Q (Lk) 9:58 ("foxes have holes . . . the Son of Man has nowhere to lay his head"); 12:51–53 (the notice of familial disruption between mothers and daughters, and mothers-in-law and daughters-in-law); Q (Lk) 14:26 (on hating family) as well as the prohibition against divorce in Q (Lk) 16:18.[35] Her apt phrasing reveals the problem: the various comments regarding familial disruption do not remove women from the home. To the contrary, they keep women in the home, albeit a home now destabilized.

The statement about the Son of Man lacking a home is about Jesus, not all of humanity and not about his followers. The call for loyalty to Jesus over family does not indicate that the women followers packed up and hit the road. Mt 10:34–37//Lk 12:51–53 need not suggest itineracy, and they may not even suggest familial breakup. Mt 10:34–37 has Jesus state, "Do not suppose that I have come to bring peace to the earth. I did not come to bring peace, but a sword. For I have come to turn 'a man against his father, a daughter against her mother, a daughter-in-law against her mother-in-law; a man's enemies will be the members of his own household.' Anyone who loves father or mother more than me is not worthy of me; anyone who loves son or daughter more than me is not worthy of me." The verse, which adverts to Mic 7:5–6, does not signal that the women are to leave home. It rather re-prioritizes loyalty, or as Tal Ilan asserts, "It is not about dissolving patriarchal structures or creating an imagined family of equals. It is about loyalty."[36]

Jesus's forbidding of divorce has the same effect: it keeps domestic relationships intact. However, in light of his message, husband and wife may have (with varying degrees of enthusiasm for the program) moved toward celibacy in light of the eschatological crisis. Focus became less on preparation for the future (the next year's harvest; the children's weddings) and more on end-time speculation. Or, husband and wife may have disagreed on the import of Jesus's messages, with the "believing" spouse staying in the relationship because of the divorce prohibition, or with (at least?) the husband deciding to leave the home in order to join the entourage, cf. Lk 18:29, "there is no one who has left house or wife or brothers or parents or children, for the sake of the kingdom of God who will not get back very much more in this age, and in the age to come eternal life."

The verse is Luke's redaction of Mk 10:29–30: "there is no one who has left house or brothers or sisters or mother or father or children or fields, for my sake and for the sake of the good news, who will not receive a hundredfold now in this age—houses, brothers and sisters, mothers and children, and fields with persecutions—and in the age to come eternal life." According to Meier, "Most of the people mentioned in Mark 10:29 are in balanced pairs—'brothers or sisters or mother or father'—and hence the absence of 'wife' may be explained rhetorically by the absence of 'husband,' the logion being addressed primarily to Peter and the Twelve."[37]

It is also possible that the term "house" *implies* wife, such that Luke was making clear the Marcan metaphor and not simply adding a sexist restriction. The use of "house" as a metaphor for "wife" appears in the Mishnah, where "setting the house in order," "cleaning the house," and "serving the house" are metaphors related to the wife's assurance of ritual purity.[38] Cynthia M. Baker, in a section entitled "'His House'—That Is, His Wife,"[39] adduces, *inter alia*, m. Mikvaot 8.4, "the woman who serves her house (האשה ששימשה את ביתה) and then goes down and immerses [in the ritual bath], and she has not [first] cleaned 'the house' [וטבלה ולא כיבדה את הבית] it is as though she has not immersed."[40] Baker details additional rabbinic connections between the terms "house" and wife," and also notes that "'Woman' and 'house' . . . intersect continually and in all manner of configurations in ancient Mediterranean discourses—discourses framed by theological/mythological, economic, political, and sociosexual propositions."[41]

If we grant that Jesus said something about "leaving house," it is possible to conclude that leaving house implied also "leaving wife." Luke's version makes explicit what was implied in the original statement: "Whoever comes to me and does not hate father and mother, wife and children, brothers and sisters, yes, and even life itself, cannot be my disciple" (14:26). Nothing here, however, about women leaving their husbands (and children).

The question of whether women accompanied Jesus in the preaching tour of lower Galilee must remain, in Meier's words, *non liquet*. There is no call of a woman, no clear notice that the women traveled since patronage does not require on-site service, and no direct evidence that the followers, called "disciples," included women.

THE HOUSEHOLD, AGAIN

If women served the Jesus movement primarily as patrons rather than as itinerant evangelists, then our understanding of these women might return to a focus on the household rather than on itineracy. Here questions remain, and perhaps these can serve, along with the issue of itineracy, as a locus for discussion.

First, Adriana Destro and Mauro Pesce propose that Jesus established interstitial voluntary associations based on loyalty to him rather than on kinship and in so doing disrupted household order. Specifically, they suggest that the women attracted to his program were elderly elites who "Broke barriers that kept them in the background or else in separate rooms"; in the presence of Jesus, they found their voice despite the expected silence they were to maintain in public, and they found their place apart from their husbands' mediation.[42] Thus the household structure prevails, but the women are no longer silent. Therefore, we might consider: is the Galilean household a place for women of confinement or openness? Does it represent an extension of, complement to, or alternative for the itinerant ministry?[43] Would women have been silent in their own homes? Would elite women, especially those with access to their own funds, have remained silent? For most homes in Galilee, was there even separate space for women?

On such questions, we should also consider recent work on domestic architecture, which suggests that categories of public and private are not secure. Sean Freyne, speaking of archaeological work in lower Galilee (e.g., Meiron and Sepphoris), finds "that a wide range of work—food preparation, spinning, iron work, grinding, et cetera—went on in adjoining rooms, all of which opened out onto a shared courtyard, in contexts where the presence of *mikvot* are clear indicators of an observant Jewish lifestyle."[44]

If Jesus disrupted household activities, what exactly was the disruption? For example, might the disruption have been in relation to sexual ethics, with both the forbidding of the divorce and the deemphasis on procreation? Given Jesus's apocalyptic warnings, might husbands and wives have lived celibately in anticipation of the in-breaking of the kingdom of Heaven?

Or, given various statements about communal disruption, did the households influenced by Jesus find themselves at odds with those who rejected his message and his missionaries (see, e.g., Mt 10:22; 24:9)?[45]

Second, if Jesus siphoned men, likely men in the middle generation, away from their homes, what roles were left to the women who remained? Had they already been sharing the running of the household, with the women now more involved in contributing to the household's economic maintenance?

Third, although the Gospels depict women as recipients of Jesus's healings, and they similarly depict the male disciples as commissioned to heal and perform exorcisms, the New Testament depicts no women as healers. Is the absence of such detail indicative of a restriction of women's roles in the Jesus movement, with the men assuming the healing functions? Or is the silence of the Gospels in relation to women's healing activities indicative of nothing?[46]

Fourth, how are we to understand the role of women who appear, according to Paul's letters, to be traveling on behalf of the Jesus movement? Paul states in 1 Cor 9:5, "we have the authority to go about with (περιάγειν) a sister wife (ἀδελφὴν γυναῖκα) as do the rest of the apostles and the Lord's brothers and Cephas." Is Paul suggesting that the women missionaries traveled only with men (cf. Rom 16:7 on Andronicus and Junia) but not by themselves? Does Paul know of single women who accompanied Jesus?

The image of women on the road with Jesus—tending to him; proclaiming his message; expressing their own freedom from traditional family life—will remain popular. For a recent version, the 2018 film "Mary Magdalene" provides a romanticized example. Could women have traveled with Jesus and the (male) disciples, as Rooney Mara does with Joaquin Phoenix, Chiwetel Ejiofor, and Tahar Rahim? Of course. But perhaps before we make this image gospel, we might look again at the evidence, or lack thereof, in the Gospels.

NOTES

1. This study draws extensively upon "John Meier, Women, and the Criteria of Authenticity," in *Jesus As a Figure of History and Theology: Essays in Honor of John P. Meier*, eds. Vincent Skemp and Kelley Coblentz Bautch (CBQMS; Washington, D.C.: Catholic University of America, in press).

2. Art. 2 (Vatican City: Holy See); cited in Chris Seeman, "Jewish-Christian Dialogue as Re-Evangelization" (manuscript, 2018).

3. *ZNW* 70.3/4 (1979).

4. Luise Schottroff, "Wanderprophetinnen: Eine feministische Analyse der Logienquelle," *EvT* 51 (1991): 332–44; ET "Itinerant Prophetesses: A Feminist Analysis of the Sayings Source Q," Institute for Antiquity and Christianity, Claremont Graduate School *Occasional Papers* 21 (1991), 261 n.129. Schottroff develops this idea in her feminist classic, *Lydia's Impatient Sisters: A Feminist Social History of Early Christianity* (Louisville: Westminster John Knox, 1995), e.g., "Of decisive importance for this model is that the praxis of the women and men who followed Jesus (whether itinerant female and male prophets or persons with fixed residences) was not an expression of an elitist special ethics but a work for the future of... the whole creation" (10). See discussion of Schottroff's thesis in Amy-Jill Levine, "Women in the Q Communit(ies) and Traditions," in *Women and Christian Origins*, eds. Ross Shephard Kraemer and Mary Rose D'Angelo (New York: Oxford, 1999), 150–71.

5. *The Historical Jesus: A Comprehensive Guide* (Minneapolis: Fortress, 1998), 222–23, my emphasis.

6. *Zealot: The Life and Times of Jesus of Nazareth* (New York: Random House, 2013), 97, 246.

7. John P. Meier, *A Marginal Jew: Rethinking the Historical Jesus*. Vol. III: *Companions and Competitors*. Anchor Bible Reference Library (New York: Doubleday, 2001), 79–80.

8. Ibid., 77. These women would not have self-identified as "Palestinian" (a term Rome promoted after 135 to erase Jewish concerns for national autonomy); the women would be Judean or Galilean.

9. The consensus requires accepting the initial hypothesis that Jesus and the male disciples also engaged in an itinerant movement. This hypothesis, like the Q hypothesis in which it is grounded, similarly requires reinvestigation. See William Edward Arnal, *Jesus and the Village Scribes: Galilean Conflicts and the Setting of Q* (Min-

neapolis: Fortress Press, 2001), 42–45. It may be equally likely that Jesus had a base of operations in Capernaum and made at most day-trips. Whether there was a Q, let alone a "Q Community," further complicates discussion.

10. Amy-Jill Levine, "Jesus, Second Temple Judaism, and Women: Yeast of Eden," *Biblical Interpretation* 2.1 (1994): 8–33; reprint: Athalya Brenner (ed.), *Feminist Companion to the Hebrew Bible in the New Testament* (Sheffield: Sheffield Academic, 1996), 302–31 (325).

11. Levine, "Jesus, Second Temple Judaism," 325.

12. They would not be in a "leadership" role because Jesus is the leader.

13. *Mary Magdalene and Many Others: Women Who Followed Jesus* (Minneapolis: Fortress, 1994), 19. Ricci's study appeals to numerous anachronistic readings of "late Judaism" (e.g., the Palestinian Talmud) to describe how "women in Palestine at the time of Jesus were subject to numerous denials" (23).

14. Schottroff, "Itinerant Prophetesses," 347.

15. Meier, *Marginal Jew* III, 630.

16. Ibid., 11.

17. Ibid., 76.

18. John Dominic Crossan, "Itinerants and Householders in the Earliest Kingdom Movement" in *Reimagining Christian Origins*, ed. E. Castelli and H. Taussig (Valley Forge: Trinity Press International, 1996), 113–29, here 120.

19. Contra Kathleen E. Corley, *Women and the Historical Jesus: Feminist Myths of Christian Origins* (Santa Rosa: Polebridge, 2002), 4, who claims that "Jesus was known . . . for associating with 'prostitutes,'" a tradition that [she argues] was originally found in Q (Q 7:29–30); she further suggests "Q indicates that the memory of the presence of these women among Jesus' disciples was controversial because of the associations of lower class women with servitude and sexual promiscuity, or the associations of independent or even elite women with liberated social behavior." Lk 7:29–30 says nothing about prostitutes; Mt 21:32 reads, "For John came to you in the way of righteousness and you did not believe him, but the tax collectors and the prostitutes believed him; and even after you saw it, you did not change your minds and believe him." The comment concerns not Jesus, but the followers of John the Baptist.

20. John P. Meier, *A Marginal Jew: Rethinking the Historical Jesus*. Vol. IV: *Law and Love*. Anchor Bible Reference Library (New York: Doubleday, 2009), 410.

21. Ibid., 475–76 n. 210.

22. See Paula Fredriksen, "Did Jesus Oppose Purity Laws?" *Bible Review* 11.3 (1995): 18–25, 42–47.

23. See Candida R. Moss and Joel S. Baden, *Reconceiving Infertility: Biblical Perspectives on Procreation and Childlessness* (Princeton: Princeton University Press, 2015), 200–6.

24. John P. Meier, *A Marginal Jew: Rethinking the Historical Jesus*. Volume II: *Mentor, Message, and Miracles;* Anchor Bible Reference Library (New York: London/ Toronto: Doubleday, 1994), 178.

25. "Who's Catering the Q Affair? Feminist Observations on Q Paraenesis," in L. G. Perdue and J. G. Gammie (eds.), *Parenesis: Moral Instruction in Judaism and Early Christianity*. Semeia 50 (1990): 145–61.

26. Against the Q hypothesis, see, e.g., Mark Goodacre, *The Case Against Q: Studies in Markan Priority and the Synoptic Problem* (Harrisburg: Trinity Press International, 2002); Idem, *The Synoptic Problem: A Way through the Maze* (London/New York: Continuum 2001; https://archive.org/details/synopticproblemw00good); Mark Goodacre and Nick Perrin (eds.), *Questioning Q* (London: SPCK, 2004); John C. Poirier and Jeff Peterson (eds.), *Marcan Priority Without Q: Explorations in the Farrer Hypothesis*, Library of New Testament Studies 455 (London: T & T Clark, 2015).

27. James Barker, *John's Use of Matthew*, Emerging Scholars Series (Minneapolis: Fortress Press, 2015).

28. Meier, *Marginal Jew* III, 75.

29. See commentary with extensive bibliography on the use of the term "disciple," in Mercedes Navarro Puerto, "Female Disciples in Mark? The 'Problematizing' of a Concept," 141–69 in *Gospels. Narrative and History*, ed. (of English publication) Amy-Jill Levine, *The Bible and Women: An Encyclopedia of Exegesis and Cultural History*, eds. Mercedes Navarro Puerto and Marinella Perroni (Atlanta: SBL, 2015), esp. 141 n. 1. For Navarro Puerto, the general category of "followers" replaces the (failed, male-only) category of "disciples": "Our first conclusion is that the women in Mark are female *followers*, but not female *disciples*" (162). Her study provides nuance to Meier's discussion of whether the women were "disciples" or not by problematizing Mark's use of "disciple" as a continuing category, especially after Judas's betrayal. No Gospel identifies the women as "disciples"; perhaps that category requires itineracy.

30. See David C. Sim, "What about the Wives and Children of the Disciples? The Cost of Discipleship from Another Perspective," *Heythrop Journal* 35.4 (1994): 373–90.

31. Meier, *Marginal Jew* III, 76. In Vol. II, 658, Meier suggests that Luke 8:1–3, "Taken as a whole, is probably a Lucan composition" despite traces of historical material.

32. Ibid., 154.

33. Meier, *Marginal Jew* III, 72.

34. Schottroff, "Itinerant Prophetesses," 360 n.1.

35. Ibid., 354–55.

36. Tal Ilan, "The Women of the Q Community within Early Judaism," in *Q in Context II: Social Setting and Archaeological Background of the Sayings Source*, ed. Markus Tiwald, Bonner Biblische Beiträge, Band 173 (Göttingen: Bonn University Press and V&R unipress, 2015), 195–209 (202).

37. *Marginal Jew* III, 110 n. 92.

38. See Mimi Levy Lipis, *Symbolic Houses in Judaism: How Objects and Metaphors Construct Hybrid Places of Belonging*; Ashgate Studies in Architecture (London: Ashgate, 2011; New York: Routledge, 2016), 132.

39. Cynthia M. Baker, *Rebuilding the House of Israel: Architectures of Gender in Jewish Antiquity* (Stanford: Stanford University Press, 2002), 48–53 (and see

m. Niddah 2.5). See also Tamara Or, *Massekhet Betsah: Text, Translation, and Commentary*, A Feminist Commentary on the Babylonian Talmud II/7 (Tübingen: Mohr Siebeck, 2010), 20–22.

40. Baker, *Building*, 53.

41. Ibid, 51. The contemporary of Jesus, Philo of Alexandria, offers the famous midrash: "Why does Moses call the likeness of the woman a 'building' man and a woman and their consummation is figuratively a house (οἶκος). And everything which is without a woman is imperfect and homeless (ἄοικος). . . ." (*Quest. Gen* 26).

42. Adriana Destro and Mauro Pesce, "In and Out of the House: Changes in Women's Roles from Jesus's Movement to the Early Churches," in *Gospels. Narrative and History*, ed. (of English publication) Amy-Jill Levine, *The Bible and Women: An Encyclopedia of Exegesis and Cultural History*, eds. Mercedes Navarro Puerto and Marinella Perroni (Atlanta: SBL, 2015), 299–320.

43. See elaboration of these questions, in conversation with the work of Carolyn Osiek, Mauro Pesce, and Adriana Destro, in *Gospels. Narrative and History*, ed. Amy-Jill Levine, "Preface to the English Edition" in Eadem, xvii–xxxi.

44. Sean Freyne, "Between Empire and Synagogue: Exploring the Roles of Women in Early Roman Palestine through a Markan Lens," in *Gospels. Narrative and History*, ed. Levine, 31–52 (37). Freyne refers to Eric Meyers, "The Problem of Gendered Space in Syro-Palestinian Domestic Architecture: The Case of Roman Period Galilee," in *Early Christian Families in Context: An Interdisciplinary Dialogue*, eds. David L. Balch and Carolyn Osiek (Grand Rapids: Eerdmans, 2003), 44–69 (esp. 58–68).

45. See Amy-Jill Levine, "The Gospel of Matthew: Between Breaking and Continuity," in *Gospels. Narrative and History*, ed. Levine, 121–44.

46. See Freyne, "Between Empire and Synagogue, 35. Freyne refers to Tal Ilan, "In the Footsteps of Jesus: Jewish Women in a Jewish Movement," in *Transformative Encounters. Jesus and Women Re-viewed*, ed. Ingrid Rosa Kitzberger (Leiden: Brill, 2000), 115–36 (128–30) and Elaine Wainwright, *Women Healing/Healing Women: The Genderization of Healing in Early Christianity* (London: Equinox, 2006).

BIBLIOGRAPHY

Arnal, William Edward. *Jesus and the Village Scribes: Galilean Conflicts and the Setting of Q*. Minneapolis: Fortress Press, 2001.

Aslan, Reza. *Zealot: The Life and Times of Jesus of Nazareth*. New York: Random House, 2013.

Barker, James. *John's Use of Matthew*, Emerging Scholars Series. Minneapolis: Fortress Press, 2015.

Corley, Kathleen E. *Women and the Historical Jesus: Feminist Myths of Christian Origins*. Santa Rosa: Polebridge, 2002.

Crossan, John Dominic. "Itinerants and Householders in the Earliest Kingdom Movement." In *Reimagining Christian Origins*, edited by Elizabeth Castelli and Hal Taussig, 113–29. Valley Forge: Trinity Press International, 1996.

Fredriksen, Paula. "Did Jesus Oppose Purity Laws?" *Bible Review* 11.3 (1995): 18–25, 42–47.
Freyne, Sean. "Between Empire and Synagogue: Exploring the Roles of Women in Early Roman Palestine through a Markan Lens." In *Gospels. Narrative and History*, edited by Amy-Jill Levine, 31–52. Atlanta: SBL Press, 2015.
Goodacre, Mark. *The Case Against Q: Studies in Markan Priority and the Synoptic Problem*. Harrisburg: Trinity Press International, 2002.
———. *The Synoptic Problem: A Way through the Maze*. London/New York: Continuum 2001.
Goodacre, Mark, and Nick Perrin, eds. *Questioning Q*. London: SPCK, 2004.
Ilan, Tal. "In the Footsteps of Jesus: Jewish Women in a Jewish Movement." In *Transformative Encounters. Jesus and Women Re-viewed*, edited by Ingrid Rosa Kitzberger, 115–36. Leiden: Brill, 2000.
———. "The Women of the Q Community within Early Judaism," In *Q in Context II: Social Setting and Archaeological Background of the Sayings Source*, edited by Markus Tiwald, 195–209. Göttingen: Bonn University Press and V & R Unipress, 2015.
Levine, Amy-Jill. "Jesus, Second Temple Judaism, and Women: Yeast of Eden." *Biblical Interpretation* 2.1 (1994): 8–33; reprint: *Feminist Companion to the Hebrew Bible in the New Testament*, edited by Athalya Brenner, 302–31. Sheffield: Sheffield Academic, 1996.
———. "John Meier, Women, and the Criteria of Authenticity." In *Jesus As a Figure of History and Theology: Essays in Honor of John P. Meier*, edited by Vincent Skemp and Kelley Coblentz Bautch. Washington, D.C.: Catholic University of America, in press.
———. "Who's Catering the Q Affair? Feminist Observations on Q Paraenesis." In *Paraenesis: Act and Form*, edited by L. G. Perdue and J. G. Gammie, 145–61. Atlanta: Scholars Press, 1990.
———. "Women in the Q Communit(ies) and Traditions." In *Women and Christian Origins*, edited by Ross Shephard Kraemer and Mary Rose D'Angelo, 150–71. New York: Oxford, 1999.
Levine, Amy-Jill, ed. *Gospels. Narrative and History*. Atlanta: SBL Press, 2015.
Lipis, Mimi Levy. *Symbolic Houses in Judaism: How Objects and Metaphors Construct Hybrid Places of Belonging*; Ashgate Studies in Architecture. London: Ashgate, 2011; New York: Routledge, 2016.
Meier, John P. *A Marginal Jew: Rethinking the Historical Jesus*. Volume II: *Mentor, Message, and Miracles;* Anchor Bible Reference Library. New York: London/Toronto: Doubleday, 1994.
———. *A Marginal Jew: Rethinking the Historical Jesus*. Vol. III: *Companions and Competitors*. Anchor Bible Reference Library. New York: Doubleday, 2001.
———. *A Marginal Jew: Rethinking the Historical Jesus*. Vol. IV: *Law and Love*. Anchor Bible Reference Library. New York: Doubleday, 2009.
Meyers, Eric. "The Problem of Gendered Space in Syro-Palestinian Domestic Architecture: The Case of Roman Period Galilee." In *Early Christian Families in*

Context: An Interdisciplinary Dialogue, edited by David L. Balch and Carolyn Osiek, 44–69. Grand Rapids: Eerdmans, 2003.

Moss, Candida R., and Joel S. Baden. *Reconceiving Infertility: Biblical Perspectives on Procreation and Childlessness*. Princeton: Princeton University Press, 2015.

Navarro Puerto, Mercedes. "Female Disciples in Mark? The 'Problematizing' of a Concept." In *Gospels. Narrative and History*, edited by Amy-Jill Levine (English publication), *The Bible and Women: An Encyclopedia of Exegesis and Cultural History*, edited by Mercedes Navarro Puerto and Marinella Perroni, 141–69. Atlanta: SBL, 2015.

Poirier, John C., and Jeff Peterson, eds. *Marcan Priority Without Q: Explorations in the Farrer Hypothesis*, Library of New Testament Studies 455. London: T & T Clark, 2015.

Ricci, Carla. *Mary Magdalene and Many Others: Women Who Followed Jesus*. Minneapolis: Fortress, 1994.

Schottroff, Luise. *Lydia's Impatient Sisters: A Feminist Social History of Early Christianity*. Louisville: Westminster John Knox, 1995.

———. "Wanderprophetinnen: Eine feministische Analyse der Logienquelle." *EvT* 51 (1991): 332–44.

Sim, David C. "What about the Wives and Children of the Disciples? The Cost of Discipleship from Another Perspective." *Heythrop Journal* 35.4 (1994): 373–90.

Theissen, Gerd and Annette Merz. *The Historical Jesus: A Comprehensive Guide*. Minneapolis: Fortress, 1998.

Wainwright, Elaine. *Women Healing/Healing Women: The Genderization of Healing in Early Christianity*. London: Equinox, 2006.

Witherington III, Ben. "On the Road with Mary Magdalene, Joanna, Susanna, and Other Disciples—Luke 8:1–3." *ZNW* 70.3/4 (1979): 242–48.

Chapter Three

Paul, the Man
Enigmatic Images
Kathy Ehrensperger

Paul does present himself as a man/male, in terms of his body as well as his gender perception. He categorizes the people he refers to in gendered form and places himself on the male side of this gender spectrum.[1] He refers to himself in gendered terms and boasts in gendered credentials as, e.g., in Phil 3:5-6 or 2 Cor 11:22-30. He claims authority and power in relation to the Christ-groups he has set up (2 Cor 10:10), asks for respect and engages in fierce competitive debates, if not fights, with people he considers to be on the wrong track (e.g. 2 Cor 11:4-15; Gal 5:7-12) or who are interfering in activity fields he considers his terrain.

On the other hand, he acknowledges his weakness and humbleness, presents himself as a fool (2 Cor 11:16, 12:11), shows himself vulnerable, unimpressive, and actually powerless, seemingly retracting from all power claims.

An irritating image of a man—an apparently unclear self-portrait, letting us see a man in a mirror dimly rather than clearly. What sort of a man is this? How can such a wavering image of a man gain trust and authority—which he seems to have achieved, at least partly?

The divergence of images is irritating in itself—and as with other Pauline themes such as the law, seemingly contradictory statements can be found in his letters. As with other themes, so also here, the starting point of the analysis should be the context of the individual letter, as far as it can be discerned. Hence I am not presenting here the solution to the conundrum of Paul, the man—if such a thing were possible, but some considerations with a particular focus on Philippians within the dominating Roman socio-political and cultural context of the colony under the early Principate.[2] For the purpose of this contribution I will focus on the Roman context of Paul's self-presentation as I consider it important not to conflate Greek and Roman culture and identity.

There existed no blended Greco-Roman culture or identity³ or sense of "Greekness and Romanness as a seamless pair" in antiquity.⁴

The focus on masculinity is of course also informed by contemporary research in gender studies. The caution raised by applying the contemporary lens to the looking glass by which we try to get a gaze of life in antiquity is certainly legitimate,⁵ however, the hermeneutical issue cannot be resolved in the end, but can only be kept at the forefront of attention as I have argued in previous publications.⁶ I will thus primarily focus on perceptions of manliness in early imperial Roman discourse on the one hand and Paul's Jewish identity on the other in order to get a sense of the manliness of Paul, the Jewish apostle to the nations.

PRESENTING CREDENTIALS

Paul presents himself in Phil 3:3 in the vein of an honorable freeborn man—in a vein which seems to somehow replicate the Roman *cursus honorum*.⁷ He mentions that he is a freeborn male member of his people by reference to his circumcision on the eight day—a clear marker, together with the following reference that he is from the people of Israel and the tribe of Benjamin, that he is not only a freeborn male but the son of freeborn ancestors according to his tradition. The addressees in Philippi most likely were not members of the Roman elite, but rather Greeks and Thracians living in the *Colonia Iulia Augusta Philippensis*, who had experienced the effects of Roman colonization. Prime land and the civil administration were firmly in the colonizers' hands, the local population were viewed as members of inferior colonized peoples/ ἔθνη in Roman ideological perception.⁸ With the Roman ideology dominating the public discourse visually and in many aspects of everyday life, the analogy of Paul's self-presentation would most likely be seen in respective Roman credentials, which certainly were propagated at the time in the *Colonia* as inscriptional evidence demonstrates.⁹

It has been noted that the reference to ἐκ γένους Ἰσραήλ resonates with the designation of a "civis Romanus" as Roman citizen, the reference to φυλῆς Βενιαμίν resonates with the accompanying necessary belonging to a Roman neighborhood, that is, a tribal designation (*Tribus Voltinia*). The reference to Ἑβραῖος ἐξ Ἑβραίων (Phil 3:5) could equal the reference to the father in Latin inscriptions whereas the reference to circumcision on the eighth day may be seen in analogy to receiving the *tria nomina* of a boy in Roman elite tradition on the ninth day after birth. With regard to his education in the traditions of his people, Paul identifies himself as a Pharisee, not in the past, but also in the present.¹⁰ The additionally acquired credentials mentioned by Paul resonate with what a free Roman citizen would need to add to his birth nobility by acquired achievements.[11] All of these credentials point to a free citizen of established ancestry, hence a full member of the assembly/ ἐκκλησία of his people.[12] So Paul here seems to replicate a dominating masculinity discourse, claiming equivalence in terms of authority and respect owed to freeborn Roman elite men. At least this is how his enumeration of manly credentials could be heard. In the Philippian context this is not such a far cry, the colony at that time was full of Latin honorary inscriptions through which the colonizing Roman elite expressed their "confidence in the flesh."[13] Clearly Paul tries to establish an authority claim in evoking male credentials of nobility, education and achievements, even though before (Phil 2:3–11) and immediately after this list of male credentials he seems to invert them (Phil 3:7–8). To invert something of high value, those addressed must be able to understand the inversion, that is, the value of credentials that Paul presents here in this comparative passage. If these credentials are supposed to resonate with the Roman elite ideal of masculinity, that is, the perception of the *vir* who embodies in his career (*cursus honorum*) the *virtutes* which guarantee his perception as a *vir* and demonstrate his *virility* in the public realm, the "saints in Christ Jesus who are in Philippi" (Phil 1:1) must be able to discern the allusion. To get a sense of what Paul's self-presentation might have implied we need to consider some exemplary aspects of this Roman discourse of virility here.[14]

ROMAN PERCEPTIONS

Although restricted and now directed toward participation in the honor/δόξα concentrated in the house of the imperial clan, the Roman perceptions of manliness and male honor were the dominating ethos of a Roman colony such as Philippi in the first century.

The status on manhood was not something that a boy arrived at automatically by coming of age, rather, "it is a precarious or artificial state that boys must win against powerful odds."[15] It had to be achieved and demonstrated in the public arena, even if the boy was freeborn into the right aristocratic clan, and thus at least had the potential of becoming a man—or in Roman terms a *vir*. One was not born a *vir*, one had to be molded into one. Although the biological status was determined at birth, through the inspection of the outer genitals, to be born male did not mean intrinsically that one had the potential to become a *vir*. Status was a decisive pre-requisite. A male slave could be referred to as a *homo* or a *puer* in Latin—and σῶμα/body in Greek but never as a *vir*, thus he also was never capable of having *virtus*/virtue; the status a former slave could achieve upon manumission was not that of a *vir* but that of a *libertus*/freedman. A good freedman (*libertus*) was not one who possessed *virtus* but loyalty (*fides,* πίστις) expressed in relation to his former master, now his patron. To become a *vir* one had to be born free and, in most cases, into the nobility, and succumb to fierce training from a young age to learn how to walk and talk, dress and relate to others (social etiquette). Rhetoric played a key role in this clearly staged education process. In addition to learning how to speak and debate in a strong, virile, not too emotional but vivid voice, the boy also had to learn how to perform in public speech and debate. The learning of the correct body language was of eminent importance. Delivery and thoughts are intimately connected, as Cicero claims "Nature has assigned to every emotion its own particular facial expression, tone of voice and gesture" (Omnis enim motus animi suum quemdam a natura habet vultum et sonum et gestum, *De Orat.* 3.56.213–58.217). In Cicero's concept what is innate in *natura* needs to be perfected by *ars* (training). Learning how to speak well included learning how to move. A speech was the enactment of thoughts, and only when body and words were in harmony was the orator trustworthy, that is a proper *vir* (Est enim actio quasi sermo corporis—For by action the body talks, *De Or* 3.59.222).[16] The mastering of this art is the pathway that leads to honor, reputation, status and glory, through fierce competition among young elite men, continuously contesting each other's status. In a realm where a young man had to be "the best, the greatest, the first, the *unus vir*"[17] to acquire and maintain his *dignitas* and *virtus* there were always others who had to be overcome.[18] Speech and performance had to be masculine in order to lead to success, and the risk of effeminacy always lured around the corner. If the voice was too high, the hand gesture too "feminine" etc., ridicule would quickly be the answer—and provide ammunition for competitors to denigrate the rhetorician as effeminate, and thus not a true man. The focus on the embodiment of masculinity in movement and gesture included the concept of the integrity of the body of a *vir*. Physical punishment was reserved for the non-elite, slaves and provincials in particular.[19] The only deviation from this rule was the option of acquiring a man-like status through an outstanding military career. By showing *virtus*, that is manly courage, in battle over the course of a long military career under the auspices of a powerful, noble patron, one could become not a *vir*, but a *homo novus* who had demonstrated and thus was acknowledged as having *virtus*.[20]

Notions of masculinity and femininity were fundamental ordering concepts in the period in question. But significantly they were not merely categorizing people along outer appearance, that is, biological appearance, as is evident in the fact that only a small section of newborn babies identified as male would be considered potential men/*viri* when living to adulthood. Not all males had the same category of a body. The male body (no less than the female) was the place upon which power relations were mapped, including social, economic, and political status. From a Roman perspective most males were *homines* and would never acquire the status of a *vir*. This not only applied to slaves and freedmen, but to all provincials prior to the granting of Roman citizenship by Caracalla in 212 CE.

With most men in the Roman empire of the first century, at least in theory, not being considered men/*viri*, it is evident that the concept of gender was not binary based on some kind of biological perception, but a socially constructed scale of degrees of masculinity and femininity respectively which marked hierarchies of status, power, and value. To be a *vir* was not a natural state—and to demonstrate *virtus* was not either. The highest value and status were attributed to the true man/*vir*, a freeborn male Roman citizen, as far as possible independent of the power of others, but most significantly, free to exercise power over others.[21] He had to be able to enact and embody this status and maintain his legal, financial, and personal autonomy lest he would lose this status, that is, would cease being a man/*vir*. The status of *vir* was that of the dominating man at the top of a pyramid of power, embodied ideally by the *pater familias* who had legal authority over the members (free and slaves) of his *familia* and *domus*. Loss of this position or not being part of the Roman elite, implied the loss of, or near impossibility to attain, the status of *vir*, sliding toward the feminine, that is, toward a category inferior to a true *vir*. The fully feminine was located at the opposite end of the gendered scale; hence the loss of, or impossibility of being a *vir*, meant to be on the slippery road from being truly masculine or being near to masculinity toward the feminine, at risk of becoming more and more effeminate, located at the lower end of the power and value categorization system.

What I briefly described here is of course not descriptive of the power relations and social categorization but what can be deduced from the prescriptive elite male literature available to us. And this is merely the social side of the categorization. With gender perceptions not being binary in antiquity, it is obvious that inherent to the categorization system are values and characteristics attributed to people, with philosophical concepts also being engendered. I have already mentioned the concept of *virtus* which was ideally embodied by a *vir*.[22] With autonomy and freedom from the power of others and the ability to exercise power over others being a key aspect of the top value attributed to manliness, it is evident that this perception impacted not only social and political interactions but also the perception of events and actions—and their interpretation.

Thus interestingly, although *virtus* is an acquired manly characteristic, it could also "unnaturally" be attributed to women who showed exceptional will and energy.[23] Although only males could acquire the status of a *vir* under certain circumstances, the notion of manliness, the manly, virtuous behavior and action could be found in bodies categorized as female as well. The perceptions of the sliding scale of male-female were categorizations of value hierarchies, embodied and lived by certain males. Moreover, they served as orientation systems for all those who could never embody them fully but were nevertheless deeply influenced by these notions. Carlin Barton has noted that emotionally the slave "was every bit as sensitive to insult as was his or her master. The plebeian was as preoccupied with honor as the patrician, the client as the patron, the woman as the man, the child as the adult."[24] And Valerius Maximus observed that "There is no status so low that it cannot be touched by the sweetness of glory" (Nulla est tanta humilitas, quae dulcedine gloriae non tangantur, 8.14.5). Hence what was the perceived ideal of a noble *vir* had implications in entangled pluriform ways in social, political, and military interactions throughout the Roman empire irrespective of the social status and actual power of those involved.

PAUL—AN EMASCULATED PROVINCIAL?

When we consider the trajectories of Paul's self-portrait that shimmers through his letters in the context of the prescriptive Roman gender discourse of the first century, clearly Paul's manly credentials do not seem to take him all that far. First and foremost, he is not born into the Roman nobility, but he is a provincial, a member of a subordinate people under Roman rule. He did thus not belong to the *populus Romanus* but to the subjugated ἔθνη/*gentes* listed in Augustus's *Res Gestae* (26–30), and visualized, e.g., in the Sebasteion of Aphrodisias.[25] As a provincial Paul did not have the prerequisites of becoming a *vir* in the Roman sense.[26] Nevertheless, he claims power and authority in relation to the addressees of his letters, clearly a manly claim according to the cultural codes of Rome, but also within Jewish tradition. He insists that he is called to be an apostle—to bring about the ὑπακοὴν πίστεως ἐν πᾶσιν τοῖς ἔθνεσιν (Rom 1:5), claims that he has the right to admonish (Rom 12:8; 15:4–5; 1 Cor 4:13; 1 Thess 4:18, 5:11) and teach (1 Cor 4:17; Phil 4:9) the Christ-following groups he had established. He even refers to himself occasionally as their father (1 Cor 4:15).[27] This seems to be a bold move by someone who hardly fit the credentials prevalent and expected by a man who had aspirations to, or defended his leadership claims. Besides these bold claims he surprisingly refers to numerous experiences which seem to directly undermine precisely such claims.

Paul thus mentions that he had been mistreated in Philippi (1 Thess 2:2), and worked hard day and night (1 Thess 2:9); he is afflicted when writing to the Corinthians (2 Cor 1:3); tells them that he was "utterly, unbearably crushed" (2 Cor 3:8). He refers directly to aspects which in the eyes of others disqualify him from any leadership claims and hence masculinity claims especially in the controversies prevalent in 2 Corinthians.

He is charged with weak performance in person and the inconsistency this indicates compared with his bold letters (2 Cor 10:10); he is an unskilled rhetorician (2 Cor 11:6a), a clearly emasculating denigration; he is working with his own hands to earn a living (2 Cor 11:7); he admits that he is not able to lord over the Corinthians like a master over slaves, or benefitting from them and in that sense he is weak (2 Cor 11:20–21), lacking the key credential of a Roman *vir*—that is, being able to exercise power over others; whether all of the hardships of the catalogue in 2 Cor 11:23–28 refer to actual real-life experiences of Paul need not deter us here, what is remarkable is that Paul lists so many emasculating mishaps in his attempt to establish his manly leadership credentials. Probably the worst of all of these is his reference to the marks of physical abuse and humiliation on his body (2 Cor 11:24–25). The scars of beatings on his back mark him as an enslaved, violated male, not able to preserve his bodily integrity, which in Roman perception meant he was at the lowest end of the gender scale. A true *vir* would maintain his physical integrity at all cost as this is clear evidence that he is in charge of his own life and is able to maintain power over others.[28]

These scars locate Paul on the feminized side of the dominant perceptions: as a provincial he was part of a subjugated, hence feminized people who in Cicero's words were born to be slaves.[29] It has to be noted that this did not attribute to Jews a slavish nature but referred to the Roman perception that peoples that were subdued by Rome were destined by the gods to be enslaved in as much as the *populus Romanus* was destined by the gods to rule. As Cicero states concerning the Jewish people "But now even more so, when that people by its armed resistance has shown what it thinks of our own rule; How dear it was to the immortal gods is shown by the fate that it has been conquered, let out for taxes, made a slave."[30]

The Philippians had obviously entered a relationship with Paul upon their first encounter (as had the other Christ-following groups from the nations except those in Rome), and thus considered him trustworthy as a leader at that point. As provincials they shared the status as members of ἔθνη/*gentes*, that is, of subjugated peoples. The addressees may have had links or occasional contacts with Jewish groups of some kind before meeting Paul, hence there might have been a level of prior trust in a member of this people among those who felt called by the message Paul conveyed to them. But it appears that subsequent events have cast some doubts about his credentials. In analogy to the dominating elite ideal where the credentials of a *vir* were not a given, but had to be established and reestablished in continuing competition with others who claimed such "virile" credentials, Paul's authority and leadership role do not seem to have been considered a given once it had been initially established. For addressees who lived in a Roman colony and hence were exposed to the claims of dominating Roman ideology on a daily basis, even if they were members of subjugated peoples (as mentioned, in Philippi most likely Greeks and Thracians), someone who wished to maintain authority and exercise power would be under continued scrutiny and had to prove again and again that he actually was at the top of the leadership game.[31]

In relation to Philippi it has been noted that the tone of the letter is mostly positive, indicating a sustained level of trust between Paul and the Christ-following group there. However, the fact that Paul feels a need to emphasize his manly credentials in 3:4–6 as mentioned above, in my view indicates that even here Paul's authority is not on as firm ground as has been assumed. At least Paul seems to consider it necessary to affirm his credentials. Given the context from which he writes—a Roman prison[32]—this should not come as such a surprise. Moreover, already in the opening of the letter he refers to his struggles, his sufferings, and hardships. Parts of the disturbing list of seemingly delegitimizing credentials in the Corinthian correspondence might well have been known also to the Philippians. Paul was beaten and thus shamed like a slave, right at the beginning of his activities in Philippi he encountered problems as he mentions to the Thessalonians (1 Thess 2:2), and now he is evidently again not in charge of himself as he is imprisoned. He clearly does not have the credentials of a man and a leader—when considered in Roman perspective.

CHANGING PERSPECTIVES

What is Paul trying to achieve? It has been argued that he is inverting the prevalent value system and thus presents a counter-cultural agenda, orienting all and everything on Christ.[33] That Paul draws some analogy to Christ cannot be doubted, but whether a mere counter-cultural argumentation would have supported him in maintaining his authority is questionable in my view. As I have argued elsewhere, for intercultural communication to be successful, there have to be links and analogies between source and target context in as much as this is necessary in linguistic translation processes.[34] Even the Christ narrative, an entirely Jewish narrative of the Second-Temple Period[35] would have been meaningless if there had been no analogies, narratives, and cultural codes in the addressees' socio-cultural context and symbolic universe that would have resonated with that of which earliest Christ-followers were convinced. That it is difficult to change ingrained perceptions—the "habitus" which molds not just our thinking but is embodied deeply in subconscious dimensions, is evident in the difficulties of inter-cultural encounters of today, manifest in many small aspects of everyday life. Trying to detach those whom Paul wants to win entirely from their "habitus" would be a difficult endeavor. The question of what Paul was trying to achieve by presenting himself as a beaten, imprisoned, suffering leader in support of his authority claims is puzzling.

It is evident that Paul does claim power and authority. Certain aspects of his self-presentation and the challenges he faces from others in the movement seem to disqualify him from the leadership competition. However, he seems to pursue a particular strategy by taking up the challenges and accusations against him. In my view he does this not in a counter-cultural vein, not so much by turning these discrediting aspects into strengths but by presenting them from a different perspective. He does not deny that he struggles, is near death, imprisoned, scared, and beaten. And he does not glorify all of this by inverting it into something that it is not. There is no glorification of suffering here, but a reinterpretation of what in Roman perspective are emasculating experiences, unworthy of a true man/*vir*. This reinterpretation does not amount to declaring weakness to be power (as in many traditional interpretations). Rather he taps into another aspect of the Roman masculinity discourse and tries to switch the perspective on these experiences not as those of a feminized, enslaved, disempowered subjugated provincial but as those of a courageous manly fighter and athlete.

Thus, apart from the fact that he makes these claims as a provincial, a member of a conquered people who is not part of the dominant nor the local elite, the masculinity Paul claims can hardly be described as counter-cultural. In order to be a trustworthy leader who exercises power in an empowering vein, he has to relate to a discourse the addressees can relate to from within their cultural context as just noted. It must make sense to them that Paul is a trustworthy representative of the message despite significant indications to the contrary. Paul is juggling a difficult balance act of cultural translation here. The message he transmits to those Christ-followers from the nations is rooted and embedded in Jewish tradition, that is, a tradition not necessarily in opposition to, but different from their own. As I have argued previously, this tradition had developed an inherently critical stance over against absolutist power claims by "rulers of this earth," that is, a perspective or view on events which might have differed from the respective dominating perspective under which Jews through various periods in history lived.³⁶ Although this did not necessarily lead to attempts at overthrowing "rulers of this earth," it enabled Jews to develop strategies "for cultural and religious self-definition and group preservation" under the conditions of foreign rule.³⁷ In Jewish tradition and life there was an element of subverting hegemonic values and being critical of dominating institutions through their own traditions. They had developed a way of accommodating to changing rulers and at the same time of maintaining some kind of independence and compensatory self-esteem.³⁸ The messianic message Paul transmits and embodies is entirely rooted in this tradition.³⁹ The challenge he faces is to translate this message into the cultural world of his non-Jewish addressees. The cultural codes and encyclopedias may have been expressed in the same language but this does not render them identical. Tessa Rajak has drawn attention to the difficulties that may have been involved for outsiders—Paul's addressees in our case—to gain understanding for a tradition whose literature is inter-textually interwoven in pluriform ways. She notes that "since any one text is only completely understood in terms of multiple allusions and resonances. . . . The full sense of the words could not be conveyed to readers not nurtured in the language and the biblical precedents."⁴⁰ Paul's addressees were only just beginning to learn what it meant to be "a gentile in Christ" in the context of precisely this tradition.⁴¹ A cultural translation process was under way with all the complexities this involves including the nontranslatability of certain aspects, understanding, transformation, and loss in translation.⁴²

In order for this translation process to have any chance of being successful, there had to be some relation in the language, codes, and encyclopedias transmitted that were either shared or understandable to some extent by those involved in this process. Paul's addressees had entered the process voluntarily. No coercive power was involved, rather the relationship may be deemed to have been based on compassionability, a willingness to listen and respond, a necessary presupposition for such a translation process to even begin.⁴³ To be heard so as the addressees would respond Paul had to be a trustworthy messenger. A trustworthy messenger had to be regarded as trustworthy according to the message he conveyed. Now, there is a tension. The message Paul conveyed did not cohere with the dominating values the addressees had been exposed to even though they most likely were not part of the group who embodied and transmitted these elite values. As to the challenges to which Paul seems to reply, these were related to the Roman perception of a true man/*vir*, who displayed the characteristics and credentials of a trustworthy leader with legitimate power and authority claims.

A COURAGEOUS FIGHTER

What is considered emasculating and disqualifying with regard to leadership credentials is in Paul's view what actually precisely does qualify him as a leader who fully embodies the message he proclaims. He sees the marks on his body, and the hardships he endures in analogy to Christ's suffering (2 Cor 1:5); his imprisonment is *for* the sake of Christ and *for* the benefit of "the brothers" (Phil 1:13–14); and his weakness (2 Cor 12:9), renders it clear that whatever is achieved is due to God's power not his own (2 Cor 13:4). But there is no identification of weakness with power. Weakness is not power, but through and despite human weakness God's power manifests itself.[44] In as much as this self-presentation is in tune with the sufferings of Christ, it is also rooted in Jewish tradition—not in glorifying suffering and weakness but in acknowledging the limits of human power and ability even when exercised in the service of the one God. In that sense, the leadership credentials Paul advocates are contrary to the leadership and masculinity ideals of the dominating imperial ideology.[45] Scriptural leadership notions paint images of kings and prophets precisely in this vein—with even Moses, although the greatest of all prophets, being depicted as sometimes doubting, loosing heart, being weak as Dennis Olson has noted

> leaders like Moses derive, on one hand, boldness, strength, and authority from their claims of relationship and connection to God. On the other hand in their relationship to God and in the face of realities of human communities, leaders like Moses come to know their own human limits, their frailty, their potential to misjudge God's will and purpose, their need for the assistance of others, and their susceptibility to God's judgment and critique as much as God's affirmation and support.[46]

Paul presents himself as a man in this vein, including a perception of power which emphasizes "not that we lord it over your faith" (2 Cor 1:24). But how would a cultural translation process in the context and under the conditions of imperial rule for people socialized so utterly differently work? Whatever Paul really thought (and I do not claim to know that), although he seems to only reluctantly and in an inverted way participate in this dominating manliness discourse (2 Cor 11:16–18), he nevertheless does actually interpret his embodiment of the message in terms of certain aspects of the dominating masculinity discourse. Whether this is to be understood as a form of accommodation in the vein of 1 Cor 9:23–33, as "becoming all things to all people" or not cannot be ascertained. But his interpretation of how he embodies the values of the movement is certainly not counter-cultural or undermining dominating masculinity perceptions as such.

What Paul challenges is the perception of others within the movement, who are questioning his role as a leader. Rather than succumbing to the perception that being beaten, naked, weak, hungry, shipwrecked (2 Cor 11:23–27) was emasculating, and thus disqualifies him as a leader, Paul maintains that these are not signs that he has been deprived of being in charge of himself, but rather that these are the battle signs of a brave virile soldier fighting for the message and for the groups that came to exist through his activities. He presents himself as a good soldier, who is able to endure hardship, is able to fight, courageous, facing up to dangers—and even risking death for the sake of those he is entrusted to lead. He defends the gospel (Phil 1:7,16), considers death for others as gain (1:21), sees himself and the Philippians as sharing in the fight (ἀγών). He faces hardship and struggle for the sake of the ἐκκλησία, but is far from being overcome by such adversities (2 Cor 4:8–12). He uses military language when taking up the challenge of so-called super-apostles and claims that "we do not wage war according to human standards; for the weapons of our warfare are not merely human, but they have divine power to destroy strongholds" (2 Cor 10:3b–4). In addition to such fighting metaphors, he also evokes the image of the athlete who does not give up, but keeps running until he reaches the goal (Phil 3:12–14). These are images, codes, and encyclopedias of masculinity which are very much in tune with certain notions of the dominant image of the true man/*vir*. Hence Paul does not deny or refute the points of reference raised in the accusations against him, but takes them up and turns them around, claiming that his credentials although different from those of others, render him precisely the credible manly/virile and virtuous leader they had trusted when they first met him. Far from idealizing weakness, he maintains "I am strong in everything through the one who empowers me"—πάντα ἰσχύω ἐν τῷ ἐνδυναμοῦντί με (Phil 4:13). He, through the power of God, remains in charge of his destiny, remains in power of himself and thus refutes the feminizing, emasculating charges raised against him. He presents himself as embodying truly virile virtues, as a credible agent of the alternative message he conveys. Since such qualities are not biologically confined to males, they could also be attributed to women as noted above. It is thus not inconsistent or surprising at all that Paul acknowledges women in the movement with reference to manly characteristics he uses for himself. Thus, Phoebe was a benefactor and mediator (Rom 1:1–2), Prisca (and Aquila) risked their necks (Rom 16:3), Mary and Persis have worked hard (Rom 16:6 and 12), Junia was imprisoned (16:7); and Evodia and Syntyche have labored with him (Phil 4:3). Leadership qualities and virtuous behavior were defined and expressed according to the prevalent masculinity discourse.

In terms of the competition for leadership in which Paul is involved, he clearly argues with reference to aspects of the dominating masculinity discourse and claims manliness in relation to it, despite indications to the contrary.

OTHER LEADERSHIP CREDENTIALS

This is not the entire picture. As mentioned, the analogy to Roman leadership credentials in Philippians 3 is preceded by the reference to the Christ hymn, introduced in Phil 2:1–4 with admonitions of how the Philippians should relate to each other in a supportive and noncompetitive way. The language expresses concern and compassion, support and other regard as core to their relationships. A very different atmosphere emerges from these words compared with the military and competitive language just mentioned. There is a high concern for the well-being of others and hope that the Philippians will be able to look after each other in the spirit of the one they follow. Here another image of Paul emerges, emotional (as in other passages of Philippians and 2 Corinthians in particular), concerned above all that there be no ἔρις among them. This coheres with the admonition later in the letter that Evodia and Syntyche be of one mind and should be supported (Phil 4:2–3). The details of the issue that led to this admonition cannot be discussed here, what is significant for the image of Paul, the man is that he appears to be concerned with harmony and reconciliation where there is potential conflict in the community. This is a concern of course not only here, but one that appears throughout Paul's letters for diverse reasons. It may cohere with an aspect in his self-understanding as a leader which he mentions briefly in 2 Cor 11:6. He admits that he is not a skilled or learned rhetorician (which disqualifies him according to the dominating masculinity discourse), but adds that he is not unskilled when it comes to knowledge. He may allude to the image of the wise, knowledgeable man here, an image of course that would resonate with philosophers of his day, but above all, when considered from the perspective of Paul's primary context, that is Jewish tradition, this might include his education in the traditions of his ancestors, as a Pharisee.[47] He would thus fall into a category of men who according to Josephus, are held in highest regard among the Jews who "give credit for wisdom to those alone who have an exact knowledge of the law and who are capable of interpreting the meaning of the holy scriptures."[48] It could well be that the knowledge Paul claims is also related to precisely such wisdom, which according to Jewish tradition attributes him high esteem, and in that sense then is the relevant credential for a true man in this perspective. If this is how Paul identifies himself from within his own tradition, there is a further aspect mentioned in Josephus which could also have impacted Paul's self-understanding. Josephus maintains that "the Pharisees are friendly among each other and cultivate harmonious relations with the community."[49] Albert Baumgarten interprets this passage as "meaning that the Pharisees worked to achieve reconciliation among members of the larger public."[50] If there is any hint of historical accuracy here, this may provide a lead into Paul's understanding and exercising of power and authority in his communities. If Paul sees himself as embodying the traditions of his ancestors as a man of knowledge and wisdom, then this role would have encompassed the notion that inherent to it was the task to settle disputes, to advocate communal care, unity, and to build up a sense of communal belonging. If there were conflicts it would thus be his task—not just since he had become convinced that Jesus was the messiah but already before that—to promote peace and reconciliation, now among the Christ-followers in a given place. Baumgarten sees a trajectory between this perception of Pharisaic leadership roles and what can be found in later rabbinical literature without claiming a direct lineage. Whatever the trajectory lines are, most likely rhizomatic rather than linear,[51] there is one known Pharisee of the first century CE who seems to fit the description of Josephus quite well.

CONCLUSION

It has become evident that Paul, by taking up the challenges to his leadership claims does not primarily subvert dominating Roman masculinity perceptions but presents experiences and bodily features which are meant to emasculate and thus disqualify him as a manly man and leader, in a different light. It is the perspective of other aspects of the dominating masculinity/gender discourse through which he interprets these very same experiences as those of a true, manly man, a courageous fighter and athlete,[52] and as someone who is more than qualified to be recognized as a leader/apostle within the movement. He does not argue in a counter-cultural vein to reestablish his leadership credentials but engages with the prevalent discourse and presents himself in light of this. In order to gain recognition there were hardly any alternative concepts available for Paul. Even though he felt commissioned to convey a message which inherently undermined the hegemonic claims of the imperial power, in order to be able to gain or re-gain respect and authority among his addressees, he had to some extent speak the embodied language of masculinity of the dominating socio-cultural context of the period. Even if he exercised his leadership role in a way that differed from that of the dominating power, as I have argued in my *Paul and the Dynamics of Power,* in order for him to be recognized as a leader, and exercise power in an empowering vein, he had to be able to demonstrate his manliness, according to the prevalent cultural notions.

One of the ways which also may have influenced Paul's perception of his leadership role, was as a conciliator in the vein described by Josephus mentioned above. Paul not only reinterpreted his experiences in light of Roman perceptions, thus playing the game of cultural accommodation, but most likely also drew for many aspects of his self-understanding from the tradition in which he was educated and embedded for his entire life, a tradition rich in knowledge and practice of playing and not playing the game of accommodation to dominating powers. The diverse glimpses on Paul, the man, thus let us see a Jewish man, who understands himself as called to be an apostle to the nations, who negotiated his credentials and the message he transmitted through a fascinating multivalent cultural translation process.

NOTES

1. An earlier version of this article has been published in Kathy Ehrensperger, *Searching Paul. Conversations with the Jewish Apostle to the Nations* (Tübingen: Mohr Siebeck 2019), 73–90.

2. For the history of the colony see, e.g., Peter Oakes, *Philippians: From People to Letter* (Cambridge: Cambridge University Press, 2001); Chaido Koukouli-Chrysanthaki, "Colonia Iulia Augusta Philippensis," in *Philippi at the Time of Paul and after his Death*, eds. Charambolos Bakirtzis and Helmut Koester (Harrisburg: Trinity Press International, 1998), 5–35.

3. Cf. the detailed arguments I presented in my *Paul at the Crossroads of Cultures: Theolgizing in the Space Between* (London/New York: Bloomsbury T & T Clark 2013), 17–38 and 76–83. Similarly, Annette Yoshiko Reed and Nathalie B. Dohrmann, "Rethinking Romanness, Provinicializing Christendom," in *Jews, Christians and the Roman Empire in Late Antiquity*, eds. Annette Yoshiko Reed and Nathalie B. Dohrmann (Philadelphia: University of Pennsylvania Press, 2013), 1–21, esp. 4–9.

4. Reed, Dohrmann, "Rethinking Romanness," 5.

5. Brooke Holmes, *Gender, Antiquity and its Legacy* (London: Tauris, 2012); Lin Foxhall, *Studying Gender in Classical Antiquity* (Cambridge: Cambridge University Press, 2013).

6. Cf. my *That We May Be Mutually Encouraged: Feminism and the New Perspective in Pauline Studies* (New York: T & T Clark, 2004), esp. 5–42.

7. The traditional *cursus honorum* had undergone changes in the transition from the Republic to the Imperial period with the competition among the aristocratic houses now giving way to competition to win the favor of the ruling imperial dynasty. Honor was now being acquired in relation to the honor and glory of the Caesar. James R. Harrison, *Paul and the Imperial Authorities at Thessalonica and Rome* (Tübingen: Mohr Siebeck, 2011), 225–32.

8. Cf. Robert Brawley, "An Alternative Community and an Oral Encomium: Traces of the People in Philippi," in *The People beside Paul: The Philippian Assembly and History from Below,* ed. Joseph A. Marchal (Atlanta: SBL Press, 2015), 223–46 (225–27); on the population of the Roman colony, see Oakes, *Philippians,* 44–63.

9. James R. Harrison, "Excavating the Urban and Country Life of Roman Philippi," in *The First Urban Churches 4*, ed. James R. Harrison and L.L. Welborn (Atlanta: SBL Press, 2018), 1–61.

10. There is an ongoing debate concerning Paul's Pharisaic credentials. Some are of the view that Paul considers these to be a matter of the past, as e.g., Daniel Boyarin in "*Ioudaismos* within Paul: Rereading Galatians 1:13–14 in the Context of Mark," paper presented at the Seminar "Reading Paul in Context: Theological and Social-Scientific Approaches," SNTS Annual Meeting Marburg 2019. I take Paul's identification as a Pharisee as ongoing also after his calling experience.

11. Peter Pilhofer, *Philippi I, Die erste christliche Gemeinde Europas* (Tübingen: Mohr Siebeck, 1995), 124–27. On the receiving of the *tria nomina* see Myles McDonnell, *Roman Manliness: Virtus and the Roman Republic* (Cambridge: Cambridge University Press, 2006), 175.

12. See Philo's reference to the third generation after the conversion of the grandfather only becoming part of the assembly (ἐκκλησία). *Virt* 108.

13. James R. Harrison, "From Rome to the Colony of Philippi: Roman Boasting in Philippians 3:4–6 in its Latin West and the Philippian Epigraphic Context," in *The First Urban Churches 4*, ed. Harrison and Welborn, 307–70 (320–27).

14. For further details, see the extensive literature e.g., Maud W. Gleason, *Making Men:Sophists and Self-Presentation in Anicent Rome* (Princeton: Princeton University Press, 1995); Lin Foxhall, Salmon John (eds.), *When Men were Men: Masculinity, Power and Identity in Classical Antiquity* (London: Routledge, 1998); Foxhall, *Studying Gender*.

15. David Gilmore, *Manhood in the Making: Cultural Concepts of Masculinity* (New Haven: Yale University Press, 1990), 11.

16. cf. also Quintillian 11.3.1.

17. Carlin A. Barton, *Roman Honor: The Fire in the Bones* (Berkley: University of California Press, 2001), 47.

18. Cf. my *Paul and the Dynamics of Power: Communication and Interaction in the Early Christ-Movement* (London/New York: T & T Clark, 2009), 102–03, also Scott S. Bartchy, "Who Should be Called Father? Paul of Tarsus between the Jesus Tradition and Patria Potestas," *BTB* 33 (2003): 135–47.

19. Cf. Jennifer Glancy, "Boasting of Beatings (2 Corinthians 11:23–25)," *JBL* 123.1 (2006): 99–135, Davina Lopez, *Apostle to the Conquered: Reimagining the Paul's Mission* (Minneapolis: Fortress, 2008).

20. On Cicero as an exception to this general rule, see McDonnell, *Roman Manliness,* 332–55. Note also that under certain circumstances, and particularly as members of the imperial household, women could be attributed *virtus*, cf McDonnell, *Roman Manliness,* 161–65 and 388 with reference to Tacitus *Ann.* 2.41.4 and *Dio* 60.22.2.

21. Cf. Richard Alston, "Arms and the Man: Soldiers, Masculinity and Power in Republican and Imperial Rome," in *When Men were Men*, ed. Foxhall and Salmon, 205–23 (206).

22. For a discussion of the concept and the changes it underwent through the intercultural interaction between Roman and Greek notions, see McDonnell, *Roman Manliness*, 12–141.

23. Cf. Barton, *Roman Honor*, 42.

24. Barton, *Roman Honor*, 11.

25. For more details on Aphrodisias, see R.R.R. Smith, "Simulacra Gentium: The Ethne from the Sebasteion in Aphrodisias," *JRS* 78 (1988): 50–77. The dating of the reliefs has been under debate, however, they do provide insight into the Roman perception of peoples under their rule/imperium. See also my *Paul at the Crossroads of Cultures*, 108–12.

26. I do not think that Paul held Roman citizenship and consider the account in *Acts* fictional serving the purpose of the theological narrative presented.

27. Cf. my *Paul and the Dynamics of Power*, 55–62;126–36.

28. Cf. Glancy, "Boasting of Beatings."

29. *De provinciis consularibus* 5, 10.

30. *Pro Flaccho* 28.69.

31. Cf. Erik Gunderson, *Staging Masculinty: The Rhetoric of Performance in the Roman World* (Ann Arbor: University of Michigan Press, 2000), 59–110.

32. Cf. Angela Standhartinger, "Letter from Prison as Hidden Transcript: What it Tells Us About the People in Philippi," in *The People Beside Paul*, ed. Joseph A. Marchal (Atlanta: SBL Press, 2015), 107–40.

33. So recently Sin-Pan Daniel Ho, *Paul and the Creation of a Counter-Cultural Community* (London: Bloomsbury T & T Clark, 2016).

34. Cf. my *Paul at the Crossroads*, 39–62.

35. The Christ-event as such including its understanding by the earliest Christ-followers must be understood as part of Jewish tradition. Cf. e.g., Daniel R. Schwartz, *2 Maccabees* (Berlin: De Gruyter, 2008); Jan W. Van Henten, *The Maccabeans as Saviours of the Jewish People. Studies in 2 and 4 Maccabees* (Leiden: Brill, 1997).

36. Cf. my *Paul at the Crossroads of Cultures*, 113–21.

37. Tessa Rajak, *Translation and Survival: The Greek Bible of the Ancient Jewish Diaspora* (Oxford: Oxford University Press, 2009), 206.

38. Rajak, *Translation and Survival*, 208. There may have been other traditions which had developed perceptions which differed from the dominating imperial discourse, but there is little literary or material evidence.

39. Cf. Ehrensperger, *Paul at the Crossroads of Cultures*, 113–21; Mark D. Nanos, *Paul within Judaism. Collected Essays Vol 1* (Eugene: Cascade, 2017); Mark D. Nanos, Magnus Zetterholm, eds., *Paul within Judaism* (Minneapolis: Fortress, 2015); Gabriele Boccaccini, Segovia Carlos eds., *Paul, the Jews: Rereading the Apostle as a Figure of Second Temple Judaism* (Minneapolis: Fortress, 2016); Paula Fredriksen, *Paul the Pagans' Apostle* (New Haven: Yale University Press, 2017).

40. Rajak, *Translation and Survival*, 207–08.

41. Steven Fowl, "Learning to be a Gentile," in *Christology and Scripture: Interdisciplinary Perspectives*, ed. Andrew Lincoln and Angus Paddison (London/ New York: T & T Clark, 2007), 22–40; also my "Embodying the Ways in Christ: Paul's Teaching of the Nations," in *Second Temple Jewish Paideia*, ed. Jason Zurawski (Berlin: De Gruyter, 2017), 239–53.

42. Cf. e.g., my *Paul at the Crossroads of Cultures*, 39–62 and Doris Bachmann-Medick, *Cultural Turns. Neuorientierung in den Kulturwissenschaften* (Reinbek bei Hamburg: Rowohlt, 2006), esp. chapter "Translational Turn," 238–83; Brigitte Wagner, "Cultural Translation: A Value or a Tool?," in *Translatio/n. Narration, Media and the Staging of Differences*, eds. Federico Italiano and Michael Rössner (Bielefeld: Transcript, 2012), 51–68, available also at http://www.goethezeitportal.de, Rubrik: "postkoloniale Studien," accessed last 01062018.

43. On such processes, see Harmut Rosa, *Resonanz: Eine Soziologie der Weltbeziehung* (Berlin: Surhkamp, 2016).

44. See also my discussion of a similar formulation to the one in 2 Cor 12:12–10 in Philo *Vit.Mos.* 1.69 in *Paul and the Dynamics of Power*, 109.

45. Although the notion of being dependent on the goodwill of the gods is also found in Roman tradition of course.

46. Dennis T. Olson, "Between Humility and Authority: The Interplay of the Judge-Prophet Laws (Deut 16:18–17:13) and the Judge-Prophet Narratives of Moses," *SBLSP* (2005): 18.

47. On the role of the Wise in Rabbinical thought, see now also Catherine Hezser, "The Rule of the Wise as an Alternative to Kingdom and Democracy in Ancient Rabbinic and Philosophical Thought," paper presented at the University of Zurich September 2019; also her *The Social Structure of the Rabbinic Movement in Roman Palestine* (Tübingen: Mohr Siebeck, 1997), 130–37.

48. *Ant.* 20.264.

49. *Bell.* 2.166.

50. Albert Baumgarten, "'Sages Increase Peace in the World': Reconciliation and Power," in *The Faces of Torah: Studies in Texts and Contexts of Ancient Judaism in Honor of Steven Fraade,* eds. Michal Bar-Asher Siegal, Tzvi Novick, Christine Hayes (Göttingen: Vandenhoeck & Ruprecht, 2017), 221–36 (235).

51. Gilles Deleuze, Félix Guattarì, *Das Rhizom* (Berlin: Merve, 1977).

52. For the image of athletics and Paul's self-representation, see now also Esther Kobel, *Paulus als Interkultureller Vermittler. Eine Studie zur kulturellen Positionierung des Apostels der Völker* (Leiden: Brill, 2019), 178–214.

BIBLIOGRAPHY

Alston, Richard. "Arms and the Man: Soldiers, Masculinity and Power in Republican and Imperial Rome." In *When Men were Men,* edited by Foxhall and Salmon, 205–23. London/ New York: Routledge, 1998.

Bachmann-Medick, Doris. *Cultural Turns. Neuorientierung in den Kulturwissenschaften*. Reinbek bei Hamburg: Rowohlt, 2006.

Bartchy, Scott S. "Who Should be Called Father? Paul of Tarsus between the Jesus Tradition and Patria Potestas." *BTB* 33 (2003): 135–47.

Barton, Carlin A. *Roman Honor: The Fire in the Bones*. Berkley: University of California Press, 2001.

Baumgarten, Albert. "'Sages Increase Peace in the World': Reconciliation and Power." In *The Faces of Torah: Studies in Texts and Contexts of Ancient Judaism in Honor of Steven Fraade*, edited by Michal Bar-Asher Siegal, Tzvi Novick, Christine Hayes, 221–36. Göttingen: Vandenhoeck & Ruprecht, 2017.

Boccaccini, Gabriele, and Carlos Segovia, eds. *Paul, the Jews: Rereading the Apostle as a Figure of Second Temple Judaism*. Minneapolis: Fortress, 2016.

Brawley, Robert. "An Alternative Community and an Oral Encomium: Traces of the People in Philippi." In *The People beside Paul: The Philippian Assembly and History from Below*, edited by Joseph A. Marchal, 223–46. Atlanta: SBL Press, 2015.

Deleuze, Gilles, and Félix Guattari. *Das Rhizom*. Berlin: Merve, 1977.

Ehrensperger, Kathy. *Paul and the Dynamics of Power: Communication and Interaction in the Early Christ-Movement*. London/ New York: T & T Clark, 2009.

———. *Paul at the Crossroads of Cultures: Theolgizing in the Space Between*. London, New York: Bloomsbury T & T Clark, 2013.

———. *Searching Paul. Conversations with the Jewish Apostle to the Nations*. Tübingen: Mohr Siebeck 2019.

———. *That We May Be Mutually Encouraged: Feminism and the New Perspective in Pauline Studies*. New York: T & T Clark, 2004.

Fowl, Steven. "Learning to be a Gentile." In *Christology and Scripture: Interdisciplinary Christology and Scripture: Interdisciplinary Perspectives*, edited by Andrew Lincoln and Angus Paddison, 22–40. London, New York: T & T Clark, 2007.

Foxhall, Lin. *Studying Gender in Classical Antiquity*. Cambridge: Cambridge University Press, 2013.

Foxhall, Lin, and John Salmon, eds. *When Men were Men: Masculinity, Power and Identity in Classical Antiquity*. London: Routledge, 1998.

Fredriksen, Paula. *Paul the Pagans' Apostle*. New Haven: Yale University Press, 2017.

Gilmore, David. *Manhood in the Making: Cultural Concepts of Masculinity*. New Haven: Yale University Press, 1990.

Glancy, Jennifer. "Boasting of Beatings (2 Corinthians 11:23–25)." *JBL* 123.1 (2006): 99–135.

Gleason, Maud W. *Making Men: Sophists and Self-Presentation in Ancient Rome*. Princeton: Princeton University Press, 1995.

Gunderson, Erik. *Staging Masculinty: The Rhetoric of Performance in the Roman World*. Ann Arbor: University of Michigan Press, 2000.

Harrison, James R. "Excavating the Urban and Country Life of Roman Philippi." In *The First Urban Churches 4*, edited by James R. Harrison and L.L. Welborn, 1–61. Atlanta: SBL Press, 2018.

———. "From Rome to the Colony of Philippi: Roman Boasting in Philippians 3:4–6 in its Latin West and the Philippian Epigraphic Context." In *The First Urban Churches 4*, edited by James R. Harrison and L. L. Welborn, 307–70. Atlanta: SBL Press, 2018.

———. *Paul and the Imperial Authorities at Thessalonica and Rome*. Tübingen: Mohr Siebeck, 2011.

Hezser, Catherine. *The Social Structure of the Rabbinic Movement in Roman Palestine*. Tübingen: Mohr Siebeck, 1997.

Ho, Sin-Pan Daniel. *Paul and the Creation of a Counter-Cultural Community*. London: Bloomsbury T & T Clark, 2016.

Holmes, Brooke. *Gender, Antiquity and its Legacy*. London: Tauris, 2012.

Kobel, Esther. *Paulus als Interkultureller Vermittler. Eine Studie zur kulturellen Positionierung des Apostels der Völker*. Leiden: Brill, 2019.

Koukouli-Chrysanthaki, Chaido. "Colonia Iulia Augusta Philippensis." In *Philippi at the Time of Paul and after his Death*, edited by Charambolos Bakirtzis and Helmut Koester, 5–35. Harrisburg: Trinity Press International, 1998.

Lopez, Davina. *Apostle to the Conquered: Reimagining the Paul's Mission*. Minneapolis: Fortress, 2008.

McDonnell, Myles. *Roman Manliness: Virtus and the Roman Republic*. Cambridge: Cambridge University Press, 2006.

Nanos, Mark D. *Paul within Judaism. Collected Essays Vol 1*. Eugene: Cascade, 2017.

Nanos, Mark D., and Magnus Zetterholm, eds. *Paul within Judaism*. Minneapolis: Fortress, 2015.

Oakes, Peter. *Philippians: From People to Letter*. Cambridge: Cambridge University Press, 2001.

Olson, Dennis T. "Between Humility and Authority: The Interplay of the Judge-Prophet Laws (Deut 16:18–17:13) and the Judge-Prophet Narratives of Moses." *SBLSP* (2005): 18.

Pilhofer, Peter. *Philippi I, Die erste christliche Gemeinde Europas*. Tübingen: Mohr Siebeck, 1995.

Rajak, Tessa. *Translation and Survival: The Greek Bible of the Ancient Jewish Diaspora*. Oxford: Oxford University Press, 2009.

Reed, Annette Yoshiko, and Nathalie B. Dohrmann. "Rethinking Romanness, Provinicializing Christendom." In *Jews, Christians and the Roman Empire in Late Antiquity*, edited by Annette Yoshiko Reed and Nathalie B. Dohrmann, 1–21. Philadelphia: University of Pennsylvania Press, 2013.

Rosa, Harmut. *Resonanz: Eine Soziologie der Weltbeziehung*. Berlin: Suhrkamp, 2016.

Schwartz, Daniel R. *2 Maccabees*. Berlin: De Gruyter, 2008.

Smith, Roland R.R. "Simulacra Gentium: The Ethne from the Sebasteion in Aphrodisias." *JRS* 78 (1988): 50–77.

Standhartinger, Angela. "Letter from Prison as Hidden Transcript: What it Tells Us About the People in Philippi." In *The People Beside Paul*, edited by Joseph A. Marchal, 107–40. Atlanta: SBL Press, 2015.

Van Henten, Jan W. *The Maccabeans as Saviours of the Jewish People. Studies in 2 and 4 Maccabees*. Leiden: Brill, 1997.

Wagner, Brigitte. "Cultural Translation: A Value or a Tool?." In *Translatio/n. Narration, Media and the Staging of Differences*, edited by Federico Italiano and Michael Rössner, 51–68. Bielefeld: Transcript, 2012.

Chapter Four

From Pain to Redemption
1 Timothy 2:15 in its Jewish Context
Sarah E. G. Fein

The creation of the first human couple, Adam and Eve, in Genesis 2 and 3 is a foundational text upon which the construction of gender roles in Judaism and Christianity is often based. One of the most important, and contested, ideas to emerge from this text is the so-called "curse of Eve." This "curse" refers to God's words to Eve after she and Adam have eaten from the Tree of the Knowledge of Good and Evil: "I will greatly multiply your toil in childbearing, in pain will you bear children."[1] The vast majority of early Christian interpreters understood this in a negative light.[2] After quoting this verse, Tertullian, a second-century North African church father, railed at the women of his day:

> And do you not know that you are (each) an Eve? The sentence of God on this sex of yours lives in this age: the guilt must of necessity live too. *You* are the devil's gateway . . . *You* destroyed so easily God's image, man. On account of *your* desert—that is, death—even the Son of God had to die.[3]

It is against this backdrop that 1 Tim 2:15 stands out all the more starkly. While 1 Tim 2:14 concedes that Eve was indeed "deceived" and is a "transgressor," the next verse counters that "She will be saved through childbearing, if she remains in faith and love and holiness, with self-control" (*sōthēsetai de dia tēs teknogonias, ean meinōsin en pistei kai agapē kai agiasmō meta sōphrosunēs*).[4] How could this note of positivity have entered 1 Timothy's exegesis of Gen 3:16? In this paper, I argue that the author's interpretation of Gen 3:16 can be understood through the lens of Jewish readings of this verse that understood childbirth—for all women—as a redemptive act. First, I will examine the gendered implications of the Hebrew and Greek texts of Gen 3:16. I will then establish that 1 Timothy demonstrates a reliance on Jewish interpretations of the larger narrative of transgression in Gen 3. Finally, I will conclude that 1 Timothy reworks Jewish ideas about women and childbirth into a Christian virtues-based framework, ultimately granting all women who physically give birth the opportunity for spiritual salvation.

THE ROOT OF ALL EVIL: GENESIS 3:16

The root of 1 Timothy's claim in 2:15 is just half a verse, Genesis 3:16a. These words are framed as divine punishment for Eve for eating from the Tree of Knowledge of Good and Evil. God says to Eve: "I will greatly multiply your toil in childbearing, in pain will you bear children" (*Harbah 'arbah 'itsvonekh veheronekh be'etsev teldi banim*).[5] The first two words, *harbah 'arbah* function together as an infinitive absolute (*harbah*) and an imperfect (*'arbah*). This combination of an infinitive absolute with a finite verb of the same stem, such as an imperfect, serves to "strengthen the idea of the verb."[6] In cases where the infinitive absolute precedes the finite verb, as here, it emphasizes the "certainty (especially in the case of threats) or the forcibleness and completeness of an occurrence."[7] Thus, one can understand *harbah 'arbah* as "greatly multiply," as I have translated it, or perhaps "certainly multiply," if you read Gen 3:16a as a threat.[8] The object of these verbs is "your toil," *'itsvonekh*. This is the same word with which God curses the man in the following verse, 3:17b: "Cursed is the earth because of you, in *toil* [*'itsavon*] you will eat from it all the days of your life" (emphasis mine). The sense of toil in verse 16a, however, is distinctly gendered. The woman's curse of toil is followed by "your childbearing" (*heronekh*). The parallelism between the two versets illuminates the meaning of the unusual noun *heron*. The more common term that refers to giving birth is found in the next line of verse 16, *teldi*, from the root *y-l-d*.[9] The parallelism of 16a suggests that the "semantics" of the first and second verset are roughly equivalent, i.e. *h-r-n* is roughly equivalent to *y-l-d* and can defensibly be translated "childbearing."[10]

The meaning of the verse is further clarified if it is understood as a hendiadys. A hendiadys, in which two words express a single idea, functions in the Hebrew Bible in one of two main ways: one, to extend the vocabulary as a "surrogate" for an adverb, and two, as hyperbole.[11] In *'itsvonekh veheronekh* the sense is more of the former, as in "your toilsome childbearing." Phyllis Trible notes that this reading is supported by its parallelism with the following line: "in pain will you bear children," *be'etsev teldi banim*.[12] The meaning of this phrase is clear for, as previously stated, the use of the root *y-l-d* to refer to bearing children is extremely common in the Hebrew Bible.

The Septuagint (LXX) translation of this passage both clarifies and muddies the issues raised by the Hebrew version of this text. The first line of verse 16a reads "I will greatly increase your pain and your groaning" (*plēthynōn plēthynō tas lypas sou kai ton stenagmon sou*).[13] The combination of *plēthynōn plēthynō*, a participle plus finite verb, echoes the *harbah 'arbah* of the Hebrew, intensifying the sense of the word "multiply." The object of these verbs are "your pain and your groaning" (*tas lypas sou kai ton stenagmon sou*), a doublet. The two terms refer to the same general idea but the second component, "groaning," is elevated to a greater importance.[14] The reference is not as explicit as it was in the Hebrew (*itsvonekh veheronekh*), but it is possible that the groaning refers to a woman's groaning during childbirth.[15] While that use is not found elsewhere in the LXX, where the term mostly refers to an outcry of oppression or injustice (as in Ex 2:24 or Judg 2:18), the next verset, in parallel with the first, makes clear the reference to childbearing. This line reads, "in pain you will bear children" (*en lypais texē tekna*).[16] Explicitly connecting the two versets is the repetition of the word "pain" (*lypais/lypas*). This parallelism illuminates the first meaning through the second, and the meaning of the second is clear: *texē*, from the verb *tiktō*, "to bear children," is the equivalent of *y-l-d* in the Hebrew, and is the most common word referring to producing offspring in the LXX.[17] Therefore, one can understand verse 16a in the LXX, like the Hebrew, to curse Eve with pain in childbirth.[18]

THE JEWISH PRESENCE AT EPHESUS

First Timothy, in which the intriguing line "She will be saved through childbearing, if she remains in faith and love and holiness, with self-control" is found, dates from the late first century or early second century CE. It is part of the Pastoral Epistles, which also includes 2 Timothy and Titus.[19] This Pastoral Epistle identifies the recipient of the letter as "Timothy," and locates him in the city of Ephesus in Asia Minor. The presumed occasion for the letter provides clues about the nascent Christian community in Ephesus.[20] In 1 Tim 1:3–7, the author warns against "certain people" teaching "myths and endless genealogies" (*mythois kai geneaogiais aperantois*) and accuses them of trying to be "teachers of the law" (*nomodidaskaloi*).[21] Paul Trebilco hypothesizes that these people could have been influenced by the "prominent and sizable" Jewish community of Ephesus, or that they were even Jewish Christians themselves.[22] In this scenario, the author would have been objecting to people "illegitimately" bringing in particularistic Jewish teachings to the Ephesian ecclesia.[23]

This sort of mixed Gentile and Jewish community was not uncommon in the early church. Adam H. Becker and Annette Yoshiko Reed make a compelling case there was no definitive "parting of the ways" of Jews and Christians until long after the first and second centuries CE, if at all:

> ... we suggest that Jews and Christians (or at least the elites among them) may have been engaged in the task of "parting" throughout Late Antiquity and the early Middle Ages, precisely because the two never really "parted" during [the first or second century CE] with the degree of decisiveness or finality needed to render either tradition irrelevant to the self-definition of the other, or even to make participation in both an unattractive or inconceivable option.[24]

In his assessment of the particular situation at Ephesus, Jörg Frey finds Reed and Becker's suggestion to hold true. He calls the separation between Jesus followers and Judaism in Ephesus a "rather incoherent process" which happened over a long period of time, for a variety of reasons, and which differed from "group to group and place to place."[25] Thus, there would have been a significant amount of time in which Jews, some of whom were probably learned, comingled with Gentiles in early Christian communities.[26] Such comingling would have resulted in interchange on a variety of levels: culture, language, diet, dress, theology, and, of course, text. It would not be surprising, therefore, to find evidence of Jewish influence in the texts produced by the Christian community of Ephesus.

FROM A JEWISH "MISOGYNISTIC TRADITION" TO 1 TIMOTHY

We cannot be sure of the identity of the author of 1 Timothy; though the book claims to be written by Paul, himself born a Jew, the authenticity of this attribution is dubious.[27] Nevertheless, it can be said with some certainty that the author, whoever he was, was familiar with Jewish scripture, theology, and liturgy. Christopher Hutson identifies four textual features of 1 Timothy that "betray a close affinity with Judaism": 1) the aforementioned *nomodidaskaloi* ("teachers of the law"); 2) the doxology in 1:17 *tō de basilei tōn aiōnōn* ("King of the Ages"), which recalls the Hebrew divine epithet *melekh haolam* (with its temporal connotation "king forever and ever"), already in use in the Second Temple Period; 3) the exhortation in 2:2 to pray *hyper basileōn kai pantōn tōn en hyperochē ontōn* ("for kings and all who are in high positions"), which "reflects a classic Jewish tactic for survival under pagan domination;" and finally 4) the affirmation in 2:5 *eis gar theos* ("for God is one"), alluding to the Shema (Deut 6:4 in the LXX): *kyrios ho theos hēmōn kyrios eis estin* ("the Lord is our God, the Lord is one").[28] These allusions to Jewish language and themes in 1 Timothy's first two chapters strengthen the case that we can identify Jewish influence in 2:15.

The influence of Jewish scriptures on 1 Timothy's understanding of gender can first be found in its interpretation of the Genesis 2–3 creation narratives. 1 Tim 2:12–14, which states that "I do not permit a woman to teach or to have authority over a man/For Adam was formed first, then Eve/And Adam was not deceived, but the woman was deceived, and became a transgressor," reveals the influence of two Jewish ideas: assigning theological significance to the order of creation and blaming Eve for the transgression in the garden of Eden. Like 1 Timothy, early rabbis preferred the creation narrative in Gen 2, in which woman is created from man's "side," to the simultaneous creation of male and female humans in Gen 1.[29] This order of creation, in which men were created first and in God's image, "maintained the primacy of the male ... with all the implications of potency, dominance, and generativity which followed from this analogy."[30] This reading of Eve as secondary, and thus inferior, coheres with the underlying message of 1 Tim 2:12–14, which justifies prohibiting women to "teach" or "have authority over a man" by appealing to the secondary creation of woman.

Jewish sources as early as the second century BCE cast blame on Eve for bringing sin into the world. Sirach 25:24 reads "From woman [*ishah/gunaikos*] sin began, and because of her we all die."[31] Jeremy Corley identifies this statement as the source of a "misogynistic tradition" which blamed human mortality on Eve.[32] This tradition was further developed in 4 Maccabees, which dates from the first century BCE or first century CE, where in 18:6–8 the mother of the seven martyred sons suggests that the nature of Eve's seduction was sexual. She claims to have been a "pure virgin" until marriage, who guarded the "side" (*pleuran*) from which woman was formed.[33] She says that "nor did the destroyer, the serpent of deceit [*apaatēs ophis*], ruin the purity of my virginity."[34] The invocation of the terms *pleuran* and *ophis* make clear the connection to Eve's transgression in Gen 2 and 3, where these same terms are used, and place the blame for being seduced by the serpent squarely upon Eve's shoulders. A clear thematic link is seen between these early Jewish texts and 1 Tim 2:14, where Adam is relieved of any responsibility for disobeying God's orders not to eat from the Tree of the Knowledge of Good and Evil, and Eve is named solely as the "transgressor."

Following in this "misogynistic tradition" (in Corley's terms), is a text which has clear parallels in 1 Tim 2:15: Mishnah Shabbat 2:6, codified circa 200 CE.[35] This verse states, "For three transgressions women die at the time of childbirth. For not being strictly observant of *niddah* [menstrual purity], *challah* [separating dough], and *hadlakat ner* [kindling the Sabbath lights]" (*'al shalosh 'averut nashim metot bish'at ledaten. 'al she'einan zehirot beniddah uvkhallah uvehadlakat haner)*.³⁶ Here, a particularly gendered "punishment" (death in childbirth) is related to the three *mitzvot* (commandments) that are reserved for women. It is possible that this verse was included in the Mishnah as a means of enforcing compliance with the *mitzvot* of *niddah, challah,* and *hadlakat ner*. Judith Romney Wegner points out that women's observance of three *mitzvot* are necessary to prevent men from transgressing—i.e., from becoming ritually impure during their wives' menstrual cycles; from failing to bake the bread themselves, which they are obligated to do according to Num 15:17–21; and from kindling the Shabbat lights after they return home from synagogue, which might be after Shabbat has started.³⁷ The rabbis would thus have had a vested interest in women's compliance with these *mitzvot* and may have attempted to enforce it by threatening women with the greatest punishment they could imagine: death in childbirth.

Yet it is possible for this statement to be construed in a more positive way. Judith Baskin proposes that perhaps the rabbis were simply connecting a common tragedy, maternal mortality, with what they perceived as women's frequent failure to observe these commandments. She wonders if the rabbis believed that "women were blessed with three empowering commandments, or cursed with three eternal punishments, or at best *three modes of atonement*. Did women view these obligations as *special opportunities for sanctity* or as deserved reminders of Eve's sin? [emphases mine]."³⁸ Reading Mishnah Shabbat as Wegner proposes, as "opportunities for sanctity," would mean that women would not die—that is, they would *be saved*—through childbirth, if they observed these three commandments. In the next section, I will argue that this redemptive possibility is the foundation upon which the formulation in 1 Tim 2:15 is built.

SAVED THROUGH CHILDBEARING: 1 TIMOTHY 2:15

We now arrive at the surprising statement in 1 Tim 2:15: "But she will be saved through childbearing, if they remain in faith and love and holiness, with self-control" (*sōthēsetai de dia tēs teknogonias, ean meinōsin en pistei kai agapē kai agiasmō meta sōphrosunēs*). There are three major parts of this verse that have puzzled interpreters for centuries. To begin, the first word, and perhaps the crux of this verse, is the future passive third-person singular verb *sōthēsetai*. From the verb *sōzō*, in its passive form it means "to be saved, preserved."³⁹ Based on how the word is used in 1 Tim 2:4, in which the author states that "[God] our Savior wants all people *to be saved* [*sōthēnai*, emphasis mine] and to come to the knowledge of truth [*epignōsin alētheias elthein*]," it is most likely that this verb means "save" in a salvific sense, equated with "coming to the knowledge of truth."[40] *Sōzō* is used elsewhere in this sense in the Pastoral Epistles, including 1 Tim 1:15 and 4:16, 2 Tim 1:9 and 4:18, and Titus 3:5. There is little reason to suppose it would have a different connotation in 1 Tim 2:15. This reading is also supported by the *de* (but/yet) in v. 15, which contrasts the woman's "saved" theological state in that verse with her state of being a "transgressor" in v. 14.[41] Second is the question of the subject of the verb *sōthēsetai*. Regarding the passive voice of this verb, Porter states that "[it] is probably a divine or theological passive, that is, God is the agent of the salvation."[42] I suggest that the ones "being saved" by God are *all* women. In the typology suggested by 1 Tim 2:14 ("And Adam was not deceived, but the woman [*gynē*] was deceived and became a transgressor"), in which all women are considered transgressors because of Eve's sin, all women are given the opportunity for salvation through childbearing. In other words, "'where someone sins, through that he is saved' (quo quis pevvat, eo salvatur)."[43] This reading is supported by the author of 1 Timothy's switch from Eve to *gynē* in v. 14, recalling earlier mentions of *gynē* as a collective (see 1 Tim 2:11 and 2:12); thus "women in general are connected to primordial woman."[44] The "she"/"they" in v. 15 ("She will be saved . . . if they remain") is therefore "women in general."[45] The evidence, therefore, suggests that this verse be understood as promising that God will bring to salvation all women "through childbearing"—the meaning of which we now turn.[46]

The noun "childbearing" (*teknogonias*) is complicated. It appears only once in any form in the entire New Testament.[47] Though some claim that this term refers to the specific childbirth of Mary, i.e., the birth of Jesus through whom salvation will come, none of the Gospels uses this language to describe Jesus's birth.[48] Nor is this the term used to refer to bearing children in the LXX of Gen 3:16 (*texē tekna*). However, these terms are clearly related: *texē* is from *tiktō*, and *teknogonias* is formed from a combination of *tiktō* + *ginomai*. Therefore, it is reasonable to connect the curse of "pain [in which women] will bear children" (*en lupais texē tekna*) in Gen 3:16 with the possibility of salvation "through childbearing" (*sōthēsetai de dia tēs teknogonias*) in 1 Tim 2:15. As all women were cursed with pain in childbirth due to Eve's transgression, this verse provides all women with the opportunity for redemption by means of that same act.

First Timothy took up the charge of early Jewish interpreters that Eve had brought all women into a state of transgression. But, like Mishnah Shabbat 2:6, it gave them a means of escape.[49] This tractate warned that women die in childbirth "for not being strictly observant of *niddah* [menstrual purity], *challah* [separating dough], and *hadlakat ner* [kindling the Sabbath lights]." As Baskin suggested, however, the reverse was also implied. If women strictly observed the *mitzvot* of *niddah, challah,* and *hadlakat ner*, they would presumably *live* through childbirth! This coheres with the teaching in Lev. 18:5, which express the idea that the commandments are a means to life: "You will keep my statutes and my judgments, which (if) a person does them, he will live in them [*vakhai bahem*]."[50] The concept of salvation in early Judaism is a complex one that cannot be fully discussed here.[51] Suffice it to say that rabbinic literature imagined salvation as having a share in the "world to come"— i.e., eternal life.[52] The means by which a Jew earned his or her share in the world to come was by participation in the covenant, and membership in the covenant was contingent upon keeping the law.[53] By observing the three women's *mitzvot* outlined above, and otherwise being full participants in the covenant, women could be "saved," and earn a share in the world to come.

First Timothy reframes the idea of a means of salvation that is particular to women in a Christian virtues-based context. This text, like the rest of the Pauline and Deutero-Pauline corpus, did not view the law, but rather "the grace of God through Jesus Christ," as necessary for salvation.[54] Abraham J. Malherbe summarizes the understanding of soteriology in the Pastoral Epistles:

> Indeed, a summary of the soteriology of the PE can begin with the observation that the PE present Jesus Christ as the sole mediator between God the Saviour (*sic*) and mankind, who gave himself as a ransom to redeem us from iniquity (1 Tim 2:3–6; cf. Tit 2:14), and it is through faith in him that people are saved (1 Tim 1:16; 2 Tim 3:15; cf. Tit 3:8: faith in God). Yet salvation depends on God's own purpose, kindness and grace, not on human works (2 Tim 1:9, Tit 3:4-7 . . .).[55]

First Tim 2:15 explains how women can access God's grace. The "means of redemption," as Anna Solevåg frames it, "is τεκνογονία and a certain set of virtues."[56] First Tim 2:15b specifies what these virtues are: "if she remains in faith and love and holiness, with self-control" (*ean meinōsin en pistei kai agape kai hagiasmō meta sōphrosynēs*).[57] Porter notes that the shift to the plural form *meinōsin* from the singular *sōthēsetai* in 15a indicates "the plural expands to include all of the individual examples of women referred to in 2:11–15a by representative or generic classification."[58] First Tim 2:15b thus gives all women the opportunity to be "saved through childbearing"—on the condition that they also practice the virtues of faith, love, holiness, and self-control. First Timothy has replaced the particularly Jewish virtues of observing *mitzvot* with virtues based in personal attitude that were particularly favored by the Pastoral Epistles. Both the rabbis and the author of 1 Timothy employed a particularly gendered experience, childbirth, in order to offer women a gender-specific means to redemption.

CONCLUSION

By the time of the composition of 1 Timothy in the late first/early second century CE, a long tradition of blaming Eve for the transgression in the Garden of Eden and the ensuing curses upon humanity had already been established in the Jewish imagination. First Timothy's reading of Genesis 3 betrays the influence of the Jewish understanding of that text. The author drew upon the tradition, also found in Mishnah Shabbat 2:6, which explained women's dying in childbirth as caused by their failure to observe the three women's *mitzvot* (*challah, niddah,* and *hadlakat ner*). Because he did not see the commandments as a means to salvation, he rearticulated this statement in a Christian virtues-based framework: women would achieve salvation through childbirth if they maintained the virtues of faith, love, holiness, and self-control. To build on these insights, future studies should attend to the motivation behind the author of 1 Timothy's choices here. Was he "marshal[ing] Jewish themes and tactics for positive engagement with the dominant society"?[59] Was his coopting of Jewish valuation of motherhood an attempt to counter an ascetic trend in his community that named celibacy as the only means of reversing Eve's curse and only path to salvation for women?[60] Whatever his reasoning, 1 Tim 2:15's declaration that women could be "saved through childbearing" would have resonated with the Jewish audience in his church community at Ephesus—just one more example of how closely intertwined Judaism and Christianity were in the first few centuries CE.

NOTES

1. Unless otherwise noted, this and all subsequent translations are my own.
2. See "Early Christian Interpretations (50–540 CE)" in *Eve and Adam: Jewish, Christian, and Muslim Readings on Genesis and Gender*, edited by Kristen E. Kvam, Linda S. Schearing, and Valarie H. Ziegler (Bloomington: Indiana University Press, 1999), 108–55. Examples include John Chrysostom, *Homilies on Genesis* 17.31: In childbirth, "you will begin with pain so that each time without fail you will personally have a reminder, through the distress and the pain of each birth, of the magnitude of this sin of disobedience . . ." (Kvam, 146); Augustine, *The Literal Meaning of Genesis* XI.37.50: ". . . the pain and anguish of childbirth belong solely to this body of death (a death engendered by the transgression) . . ." (Kvam, 152).
3. *On the Apparel of Women,* I.I.2. S. Thelwall, trans., and Alexander Roberts, James Donaldson, and A. Cleveland Coxe, eds., *Ante-Nicene Fathers, Vol. 4* (Buffalo, NY: Christian Literature Publishing Co., 1885).
4. 1 Tim 2:15: σωθήσεται δὲ διὰ τῆς τεκνογονίας, ἐὰν μείνωσιν ἐν πίστει καὶ ἀγάπῃ καὶ ἁγιασμῷ μετὰ σωφροσύνης.

5. Gen 3:16a: הַרְבָּה אַרְבֶּה עִצְּבוֹנֵךְ וְהֵרֹנֵךְ בְּעֶצֶב תֵּלְדִי בָנִים
6. E. Kautzsch, ed., *Gesenius' Hebrew Grammar* (Mineola, NY: Dover Publications, Inc., 2006), §113 l-n.
7. Kautzsch, §113 l-n.
8. Carol Meyers understands both forces to be at play here, noting that "the absolute certainty of the verbal action is thus expressed ... the simple notion of quantitative 'increase' in the verb alone is intensified, thus implying even greater quantity." Meyers, "Gender Roles and Genesis 3:16 Revisited," in *A Feminist Companion to Genesis,* ed. Athalya Brenner (Sheffield, England: Sheffield Academic Press, 1997), 130. Some exegetes prefer to read the two nouns "toil" and "childbearing" (*'itsvonekh veheronekh*) as two separate objects of the verbs *harbah 'arbah*. Meyers, for example, understands the text to mean that the woman's "productive work" *and* her "procreative role" will both be increased. Meyers, 131.
9. *H-r-n* is found just two other places in the Hebrew Bible, in Hosea 9:11 and Ruth 3:14. Hosea 9:11: "from birth, from pregnancy, from conception" (*miledah umibeten umaherayon*) and Ruth 3:14: "the LORD gave her conception" (*vayiten Adonai lah herayon*). *Y-l-d*, on the other hand, occurs 495 times as a verb in the entire Hebrew Bible, and 179 times as a verb in Genesis alone.
10. For more on parallelism, see Robert Alter, *The Art of Biblical Poetry* (New York: Basic Books, 2011), especially ch. 1.
11. Wilfred G.E. Watson, *Classical Hebrew Poetry* (Sheffield, England: JSOT Press, 1986), 327–28.
12. Phyllis Trible, *God and the Rhetoric of Sexuality* (Philadelphia: Fortress Press, 1978), 127. Interestingly, the term "pain" (*'atsev*) is most often used in the Hebrew Bible to express emotional pain, such as grief or anxiety. Only in 1 Chron 4:9 does this pain refer to the physical pain of childbearing, in what seems like a deliberate invocation of Gen 3:16a: "... his mother called his name Jabetz, saying 'Because I bore him in pain'" (*be'otsev*). The exact nature of the woman's suffering, whether physical or emotional, is not germane to my argument here.
13. Gen 3:16aα: Πληθύνων πληθυνῶ τὰς λύπας σου καὶ τὸν στεναγμόν σου
14. I am grateful to Dr. Joel Christensen for this explanation. In a personal correspondence from December 14, 2016, he states that "the latter [component] cannot exist without the former, but the meaning of both is increased by the combination."
15. Jacques van Ruiten notes that the use of *stenagmos* for *heron* is "quite odd." He suggests that either the LXX translator had a different word in his *Vorlage* than the one that appears in the Masoretic text, or that he gave a "free rendering" of *heron* because he did not associate it with a verb meaning "to conceive" or "to be pregnant." "Eve's Pain in Childbearing? Interpretations of Gen 3:16a in Biblical and Early Jewish Texts," in *Eve's Children: The Biblical Stories Retold and Interpreted in Jewish and Christian Traditions*, ed. Gerard P. Luttikhuzien (Leiden, NL: Brill, 2003), 13.
16. Gen 3:16aβ: ἐν λύπαις τέξῃ τέκνα.
17. It occurs 236 times in the LXX, not including prefixed forms.
18. This is the majority, though by no means the consensus view. Detractors include Christine Curley and Brian Peterson, who argue that Eve's curse is an increase of "barrenness and infertility." "Eve's Curse Revisited: An Increase of 'Sorrowful

Conceptions,'" *Bulletin for Biblical Research* 26, no. 2 (2016): 157–72. Carol Meyers, above, sees the curse as an increase in women's procreative *and* productive (i.e., substantive labor) role.

19. I follow most scholars who view the Pastoral Epistles as a pseudonymous, post-Pauline collection. See the useful review of scholarship in Anna Rebecca Solevåg, *Birthing Salvation: Gender and Class in Early Christian Childbearing Discourse* (Leiden, NL: Brill), 85–87, notes 1–10.

20. The certainty with which we can locate the recipient of 1 Timothy in Ephesus is, like much of the history of the Pastoral Epistles, debated. Paul Trebilco, however, concludes on the basis of literary analysis of 1 and 2 Timothy that the epistles "were sent by the pastor to Christians in Ephesus with particular application to their situation, and can provide us with information about Christians in the city." Trebilco, *The Early Christians in Ephesus from Paul to Ignatius* (Tübingen: Mohr Siebeck, 2004), 209. See also pp. 205–9.

21. 1 Tim 1:4 warns against μύθοις καὶ γενεαλογίαις ἀπεράντοις, and 1 Tim 1:7, against νομοδιδάσκαλοι.

22. Paul Trebilco, "The Jewish Community in Ephesus and their Interaction with Christ-Believers in the First Century CE and Beyond," in *The First Urban Churches 3: Ephesus,* ed. James R. Harrison and L.L. Welborn (SBL Press: 2018), 109. He also notes that Titus 1:14 warns people not to pay attention to *Jewish* myths (*Ioudaiikos mythois*), suggesting 1 Timothy's opponents teaching *mythois* in 1:3–7 could have been Jews or influenced by Jews, as well. Trebilco, "Jewish Community," 107. See also Michael Goulder, "The Pastor's Wolves: Jewish Christian Visionaries behind the Pastoral Epistles," *Novum Testamentum* 38.3 (1996): 242–56; Jerry L. Sumney, "The Pastoral Epistles," chap. 9 in *"Servants of Satan," "False Brothers," and Other Opponents of Paul, Journal for the Study of the New Testament Supplement* 188 (Sheffield: Sheffield Academic Press, 1999).

There is, additionally, archaeological evidence for a Jewish community at Ephesus. Acts 18 testifies to the presence of a synagogue and Jewish community there. Additionally, artifacts and inscriptions confirm a Jewish presence at the site. See George Kalantzis, "Ephesus as a Roman, Christian, and Jewish Metropolis in the First and Second Centuries CE," *Jian Dao: A Journal of Bible and Theology* 8 (1997): 113–18.

23. See Trebilco, *From Paul to Ignatius,* 215–17.

In 1 Tim 1:17, Τῷ δὲ βασιλεῖ τῶν αἰώνων parallels מלך העולם. ὑπὲρ βασιλέων καὶ πάντων τῶν ἐν ὑπεροχῇ ὄντων is found in 1 Tim 2:2; Εἷς γὰρ θεός in 1 Tim 2:2 parallels the LXX version of Deut. 6:4: κύριος ὁ θεὸς ἡμῶν κύριος εἷς ἐστιν.

24. Adam H. Becker and Annette Yoshiko Reed, *The Ways that Never Parted: Jews and Christians in Late Antiquity and the Middle Ages* (Minneapolis: Fortress Press, 2007), 22–23.

25. Jörg Frey, "Towards Reconfiguring Our Views on the 'Parting of the Ways': Ephesus as a Test Case," in *John and Judaism: A Contested Relationship in Context,* ed. R. Alan Culpepper and Paul N. Anderson (Atlanta, GA: SBL Press, 2017), 238.

26. Raymond E. Brown describes a variety of "Hebrew Christians" active in the first century, ranging from those who insisted on the full observance of the Mosaic law to those who saw no continuing relevance of the Law or the Temple. Brown, "Not

Jewish Christianity and Gentile Christianity but Types of Jewish/Gentile Christianity," *Catholic Biblical Quarterly* 45, no. 1 (1983): 77–78.

27. Martin Dibelius and Hans Conzelmann, *The Pastoral Epistles,* Hermenia (Philadelphia: Fortress Press, 1972), 1. See also discussion in Luke Timothy Johnson, *The First and Second Letters to Timothy,* Anchor Bible Commentary (New York: Doubleday, 2001), especially "Introduction."

28. Christopher R. Hutson, "Saved Through Childbearing: The Jewish Context of 1 Timothy 2:15," *Novum Testamentum* 56 (2014): 395–97.

29. B. Ketubot 8a attests: "The whole world agrees that there was only one formation [and it was of man alone] . . . How is this [to be understood]? [In this way:] In the beginning it was the intention [of God] to create two [human beings in the divine image], and in the end [only] one was created." Translation from Judith R. Baskin, *Midrashic Women: Formations of the Feminine in Rabbinic Literature* (Hanover, NH: Brandeis University Press, 2002), 49.

30. Baskin, 49.

31. אשה/γυναικὸς. The majority of interpreters understand the "woman" in this verse to be Eve; they include, but are not limited to, early twentieth-century scholars such as Rudolf Smend, *Die Weisheit des Jesus Sirach erklärt* (Berlin: Reimer, 1906), 232; and more recent scholars such as Warren Trenchard, *Ben Sira's View of Women: A Literary Analysis* Brown Judaic Studies 38 (Chico, CA: Scholars, 1982), 82.

32. Jeremy Corley, "Divine Creation and Human Mortality from Genesis to Ben Sira," *Irish Theological Quarterly* 81, no. 4 (2016): 358.

33. πλευράν

34. ἀπάτης ὄφις

35. Hutson anticipates possible objections to the use of Mishnah Shabbat to explain 1 Timothy as anachronistic. He states that the Mishnah "does not purport to be innovating" and in fact "explicitly intends to record opinions of rabbis from the Second Temple period. The Mishnah, therefore, offers circumstantial evidence that the tradition about women dying in childbirth was established as early as the first century." Hutson, 406.

36. Mishnah Shabbat 2:6: על שלש עבירות נשים מתות בשעת לדתן. על שאינן זהירות בנדה ובחלה ובהדלקת הנר.

In later commentaries, such as Yerushalmi Shabbat 2:6 (5b) and Bereshit Rabbah 17, these *mitzvot* are explicitly identified as means of atoning for Eve's sin. Because they can be dated to *after* the composition of 1 Timothy, and are farther removed from earlier traditions, I am excluding them from consideration in this paper. However, they do suggest a chain of tradition in which 1 Timothy could comfortably reside. Judith Hauptman, "A Synchronic and Diachronic Reading of Mishnah Shabbat 2:6: Why Women Die in Childbirth," in *Envisioning Judaism: Studies in Honor of Peter Schäfer on the Occasion of his Seventieth Birthday* (Tubingen: Mohr Siebeck, 2013), 478–82.

37. Wegner, *Chattel or Person? The Status of Women in the Mishnah* (New York: Oxford University Press, 1998), 155–56.

38. Baskin, 72–73.

39. *Liddell and Scott's Greek-English Lexicon* gives the first definition of *sōzō* as "to save, keep, especially to keep alive, preserve;" the second definition is "to keep alive, preserve." *Liddell and Scott's Greek-English Lexicon Abridged* (2007), s.v. σώζω.

40. Come to knowledge of truth: ἐπίγνωσιν ἀληθείας ἐλθεῖν. Others have read *sōthēnai* differently, such as Moyer Hubbard, who argues that "to be saved" means "to be kept safe through the ordeal of childbearing;" i.e., to survive what was in antiquity an often life-threatening experience. Hubbard, "Kept Safe Through Childbearing: Maternal Mortality, Justification by Faith, and the Social Setting of 1 Timothy 2:15," *Journal of the Evangelical Theological Society,* 55, no. 4 (2012): 743–62. Still others understand this verse as referring to Mary, who in the "Eve-Mary typology" saved humanity by giving birth to Jesus. See Walter Lock, *A Critical and Exegetical Commentary on the Pastoral Epistles* (ICC; Edinburgh: T & T Clark, 1924), 32–33; George W. Knight, III, *Commentary on the Pastoral Epistles* (NIGTC; Grand Rapids: Eerdmans 1992), 215; Ben Witherington III, *Letters and Homilies for Hellenized Christians I: A Socio-Rhetorical Commentary on Titus, 1–2 Timothy and 1–3 John* (Downers Grove: IVP Academic, 2006), 229–30.

41. Stanley E. Porter, "What Does it Mean to be 'Saved by Childbirth'?" *Journal for the Study of the New Testament* 49 (1993): 94. Dibelius and Conzelmann note that "Since the word 'sin,' 'transgression' (παράβασεις) has been mentioned, the question of salvation from divine wrath becomes an urgent one." Dibelius and Conzelmann, 48.

42. Porter, 94.

43. Dibelius and Conzelmann, 48.

44. Solevåg, 124. See 1 Tim 2:11 and 12.

45. The shift from singular to plural in v. 15 persuades some scholars to imagine that it is the women's *children,* not the women themselves, who must continue in "faith, love, and holiness," implying that it is the mother's responsibility to raise them with these virtues. Solevåg argues convincingly against this, pointing out that "the focus has been on women throughout this passage, and their virtues, particularly connected to sexuality, seem to be a major concern." See Solevåg, 131–32.

46. *dia* +genitive is a common way of expressing means or instrument, i.e., "arising from, through, by means of, by." Liddell and Scott, s.v. διά. Porter and Solevåg agree that "'childbearing' is the means or channel by which salvation is accomplished." Porter, 98 quoted in Solevåg, 130.

47. First Tim 5:14 uses the verbal form, *teknogonein.* While *teknogonias* is a *hapax legomenon* in the New Testament, its usage in roughly contemporaneous texts outside of the NT can nuance our understanding of it. See the comprehensive list in Kenneth L. Waters "Revisiting Virtues as Children: 1 Timothy 2:15 as Centerpiece of an Egalitarian Soteriology," *Lexington Theological Quarterly* 42, no 1 (Spring 2007): 47, n.2: "The term τεκνογονία (*teknogonia,* 'childbirth') appears also in the writing of the physicians Hippocrates (460–377 BCE) and Galen (129–216 CE) and also in the works of Aristotle (384–322 BCE) and Stobaeus (c. 455 BCE)." Solevåg notes that Aristotle *Historia animalium* 582a uses it when discussing women's "particular role in procreation," and medical-philosophical texts (like Areimus Didymus, *Liber*

de philisophorum sectis 76.1 and Chrysippus, *Fragmenta moralia* 611) use it when discussing "household management." Solevåg, 130.

48. Porter, 92. Matthew uses *hē genesis* (1:18), Luke says the time came for Mary to *tekein* (2:6), and John refers to Jesus "coming into the world" (*erchomeon eis ton kosmon*) (1:9).

49. In 1988, Jouette M. Bassler made the intriguing suggestion that the "heretics, who were skilled in manipulating Jewish myths, may have already exploited the potential" of the idea that childbirth was *not* as curse, as Genesis made it seem. "The pastor, then, polemically transformed the Genesis curse into a Christian blessing. A woman will be saved *from the allure of the heretical message* by bearing children... she will also be saved in the absolute sense of the word," provided she continue in the virtues described. Bassler, "Adam, Eve, and the Pastor. The Use of Genesis 2–3 in the Pastoral Epistles," in *Genesis 1-3 in the History of Exegesis. Intrigue in the Garden*, edc G.A. Robbins (Lewiston, Queenston: The Edwin Mellen Press, 1998), 55–56.

50. Live in them וָחַי בָּהֶם.

51. See Daniel M. Gurtner, *This World and the World to Come: Soteriology and Rabbinic Judaism* (London: Bloomsbury T & T Clark, 2011), especially Jacob Neusner, "The Restoration of Israel: Soteriology in Rabbinic Judaism," 285–98.

52. Mishnah Sanhedrin 10:1. Neusner summarizes the rabbinic system thus: "At the end of days the individual Israelite will rise from the dead, and all Israel will be restored to the Land of Israel for eternal life." Neusner, 285.

53. E. P. Sanders, *Comparing Judaism and Christianity: Common Judaism, Paul, and the Inner and the Outer in Ancient Religion* (Philadephia: Fortress Press, 2016), 168–71.

54. Johnson, 77.

55. Abraham J. Malherbe, "'Christ Jesus Came Into the World to Save Sinners': Soteriology in the Pastoral Epistles," in *Salvation in the New Testament: Perspectives on Soteriology*, ed. Jan G. van der Watt (Leiden: Brill, 2005), 332–33.

56. Solevåg, 129.

57. Waters takes this one step further to argue 2:15 is an allegory in which "the women give birth to these virtues [of faith, love, holiness, and self-control] and then they *continue* or *abide* in them in order to be saved." Waters, 705. He compares this verse with contemporaneous Hellenistic texts such as Philo's *Legum allegoriae* that also imagine virtues as children. His ultimate conclusion is that it is unreasonable to understand *teknogonia* in 1 Timothy 2:15 as *literal* childbearing; a view, of course, which is in direct contrast with my own.

58. Porter, 98.

59. Hutson, 409.

60. See J. Bassler, *1 Timothy, 2 Timothy, and Titus,* Abindgton NTC (Nashville: Abington, 1996).

BIBLIOGRAPHY

Baskin, Judith R. *Midrashic Women: Formations of the Feminine in Rabbinic Literature.* Hanover, NH: Brandeis University Press, 2002.

Bassler, Jouette M. "Adam, Eve, and the Pastor. The Use of Genesis 2–3 in the Pastoral Epistles." In *Genesis 1-3 in the History of Exegesis. Intrigue in the Garden*, edited by Gregory Robbins, 43–65. Lewiston, Queenston: The Edwin Mellen Press, 1998.

Becker, Adam H., and Annette Yoshiko Reed. *The Ways that Never Parted: Jews and Christians in Late Antiquity and the Middle Ages.* Minneapolis: Fortress Press, 2007.

Brown, Raymond E. "Not Jewish Christianity and Gentile Christianity but Types of Jewish/Gentile Christianity." *Catholic Biblical Quarterly* 45, no. 1 (1983): 74–79.

Corley, Jeremy. "Divine Creation and Human Mortality from Genesis to Ben Sira." *Irish Theological Quarterly* 81, no. 4 (2016): 343–61.

Dibelius, Martin, and Hans Conzelmann. *The Pastoral Epistles.* Hermenia. Philadelphia: Fortress Press, 1972.

Frey, Jörg. "Towards Reconfiguring Our Views on the 'Parting of the Ways': Ephesus as a Test Case." In *John and Judaism: A Contested Relationship in Context*, edited by R. Alan Culpepper and Paul N. Anderson, 221–39. Atlanta: SBL Press, 2017.

Hauptman, Judith. "A Synchronic and Diachronic Reading of Mishnah Shabbat 2:6: Why Women Die in Childbirth." In *Envisioning Judaism: Studies in Honor of Peter Schäfer on the Occasion of his Seventieth Birthday.* Tübingen: Mohr Siebeck, 2013.

Johnson, Luke Timothy. *The First and Second Letters to Timothy.* Anchor Bible Commentary. New York: Doubleday, 2001.

Kvam, Kristen E., Linda S. Schearing, and Valarie H. Ziegler. *Eve and Adam: Jewish, Christian, and Muslim Readings on Genesis and Gender.* Bloomington: Indiana University Press, 1999.

Malherbe, Abraham J. "'Christ Jesus Came Into the World to Save Sinners': Soteriology in the Pastoral Epistles." In *Salvation in the New Testament: Perspectives on Soteriology*, edited by Jan G. van der Watt, 331–58. Leiden: Brill, 2005.

Meyers, Carol. "Gender Roles and Genesis 3:16 Revisited." In *A Feminist Companion to Genesis*, edited by Athalya Brenner, 118–41. Sheffield, England: Sheffield Academic Press, 1997.

Porter, Stanley E. "What Does it Mean to be 'Saved by Childbirth'?" *Journal for the Study of the New Testament* 49 (1993): 87–102.

Sanders, E. P. *Comparing Judaism and Christianity: Common Judaism, Paul, and the Inner and the Outer in Ancient Religion.* Philadelphia: Fortress Press, 2016.

Solevåg, Anna Rebecca. *Birthing Salvation: Gender and Class in Early Christian Childbearing Discourse.* Leiden, NL: Brill, 2013.

Trebilco, Paul. *The Early Christians in Ephesus from Paul to Ignatius.* Tübingen: Mohr Siebeck, 2004.

———. "The Jewish Community in Ephesus and its Interaction with Christ-Believers in the First Century CE and Beyond." In *The First Urban Churches 3: Ephesus*, edited by James R. Harrison and L. L. Welborn, 93–126. Atlanta: SBL Press, 2018.

Trible, Phyllis. *God and the Rhetoric of Sexuality*. Philadelphia: Fortress Press, 1978.

Van Ruiten, Jacques. "Eve's Pain in Childbearing? Interpretations of Gen 3:16a in Biblical and Early Jewish Texts." In *Eve's Children: The Biblical Stories Retold and Interpreted in Jewish and Christian Traditions*, edited by Gerard P. Luttikhuzien, 3–26. Leiden, NL: Brill, 2003.

Waters, Kenneth L. "Revisiting Virtues as Children: 1 Timothy 2:15 as Centerpiece of an Egalitarian Soteriology." *Lexington Theological Quarterly* 42, no 1 (Spring 2007): 37–49.

Wegner, Judith Romney. *Chattel or Person? The Status of Women in the Mishnah*. New York: Oxford University Press, 1998.

Chapter Five

Traversing the Boundaries of Gender

Rebekah's Usurpation of the Patriarchal Role in the Book of Jubilees

Chontel Syfox

It has long been noticed that women feature far more prominently in the Book of *Jubilees*[1] than in the Book of Genesis. Rebekah, in particular, has been the focus of much scholarly attention,[2] and the general consensus is that she is portrayed as the *matriarch par excellence* in *Jubilees*. This paper utilizes the concepts of gender performativity and multiple masculinities/femininities as hermeneutical lenses through which to examine the depiction of the rewritten Rebekah. It proffers that when *Jubilees* rewrites the events recorded in Genesis, Rebekah does her gender, performing the reproductive and protective feminine functions already ascribed to her in the biblical text. When *Jubilees* creates new episodes for her, however, Rebekah moves beyond these feminine functions. She takes up the mantle of the patriarch, performing masculine functions such as passing on the covenantal blessings to the correct heir and providing moral instruction for her sons. It is specifically in these instances in which Rebekah is depicted acting like a man that the matriarch's stature is dramatically heightened in *Jubilees*. Yet, this does not last. Once Rebekah ensures that Jacob received the patriarchal blessing and he was protected from his scorned brother, her gender-bending behavior decreases; her words bear less authority in Jacob's eyes, and Isaac resumes his duties as the head of the family. Thus, Rebekah is allowed to traverse gender boundaries, but only temporarily.

DOING ONE'S GENDER: METHODOLOGICAL CONSIDERATIONS

Judith Butler explains that gender is culturally constructed. Gender identities are "instituted through a stylised repetition of acts" in a "culturally restricted corporeal space." The repetition and eventual sedimentation of these "public actions and performative acts" leads to them simultaneously establishing gender identity and becoming the criteria by which one is judged as complying with or flouting gender expectations in a particular time and space. Behavior is the key to understanding the construction of gender in this model. Gender is "dramatised," "acted out,"—it is "done."[3] Moreover, gender is relational and oppositional, meaning certain acts are understood as "masculine" or appropriate behavior for a man, whilst others are contrastingly understood as "feminine" or appropriate for a woman.[4]

R. W. Connell observes, however, that gender cannot be reduced to "two homogenous categories."[5] In a single culture there may be "multiple masculinities" and multiple femininities; meaning, there are many different ways of expressing a particular gender identity. "At any given time," Connell theorizes, "one form of masculinity rather than others is culturally exalted." This exalted form is termed "hegemonic masculinity."[6] It is "the specific gender construction that is dominant in cultural and political power structures."[7] Other, "subordinate" and "marginalised" forms of masculinity are in constant tension with the hegemonic construction of masculinity. Subordinate masculinities "lack or differ in some crucial characteristics of hegemonic masculinity and [signify] a lower status in male hierarchy." Marginalized masculinities, meanwhile, represent "illegitimate type[s] of male performance."[8] I contend that the same holds true *vis-à-vis* femininity. In a single culture there may be a hegemonic femininity, which is the social construction of femininity that is exalted; subordinate femininities, which are accepted but considered to be lesser types of femininity; and marginalized femininities, which are considered wrong and illegitimate expressions of femininity.

Hegemonic masculinity is by no means a "fixed character type, always and everywhere the same,"[9] but across many cultures, times, and places, it has often been linked to military prowess, virility, self-mastery, and the ability to control subordinates (wives, children, and slaves). This construction of masculinity is seen in various parts of the Hebrew Bible (HB),[10] but it is not the dominant construction in the patriarchal narratives. These stories are marked by a subordinate masculinity. For the male protagonists in the patriarchal narrative cycles, doing their gender means covenant-making, covenant-sustaining, and covenant-transferring. Their gender performance is judged, first in terms of their relationship with God. The patriarchs enter into a covenant with God, from whom they receive certain promises. In order to bring these divine promises to fruition the patriarchs must show faith in, devotion, and obedience to God. It is precisely this relationship to God that permits the subordinate masculinity of the patriarchs to be acceptable. "The man before God," explains Martti Nissinen, "does not need to conform to the ideals of hegemonic masculinity." He is accepted because he "serves even higher ideals."[11] Second, the patriarchs' gender performance is judged in terms of their relationships with their offspring. They must produce a male heir, and to prove their virility many spares, who will succeed them in the covenant relationship with God. The patriarchs must instruct the heir in the ways of keeping the covenant and transfer the covenant promises and responsibilities to him.

In ancient Israelite society, marriage was one of the primary ways of achieving status for women.[12] Second to becoming a wife was becoming a mother, which "conferred social and cultural validation on a woman within the family unit."[13] Hegemonic femininity in the HB, therefore, entails being a wife and a mother. The "Woman of Valour" in Prov 31:10–31 embodies a well-attested view of hegemonic femininity in the ancient Mediterranean world. She does her gender within the private domestic sphere, tending to women's work, such as childcare and preparing food and clothing (Prov 31:13–15, 19, 21). She is pious, dignified, and speaks with wisdom (Prov 31:25–26, 30).[14] This is not exactly the femininity that is presented in the patriarchal narratives, however. Motherhood is still a dominant feature of the subordinate construction of femininity present in these narratives, as the production of the male heir for the patriarch is wholly contingent upon the wombs of women. But, a recurring trope subverts the hegemonic construction of femininity—the female protagonists, often infertile, do whatever it takes to realize their personal dreams of motherhood, even at the cost of discord with their husbands and rivalry with co-wives. Furthermore, the matriarchs are portrayed "not only as desirous of children but also as protective of their children and relentlessly devoted to them."[15] Once a child is born, doing whatever it takes to ensure that her personal dreams for the survival and prosperity of that child becomes the matriarch's priority. For a matriarch, therefore, doing her gender means performing "reproductive and protective functions."[16]

GEN 27: FEMININE TRICKERY AND FAILING MASCULINITY

Based on her actions in Gen 27, the biblical Rebekah has long been interpreted as an example of the universal literary type known as the "trickster" character.[17] The chapter begins with Isaac, in anticipation of his death, summoning Esau to give him his final blessing, saying, "Prepare for me savoury food, such as I like, and bring it to me to eat, so that I may bless you before I die" (Gen 27:4). Eavesdropping, Rebekah heard her husband's plan and determined to supplant Esau with Jacob. Summoning Jacob, Rebekah manipulated Isaac's words, reporting, "I heard your father say to your brother Esau, 'Bring me game, and prepare for me savoury food to eat, that I may bless you *before the Lord* before I die'" (Gen 27:6). Then she instructed Jacob, saying, "Obey my word as I command you . . . get me two choice kids, so that I may prepare from them savoury food for your father . . . and you shall take it to your father to eat, so that he may bless you before he dies" (Gen 27:8–10). His initial fears having been brushed aside by his mother, Jacob obediently complied (Gen 27:12–13). Meanwhile, Rebekah fetched Esau's best clothes to dress Jacob in. Next, receiving the kids from Jacob, she prepared the food Isaac requested and fashioned accoutrements to cover Jacob's hands and neck so that his glabrous skin would not reveal his true identity (Gen 27:15–17). Then she sent Jacob to his father to purloin Esau's blessing (Gen 27:18–29).

When Esau returned to Isaac, stew in hand, Isaac became aware of what had occurred, informing Esau that Jacob "deceitfully" (במרמה) took away the blessing (Gen 27:35). Filled with resentment, Esau determined to kill Jacob (Gen 27:38–41). Discovering Esau's fratricidal intent, Rebekah contrived to spirit Jacob away to safety. To Jacob she said, "My son, obey my voice; flee at once to my brother Laban in Haran and stay with him a while, until your brother's fury turns away" (Gen 27:44). Rebekah disguised her worry about Jacob's life as concern for ensuring an endogamous union for him, saying to Isaac, "If Jacob marries one of the Hittite women such as these . . . what good will my life be to me?" (Gen 27:46). Oblivious to Esau's and Rebekah's opposing plots, Isaac then sent Jacob to Laban in Paddan-Aram to find a wife (Gen 28:1–5).

As Genesis does not provide an explicit reason for Rebekah deciding that Jacob should receive Esau's blessing, her scheme appears to be a whim. Esther Fuchs point outs, however, that "it is implied that [Rebekah's] actions are in harmony with Yahweh's plan."[18] As Jacob and Esau struggled in-utero, a distressed Rebekah was appeased by a revelation in which God told the expectant mother that "the older will serve the younger [son]" (Gen 25:23). Following this, the text reports the boys' birth and explains that Esau grew up to be a skilled hunter and Jacob a quiet man of tents (Gen 25:28). Then we learn of their parents' favoritism; Isaac loved Esau, but Rebekah loved Jacob. Although a basis for Isaac favoring Esau is provided—Isaac was fond of the game that Esau hunted (Gen 25:28)—no justification is given for Rebekah favoring Jacob.[19] The statement of Rebekah's partiality toward Jacob being given in the context of the revelation she received "gives rise to the possibility that God's destiny for her sons . . . impact[ed] Rebekah's feelings for them."[20] If so, Rebekah acted, "on an understanding that Isaac's actions [to bless Esau] conflict[ed] with the words that the Israelite Deity [gave] her prior to her children's birth,"[21] and provided a divinely inspired corrective to Isaac's misapprehension of who was to succeed him. Yet, while acting as an instrument for the Lord's purposes, Rebekah remained "subservient to her husband's authority over her and her children,"[22] making deceit her only option. This is never made clear, however, and Rebekah appearing to play Isaac like a fiddle further distracts from the divine purpose behind her actions.

Rebekah's trickery was also partially necessitated by Isaac's inability to adequately perform his own gender. Among the ways that masculinity is undermined in the HB, Hilary Lipka lists "growing old, which results in the loss of strength in several areas and the loss of control over one's own body."[23] For Isaac, who became "old and enfeebled before his time,"[24] losing his sight was the initial sign of masculinity on the decline. Then he miscalculated the time of his death and determined to confer his final blessing upon Esau. Two signs evinced that Esau was not fit for this. Firstly, Esau sold his birthright for a bowl of lentil stew, showing no "regard for the sacred institution of the first born" (Gen 25:34).[25] Secondly, he married Hittite women (Gen 26:34–35). After receiving the birthright an appropriate marriage was "the second *sine qua non* for being reckoned as heir,"[26] and Esau did not meet either of these criteria. Nevertheless, "Isaac apparently remain[ed] eager to confer the better blessing on Esau,"[27] jeopardizing the future of the covenant. Failing to adequately perform the masculine function of covenant-transferral, Isaac proved himself to be inept at performing his gender. Had Isaac recognised that Esau was an unfit heir, Rebekah's deceit would have been unnecessary.

REHABILITATING REBEKAH

Fuchs comments: "Even when women's motivation for deceiving is defensible, the very act of deception produces an ambivalent effect that is bound to compromise their character as a whole."[28] Indeed, although Genesis implies that Rebekah's deception was in harmony with God's covenantal plan, her actions seem to point only toward a "moral deficiency"[29] on her part. *Jubilees* mitigates this ambivalence by giving Rebekah's partiality toward Jacob clear sanctioning.

The first form of sanction comes in *Jub* 19:13–15 from Abraham. *Jubilees* omits the narrative concerning Jacob's and Esau's in-utero struggles and the subsequent oracle foretelling Jacob's election as heir to the covenant (Gen 25:19–23), which as aforementioned may provide an implicit explanation for Rebekah's preference for Jacob in Genesis. Instead, in *Jubilees*, the biblical chronology is exploited so that Abraham was alive to see the early lives of his grandsons.[30] After Esau's and Jacob's birth notice we learn that Jacob, who was "perfect and upright" (*feṣṣum warāte'*),[31] learned the art of "writing"(*maṣḥaf*) and lived in tents.[32] Esau meanwhile was a "rustic man" (*be'esi ḥaqqālāwi*) and "hunter" (*wana'āwi*). He learned the art of "war" (*dabʼa*), and "everything that he did was harsh" (*wakʷellu geberā deruq*; *Jub* 19:13–14).³³ This is followed by the statement that "Abraham loved Jacob, but Isaac (loved) Esau" (*Jub* 19:15), with Abraham replacing Rebekah in the biblical formulation (Gen 25:28). The reason for Isaac's fondness for Esau is omitted, but Abraham's feelings for Jacob are given some explanation: "As Abraham observed Esau's behaviour, he realised that through Jacob he would have a reputation and descendants" (*Jub* 19:16). These changes result in Isaac's feelings for Esau being "reduced ... to the level of personal favouritism,"³⁴ while Abraham's decision was reasonably based on observing the boys' behavior. Abraham, described as "perfect in all things" (*bakʷellu feṣṣum*; *Jub* 23:10), perhaps recognized that Jacob's personality was most like his own and he would thus be an appropriate heir for his grandfather. Moreover, Abraham learned "(the art of) writing" (*maṣhafa*; *Jub* 11:16), like his ancestors before him (*Jub* 4:17; 10:13–14; 11:16). Jacob continuing this tradition signaled that he was a fitting candidate to continue the line of succession. Esau, however, was the opposite of his grandfather; rather than learning what was equated with rightness (i.e., writing), he learned what was "harsh" or "savage" (i.e., hunting and warfare).³⁵

Approaching Rebekah, Abraham said to her, "My son Isaac now loves Esau more than Jacob, but I see that you rightly love Jacob" (*Jub* 19:19). Thus, Abraham instructed her, "Take care of my son Jacob because he will occupy my place on the earth ... increase your favour to him still more" (*Jub* 19:17–20). Abraham then blessed Jacob before Rebekah (*Jub* 19:26–29). When the mother and son departed together at the blessing's conclusion, the text states that Rebekah loved Jacob "with her entire heart and her entire being (*bakʷellu lebbā wakʷellu manfasā*) very much more than Esau; but Isaac loved Esau much more than Jacob" (*Jub* 19:31; cf. Gen 25:28). John Endres suggests that Rebekah's preference for Jacob was "rooted in Abraham's command to favour the young man,"³⁶ but this assertion does not fully take into account the words spoken by Abraham at the beginning of the scene; his statement, "I see that you rightly love Jacob," indicates that Rebekah already favored Jacob before Abraham's intervention. By the end of the scene, Rebekah's affection for Jacob developed considerably. The statement that Rebekah loved Jacob with her entire being and spirit (*bakʷellu lebbā wakʷellu manfasā*) echoes the *Shema*'s instruction to love God "with all your heart and all your soul" (בכל לבבך ובכל נפשך; Deut 6:4). The use of Deuteronomic language likens Rebekah's feelings for Jacob to the "intense devotion" Israel is required to show to God.³⁷ It is not, says James VanderKam, "just a preference ... [it] is a total love for him that far exceeds her feelings toward her other son Esau."³⁸ Coming at the end of the episode, after Abraham's instructions have been given to her, the description of Rebekah's intensified love indicates that she heeded the words of her father-in-law to *increase* her love toward her favored son. When all of the actions Rebekah will take to elevate Jacob above his brother are considered in light of this instruction, the matriarch's trickery is less damning as she appears to be following Abraham's express instruction to "increase her favour" toward his true heir. Consequently, Abraham appears as "the catalyst for the assertiveness of Rebekah's character," while his instructions to Rebekah "help to vitiate the moral ambiguity of her subsequent initiation of the deception of Isaac."[39]

Rebekah's plan to deceive Isaac is "the same seemingly implausible one in *Jubilees* as it is in Genesis: she puts some of Esau's finest clothing on [Jacob], and lays the hides of the kids/goats on his hands or arms and on the exposed part of his neck."[40] But, a notable change in the episode gives Rebekah's actions to elevate Jacob above his brother sanction from the heavenly realm. According to the rewritten work, when a disguised Jacob approached Isaac "there was a turn of events in heaven," which distracted Isaac, preventing him from recognizing his younger son (*Jub* 26:18). The addition of heavenly beings seemingly running interference to ensure Rebekah's and Jacob's success in tricking Isaac indicates that "the plan . . . was actually the will of the Lord who intervened to make sure it succeeded in order that Jacob, not Esau, would receive the blessing."[41] As Piet Van Boxel proffers, "this means that the way Jacob will receive his father's blessing has gone beyond the level of trickery and imperfect morality. This procedure was foreseen by God."[42] Furthermore, Genesis merely tells that Esau's plot to kill Jacob was "told to Rebekah" (Gen 27:42), although from where or whom she received this information is unclear. *Jubilees*, on the other hand, reports that Rebekah "was told in a dream what her older son Esau had said" (*Jub* 27:1). As dreams often convey divine information, it is implied that Rebekah received a revelation from God concerning Esau's plan to kill Jacob.[43] Thus, her deception to save Jacob also implicitly receives divine sanctioning.

In Genesis, Rebekah's sudden concern about Jacob marrying outside of the family line appears to be "an excuse to compel Isaac to send Jacob away."[44] This is not the case in *Jubilees*. Her fears about Jacob marrying women of the land are shown to be "sincere,"[45] as she expressed the very same worries directly to Jacob (*Jub* 25:1). Her worry is justified too, as Esau spent twenty-two years attempting to persuade Jacob to marry a Canaanite woman (*Jub* 25:8). Given Rebekah's legitimate concerns about Jacob's future marriages, this second instance of her deceiving Isaac seems less conniving and less of a blemish upon her character.[46]

In *Jubilees*' rewriting of Rebekah's deceptions, she is still a woman doing her gender by performing reproductive and protective functions. Her knowledge that Jacob would succeed Abraham explicitly becomes the basis for her actions on Jacob's behalf, thereby mitigating negative evaluations of her moral character. Her stature is not increased, however; she still had to deceive Isaac because in the gendered power dynamic of their marriage she was in a subordinate position.

REBEKAH'S PATRIARCHAL BEHAVIOR

Rebekah truly shines in *Jubilees* when the author of the rewritten work creates new scenes for her, in which she delivers impressive speeches. In these scenes she usurps Isaac's role, becoming "in effect, . . . a patriarch by carrying out functions normally reserved for male ancestors."[47] For instance, before reporting the theft of the blessing, *Jubilees* tells that Rebekah called Jacob to her to instruct him against marrying a Canaanite woman (*Jub* 25:1–4). The very act of summoning her son is remarkable. As VanderKam highlights, "in bidding him to come to her, this redoubtable mother did something that no other woman does in Genesis . . . where patriarchs are the ones who require the presence of others."[48] Rebekah warned Jacob against unions with women of the land, saying their deeds consisted of "sexual impurity" (*rek^{w}es*) and "lewdness" (*zemmut*). She added, "Do as your mother wishes . . . [and] the most high God will bless you; your family will become a righteous family and your descendants (will be) holy" (*Jub* 25:3). Jacob explained to his mother that, although Esau had attempted to convince him to do so, he had not touched or considered marrying any Canaanite women because Abraham cautioned him against such behaviour (*Jub* 25:4–9). Rebekah's "words to Jacob echo faithfully [Abraham's] injunctions" against "sexual impurity and uncleanness" (*rek^{w}es wazemmut*; *Jub* 20:3). This correspondence in their language indicates that Rebekah had risen to the status of "mediator" of her father-in-law's commands.[49] Moreover, it is quite extraordinary that the author of *Jubilees* assigns the task of providing instruction about endogamy, perhaps his chief concern, to a woman, as this kind of instruction was typically delivered by a father to his son.[50] As she gives this important parenetic speech, Rebekah is cast as the "chief guardian of Abraham's moral legacy," instead of his son, Isaac.[51]

As explained by Fuchs, "within biblical patriarchy, the institute of . . . parental blessings applied strictly to males [and] mothers could not give blessings to their children."[52] In fact she says, "had Rebekah been able to express her love for Jacob through maternal blessings, she would not have needed to use deception. She would have in all probability blessed Jacob by herself."[53] *Jubilees* gives Rebekah the power to do just that. Inspired by "a spirit of righteousness" (*Jub* 25:14), Rebekah conveyed to Jacob the threefold promises originally sworn to Abraham (*Jub* 25:16, 17, 22; cf. Gen 22:17). This task should have been performed by Isaac, but as Michel Testuz notes Rebekah "obéissant aux recommendations d'Abraham et à sa propre inclination pour [Jacob], le bénit très longuement."[54] This "extraordinary act of conferring the blessings on the correct son," says VanderKam, "ensure[s] that the line of Abraham would remain pure so that the promises could someday be realised"[55] and shows that Rebekah was Abraham's "true successor."[56] Betsy Halpern-Amaru maintains that since Rebekah utilized maternal images in her blessing, speaking of "the womb that bore her son, of breasts that bless him (25:19), and of the maternal nature of God's love (25:23)" she gives a "matriarchal blessing."[57] Rebekah's blessing is indeed flavored with feminine touches, but this is a common feature of biblical women's prayers.[58] Halpern-Amaru does not seem to take into account that Rebekah's blessing is "similar to the prayers of men in structure, content, and social location."[59] The words of Rebekah's blessing—she "blessed the Most High God, who created heaven and earth"—and the gestures that accompany it—"she lifted her face to heaven and extended the fingers of her hands" (*Jub* 25:11)—are those of priestly men, such as Melchizedek (Gen 14:18–19) and Levi (ALD 3:1–2).[60] The sentiments she expresses and blessings she transmits are those of Abraham, the father of the covenant (*Jub* 19:18, 27, 29; 22:10, 11, 14, 15, 19, 24, 28–30).[61] Thus, although Rebekah's blessing is couched in "gynocentric language," she gives the performance of a man. As VanderKam asserts, then, with this speech Rebekah "adopted the role of the patriarch."[62]

Rebekah's testament is also noteworthy. Testamentary speeches are uniquely male performances. These discourses delivered in anticipation of imminent death"[63] often consist of "two major components: exhortations and moral and cultic instructions on the one hand, and future foretellings on the other hand."[64] Summoning Esau first, Rebekah began her testament by making arrangements for her burial, asking to be interred near Sarah in the family cave at Machpelah. Following this, she provided moral instruction, entreating Esau to love his brother (*Jub* 35:20). Then she summoned Jacob and repeated to him all that she had said to Esau (*Jub* 25:25). Concluding her speech, she ate and drank with her sons and died at the age of 155 years old (*Jub* 35:27). Rebekah's delivery of a testamentary speech is quite a remarkable feat, as she is one of only two female characters to do so in ancient Jewish literature.[65] By writing such a speech onto Rebekah's lips, *Jubilees* depicts her acting like a patriarch yet again. Further, Rebekah once again pips Isaac to the post in providing moral instruction for her sons that should have been conveyed by their father.[66]

In these scenes, Rebekah crosses gender boundaries. She provides instruction in the ways of the covenant, ensuring that the genealogical line from which future heirs will arise remains pure and she blesses her sons. She becomes the "bridge"[67] between Abraham and Jacob and "Jacob's spiritual guardian."[68] In short, she performs the gendered behaviors expected of a patriarch. Rebekah's status is amplified in these scenes because the author permits her to act like a man.

REESTABLISHING A GENDERED STATUS QUO

William Loader proposes that the image of Rebekah in *Jubilees* "assumes the possibility of strong leadership" roles for women within the "traditional patriarchal structure" of the family.[69] I proffer that *Jubilees'* author was not entirely comfortable with this possibility. After serving the needs of Abraham and God by securing Jacob's blessing and safety, Rebekah's role as patriarchal proxy diminishes. This is seen in the fact that after the blessing had been conferred to him Jacob stopped heeding his mother's instructions. Firstly, Rebekah told Jacob of the dream she received about Esau's plan to kill him, instructing Jacob to flee to safety. He refused, responding, "I will not go. If [Isaac] sends me only then will I go." Heeding her son's demands Rebekah replied, "I will go in and tell him. Then he will send you" (*Jub* 27:7). Hanna Tervanotko highlights that Jacob "does not reject the content of the dream;" this much is clear as he declared, "I am not afraid. If [Esau] wishes to kill me, I will kill him" (*Jub* 27:4). Nonetheless, Jacob was "not willing to follow his mother's instruction."[70] Jacob explained to his mother that leaving without his father's permission "would be a bad thing," adding, "My father would be angry and curse me" (*Jub* 27:6). Despite the new divinely determined validity of Rebekah's concern in *Jubilees,* Jacob is now strangely concerned that his mother is leading him astray.

When Rebekah later spoke to Jacob about another of her dreams she was met with outright disbelief. She told her son that she had seen "the day of [her] death in a dream" (*Jub* 35:6). In response, Jacob "laughed at what his mother was saying" and replied, "You are not going to die but rather have spoken idle nonsense with me about your death" (*Jub* 35:8). There is a marked shift in the relationship between Rebekah and Jacob in these episodes; the unique closeness between mother and son that compelled Jacob to hang on Rebekah's words now gives way to a closeness between him and his father that sees him refuse to heed his mother's instruction. Previously recognized by the "perfect" Abraham for her wisdom, Rebekah now has her words met with suspicion and ridicule by Abraham's heir. This is evidence of her diminishing authority; of her being treated more like a woman than a patriarch.

Upon Jacob's return to his parents' house with his children, Rebekah greeted her grandsons with a blessing, saying, "Through you Abraham's descendants will become famous. You will become a blessing on the earth" (*Jub* 31:7). Jacob and his sons then went in to visit Isaac, who proceeded to offer a similar, albeit longer, blessing (*Jub* 31:11–21). Whereas Rebekah was previously present for Abraham's blessing of Jacob, transmitted the patriarchal blessing to Jacob herself, and was instrumental in Jacob receiving the blessing from Isaac too, in this instance her intervention is unnecessary. With Isaac competently fulfilling the patriarchal duty of blessing-conferral, Rebekah was not needed to protect the family's future.

The role reversal that sees Jacob dismissing his mother's words and Isaac correctly transmitting the covenant to his grandsons may reveal the ideal male-female power dynamic the author of the text wished to prescribe for his readers. Accordingly, Rebekah's gender nonconformity is not a marker of the hegemonic construction of femininity in *Jubilees*, but rather a subordinate femininity that is temporarily permissible in order to serve divine purposes.

CONCLUSION

When *Jubilees* rewrites Genesis, Rebekah performs her femininity as she is expected to, producing children and protecting the child who will inherit the covenant. *Jubilees* provides justifications for Rebekah's deceptive behavior, which rehabilitates her moral character. But, as she must still utilize trickery to overcome the power limitations forced upon her by her gender, her stature is hardly elevated. In the new episodes the author of *Jubilees* wrote for her, Rebekah's role extends beyond reproductive and protective feminine functions. She usurps Isaac's patriarchal role, performing the masculine functions of passing on the covenant and providing moral instruction. It is in these instances that Rebekah's stature is amplified because she moves beyond the limits of her gender. Yet, she is only temporarily permitted to play the patriarch. Eventually, Isaac resumes his patriarchal duties and Jacob is dismissive of his mother. Rebekah thus traverses gender boundaries, at times performing feminine functions and at times performing masculine functions.

NOTES

1. *Jubilees*, widely regarded as belonging to the corpus of texts known as "Rewritten Scripture," is thought to have been composed circa 160–140 BC. On the category of "Rewritten Scripture," see Moshe J. Bernstein, "'Rewritten Bible': A Generic Category Which Has Outlived its Usefulness?" *Textus* 22 (2005), 169–96; On dating

Jubilees, see James C. VanderKam, *Textual and Historical Studies in the Book of Jubilees* (Missoula, MT: Scholars Press, 1977), 214–85.

2. See Betsy Halpern-Amaru, *The Empowerment of Women in the Book of Jubilees* (JSJSup 60; Leiden: Brill, 1999), 55–64; John C. Endres, *Biblical Interpretation in the Book of Jubilees* (CBQMS 18; Washington D.C.: Catholic Biblical Association of America, 1987), 51–176; Endres, "Revisiting the Rebekah of the Book of Jubilees," in *A Teacher for All Generations: Essays in Honour of James C. VanderKam* (JSJSup 151/I-II; eds. Eric F. Mason et al.; Leiden: Brill, 2012), 765–82; James C. VanderKam, *The Book of Jubilees* (Sheffield: Sheffield Academic Press, 2001), 116–17; Piet van Boxel, "The God of Rebekah," *SIDIC* 9 (1976): 14–18.

3. Judith Butler, "Performative Acts and Gender Constitution: An Essay in Phenomenology and Feminist Theory," *Theatre Journal* 40.4 (1988), 519, 526, 521.

4. Judith Butler, *Gender Trouble* (New York: Routledge, 1990; repr., New York: Routledge Classics, 2006), 24.

5. R. W. Connell, *Masculinities* (Berkeley: University of California Press, 2005), 26.

6. Connell, *Masculinities*, 76–77.

7. Susan Haddox, "Masculinity Studies of the Hebrew Bible: The First Two Decades," *CBR* 14.2 (2016): 179.

8. Martti Nissinen, "Relative Masculinities in the Hebrew Bible and Old Testament," in *Being a Man: Negotiating Ancient Constructions of Masculinity* (ed. Ilona Zsolnay; New York: Routledge, 2017), 222.

9. Connell, *Masculinities*, 76.

10. Use of the term "Hebrew Bible" does not assume that at the time of *Jubilees'* composition the biblical canon had closed; it designates the texts we have reasonable evidence to believe were considered sacred and authoritative by *Jubilees'* author and his contemporaries.

11. Nissinen, "Relative Masculinities," 222.

12. Phyllis Bird, "Images of Women in the Old Testament," in *Religion and Sexism: Images of Women in the Jewish and Christian Traditions* (ed. Rosemary Radford Ruether; New York: Simon and Schuster, 1974), 62–63.

13. Naomi Steinberg, "Gender Roles in the Rebekah Cycle," *USQR* 39.3 (1984): 180.

14. Sir 26:1–23; Xenophon, *Econ.* 7.10–12; Plutarch, *Mor.* 141.22, 26.

15. Esther Fuchs, "The Literary Characterisation of Mothers and Sexual Politics in the Hebrew Bible," in *Feminist Perspectives on Biblical Scholarship* (ed. Adela Yarbro Collins; Chico: Scholars Press, 1985), 133.

16. Fuchs, "Sexual Politics," 134.

17. Susan Niditch, *Underdogs and Tricksters: A Prelude to Biblical Folklore* (San Francisco: Harpers Row Publishers, 1987), 1: The underdog is "the person . . . who is least likely to succeed and yet does." The trickster is a "subtype of the underdog" who "brings about change in a situation via trickery . . . they never gain full control of the situation around them and often escape difficulties in a less than noble way."

18. Fuchs, "Sexual Politics," 138.

19. Nahum M. Sarna, *Genesis: The Traditional Hebrew Text with New JPS Translation* (Philadelphia: Jewish Publication Society, 1989), 174.

20. Sharon Pace Jeansonne, "Images of Rebekah: From Modern Interpretations to Biblical Portrayal" *BR* 35 (1989), 41.

21. Tammi J. Schneider, *Mothers of the Promise: Women in the Book of Genesis* (Grand Rapids: Baker Academic, 2008), 51.

22. Fuchs, "Sexual Politics," 134.

23. Hilary Lipka, "Shaved Beards and Bared Buttocks," in *Being a Man: Negotiating Ancient Constructions of Masculinity*, 180.

24. Susan Haddox, "Favoured Sons and Subordinate Masculinities," in *Men and Masculinity in the Hebrew Bible and Beyond* (ed. Ovidiu Creanga; Sheffield: Phoenix Press, 2010), 10.

25. Sarna, *Genesis*, 175.

26. Steinberg, "Gender Roles," 181.

27. Lori Hope Lefkovitz, "Passing as a Man: Narratives of Jewish Gender Performance," *Narrative* 10:1 (2002): 93.

28. Esther Fuchs, "Who's Hiding the Truth? Deceptive Women and Biblical Androcentrism," in *Feminist Perspectives on Biblical Scholarship*, 140.

29. Ibid, 144.

30. James C. VanderKam, *Jubilees: A Commentary in Two Volumes* (Philadelphia: Fortress Press, forthcoming): VanderKam highlights that in Genesis there is already a fifteen-year overlap in the lifetimes of Abraham and Jacob, but the placement of Abraham's death notice before the birth notice for Esau and Jacob excludes the possibility of the grandfather interacting with his grandsons.

31. See Gen 25:27 where Jacob is called an איש תם.

32. See *Gen. Rab.* 63:10; *Tg. Onq.* Gen 25:27; *Tg. Neof.* Gen 25:2; *Tg. Ps.-J.* Gen 25:27; *Sifre Deut.* 336.

33. cf. *Tg. Ps.-J.* Gen 25:27.

34. Endres, *Biblical Interpretation*, 26.

35. In Genesis, the hirsute hunter Esau represents ideal masculinity. In *Jubilees* Abraham and Jacob's intellectual pursuits are instead painted as traits of ideal masculinity.

36. Endres, *Biblical Interpretation*, 25.

37. VanderKam, *Jubilees: A Commentary* (forthcoming).

38. Ibid.

39. Halpern-Amaru, *Empowerment*, 83.

40. VanderKam, *Jubilees: A Commentary* (forthcoming).

41. Ibid; cf. Philo, *QG* 4.196.

42. Piet Van Boxel, "The God of Rebekah," 17.

43. See Moshe Bernstein, "The Genesis Apocryphon: Compositional and Interpretative Perspectives," in *A Companion to Biblical Interpretation in Early Judaism* (ed. Matthias Henze; Grand Rapids: Eerdmans, 2001), 171; Sidnie White Crawford, *Rewriting Scripture in Second Temple Times* (Grand Rapids: Eerdmans, 2008), 118; cf. 1Qap Genar 19:14–19.

44. VanderKam, *The Book of Jubilees*, 116.

45. Halpern-Amaru, *Empowerment*, 89.

46. Before dying, Rebekah finally reveals Esau's wish to kill Jacob to Isaac (*Jub* 35:9).

47. James C. VanderKam, "Rebekah's Patriarchal Prayers," in *Prayer and Poetry in the Dead Sea Scrolls and Related Literature: Essays in Honour of Eileen Schuller on the Occasion of Her 65th Birthday* (eds. Jeremy Penner et. al.; Leiden: Brill, 2011), 425.

48. VanderKam, *Jubilees: A Commentary* (forthcoming).

49. Helena Zlotnick, *Dinah's Daughters: Gender and Judaism from the Hebrew Bible to Late Antiquity* (Philadelphia: University of Pennsylvania Press, 2002), 70.

50. cf. Tob 4:12; Prov 7.

51. Zlotnick, *Dinah's Daughters*, 70.

52. Fuchs, "Deceptive Women and Biblical Androcentrism," 138.

53. Ibid.

54. Michel Testuz, *Les Idées Religieuses du Livre des Jubilés* (Geneva: Librairie E. Droz and Paris: Librairie Minard, 1960), 65.

55. VanderKam, "Rebekah's Patriarchal Prayers," 436.

56. VanderKam, *Jubilees: A Commentary* (forthcoming).

57. Halpern-Amaru, *Empowerment*, 87.

58. Markus Holland McDowell, "'As I Prayed Many Things:' Patterns of Prayer in the Portrayal of Jewish Women in the Literature of the Second Temple Period" (PhD diss., Fuller Theological Seminary, 2004), 258.

59. Markus McDowell, *Prayers of Jewish Women: Studies of Patterns of Prayer in the Second Temple Period* (Tübingen: Mohr Siebeck, 2006), 61.

60. In classical iconography, however, the frequently found *Orans* figure is usually depicted as a woman with hands stretched outward and upward in prayer. Many thanks to Sari Fein and Gillian Glass for bringing this to my attention.

61. James C. VanderKam, *Jubilees: A Commentary in Two Volumes* (Minneapolis: Fortress Press, 2018).

62. Ibid.

63. John J. Collins, "Testaments," in *Jewish Writings of the Second Temple Period: Apocrypha, Pseudepigrapha, Qumran Sectarian Writings, Philo, Josephus: The Literature of the Jewish People in the Period of the Second Temple and the Talmud*, Vol. 2 (CRINT 2; ed. M. E. Stone; Philadelphia: Fortress Press, 1984), 324.

64. Devorah Dimant, "The Testament as a Literary Form in Early Jewish Pseudepigraphic Literature," in *Proceedings of the Eighth World Congress of Jewish Studies: Division A, The Period of the Bible* (Jerusalem: World Union of Jewish Studies, 1982), 81; e.g. Gen 49; Josh 22–24; 1 Sam 12; 1 Kgs 2:1–9; 1 Chron 28–29; *ALD* 5–10; *Jub* 20:1–12; 21:1–26; 22:10–23:7; *T. 12 Patr.*

65. See Pseudo-Philo, *L.A.B.* 33 for Deborah's testament.

66. Following Rebekah's request (*Jub* 35:9), Isaac repeats the instruction on brotherly love (*Jub* 36:1–11).

67. Randall Chesnutt, "Revelatory Experiences Attributed to Biblical Women in Early Jewish Literature," in *"Women Like This:" New Perspectives on Jewish Women in the Greco-Roman World* (ed. Amy-Jill Levine; Atlanta: Scholars Press, 1991), 108–11.

68. Halpern-Amaru, *Empowerment*, 84.

69. William Loader, *Enoch, Levi, and Jubilees on Sexuality: Attitudes towards Sexuality in the Early Enoch Literature, the Aramaic Levi Document, and the Book of Jubilees* (Grand Rapids: Eerdmans, 2007), 260.

70. Hanna Tervanotko, "Unreliability and Gender: Untrusted Female Prophets in Ancient Greek and Jewish Texts," *Journal of Ancient Judaism* 6 (2016): 366.

BIBLIOGRAPHY

Bernstein Moshe. "The Genesis Apocryphon: Compositional and Interpretative Perspectives." In *A Companion to Biblical Interpretation in Early Judaism*, edited by Matthias Henze, 157–79. Grand Rapids: William B. Eerdmans Publishing Company, 2001.

———. "'Rewritten Bible': A Generic Category which has Outlived its Usefulness?" *Textus* 22, edited by Alexander Rofé, 169–96. Jerusalem: Magnes Press, 2005.

Bird, Phyllis. "Images of Women in the Old Testament." In *Religion and Sexism: Images of Women in the Jewish and Christian Traditions*, edited by Rosemary Radford Ruether, 41–88. New York: Simon and Schuster, 1974.

Butler, Judith. *Gender Trouble*. New York: Routledge, 1990. Repr., New York: Routledge Classics, 2006.

Butler, Judith. "Performative Acts and Gender Constitution: An Essay in Phenomenology and Feminist Theory." *Theatre Journal* 40.4 (1988): 519–31.

Chesnutt, Randall D. "Revelatory Experiences Attributed to Biblical Women in Early Jewish Literature." In *"Women Like This": New Perspectives on Jewish Women in the Greco-Roman World*, edited by Amy-Jill Levine, 107–25. Atlanta: Scholars Press, 1991.

Collins, John J. "Testaments." In *Jewish Writings of the Second Temple Period: Apocrypha, Pseudepigrapha, Qumran Sectarian Writings, Philo, Josephus: The Literature of the Jewish People in the Period of the Second Temple and the Talmud*, edited by M. E. Stone, vol. 2, 325–56. Philadelphia: Fortress Press, 1984.

Collins, Adela Yarbro. *Feminist Perspectives on Biblical Scholarship*. Chico: Scholars Press, 1985.

Connell, Raewyn W. *Masculinities*. Berkeley: University of California Press, 2005.

Crawford, Sidnie White. *Rewriting Scripture in Second Temple Times*. Grand Rapids: Eerdmans, 2008.

Dimant, Devorah. "The Testament as a Literary Form in Early Jewish Pseudepigraphic Literature." In *Proceedings of the Eighth World Congress of Jewish Studies: Division A, The Period of the Bible*, 79–83. Jerusalem: World Union of Jewish Studies, 1982.

Endres, John. *Biblical Interpretation in the Book of Jubilees*. Washington: Catholic Bible Association of America, 1987.

———. "The Empowerment of Rebekah in the Book of *Jubilees*." *Proceedings of the World Congress of Jewish Studies* (1997): 189–97.

———. "Revisiting the Rebekah of the Book of *Jubilees.*" In *A Teacher for All Generations Essays in Honour of James VanderKam Vol. 1*, edited by Eric F. Mason Samuel I. Thomas, Alison Schofield, and Eugene Ulrich, 765–82. Boston: Brill, 2012.

Fuchs, Esther. "The Literary Characterisation of Mothers And Sexual Politics in the Hebrew Bible." In *Feminist Perspectives on Biblical Scholarship*, edited by Adela Yarbro Collins, 117–36. Chico: Scholars Press, 1985.

———. "Who's Hiding The Truth? Deceptive Women and Biblical Androcentrism." In *Feminist Perspectives on Biblical Scholarship*, edited by Adela Yarbro Collins, 137–44. Chico: Scholars Press, 1985.

Haddox, Susan. "Favoured Sons and Subordinate Masculinities." In *Men and Masculinity in the Hebrew Bible and Beyond*, edited by Ovidiu Creanga, 2–19. Sheffield: Phoenix Press, 2010.

———. "Masculinity Studies of the Hebrew Bible: The First Two Decades." *Currents in Biblical Research* 14.2 (2016): 176–206.

Jeansonne, Sharon Pace. "Images of Rebekah: From Modern Interpretations to Biblical Portrayal." *Biblical Research* 35 (1989): 33–52.

Lefkovitz, Lori Hope. "Passing as a Man: Narratives of Jewish Gender Performance." *Narrative* 10.1 (2002): 91–103.

Lipka, Hilary. "Shaved Beards and Bared Buttocks." In *Being a Man: Negotiating Ancient Constructions of Masculinity*, edited by Ilona Zsolnay, 176–97. New York: Routledge, 2017.

Loader, William. *Enoch, Levi and Jubilees on Sexuality: Attitudes Towards Sexuality in the Early Enoch Literature, the Aramaic Levi Document, and the Book of Jubilees*. Grand Rapids: Eerdmans, 2007.

McDonald, Markus Holland. "'As I Prayed Many Things:' Patterns of Prayer in the Portrayal of Jewish Women in the Literature of the Second Temple Period." PhD diss., Fuller Theological Seminary, 2004.

McDowell, Markus. *Prayers of Jewish Women: Studies of Patterns of Prayer in the Second Temple Period.* Tübingen: Mohr Siebeck, 2006.

Niditch, Susan. *Underdogs and Tricksters: A Prelude to Biblical Folklore.* San Francisco: Harpers Row Publishers, 1987.

Nissinen, Martti. "Relative Masculinities in the Hebrew Bible and Old Testament." In *Being a Man: Negotiating Ancient Constructions of Masculinity*, edited by Ilona Zsolnay, 221–47. New York: Routledge, 2017.

Sarna, Nahum M. *Genesis: The Traditional Hebrew Text with new JPS Translation.* Philadelphia: Jewish Publication Society, 1989.

Schneider, Tammi J. *Mothers of the Promise: Women in the Book of Genesis.* Grand Rapids: Baker Academic, 2008.

Steinberg, Naomi. "Gender Roles in the Rebekah Cycle." *Union Seminary Quarterly Review* 39.3 (1984): 175–88.

Tervanotko, Hanna. "Unreliability and Gender: Untrusted Female Prophets in Ancient Greek and Jewish Texts." *Journal of Ancient Judaism* 6 (2016): 358–81.

Testuz, Michel. *Les Idées Religieuses du Livre des Jubilés.* Geneva: E. Droz, 1960.

van Boxel, Piet. "The God of Rebekah." *SIDIC* 9.3 (1976): 14–18.

VanderKam, James C. *Book of Jubilees.* Sheffield: Sheffield Academic Press, 2001.
———. *Jubilees: A Commentary in Two Volumes.* Minneapolis: Fortress Press, 2018.
———. "Rebekah's Patriarchal Prayers." In *Prayer and Poetry in the Dead Sea Scrolls and Related Literature: Essays in Honor of Eileen Schuller on the Occasion of her 65th Birthday*, edited by Jeremy Penner, Ken M. Penner, and Cecilia Wassen, 421–36. Leiden: Brill, 2012.
———. *Textual and Historical Studies in the Book of Jubilees.* Missoula: Scholars Press, 1977.
Zlotnick, Helena. *Dinah's Daughters: Gender and Judaism from the Hebrew Bible to Late Antiquity.* Philadelphia: University of Pennsylvania Press, 2002.
Zsolnay Ilona, ed. *Being a Man: Negotiating Ancient Constructions of Masculinity.* New York: Routledge, 2017.

Chapter Six

The Reinforcement of Patriarchy and the (De)Construction of Gender Roles in *Jubilees'* Reception of the Jacob-Esau-Narrative

Daniel Vorpahl

From Cain and Abel through to Joseph and his brothers, siblings-stories within the book of Genesis function as a matrix of socio-ethical development within the familial pre-society of ancient Israel.[1] Likewise, within an androcentric social order siblings rivalry appears as a counterdraft to male bonding. That androcentric order is generally called patriarchy, understood as a social system in which men hold power and women are largely excluded from it. But patriarchy in the narrow sense of the word is actually a familial system that is reckoned through the male line, representing the power of fathers.[2] In both senses the narratives of Gen 12–50 are broadly called stories of the patriarchs, although correctly these are stories about families.

A patriarchal system does not work by fathers alone, as their status requires the existence of mothers and descendants. Carol Meyers speaks therefore rather of a patrilineality than a patriarchy in ancient Israel, emphasizing that male control in certain areas does not mean absolute authority in all social areas of daily life.[3] As antique societies had no strict separation of households and workplaces, women and men had overlapping tasks within these areas,[4] as biblical narratives document as well.[5] Furthermore the matriarchs Sarah, Rebekah, Leah, and Rachel impinge upon the patriarchs, especially upon the emergence of the people of Israel.[6] But in my assessment they do so within a patriarchal system. That women develop special skills and operate households[7] does not restrain men from ignoring or downgrading that work until today.[8] And biblical or archaeological witness for examples of women holding communal positions[9] does not negate the fact that they did so within a patriarchal structure.

Even as a familial system, patriarchy depends on a fundamental differentiation and hierarchical classification between males and females.[10] The very existence of patrilineality downgrades the female newborn, and male circumcision as Israel's sign of the covenant demotes women as well.[11] Not least, most recorded biblical texts were presumably written by men.[12] Accordingly we have to assume that sovereignty about the construction of gender within biblical as well as Second-Temple literature lay foremost in the hands of men. Nevertheless, male dominance in Jewish antiquity cannot be taken as a solid fact of absolute power and control. As patriarchy is not a natural phenomenon[13] but a social construction, it must have been constructed as well in patrilineal families of ancient Israel. Within this paper I will analyze textual witnesses for the social construction of patriarchy and its impact on the creation of gender roles in the book of Jubilees' reception of the Jacob-Esau-narrative in comparison to its biblical source.[14]

To examine how assumptions of patriarchy are reflected and reinforced with impact on the construction of gender roles I will start by looking for appropriate indicators within related motifs and categories of the biblical narrative of the siblings Jacob and Esau in the Masoretic Text of Gen 25:19–28:9.[15] The developed motifs and categories will build the framework for the comparison of the biblical story and its reception in Jub 19:13–27:18, focused on the promotion of patriarchy and its impact on gender roles.

To analyze how, and for which criteria, gender is ordered as a universal and central social category[16] within a patriarchal structure we have to consider that structure's implemented binarity of sex. The assumption of binary sexes and the construction of genders within Jewish antiquity might differ from the binary idea of sex that postmodern feminism and gender studies try to deconstruct nowadays.[17] It has to be carefully reconstructed from the textual presentation of Jewish society preserved within extant antique literary sources. Generally, the cultural construction of gender is based on the identification of a biological sex, followed by its social grading. As we have no ensured information about the biological characteristics of biblical figures, we must infer these, based on the few hints biblical texts offer, combined with a rudimentary assumption of a plain idea of male and female biology. At least the biblical stories of creation present two biological sex-categories (male and female) according to the immediately following instruction to reproduce (Gen 1:27–28), and two social genders that cannot live without each other (Gen 2:18–24). And as Betsy Halpern-Amaru shows, within the reception of the creation of men in Jubilees, masculinity is understood as the natural dominant principle of the human being with femininity a potential that needs to be developed.[18]

A PLACE OF RIVALRY:
THE BIBLICAL JACOB-ESAU-NARRATIVE

The biblical Jacob-Esau-narrative is a fruitful example to examine familial powers concerning the determination and development of gender roles. I have analyzed its first half (Gen 25:19–28:9) for motifs and categories with potential for later reception and will now observe which patriarchal structure and gender-related aspects are implemented in their respective appearances.

From the very beginning, the biblical narrative of Jacob and Esau oscillates between the micro level of family and the meta level of peoples (Israel and Edom), based on the divine explanation of Rebekah's painful pregnancy as two stocks, separating from one root, with the prediction that the smaller people will rule over the bigger people (Gen 25:23).[19] While God's revelation is highly relevant for the further story and the development of Rebekah's and Jacob's actions in particular,[20] we have to focus on the micro level of the familial storyline to ascertain elements of a patriarchal structure and gender roles. The first observable category of *intra-familial relations* can be subdivided into the siblings' relation and the relation of Rebekah and Isaac.

The revelation in Gen 25:23 overshadows the reader's view on the relation of Esau and Jacob with upcoming rivalry. The use of the terms twins (תומם, 25:24) and brother (אח, 25:26) in the following verses may harmonize their relation verbally, but likewise tightens the smoldering conflict by the fact that the opposing parties are related to one another. The descriptions of the brothers as they grow up highlight the distinctions between Jacob and Esau: Esau becomes a skillful hunter and Jacob a civilized man who stays in camp (25:27), obviously becoming a farmer (25:29, 34; 27:9). The text's creators do not incline any hegemonic form of maleness, as both kinds of grown men are differentiated but not judged. Nevertheless, the differences of the brothers' characters turn their relation into a struggle for power, so that Jacob buys Esau's birthright under disputable circumstances (25:29–34) and finally defrauds him of their father's blessing (27:18–29).[21] The brothers' rivalry is a typical form of sibling relation in Genesis, without direct gender relevance. But the chosen objects of their rivalry—birthright (הרכב) and blessing (הכרב)—are components of a patriarchal structure. That this structure builds the framework of the brother's rivalry becomes obvious when the imminent escalation of Esau's will to kill his brother is deferred until their father's time of death (27:41). Here the siblings' rivalry is subordinated to the deference to the patriarch.

Turning to the second *intra-familial relation*, it shows that within the parental household the Jacob-Esau-narrative is as well about a rivalry between Isaac and Rebekah. Isaac loves Esau, but Rebekah loves Jacob (Gen 25:28). Weird enough that both parents have an opposing preference for one of their grown-up children, it seems absurd that Isaac's love for Esau is caused by his "taste for game" (ibid. JPS). This looks like a superficial reason, but on a meta level it refers to the important *feeding* motif I will discuss below.

Indeed, Rebekah acts against her husband, as well as against her older son. She intervenes proactively and deceitfully in Isaac's blessing (Gen 27:6–13, 15–17) and acts also very self-referentially (27:8, 9, 13), as well concerning her sons' escalating conflict and Jacob's flight (27:42–45). But Rebekah's intention might be not to harm Isaac and Esau but to support Jacob to receive his father's blessing (27:8–13). From Esau's and Isaac's point of view one might say that Rebekah is fighting the patriarchal structure of succession. But from her point of view she might even follow that structure in her legal understanding. As it is the matriarch's firstborn son who owns the birthright to be the first in the patrilineal inheritance, Rebekah decides under the impression of the divine revelation (25:23) that her younger son Jacob is going to be the first successor, while Jacob himself might feel legitimated by the birthright he purchased from his brother.

We see that the *intra-familial relations* are closely intertwined, while that category is weaving a field of tension of patriarchal structure to which four characters are assigned. This process is deeply infiltrated with the motif of these characters *emotions*: Rebekah's despair during her pregnancy (Gen 25:22) and concerning the rivalry of her sons (27:45), Isaac's reasonable love for Esau and Rebekah's unreasonable love for Jacob (25:28), Esau's despair out of hunger (25:29–32), Rebekah's and Isaac's bitterness because of Esau's two Hittite wives (26:34; 27:46), Isaac's and Esau's shock and despair about Jacob's betrayal (27:33–34, 38) and Esau's following anger (27:41).[22] The narrative's creators portray the negotiation processes of the construction of familial patriarchy in a highly emotional manner.

Likewise, these processes are associated with the relevant category of *legal issues*: The birthright is a directly gender-related element of a patriarchal structure, as it goes only to the firstborn male descendant (Deut 21:15–17). Nevertheless, Esau's selling of his birthright seems to be legally alright.[23] According to Gen 27:36 it is separated from the father's blessing, while Esau feels deceived in both cases by his brother. The content of Isaac's blessing corresponds to a hierarchically patriarchal structure: The firstborn shall suppress his brothers, his mother's sons (27:29, 37), and shall be blessed with ecological wealth (27:28). Eventually this defines the role of the next patriarch, being the potentate and nurturer of the family.

This leads us to two further relevant motifs: *power and obedience* and *feeding*. The power relations are easily outlined: Jacob controls Esau (Gen 25:29–34) and Isaac (27:19–23) concerning birthright and blessing and shall finally have power over other peoples and his brothers (27:29). Esau has unconscious power over Jacob and Rebekah by his will to murder his brother (27:42–45). Isaac controls Esau (27:1–5) and Jacob (28:1–5) by telling them where to go and what to do. And Rebekah controls Jacob (27:6–14, 42–45) and Isaac

(27:46) in telling them what to do.[24] But she cannot control Esau as he is driven by his privileges of the firstborn son (27:36) while Rebekah has no legal impact on this social status that is defined by the patriarchal system. Nevertheless, the power relations within the Jacob-Esau-narrative are not all legally based but often driven by interpersonal forces and thereby gender-balanced.

A highly relevant motif within the Jacob-Esau-narrative is *feeding*, which runs like a golden thread through the whole story. In Gen 25:29, 34 Jacob cooks lentils, obviously able to fulfill the household duty of preparing a meal. This is neither an attribute nor an exception of a male gender role, as Rebekah and Esau are capable of the same skill (Gen 27:14, 31). But Jacob distinguishes himself as an autarchic breadwinner, as he does again when he fetches two young goats from the flock in Gen 27:9–14. Esau by contrast is no regularly successful hunter, failing in Gen 25:29–32 and taking too long in Gen 27. It might be morally unfair of Jacob to take advantage of Esau being starving, forcing him to sell his birthright.[25] But especially with this and the meta level of future peoples in view it is mostly relevant that Jacob is able to ensure food supply and Esau is not, as the following chapter emphasizes by the mention of a famine (26:1).[26] This correlation becomes obvious again within the repeated combination of eating and blessing in Gen 27:4, 7, 10, 19, 25, 31, 33 and the emphasis on agricultural wealth within Isaac's blessing (27:28, 39). Consequently, the ability to prepare food seems to be gender-equal within the Jacob-Esau-narrative while the food supply seems to be a patriarchal attribute and hence a demand on the male gender role.

A more explicit distinction of gender roles appears within the motif of *communication with God*. When Isaac pleads to God on his wife's behalf (Gen 25:21), God finally replies by action resulting in Rebekah's pregnancy (ibid.). Both Isaac and God are active. Rebekah on the contrary is passive, although the verse is primarily about her. She is the object of a discourse but no part of it. One verse later, caused by the struggle of the fetuses in her womb, Rebekah herself turns to the inventor of reproduction and is going to ask God (25:22). Actually, it is not said that she asks God, but that she is going to (ותלך לדרש ת־יאהוה, 25:22). Meanwhile God already talks to her, unfolding the revelation of two rivaling peoples coming out of Rebekah's womb (25:23). Again, Rebekah remains passive as she is not talking to God but God is talking to her. Instead of his action she receives a reply by God, explaining not the cause but the meaning of her problem that remains unresolved.[27] This motif is closely related to the one of *infertility*, which appears only in Gen 25:21, where Rebekah is mentioned four times, but only once by name, once as a female pronoun and two times as Jacob's wife. It seems that because fertility is a matter of God, it is the man as God's communication partner who has to handle it. The woman's role is downgraded to be a passive object that is moreover damaged with infertility.

This leads us to the category of *embodiment*, starting with Rebekah remaining passive when the two fetuses struggle in her womb in Gen 25:22. By wondering why this is happening to her, the topic of the right of physical self-determination is raised. Of course, this lies in the very nature of pregnancy, as a pregnant woman's body is no longer hers alone, a growing fetus is occupying space and has impact on somatic functions.[28] Within God's reply to Rebekah the womb[29] is called hers (25:23–24), as it is called her birth (25:24). But the very moment the twins are born the text focuses on them (25:25–27). Rebekah is just described as the vessel of her unborn children's rivalry. Measured against the highly intense use of physical strength that a woman achieves during a pregnancy and birth, it becomes obvious that the text downgrades Rebekah within passive embodiment.

In Gen 25:27 the boys (נערים) each become a man (איש). It seems as if maleness naturally takes place by itself, while the text does not say how the distinction between Esau and Jacob came about. The different skills of the different kinds of men (hunter and farmer) are further augmented by the bodily criteria of being hairy or smooth-skinned (27:11). Based on that bodily ascription, Jacob's mimesis of his brother Esau to get the father's blessing in Gen 27:15–16 might be seen as some kind of body-switching experience. Although it is just about the surface of the skin and its hair than about the whole body, from a modern perspective the skin is the biggest organ of the human body. Jacob's switch from one man to the other to receive his father's blessing is a most visible example of patriarchy suppressing inappropriate males. The text emphasizes that Jacob does not completely change his identity but becomes a hybrid creature with Jacob's voice and Esau's hands (27:22). Jacob keeps his gender but strengthens it situationally. According to that there is not just one kind of being male, as Jacob changes his variant of social gender temporarily under the influence of Rebekah.[30]

The Rebekah-Isaac-rivalry becomes as well a matter of embodiment when Isaac's eyes do not see anymore (Gen 27:1) but Rebekah hears him and Esau talking (27:5). Obviously, Isaac is capable of hearing as well, but Rebekah uses the same receiving organ to intervene against her husband for the benefit of Jacob. Isaac on the contrary hears that it is Jacob who speaks to him, but still trusts his bad eyes (27:22–23) and is infatuated by the smell he likes so much (27:27).

As a counterpart of constructed bodies, the category of *constructed spaces* can as well have impact on the construction of gender as certain attributed fields of action. The male successors' characters are hereby more active than the one female, while we cannot say anything relevant about Isaac's fields of action. Esau, being sent out to the field (Gen 27:3.5) to return to his home with success (27:5), is leaving a place to return to it. For a similar success Jacob goes to the flock, fetching young cattle just within his home area (27:9–14). While his brother has to leave for a living, Jacob has to leave to survive (27:43–45) and to get married (28:2, 5), once the siblings' rivalry escalates. About Rebekah we can note that in Gen 27:5 she is acting from or within the hidden. Likewise, this is her most active part within the whole story.

Finally, as a word statistic reveals, the quantitative relations of descriptive narration, amount of action and speech in Gen 25:19–28:9 are reasonably balanced between the four characters. There is one third more descriptive text concerning Jacob in comparison to the other characters, which is no substantial difference. More significant is that Rebekah has half as much action than Isaac and Jacob, but almost as much as Esau. This means it is not simply the men being described more actively than the woman, but it is the two progenitors of Israel that get a higher amount of action. Rebekah is as much described as she is active, but as we have seen, her field of action is hidden in the background. She is indeed active and influential, but nevertheless structurally suppressed within the patriarchal system.

Collectively Isaac has more than twice as much direct speech than the other three characters. Thereby, on the textual level Isaac has the say-so, he is in charge over his wife and his children, which exhibits a verbal expression of patriarchy. As we have seen, within that structure Isaac's wife and younger son are legally suppressed. But neither Rebekah nor Jacob rebel against that situation, as their goal is at least to profit from the very same system. Therefore, Rebekah and Jacob trick their family's patriarchal structure without putting itself into question.

The gender roles that are derived within that patriarchal structure are two-part: They consist firstly of a relevant but passive mother's role, as represented within Rebekah's passive embodiment of being object but not a part of a discourse on infertility, and her main acting in a hidden space. And secondly, an unstable male role finds its embodiment in the hybrid Jacob-Esau-creature during the fraud scene, and is further represented in the home space area that Esau has to leave for a living and Jacob has to leave to survive. As its intra-familial relations reveal, the biblical Jacob-Esau-narrative consists of a siblings-rivalry that concerns legal issues of a patriarchal structure, such as birthright, blessing, potentate, and food supply, but that does not judge the brothers' different forms of male gender. Likewise, it consists of a parents-rivalry, revealed in their opposing preferences for one of their children and Rebekah's intervening against her husband. Accordingly, the patriarchal familial system knows two hierarchies: male over female, and firstborn over younger brother(s), expressed mainly through the motifs or categories of *communication with God, embodiment, constructed spaces* and fields of action. Within the highly emotional negotiation processes of that patriarchy's construction in the Jacob-Esau-narrative, both hierarchies are subverted without attacking the structure of patriarchy itself.

CAGED IN A STRUCTURE: THE RECEPTION OF THE JACOB-ESAU-NARRATIVE IN JUBILEES

The book of Jubilees adapts most of the content of Genesis and parts of Exodus in the style of rewritten scripture, arranged as a revelation to Moses and consequently following its own structure of annual cycles. Probably of priestly origin, Jubilees is focused on topics such as purity, cult, and law[31] and emphasizes the relevance of endogamy, ideal progenitors, and selecting appropriate brides.[32] In this regard, the presumably male author(s)[33] of Jubilees "expands and enriches the depiction of female characters."[34] More pronounced than within Genesis, women in Jubilees become cooperatively engaged in parenting and the "workings of the covenant."[35] And as Halpern-Amaru demonstrates further, especially Rebekah's role is emphasized "as the matriarch par excellence."[36]

Presumably written in Palestine in the second century BCE,[37] the sociocultural context of Jubilees is set in a controversially debated social construction of gender within the Jewish-Hellenistic literature.[38] Based on these preliminary considerations it is obviously worth analyzing how the reception of the Jacob-Esau-narrative in Jub 19:13–27:18 was realized concerning the promotion of patriarchy and its impact on gender roles.

A look at the word statistics of the Jubilees text reveals a significant contrast to Genesis, particularly caused by the additional presence of Abraham. His amount of direct speech is four times as much compared to the other characters and even more extensive than all other direct speech together. Apart from that, the statistical relations of descriptive narration and amount of action and speech are quite similar to Genesis, with a slightly higher proportion of description in general and two relevant exceptions: in Jubilees, Rebekah's amount of direct speech is as much as Isaac's, and Esau is far less present than all other characters. Compared quantitatively, in Jubilees, Rebekah speaks more, while Isaac speaks a little less than in Genesis.

A major intervention is indeed the additional appearance of Abraham within the Jacob-Esau-narrative. According to biblical information Abraham was one hundred years old when Isaac was born (Gen 21:5) and died at the age of 175 (25:7). Within the text's chronology, this happened shortly before Jacob and Esau were born (25:24–26). However, biographically Isaac was sixty years old by then (25:25), hence Abraham was at the age of one hundred sixty and lived on until the siblings turned fifteen.[39] The extending of Abraham's appearance therefore fits with the biblical timetable. Furthermore, Abraham's presence is intensified by intertextual linkage, when he says that Jacob's descendants shall be counted like the sands on the earth (Jub 19:22 cf. Gen 22:17), or his blessings of Jacob refer to elements of Isaac's blessing of the Jacob-Esau-hybrid.[40]

That Abraham is so deeply woven into the DNA of the Jacob-Esau-story, also has impact on the *intra-familial relations* in Jubilees' reception of the Genesis narrative. Without the impression of a divine revelation, the siblings' relationship is here more focused on the familial micro level. Likewise, the distinction between the siblings is enhanced. Their more detailed description emphasizes the first-mentioned Jacob as being perfect and upright, and strengthens the downgrading of Esau, who is called harsh, rustic, and hairy (Jub 19:13). The additional characteristics animalize Esau, whereby it becomes relevant that only Jacob's place of living is mentioned, although Esau might live as well in tents (ibid.). The brothers' differences are prioritized over their equivalent gender. While Jacob learns how to write,[41] Esau does not, becoming a wild man, a hunter, learning war and being rough in everything he does (19:14). Interesting enough, only Esau is called a man (19:13–14), although this gender is not positively described. Through the description of Esau's behavior Abraham realizes that it is "through Jacob he would have a reputation and descendants" (19:16),[42] which appears less as a qualification of Jacob but a disqualification of Esau.[43] The author(s) of Jubilees, therefore, replace(s) the divine revelation of the Jacob-Esau relationship to the matriarch Rebekah (Gen 25:23) by the reasonable knowledge of the patriarch Abraham and therefore erase(s) the idea that "Isaac is not privy to the same knowledge."[44] This strengthens the role that patriarchy plays in Jubilees through the appearance of Abraham.

In Jubilees' reception of the Jacob-Esau-narrative the siblings' rivalry itself is more pronounced while objects of birthright and blessing are less focused. Nonetheless, the rivalry is here much more intertwined with the category of *legal issues* than in Genesis: Rebekah stresses that Jacob shall not take a woman from Canaan as Esau did (Jub 25:1) and Jacob replies that he will not act as evil as his brother (25:9). Moreover, Esau actively attempts to force Jacob to marry one of his sisters-in-law, while Jacob had been instructed by Abraham not to do so (25:7–8). It is only within the legal issue of foreign women that Esau's struggle with Jacob turns into a conflict with the tradition of Abraham and so becomes a struggle with patriarchy, as it is the patriarch here who predetermines appropriate brides. This is highlighted by the alteration of Esau not deferring the killing of his brother until his father's death time but wishing his father's death to come to make this happen (26:35). Again, the denigration of the rough and harsh, male character of Esau is spelled out much more than in the biblical narrative. However, the siblings' rivalry itself is not directly gender-related. So, Isaac warns Esau not to act against his brother (26:34), while Jacob will not adopt his mother's fear of getting killed by Esau but instead aims to kill him (27:4). In Jubilees' reception of the biblical story Esau's generally rude behavior is clearly depicted as a violation of patriarchic rules, which is furthered by the addition of Abraham. However, violence itself is not in a breath discredited as a male characteristic, but is presented without judgment, as the example of Jacob in Jub 27:4 shows.

The figure of Abraham has an even bigger impact on the *intra-familial relation* of Rebekah and Isaac. As the motifs of *communication with God* and *infertility* are deleted from the narrative's reception in Jubilees, Isaac does not plead for Rebekah's sake, she receives no revelation, and her pregnancy is not brought up. Jubilees just mentions that Rebekah gives birth to two sons for Isaac (Jub 19:13), focusing as well on the familial micro level.[45] Reduced to that statement, Rebekah's role within a patriarchal system that is focused on male successors is simply functional. It is now Abraham who loves Jacob, while Isaac loves Esau (19:15), both without mentioning any reason. By Abraham overtaking Rebekah's role—contrary to Genesis—the Rebekah-Isaac-rivalry within the birth scene becomes one between Abraham and Isaac, and thus a rivalry between father and son, further embedding the narrative into a patriarchal system. Nevertheless, a rivalry between Isaac and Rebekah is also established in Jubilees, as Esau is called Isaac's son (26:1–2) and Rebekah talks to Jacob as her son (26:5–6). As well, Rebekah still intervenes proactively and deceitfully in Isaac's blessing (26:5–6, 9–12). Jubilees also adds the expression of an emotional bond between Isaac and Rebekah when he consoles her at the moment that Jacob is leaving (27:14–18), which demonstrates the ideality of their marriage[46] and reduces the intensity of their rivalry. Parallel to that, the relation of Jacob and Rebekah is emphasized in Jubilees, for instance in movements, as when both leave Abraham's place together (Jub 19:30) or Jacob runs to his mother after Abraham's death and just then Rebekah talks to Isaac until all three went together to the dead Abraham (23:4). Furthermore, Rebekah repeats calling Jacob her son (25:2, 3, 15, 18.) and he calls her mother (25:5, 9, 10). Similar to the brothers Jacob and Esau their parents' rivalry is shifted in Jubilees' reception of the biblical narrative. Concerning the preference of Jacob, Abraham is overtaking Rebekah's role, turning her conflict with Isaac into a patriarchal controversy, while the parents' bonding on each one of their sons is only intra-familial and emotional, and does not burden their spousal relationship.

Although Abraham occupies Rebekah's emotional space in loving Jacob in the birth scene (Jub 19:15), the matriarch's love for Jacob is nevertheless stressed more than in the biblical text through the use of modifiers, described as truly (19:19) and whole-hearted (19:31; 25:2) and even stronger than her feelings for Esau (19:16, 31). But the same applies to Isaac's love for Esau (19:19, 31) and Abraham's love for Jacob (19:21, 27; 22:26). The relevance of the motif of *emotions* is as high as in the biblical narrative, and is even further highlighted with respect to love, and there is no gender distinction in the representation of emotions.[47]

The category of *legal issues* is emphasized especially within the integrity of Abraham, and in general concerning birthright and blessing. So is Jacob's role as the firstborn son transferred into the meta level of God as his father (Jub 19:29).[48] And by purchasing the birthright from his brother Jacob gets also his higher age (24:3–5), becoming the older while Esau is degraded in his size (24:7), as a physical representation of his social status. These variances within Jubilees' reception of the biblical brothers strengthen Jacob's final legal status, no matter how he got it, and therefore enshrine the system of patrilineal succession. This patriarchal structure is further confirmed when Rebekah sends Jacob not to her brother's (Gen 27:43) but to her father's house (Jub 25:3), and Jacob agrees to his mother's suggestion only with reference to the patriarch Abraham (25:4–5). Likewise, Rebekah's blessing of Jacob is "an abbreviated reflection of the one she witnessed Abraham bestow upon Jacob."[49] Her maternal concern is of high relevance and influence in Jubilees as well.[50] But even more than in Genesis it is actively expressed only in the scope of a patriarchal structure, additionally enhanced by Rebekah's strong ideological and emotional parallelization with Abraham.

Concerning the motif of *power and obedience* the influence of Abraham's presence within Jubilees' reception of the Jacob-Esau-narrative is widely noticeable. Abraham controls Rebekah, his daughter-in-law, by calling her and telling how to treat Jacob (Jub 19:16, 20–21), who shall stay in his direct succession to take his place on earth (19:17, 20–21, 23–24, 27). Thereby, Abraham's structurally patriarchal intent is not a matter of material inheritance but of spiritual succession. His power over Rebekah is internalized by her to the point that she functions as a substitute for Abraham toward Jacob and an intermediary between Isaac and his father, as Halpern-Amaru has demonstrated.[51] Beside all expressions of emotional closeness, Abraham is taking possession of Rebekah and Jacob by calling them his daughter and son (19:17, 21; 22:10, 11, 16, 19, 20, 23, 28) to instruct them, and he also overpowers Isaac by instructing Rebekah to bless Jacob (19:26). Abraham's intervention is justified by his knowledge that God will choose Jacob already as a people above all other peoples on earth (19:18). It is most relevant that

Jubilees does not document that God spoke to Abraham, but it is Abraham's knowledge that justifies his power.

Most of the other relations of power and obedience are similar to the biblical Jacob-Esau-narrative. But when Rebekah tries to control her son Jacob, his reply does occasionally refer to Abraham's authority (Jub 25:3–5). Even if Jacob follows his mother's will (25:9–10) he does so because it corresponds to the will of the patriarchs Abraham or Isaac (27:2–6). In Genesis, Jacob is also sent away by his father Isaac (Gen 28:1–2), while in Jubilees' reception of the biblical narrative this situation is based on Rebekah's confident influence on Isaac (Jub 27:7). Nevertheless, in Jub 27:2–6 Jacob will bow only to the patriarchal authority of his father. In contrast to the biblical Jacob-Esau-narrative, Jubilees strengthens—at least partially—the legal formalities of the exercise of power within the patriarchal system, especially with adding Abraham's impact on Rebekah and Jacob. Within the patriarchal structure Jacob and Rebekah are both legally suppressed. That they appear nevertheless active and successful within Jubilees' reception of the Jacob-Esau-narrative, is enabled by the authority of Abraham.

The motif of *feeding* appears in Jubilees' reception in constant analogy to its function within the biblical Jacob-Esau-narrative, just being widened to Abraham receiving bread and eating it before he blesses Jacob (Jub 22:4). As in the biblical narrative, the preparation of food is a gender-equal skill while the food supply is a male skill of patriarchal relevance. And also, the category of *constructed spaces* is adopted equally to the biblical source of reception.

The first manifestation of the mostly gender-related category of *embodiment* is the fact that in Jubilees' reception Esau's and Jacob's most distinguishable characteristics are already mentioned before they grew up (Jub 19:13–14). The more detailed the siblings' descriptions turn out, the more distinct is their predestination according to Jub 19:13. Nevertheless, while the different bodily criteria of the siblings are maintained and extended, only Esau is called a man (19:3–4). It seems as if Jacob is first and foremost the son, especially for Abraham. Male gender characteristics become of secondary interest as Jubilees' reception of the Jacob-Esau-narrative is less focused on individual genders but instead focused on structural roles within a patriarchal system in which the male-female-hierarchy is immanent. Precisely because the succession of Jacob and Esau is a controversial matter of rivalry their gender roles are relevant, as we have seen within Genesis. But within Jubilees' reception of the Jacob-Esau-narrative that aspect is overpowered by the knowledge and authority of Abraham. Ironically, this proves that gender inequality is not a matter of "natural" characteristics of biological sexes but of power.

Most observations concerning the category of embodiment within the biblical Jacob-Esau-narrative appear equally in Jubilees. A stronger bodily presence can be recognized within the kissing that accompanies each situation of blessing (Jub 19:26; 22:10, 11; 25:23; 26,21). Especially Abraham's relation to Jacob is as well expressed physically, as Jacob falls asleep on Abraham's lap and he kisses him seven times (22:26), finally laying two fingers on his grandfather's eyes before he dies (23:1) until Jacob wakes up in Abraham's ice-cold lap (23:2–3). Thus, patriarchy in Jubilees is even embodied in male physical bonding.

As Rebekah's pregnancy is not a topic in Jubilees but a note (Jub 19:13), her bodily presence as a mother is reduced but does not fully disappear. She blesses Jacob through the power of God, but also with her love and her breasts, while her mouth and her tongue might praise him (25:19). Rebekah functions as a medium for God, a pure vessel for his blessing (25:13–14). The blessing that comes from her is mainly given by her body and through her motherly feelings (25:19). Within the Jubilees' reception of the Jacob-Esau-narrative even this is an exception, as Rebekah's enhanced speech and action is mainly oriented on and justified by "overriding patriarchal and patriotic concerns."[52] These are established by the additional strong appearance of Abraham, taking control on the whole familial micro level through his power of knowledge.

That knowledge is neither constructive nor destructive but it is consolidating a patriarchal structure. Therefore, Jacob's legal position is strengthened as well, while Esau's behavior is described as anti-patriarchic. From the very moment of their first description in Jub 19:13, the siblings' distinction into Jacob's values (perfect, upright) and Esau's characteristics (harsh, rustic, hairy) follows that patriarchal structure in a much stronger and less gender-constructing way than its biblical source. While only Esau is called a man, it is Jacob who appears as the ideal male successor, being bonded emotionally and physically to the patriarch Abraham and his female substitute, Rebekah, whose expanded presence in Jubilees' reception of the Jacob-Esau-narrative is overshadowed by the fencing of patriarchal structure.

NOTES

1. While Cain kills his brother Abel, within the further siblings-stories in Genesis brothers and sisters evolve increasingly into ending their rivalries not in violence but solving them interpersonally. See Daniel Vorpahl, "Geschwisterlichkeit als sozial-ethische Matrix des Volkes Israel in der *Tora*," in *Zwischen Ideal und Ambivalenz: Geschwisterbeziehungen in ihren soziokulturellen Kontexten*, eds. Ulrike Schneider et al. (Frankfurt am Main: PL Academic Research, 2015), 85–103, here 97–101.

2. Above all, the father has "legal power over his wife, his children, and his servants/slaves, who are regarded as his property alongside his land." Deborah W.

Rooke, "Patriarchy/Kyriarchy," in *The Oxford Encyclopedia of the Bible and Gender Studies*, ed. Julia M. O'Brien (New York: Oxford University Press, 2014), Vol. 2, 1–9, here 1. See Carol L. Meyers, "Was Ancient Israel a Patriarchal Society," *JBL* 133/1 (2014): 8–27, here 8–15 and Laurie Penny, *Unspeakable Things: Sex, Lies and Revolution* (London: Bloomsbury, 2015), 69–70.

3. See Meyers, "Was Ancient Israel," 16–17.

4. See ibid., 18, 20–22 and Regine Gildemeister and Katja Hericks, *Geschlechtersoziologie: Theoretische Zugänge zu einer vertrackten Kategorie des Sozialen* (München: Oldenbourg, 2012), 10–11.

5. See e.g., Jacob, Rebekah and Esau cooking meals in Gen 25:29, and 27:14, 31, Abraham instructing Sarah how to bake in Gen 18:6, or Rachel tending sheep among men in Gen 29:2–9.

6. See Rachel's and Leah's birth-rivalry in Gen 29:31–30:24 and hereof Vorpahl, "Geschwisterlichkeit," 100.

7. See Meyers, "Was Ancient Israel," 21.

8. See Penny, *Unspeakable Things*, 225–26.

9. See Meyers, "Was Ancient Israel," 23 and Angela Standhartinger, *Das Frauenbild im Judentum der hellenistischen Zeit: ein Beitrag anhand von Joseph und Aseneth'* (Leiden: Brill, 1995), 72.

10. See Rooke, "Patriarchy," 5.

11. See ibid., 1.

12. See Claudia V. Camp, "Understanding a Patriarchy: Women in Second Century Jerusalem Through the Eyes of Ben Sira," in *"Women Like This": New Perspectives on Jewish Women in the Greco Roman World*, ed. Amy-Jill Levine, EJL 1 (Atlanta: Scholars Press, 1991), 1–39, here 1.

13. See Janice Capel Anderson, "Mary's Difference: Gender and Patriarchy in the Birth Narratives," *JR* 67/2 (1987): 183–202, here 185–86 (n. 7); Meyers, "Was Ancient Israel," 24, 26 and Rooke, "Patriarchy," 5–6. The "naturalization" of the social and legal subordination of women to men is mainly a product of the enlightenment in the eighteenth/nineteenth century. See Gildemeister and Hericks, *Geschlechtersoziologie*, 13–15 and Nina Degele, *Gender/Queer Studies: Eine Einführung* (Paderborn: Fink, 2008), 60–66.

14. Within this article the Jacob-Esau-narrative in the book of Jubilees is fully treated as a productive reception of the biblical Jacob-Esau-narrative in the book of Genesis. Proceeding on the assumption that this reception is based on a monogenetic relation, namely the Jubilees' author(s') direct knowledge of the Genesis narrative, I will primarily compare both versions of the Jacob-Esau-story. Regarding the term of reception and the idea of monogenetic relation see Susan Gillingham, "Biblical Studies on Holiday? A Personal View of Reception History," in *Reception History and Biblical Studies*, ed. Emma England and William J. Lyons (London: Bloomsbury, 2015), 17–30, here 19–20; Hannelore Link, *Rezeptionsforschung. Eine Einführung in Methoden und Probleme* (Stuttgart: Kohlhammer, 1980), 99 and Evi Zemanek, "Was ist Komparatistik?," in *Komparatistik*, ed. idem and Alexander Nebrig (Berlin: Akademie-Verlag 2012), 7–20, here 16–18.

15. Gen 25:19–28:9 covers the birth narrative and grow-up story of the siblings within their close family household until Jacob flees to Haran. Gen 28:10–33:20 is focused on Jacob's family, developing their own familial structure. Especially the further siblings-rivalry between Leah and Rachel in that second part needs a separate research beyond the manageable scope of this paper. See Atar Livneh, "Not at First Sight: Gender Love in *Jubilees*," *JSPE* 23/1 (2013): 3–20, here 14; Daniel Vorpahl, *"Es war zwar unrecht, aber Tradition ist es": Der Erstgeburtsrechts- und Betrugsfall der Brüder Jakob und Esau*, Pri ha-Pardes 4 (Potsdam: Universitätsverlag Potsdam, 2008), 36–50 and idem, "Geschwisterlichkeit," 98–100.

16. See Edith Franke and Verena Maske, "Religionen, Religionswissenschaft und die Kategorie Geschlecht/Gender," in *Religionswissenschaft*, ed. Michael Stausberg (Berlin: de Gruyter, 2012), 125–140, here 127.

17. As well as the wider terms of patriarchy, childhood, and motherhood, the modern binary idea of sex was developed within the eighteenth/nineteenth century. See Meyers, "Was Ancient Israel," 18; Degele, *Gender/Queer Studies*, 60–62 and Gildemeister and Hericks, *Geschlechtersoziologie*, 10–12.

18. See Betsy Halpern-Amaru, *The Empowerment of Women in the* Book of Jubilees, JSJ.S 60 (Leiden: Brill, 1999), 11. On the social phenomenon of women as defective variant of men see Gildemeister and Hericks, *Geschlechtersoziologie*, 14.

19. Concerning the translation, see Vorpahl, *"Es war zwar unrecht,"* 11–13.

20. See ibid., 25–29, 80–83.

21. Here it becomes a conflict between Jacob and Isaac, as he also betrays his father in Gen 27:19–20, 24.

22. A key word thereby is the helpless interrogative 'Why?' (למה): למה זה אנכי (27:45), שניכם למה אשכל גם־ (27:46) and למה לי חיים (25:32), לי בכרה למה־זה (Gen 25:22).

23. See Vorpahl, *"Es war zwar unrecht,"* 16–17.

24. Concerning Esau's marriages, Rebekah talks to Isaac (Gen 27:46) with the outcome that Isaac blesses Jacob, telling him not to marry Canaanite women (28:1). From a literary critical perspective Gen 26:34; 27:46, and 28:1 seem to be related.

25. Jacob's dish is not the price for the birthright. See Vorpahl, *"Es war zwar unrecht,"* 16.

26. See ibid., 17–18 and Diana Lipton, *From Forbidden Fruit to Milk and Honey: A Commentary on Food in the Torah* (Jerusalem: Urim Publications, 2018), 53.

27. Rebekah's problem can probably not be solved because of its meaning on the nonfamilial meta level of the story. Also, we cannot say if God describes in Gen 25:23 the reason for the siblings' rivalry or its consequence.

28. The first time they are mentioned at the beginning of Gen 25:22 the siblings are called בנים, sons. Although the term can include females as well, and is therefore nowadays sometimes translated as children, it is distinctive that a grammatically male form is the rule.

29. In Gen 25:23 two terms for womb (בטן and מעה) are used to separate the two foetuses resp. peoples.

30. Observing the complete biblical story of Jacob, it turns out that he actually is "the kind of male" that constantly changes.

31. See Halpern-Amaru, *Empowerment*, 1.

32. See ibid., 38, 47; Livneh, "Not at First Sight," 6, 8; Friedemann Schubert, *Tradition und Erneuerung: Studien zum Jubiläenbuch*, EHS.G 771 (Frankfurt am Main: Lang, 1998), 137 and Helena Zlotnick, *Dinah's Daughters: Gender and Judaism From the Hebrew Bible to Late Antiquity* (Philadelphia: University of Pennsylvania Press, 2002), 70.

33. Although I address the book of Jubilees' Jacob-Esau cycle here as a literary unit, I cannot bindingly say if it had one or multiple author(s). For a redaction-critical analysis of the book, see Michael Segal, *The Book of Jubilees* (Leiden: Brill, 2007).

34. Halpern-Amaru, "The First Women, Wives, and Mothers in Jubilees," *JBL* 113/4 (1994): 609–26, here 609.

35. Halpern-Amaru, *Empowerment*, 34. "For the author of *Jubilees*, all women, even the matriarchs, function only within the circle of family. But since the dynamic of the family and covenant history intersect, the matriarchs have the potential to influence the movement of that history in the direction in which it is intended to go." Ibid., 75. See also ibid., 28 and idem, "The First Woman," 622.

36. Halpern-Amaru, "The First Woman," 616. See also idem, *Empowerment*, 37 and John C. Endres, "Scriptural Authority in the Book of Jubilees," in *Scriptural Authority in Early Judaism and Ancient Christianity*, ed. Isaac Kalimi et al., DCLS 16 (Berlin: De Gruyter, 2013), 185–205, here 185.

37. Jubilees was originally written in Hebrew but is fully preserved just in Ethiopic and early translated into Syriac, Greek, and Latin. See Endres, "Scriptural Authority," 188 and Halpern-Amaru, *Empowerment*, 2.

38. See Standhartinger, *Das Frauenbild*, 59, 71–74 and e.g. Ben Sira 26:14–16, 25:21–22, and 33:20.

39. See Halpern-Amaru, *Empowerment*, 38f. (n. 11).

40. See ibid., 83. The first blessing takes place because Abraham is old and does not know how soon he may die (Jub 21:1 cf. Gen 27:1), in the second one Abraham says that the peoples may serve Jacob (Jub 22:11 cf. Gen 27:29).

41. Concerning the important issue of writing, see Jacques T.A.G.M. von Ruiten, *Abraham in the Book of Jubilees*, JSJ.S 161 (Leiden: Brill, 2012), 243.

42. All quotations from Jubilees are taken from *The Book of Jubilees*, trans. James C. Vanderkam, CSCO 511 (Lovanii: Peeters, 1989).

43. See Halpern-Amaru, *Empowerment*, 81–82.

44. Ibid., 83.

45. See ibid., 57.

46. See ibid., 60.

47. Concerning the relation of parental and godly love for Jacob see Atar Livneh, "The 'Beloved Sons' of Jubilees," *JAJ* 6 (2015): 85–96, here 90–95.

48. See ibid.

49. Halpern-Amaru, *Empowerment*, 62.

50. See ibid., 63.

51. See ibid., 84, 87, 90.

52. Zlotnick, *Dinah's Daughters*, 69.

BIBLIOGRAPHY

Anderson, Janice C. "Mary's Difference: Gender and Patriarchy in the Birth Narratives." *JR* 67/2 (1987): 183–202.
Biblia Hebraica Stuttgartensia. Edited by Rudolph Kittel et al. Stuttgart: Deutsche Bibelgesellschaft, 1997.
The Book of Jubilees. CSCO 511. Translated by James C. Vanderkam. Lovanii: Peeters, 1989.
Camp, Claudia V. "Understanding a Patriarchy: Women in Second Century Jerusalem Through the Eyes of Ben Sira." In *"Women Like This": New Perspectives on Jewish Women in the Greco Roman World*, edited by Amy-Jill Levine, 1–39. Atlanta: Scholars Press, 1991.
Degele, Nina. *Gender/Queer Studies: Eine Einführung.* Paderborn: Fink, 2008.
Endres, John C. "Scriptural Authority in the Book of Jubilees." In *Scriptural Authority in Early Judaism and Ancient Christianity*, edited by Isaac Kalimi et al, 185–205. Berlin: De Gruyter, 2013.
Franke, Edith, and Verena Maske. "Religionen, Religionswissenschaft und die Kategorie Geschlecht/Gender." In *Religionswissenschaft*, edited by Michael Stausberg, 125–40. Berlin: De Gruyter, 2012.
Gildemeister, Regine, and Katja Hericks. *Geschlechtersoziologie: Theoretische Zugänge zu einer vertrackten Kategorie des Sozialen.* München: Oldenbourg, 2012.
Gillingham, Susan. "Biblical Studies on Holiday? A Personal View of Reception History." In *Reception History and Biblical Studies*, edited by Emma England and William J. Lyons, 17–30. London: Bloomsbury, 2015.
Halpern-Amaru, Betsy. *The Empowerment of Women in the Book of Jubilees.* JSJ.S 60. Leiden: Brill, 1999.
———. "The First Women, Wives, and Mothers in Jubilees." *JBL* 113/4 (1994): 609–26.
The Jewish Study Bible. Edited by Adele Berlin and Marc Zvi Brettler. New York: Oxford University Press, 2014.
Link, Hannelore. *Rezeptionsforschung. Eine Einführung in Methoden und Probleme.* Stuttgart: Kohlhammer, 1980.
Lipton, Diana. *From Forbidden Fruit to Milk and Honey: A Commentary on Food in the Torah.* Jerusalem: Urim Publications, 2018.
Livneh, Atar. "Not at First Sight: Gender Love in *Jubilees*." *JSPE* 23/1 (2013): 3–20.
Meyers, Carol L. "Was Ancient Israel a Patriarchal Society." *JBL* 133/1 (2014): 8–27.
Penny, Laurie. *Unspeakable Things: Sex, Lies and Revolution.* London: Bloomsbury, 2015.
Rooke, Deborah W. "Patriarchy/Kyriarchy." In *The Oxford Encyclopedia of the Bible and Gender Studies*, edited by Julia M. O'Brien, vol. 2, 1–9. New York: Oxford University Press, 2014.
Schubert, Friedemann. *Tradition und Erneuerung: Studien zum Jubiläenbuch.* EHS.G 771. Frankfurt am Main: Lang, 1998.
Segal, Michael. *The Book of Jubilees.* Leiden: Brill, 2007.

Standhartinger, Angela. *Das Frauenbild im Judentum der hellenistischen Zeit: ein Beitrag anhand von Joseph und Aseneth.* Leiden: Brill, 1995.

von Ruiten, Jacques T.A.G.M. *Abraham in the Book of Jubilees.* JSJ.S 161. Leiden: Brill, 2012.

Vorpahl, Daniel. *"Es war zwar unrecht, aber Tradition ist es": Der Erstgeburtsrechts- und Betrugsfall der Brüder Jakob und Esau.* Pri ha-Pardes 4. Potsdam: Universitätsverlag Potsdam, 2008.

———. "Geschwisterlichkeit als sozialethische Matrix des Volkes Israel in der *Tora.*" In *Zwischen Ideal und Ambivalenz: Geschwisterbeziehungen in ihren soziokulturellen Kontexten,* edited by Ulrike Schneider et al., 85–103. Frankfurt am Main: PL Academic Research, 2015.

Zemanek, Evi. "Was ist Komparatistik?" In *Komparatistik,* edited by idem and Alexander Nebrig, 7–20. Berlin: Akademie-Verlag 2012.

Zlotnick, Helena. *Dinah's Daughters: Gender and Judaism From the Hebrew Bible to Late Antiquity.* Philadelphia: University of Pennsylvania Press, 2002.

Chapter Seven

Women and Gender in the Gospel of John

Adele Reinhartz

If the topic of gender has not received the attention it warrants in the study of Second-Temple Judaism,[1] the same cannot be said with respect to the Gospel of John. To be sure, the Fourth Gospel is generally dated to the late first century, after the destruction of the Second Temple. Nevertheless, it can be included in Second-Temple Judaism insofar as it shares some important ideas, perspectives, and contexts, with apocalyptic Jewish literature, Philo's treatises, and other Second-Temple texts.[2] Numerous articles and books have been written on women and gender in the Fourth Gospel, beginning perhaps with Raymond Brown's oft-cited article on the roles of women in the Fourth Gospel,[3] the work of Sandra Schneiders and Elisabeth Schüssler Fiorenza,[4] and, my personal favorite, *A Feminist Companion to John*, edited by Amy-Jill Levine with Marianne Blickenstaff.[5] Indeed, the terrain has been covered so thoroughly that one might despair of having anything new or, at least, moderately interesting, to say on the topic.

The reasons for this interest, I suggest, are twofold. The first concerns the prominence of female characters, and what can conventionally be seen as female imagery in the Gospel. Although the Fourth Gospel, in contrast to the gospels of Matthew and Luke, devotes little attention to Jesus's mother, it does assign substantial narrative roles to several other female characters: the Samaritan woman (4:7–26); Mary and Martha of Bethany (11:1–44); and Mary Magdalene (20:1–18). John also draws amply on gendered undertones in these and other passages. In the Prologue, Jesus is the Word, God's intimate, who is endowed with the creative ability of Lady Wisdom—*sophia* in Greek, *ḥokhmah* in Hebrew—and yet incarnated as a man. Imagery related to childbirth emerges in Jesus' conversation with Nicodemus as well as in the crucifixion scene (3:4–6; 19:34).[6] In his Farewell Discourses, John's Jesus evokes female experience—the pain of labor followed by the joy of childbirth

—to assure the disciples that their distress at his impending death will be followed by their joy when they see him again (16:20–22).

The second concerns the ongoing authority ascribed to the Gospel of John by virtue of its inclusion in the Christian canon. In this regard, the Fourth Gospel differs from many other Second-Temple Jewish texts. Some wisdom texts and some of the Dead Sea Scrolls, for example, may have been authoritative for some Jews in their time, but such authority had waned long before their modern study was undertaken. Other works, such as the treatises of Josephus and Philo, never had such authority. For many modern Christians, however, the Gospel of John and other New Testament books continue to be authoritative, not only for matters of theology but also for their understanding of gender roles within the family and within the church. Arguments for or against the inclusion of women in present-day leadership within the churches often entail arguments about whether the New Testament does or does not testify to the role of women in the early Jesus movement.[7]

My modest contribution to the well-studied topic of women and gender in John concentrates specifically on methodology, the stated theme for our conference. I will consider three interrelated questions. First, given the authoritative status of the New Testament for many Christians, how, if at all, should concerns about the role of women in twenty-first-century churches affect our assessment of their representation in the Gospel of John and/or their historical role in the early Jesus movement? Second, how should we situate John's Gospel, and specifically John's Jesus, in the context of Second-Temple or first-century Judaism?[8] Is John's portrayal of Jesus's encounters with women meant to be representative of or a departure from first-century Jewish norms and practices? And third, what is the significance of John's portrayal of female characters and use of female imagery for our understanding of the early Jesus movement?

I will lay my cards on the table. My answers to all of these questions are negative. Briefly, I argue that despite the interesting work done by activist feminist theologians, contemporary concerns should not guide our historical investigations. There are other ways to bring canonical texts into conversation with contemporary practice without allowing the latter to shape our construction of the history of the early Jesus movement. On the question of John and ancient Judaism, I agree that Second-Temple and first-century Jewish sources can shed light on many aspects of the Fourth Gospel. This is not the case, however, with regard to John's representation of women. That John's Gospel, and John's Jesus, should be situated within a first-century Jewish spectrum is obvious. But neither the female characters within the narrative nor the presence of female imagery allows us to situate John or John's Jesus more specifically within that spectrum. Finally, and most important for our purposes, I do not believe John tells us very much about the role of women in the early Jesus movement. In this pessimistic assessment, I realize I am going against the current grain. In what follows, I will try to explain.

AUTHORITY

Raymond E. Brown's essay on the role of women in the Gospel of John, first published in *Theological Studies* in 1975, was perhaps the first systematic treatment of the topic.[9] In the reprinted version in his 1979 book *The Community of the Beloved Disciple*, Brown states that the article "was originally intended as a contribution to the discussion of the ministry of women in the Roman Catholic Church today."[10] He included it in his book on the Johannine community because "the unique place given to women in the Fourth Gospel reflects the history, the theology, and the values of the Johannine community."[11] Although the *Community* book is historical-critical in approach, Brown's pastoral interest in the question of women is evident throughout his essay. He articulates it directly in the concluding paragraph, where he notes that "even John has left us with one curious note of incompleteness: the disciples, surprised at Jesus' openness with a woman, still did not dare to ask him, 'What do you want of a woman'? (4:27). That may well be a question whose time has come in the church of Jesus Christ."[12]

Brown's essay as a whole emphasizes the uniqueness of John's representation of women; it intertwines exegesis and historical reconstruction, and views them in light of the ongoing authority of the Fourth Gospel for the modern church. This approach is shared by others who, as Mary Rose D'Angelo commented, turned to John as a first attempt "to reread the Gospels in search of authority for a more inclusive treatment of women" in the church.[13]

Two examples of such readings are provided by the work of Sandra Schneiders and Elisabeth Schüssler Fiorenza, both written in the early 1980s. Schneiders tackles the issue of authority directly in her article, "Women in the Fourth Gospel and the Role of Women in the Contemporary Church."[14] At the outset, it seems that Schneiders is making a nuanced case for why scripture should not necessarily be set up as the paradigm for contemporary practice. When it comes to slavery, she argues, it is clear from passages such as Philemon 16 that Christians held slaves. Slavery was a social institution that was not explicitly criticized in any New Testament book. Nevertheless, today's churches would by no means support the return of this institution and indeed they consider it morally wrong and "unchristian." The same, in Schneiders' view, should hold in the case of women: "In every other sphere of modern life discrimination on the basis of sex is being recognized as baseless, unjust and dysfunctional."[15] Rather than search the Scriptures for paradigms that support contemporary values such as feminism, she suggests, we should recognize that the New Testament is "not primarily a source of historical information but religious literature whose purpose is to bear witness to the faith of the first Christians. . . ."[16]

Nevertheless, Schneiders argues, the Scriptures as such are not patriarchal; the problem over the past two millennia has resided with patriarchal modes of exegesis and appropriation. She then undertakes an analysis of the Johannine pericopes in which women are major characters, and draws the following conclusions: 1. All the women in the Fourth Gospel are presented "positively and in intimate relation to Jesus." 2. Their presentation is not one-dimensional; all are "strikingly individual and original characters." 3. They play unconventional roles, though the background against which these roles are unconventional (Jewish, Greco-Roman, Jesus movement) is not made clear.[17]

Schneiders then transposes these literary and exegetical observations to the historical realm; in her view the Johannine passages show that "the women Christians in at least one of the earliest communities, John's, were fully participating and highly valuable community members"[18] and that "the evangelist considered such feminine behavior as fully according to the mind of Jesus who is never presented as disapproving of the women. . . ."[19] She concludes the essay by stating that John provides us "with a picture of a first century community in which original and loving women played a variety of unconventional roles which the Fourth Evangelist presents as approved by Jesus and the community despite the grumblings of some men."[20] Despite her introductory critique of others' efforts to ground modern behavior in scriptural paradigms, Schneiders has provided an analysis that allows Christian feminists to do precisely that.

Elisabeth Schüssler Fiorenza's approach is similar to that of Schneiders, except that it is not an apologetic for the Gospel. In the introduction to her important book, *In Memory of Her*, Schüssler Fiorenza writes that "feminist biblical scholarship and historical biblical scholarship share as their common hermeneutical perspective a critical commitment to the Christian community and its traditions . . . the Bible is not just a document of past history but functions as Scripture in present day religious communities."[21] She presents her book as a new lens that enables us "to read the biblical sources in a new feminist light, in order to engage in the struggle for women's liberation inspired by the Christian feminist vision of the discipleship of equals."[22]

Like Schneiders, Schüssler Fiorenza argues that the history of patriarchal exegesis and hermeneutics has obscured the central role of women in the earliest stages of the Jesus movement. Reading the New Testament through a feminist lens allows us to recuperate that role, and to use it productively as a foundation for contemporary feminist praxis. She concludes that

> only in and through a critical evaluative process of feminist hermeneutics can Scripture be used as a resource in the liberation struggle of women and other "subordinated" people. The vision and praxis of our forecasters who heard the call to coequal discipleship and who acted in the power of the Spirit must be allowed to become a transformative power that can open up a feminist future for women in biblical religion.[23]

I agree with Schneiders and Schüssler Fiorenza about the history of patriarchal exegesis. I also applaud the new perspectives that feminist interpretation can provide on many issues. And, although I am not a Christian, I strongly support the rights of women to full liturgical and institutional participation in the Christian churches. Nevertheless, it seems to me that the results of feminist historical investigation can sometimes be skewed precisely by an underlying belief that the challenge to patriarchal power must be grounded in scriptural authority. My discomfort may of course simply betray the degree to which I remain hopelessly stuck in the pre-post-modern historical-critical approaches that were the backbone of New Testament scholarship in the last century, when I received my academic formation. Nevertheless, this seems to be a case where that old-time distinction between eisegesis and exegesis is still apt. My own inclination would be, as Sandra Schneiders suggests at the outset of her article, to challenge the view that contemporary practice must be tied closely to scriptural paradigms. If we do not require this tie for the practice of slavery, why do we do so for the practice of patriarchy?

CONTEXT IN FIRST-CENTURY JEWISHNESS

The first-century Jewish context of John's female characters and images has often been noted. Studies of John's female imagery have noted parallels to Second-Temple Jewish literature. John's prologue, for example, refers to "the Word" in terms that closely parallel the role of Sophia or *hokhmah* in Proverbs and Sirach.[24] The eschatological metaphor of a woman in labor is evident not only in the LXX (see Isa 21:3; 26:17–18; 42:14) and in Revelation 12:2–5, but also prominently in 4 Ezra 4:40, 42; 9:38–10:57. Some scholars also examine John's female characters in the context of Jewish wisdom literature and, especially, the allusions to the Song of Songs and its Jewish interpretations in John's story of Mary Magdalene at the empty tomb (20:1–18).[25] These examples help us to see John in its first-century Jewish context, but otherwise, I would suggest, does not alter our understanding either of John or of first-century Judaism.

Situating John's female characters in a Jewish context has on occasion led to the explicit or implicit construction of John and/or Jesus's positive stance towards women over against the attitudes towards and roles of women in first-century Jewish society. For example, in his 1984 book, *Women in the Ministry of Jesus*, Ben Witherington III states "That Jesus taught women and allowed them to follow Him reveals how very different He was from other rabbis in His treatment of women." In Witherington's view, John in particular includes "a considerable amount of material revealing women's new freedom and equality in the presence of Jesus and in the midst of His community."[26] This tendency to use patriarchal Judaism as a negative backdrop to a "feminist" Jesus is widespread, and, as Judith Plaskow, Amy-Jill Levine, among others, have commented, both ahistorical and lamentable.[27]

The opposite position is taken by Elisabeth Schüssler Fiorenza, who argues that Jesus's inclusive stance toward women is understandable only if Judaism had already within it the elements of what she refers to as a critical feminist impulse. Schüssler Fiorenza notes that Jewish sources demonstrate both positive and negative views of women, and, in any case, do not capture the social realities, in which actual interactions between men and women were often less restrictive than the negative sources would suggest.[28] On the basis of Judith and other Second Temple sources, she concludes that "it seems greatly misleading . . . to picture Jewish women of the first century in particular, and Jewish theology in general, in predominantly negative terms."[29]

At least one Jewish feminist scholar, Judith Hauptman, detects in Schüssler Fiorenza's work a hint of the same negative construction that is explicit in Witherington's book. Hauptman acknowledges that Schüssler Fiorenza posits "the existence of a critical feminist impulse" in Judaism. She also argues that by saying that feminist elements "came to the fore in the vision and ministry of Jesus, [Schüssler Fiorenza] suggests that Jesus was the first to synthesize these ideas and produce a feminist ideology."[30]

Pace Hauptman, Schüssler Fiorenza does not, in fact, claim that these elements "came to the fore" only or for the first time in Jesus's interactions with women. This undercurrent is present, however, if unarticulated, in the work of some other scholars. Scot McKnight, for example, comments that the Jewish context of Jesus's interactions with women was well known, citing Witherington's earlier work as his source. He softens this comment, however, by adding that "scholars have too often exaggerated the ugliness of Jewish treatment of women in order to cast Jesus' practice in a more favorable light. The reality of Jewish practice was probably far more humane than some of the ancient texts assert."[31]

Most recent scholarship evinces a desire to avoid anti-Judaism. These studies also avoid contrasting the views and actions ascribed to Jesus with those that are mentioned in Second-Temple or first-century Jewish texts what we know about first-century Judaism. One strategy for doing so is to avoid comparative language. Margaret Elizabeth Köstenberger, for example, outlines several aspects of Jesus's interactions with women based on the Gospels: 1) he treated women with respect, honesty, and sensitivity; 2) he used women alongside men as illustrations; 3) women supported him financially and bore witness to him. What is significant here is not so much the descriptors themselves (or the concerns one might raise about presuming that the Gospels depict the actual interactions of the historical Jesus) but the absence of comparative language. Jesus is praised, but he is not compared with any other individual or group, but simply described.[32]

EARLY JESUS MOVEMENT

In her introduction to *A Feminist Companion to John*, Volume I, published in 2003, A.-J. Levine comments that in the decades since the publication of Brown's article, "most biblical scholars recognize that the Fourth Gospel's women . . . are at the heart of the gospel text and quite possibly the community behind it."[33] I would modify this statement only slightly; given the Gospel's relentless Christocentrism, it is only Jesus who is at the heart of this Gospel. But it is fair to say that most biblical scholars recognize that women play a more central role in John's narrative than in the Synoptic versions of Jesus's story, and that many view the narrative importance of female characters as evidence of their importance within a putative Johannine community.

Some scholars, to be sure, explicitly refrain from using the Gospel's representation of women to describe the role of women in a Johannine community. In her 1986 study, Turid Seim expressed her concerns about the ease with which Brown and Schneiders moved from text to history. For her part, Seim hesitated "to infer from text to socio-historical background" and refrained from presupposing "that the roles of women as described in the text correspond to or mirror without reservation and practical function in a specific historical situation."[34]

Wolfgang and Ekkehard Stegemann voiced their concerns even more strongly, stating categorically that one cannot derive significant socio-historical information about women in the Johannine community based on the texts about women in the Fourth Gospel.[35] Colleen Conway critiqued the trend to read Johannine female characters as evidence of an egalitarian Johannine community,[36] while Jo-Ann Brant engaged in a purely literary-critical study that did not address the historical question at all.[37] Adeline Fehribach undertakes what she calls a feminist historical-literary approach which attempts to construct not the role of women in the Johannine community but the manner in which a first-century reader would have understood the Gospel and its depiction of women.[38]

Some scholars, however, succumb to the strong desire—often, as I have already noted, grounded in concerns for contemporary women in the church—to extrapolate history from the Gospel's literary presentation. Schneiders goes so far as to suggest that the Gospel's author may have been a woman, or, at least, that the putative author, the Beloved Disciple, is a composite character that includes both men and women.[39]

Others prefer to remain agnostic on authorship but argue that the roles played by women in the narrative correspond quite specifically to those played by women in the Johannine community. Raymond Brown, for example, sees both the Samaritan woman and Mary Magdalene as playing quasi-apostolic roles in the narrative, and argues that all of John's women are portrayed positively as disciples. Without providing a methodological justification for his position, he sees these portrayals as reflecting directly the role of women in the community. He concludes that the Johannine community was one "where in the things that really mattered in the following of Christ there was no difference between male and female—a Pauline dream (Gal 3:28) that was not completely realized in the Pauline communities."[40] Brown's wording is very careful here, and throughout. The "things that really mattered" seems implicitly to rule out formal leadership roles of the sort that were controversial in the Catholic Church at the time he wrote, as indeed they remain today.

In a similar vein, Elisabeth Schüssler Fiorenza assumes that the portrayal of women in the Fourth Gospel reflects directly their role within the community. She states that the community's inclusion of women was controversial, as reflected in 4:27 in which the disciples express their shock that Jesus is speaking with a woman.[41] She concludes that the Gospels of both John and Mark "accord women apostolic and ministerial leadership" on the basis of their representation of women within their narratives.[42]

Brown, Schneiders, and Schüssler Fiorenza wrote the works I have been describing some thirty to forty years ago. At about this same time, in the late 1970s and early 1980s, literary criticism was just entering into the mainstream of biblical studies, and had yet to set the field on course toward greater methodological reflection that included the reexamination and articulation of basic assumptions. Yet it is not difficult to discern the fundamental presupposition that undergirds their approach: that the Gospel tells its story of Jesus in a way that reflects both the history and social structure of a community within which and for which it is written. This assumption is based on J. Louis Martyn's highly influential book, *History and Theology in the Fourth Gospel*, which was first published in 1968, with a second edition in 1979 and a third in 2003.[43] The 1979 edition in particular was widely read and it continues to shape the historical study of the Gospel of John, at least in the English-speaking world, to this very day.

Martyn argued that the Gospel is a two-level narrative that tells the story of Jesus in a way that also describes the historical experience of a community—dubbed the Johannine community—that already existed at the time the Gospel reached its final form in the late first century. Martyn developed this approach as a way of explicating the Gospel's curious references to expulsion from the synagogue. Because such an expulsion could not have occurred in Jesus's time, Martyn reasoned, these verses must refer to an event that happened some time later, when the Gospel reached its final form. The two-level reading strategy makes several assumptions: 1) that the Gospel was a central, perhaps foundational document for a particular community that already existed at the time that the Gospel was written; 2) that the particulars of the community's history and social structure were encoded in the Gospel narrative and hence transparent to its earliest readers; 3) that this community read the Gospel both as a story of Jesus and as its own story. Martyn's book does not address the role of women but the methodological principles upon which it is based are easily applied to the social structure of the Johannine community, as the studies of Brown, Schneiders, and Schüssler Fiorenza demonstrate.

By the late 1990s, I had become critical of Martyn's hypothesis that the Gospel encoded the community's traumatic expulsion from the synagogue. My critique was based primarily on historical-critical considerations related to the evidence that Martyn summoned in favor of the expulsion theory.[44] But I remained intrigued by the idea of discerning the social composition of John's ancient community through a two-level reading of the Gospel. And so, when Amy-Jill Levine asked me to write a chapter for her Feminist Companion series, I tried my hand at an imaginative exercise in which I applied the two-level reading strategy to the stories about women. On that basis, I speculated about the role of women in the community, without, however, insisting that my speculations corresponded to the actual facts on the ground.[45]

The conclusions I came to at that time can be summarized briefly. I argued that the content of the stories suggests that women may have held roles as teachers, spiritual leaders, prophets, apostles, and even theologians; the positive tone suggests that women may have been admired in the community. Nevertheless, the presentation of these women, and hence perhaps their status in the group, was not altogether free of tension. This comes to the fore particularly in John 20:1–18. In this story Jesus instructs Mary Magdalene to "go to my brothers and say to them, 'I am ascending to my Father and your Father, to my God and your God'" (20:17). Mary does so, but, as far as we know, this message had no impact whatsoever on the disciples. Within the Gospel's narrative pattern, the disciples should have believed that Jesus had risen on the basis of her testimony, just as Thomas should have believed that Jesus had returned on the basis of the disciples' testimony (20:25; cf. 20:29). Yet, in contrast to the Thomas situation, neither Jesus nor the narrator comments on the disciples' lapse. Finally, I suggested that far from being a closed community, as Wayne Meeks had argued,[46] Jesus' openness to Samaritans, gentiles, and women suggested that the Johannine community may have been far more open than some scholars assumed.

Some fifteen or more years after writing that essay, I would now disagree with just about all of it, including its presuppositions. I would now argue, along with Wolfgang and Ekkehard Stegemann, that the Gospel of John's stories about women do not provide any foundation for speculating about the role of women in the Johannine community. Indeed, I would go further than this to argue that the very assumption that a Johannine community already existed at the time the Gospel was written is open to serious question. While it is reasonable to assume that one or more groups may have formed in response to the Gospel—the fact that it circulated and was eventually canonized implies as much—there is no evidence for the prior existence of a Johannine community.

Furthermore, it now seems to me that viewing the Gospel as a two-level drama that encodes a community's history into its story of Jesus fundamentally misconstrues the nature of this book. Although we have become accustomed to viewing the Gospel as a window to the past experience of a historical community, the Gospel presents itself in a different light: as a rhetorical text meant to persuade its audience to take on a certain course of action—belief that Jesus is the messiah and Son of God—that will lead to a positive outcome—life in his name. This is stated explicitly in the Gospel's conclusion and statement of purpose in 20:30–31. This statement prompts us to view the Gospel not as a retrospective document about the supposed experience of a hypothetical community but as a dynamic force that aims to shape the beliefs, attitudes, and actions of its audience.[47]

The numerous communal metaphors within the Gospel, such as the sheepfold and the grape vine, imply that such action includes the future banding together, perhaps even in a discrete community, as the Johannine letters themselves might suggest, but they do not support the hypothesis that such a community already existed in the period prior to the Gospel itself. What can safely be assumed, however, is that enough people among its audience responded to the Gospel's rhetoric to ensure, over time, that it was copied and recopied, distributed widely, and eventually incorporated into the New Testament canon. The letters of John imply the existence of a church or churches for which the Gospel was formative.[48] These churches, and all others who were persuaded by the Gospel's message, constitute a Johannine community at least in a conceptual, perhaps even imagined sense, but it is a community that postdates rather than predates the Gospel's own time of writing.[49] Of course, none of these considerations in themselves rule out the possibility that a Johannine community already existed prior to the final version of the Gospel, but the absence of incontrovertible evidence to that effect suggests that we would do well to refrain from positing such a community a priori.

Perceiving the Gospel as a rhetorical and dynamic text that is oriented toward the present and future rather than the past suggests that the Gospel's women may have been intended in the first instance to appeal to the women in the Gospel's audience. The relatively active roles that John's women play—in prompting Jesus to turn water into wine (Jesus's mother), in bearing witness to others (the Samaritan woman and Mary Magdalene), and in calling on Jesus to heal their brother (Mary and Martha)—may potentially ascribe agency to the female members of John's audience when it comes to making the choice of whether or not to adopt the Gospel's perspective on Jesus. The stories, however, do not necessarily demonstrate that women did or would have specific leadership positions in the church. The same is true for the stories about men. Even the Beloved Disciple, identified as the authority behind the Gospel account, is not described in a way that unequivocally points to a leadership role within the community. These points should caution us against concluding too quickly that the Gospel laid out an institutional structure. It stands to reason, of course, that any community that might have developed in response to the Gospel would have required at least an informal leadership mechanism. But this does not mean that the Gospel reflects this aspect of community formation.

Nor should we assume that (our own interests to the contrary) the Gospel writer(s) told stories about women with the primary intention of conveying a message about women's role in the past, present, or future. Aside from the Samaritan woman, all of the women mentioned in the Fourth Gospel are known to the Synoptics, even if the stories that John tells about them differ from those told in the Synoptics. If we take seriously the idea that John had access to a different set of traditions in addition to those he shares with the Synoptics, then we also cannot rule out that at least some of his narrative may have been motivated by the desire to recount those traditions.

What, then, can we say about the role of women in the early Jesus movement, based on the Gospel of John? Only that women were included. I share the desire of feminist historians and theologians to imagine that women had leadership positions in the ancient church, but I do not believe that the Gospel of John gives us anything to go on. I also sympathize with the desire of Christian feminists for full access for women to leadership positions in the today's churches and I do not believe that the vagueness and even silence of our sources on this matter is a reason to prevent such access. Finally, the stories about women in the Gospel of John do not amplify our understanding of Second-Temple or first-century Judaism, nor does this context help us to understand these stories.

NOTES

1. See, however, Marie-Theres Wacker and Eileen Schuller, eds., *Early Jewish Writings*, Bible and Women, 3.1 (Atlanta: SBL Press, 2017).
2. Gabriele Boccaccini and Benjamin Reynolds, eds., *Reading the Gospel of John's Christology as Jewish Messianism: Royal, Prophetic, and Divine Messiahs* (Leiden: Brill, 2018).
3. Raymond Edward Brown, *The Community of the Beloved Disciple* (New York: Paulist Press, 1979), 183–98.
4. Sandra M. Schneiders, "Women in the Fourth Gospel and the Role of Women in the Contemporary Church," *Biblical Theology Bulletin* 12, no. 2 (May 1, 1982): 35–45, https://doi.org/10.1177/014610798201200202. Elisabeth Schüssler Fiorenza, *In Memory of Her: A Feminist Theological Reconstruction of Christian Origins.* (New York: Crossroad, 2002).
5. Amy-Jill Levine and Marianne Blickenstaff, *A Feminist Companion to John*, vol. 1 (London; New York: Sheffield Academic Press, 2003), http://public.eblib.com/choice/publicfullrecord.aspx?p=1748783; Amy-Jill Levine and Marianne Blickenstaff, *A Feminist Companion to John*, vol. 2, 2003, http://site.ebrary.com/id/10869591.
6. John Wilkinson, "Incident of the Blood and Water in John 19:34," *Scottish Journal of Theology* 28, no. 2 (January 1, 1975): 149–72; Adeline Fehribach, "The 'Birthing' Bridegroom: The Portrayal of Jesus in the Fourth Gospel," in *A Feminist Companion to John*, ed. Amy-Jill Levine and Marianne Blickenstaff, vol. 2, 2003, 104–29, http://site.ebrary.com/id/10869591; Deborah Sawyer, "John 19:34: From Crucifixion to Birth, or Creation?," in *A Feminist Companion to John*, ed. Amy-Jill Levine and Marianne Blickenstaff, vol. 2, 2003, 130–39, http://site.ebrary.com/id/10869591.
7. See https://www.cbeinternational.org/resources/article/priscilla-papers/role-women-church-society-and-home for an example of how scriptural verses are deployed in both sides of the egalitarian argument. Unchallenged is the basic assumption that scriptural authority is key to determining women's roles at home and at church.
8. My preference for "first-century Judaism" stems from the sense that the Gospel was influenced not only by the cultural and historical currents in the Second-Temple

period but also by the events of 70 CE including the revolt against Rome and the destruction of the second temple, which, technically, ended the second temple period. The idea that the Gospels emerged during this time needs no defense. The Gospel's debt to Hellenistic Jewish thought and practice is well-documented.

9. *Theological Studies* 36 (1975): 688–99. Reprinted in Brown, *The Community of the Beloved Disciple*, 183–98.

10. See Brown, *Community*, 183.

11. Brown, *Community*, 183.

12. Brown, *Community*, 198.

13. Mary Rose D'Angelo, "(Re)Presentations of Women in the Gospels: John and Mark," in *Women & Christian Origins*, ed. Ross Shepard Kraemer and Mary Rose D'Angelo (New York: Oxford University Press, 1999), 131, http://search.ebscohost.com/login.aspx?direct=true&scope=site&db=nlebk&db=nlabk&AN=23653.

14. Schneiders, "Women."

15. Schneiders, "Women," 36. One might observe that in many spheres of endeavour such discrimination continues to exist, even some thirty-five years after Schneiders wrote her article.

16. Schneiders, "Women," 36.

17. Schneiders, "Women," 38.

18. Schneiders, "Women," 38.

19. Schneiders, "Women," 38–39.

20. Schneiders, "Women," 44.

21. Schüssler Fiorenza, *In Memory of Her*, xxii. The original publication date is 1983.

22. Schüssler Fiorenza, *In Memory of Her*, xxiv.

23. Schüssler Fiorenza, *In Memory of Her*, 343.

24. For detailed discussion, see Martin Scott, *Sophia and the Johannine Jesus*. (Sheffield: JSOT Press, 2016). This is a reprint of the 1992 edition.

25. Adele Reinhartz, "To Love the Lord: An Intertextual Reading of John 20," in *The Labour of Reading:* Desire, Alienation, and Biblical Interpretation, ed. Fiona Black et al., Semeia Studies (Atlanta: Scholars Press, 1999), 56–69; Ann Roberts Winsor, *A King Is Bound in the Tresses: Allusions to the Song of Songs in the Fourth Gospel* (New York: P. Lang, 1999).

26. Ben Witherington III, *Women in the Ministry of Jesus: A Study of Jesus' Attitudes to Women and Their Roles as Reflected in His Earthly Life* (Cambridge/ New York: Cambridge University Press, 1984; 2001), 123.

27. Judith Plaskow, "Feminist Anti-Judaism and the Christian God," *Journal of Feminist Studies in Religion* 7, no. 2 (1991): 99–108; Amy-Jill Levine, "The Disease of Postcolonial New Testament Studies and the Hermeneutics of Healing," *Journal of Feminist Studies in Religion* 20, no. 1 (2004): 91–99.

28. Schüssler Fiorenza, *In Memory of Her*, 109.

29. Schüssler Fiorenza, *In Memory of Her*, 109.

30. Judith Hauptman, "Feminist Perspectives on Rabbinic Texts," in *Feminist Perspectives on Jewish Studies*, ed. Shelly Tenenbaum and Lynn Davidman (New Haven: Yale University Press, 1994), 50.

31. Scot McKnight, *A New Vision for Israel: The Teachings of Jesus in National Context* (Grand Rapids: William B. Eerdmans, 1999), 222. Underlying the contrast that some scholars wish to draw is not necessarily a deep-seated anti-Judaism, though that may be the case at times. Most often, however, the contrast stems from the conviction that Jesus, as the messiah and God's son, had to be unique over against his background and context. This principle is even enshrined in the criterion of uniqueness that for decades was a staple of historical Jesus research. Recent methodological analyses of historical Jesus research, however, tend to point out the implicit anti-Judaism of this criterion and to use it only in very nuanced ways, if at all. See, for example, the essays in Chris Keith and Anthony Le Donne, eds., *Jesus, Criteria, and the Demise of Authenticity* (London/ New York: T & T Clark, 2012).

32. Margaret Elizabeth Köstenberger, *Jesus and the Feminists: Who Do They Say That He Is?* (Wheaton: Crossway Books, 2008), 211–12.

33. Amy-Jill Levine, "Introduction," in *A Feminist Companion to John*, ed. Amy-Jill Levine and Marianne Blickenstaff, vol. 2 (London/ New York: Sheffield Academic Press, 2003), 1, http://public.eblib.com/choice/publicfullrecord.aspx?p=1748783.

34. Turid Karlsen Seim, "Roles of Women in the Gospel of John," in *Aspects on the Johannine Literature: Papers Presented at a Conf of Scandinavian NT Exegetes at Uppsala, June 1986,* eds. Lars Hartman and Birger Olsson (Uppsala: Almqvist & Wiksell, 1987), 57.

35. Ekkehard Stegemann and Wolfgang Stegemann, *The Jesus Movement: A Social History of Its First Century* (Minneapolis: Fortress Press, 1999), 388.

36. Colleen M. Conway, *Men and Women in the Fourth Gospel: Gender and Johannine Characterization* (Atlanta: Society of Biblical Literature, 1999).

37. Jo-Ann A. Brant, "Husband Hunting: Characterization and Narrative Art in the Gospel of John," *Biblical Interpretation* 4, no. 2 (June 1996): 205–23.

38. Adeline Fehribach, *The Women in the Life of the Bridegroom: A Feminist Historical-Literary Analysis of the Female Characters in the Fourth Gospel* (Collegeville: Liturgical Press, 1998), 6–7.

39. Sandra M. Schneiders, "'Because of the Woman's Testimony . . .': Reexamining the Issue of Authorship in the Fourth Gospel," *New Testament Studies* 44 (1998): 513–35.

40. Brown, *The Community of the Beloved Disciple*, 198.

41. Schüssler Fiorenza, *In Memory of Her*, 326.

42. Schüssler Fiorenza, *In Memory of Her*, 334.

43. J. Louis Martyn, *History and Theology in the Fourth Gospel* (Louisville: Westminster John Knox Press, 2003).

44. Adele Reinhartz, "The Johannine Community and Its Jewish Neighbors: A Reappraisal," in *What Is John?* (Atlanta: Scholars Press, 1998), 111–38.

45. Adele Reinhartz, "Women in the Johannine Community: An Exercise in Historical Imagination," in *A Feminist Companion to John*, ed. Amy-Jill Levine and Marianne Blickenstaff, vol. 2 (London/ New York: Sheffield Academic Press, 2003), 14–33, http://public.eblib.com/choice/publicfullrecord.aspx?p=1748783.

46. Wayne A. Meeks, "The Man from Heaven in Johannine Sectarianism," *Journal of Biblical Literature* 91, no. 1 (March 1, 1972): 44–72, https://doi.org/10.2307/3262920.

47. For detailed discussion of the views articulated here, see Adele Reinhartz, *Cast out of the Covenant: Jews and Anti-Judaism in the Gospel of John* (Lanham: Lexington Books/Fortress Academic, 2018).

48. For a recent survey and discussion of the relationship between John and 1 John, see R. Alan Culpepper, "The Relationship between John and 1 John," in *Communities in Dispute: Current Scholarship on the Johannine Epistles*, ed. R. Alan Culpepper and Paul N. Anderson (Society of Biblical Literature, 2014), 95–120, http://www.jstor.org.proxy.bc.edu/stable/j.ctt9qh1w6; R. Alan Culpepper, *The Gospel and Letters of John* (Nashville: Abingdon Press, 1998).

49. For the concept of imagined communities, see Benedict R. O'G Anderson, *Imagined Communities: Reflections on the Origin and Spread of Nationalism*, 2016. This book was first published in 1983.

BIBLIOGRAPHY

Anderson, Benedict R. O'G. *Imagined Communities: Reflections on the Origin and Spread of Nationalism*, London: Verso, 2016.

Boccaccini, Gabriele, and Benjamin Reynolds. *Reading the Gospel of John's Christology as Jewish Messianism: Royal, Prophetic, and Divine Messiahs*. Leiden: Brill, 2018.

Brown, Raymond Edward. *The Community of the Beloved Disciple*. New York: Paulist Press, 1979.

Culpepper, R. Alan. *The Gospel and Letters of John*. Nashville: Abingdon Press, 1998.

———. "The Relationship between John and 1 John." In *Communities in Dispute: Current Scholarship on the Johannine Epistles*, edited by R. Alan Culpepper and Paul N. Anderson, 95–120. Society of Biblical Literature, 2014. http://www.jstor.org.proxy.bc.edu/stable/j.ctt9qh1w6.

D'Angelo, Mary Rose. "(Re)Presentations of Women in the Gospels: John and Mark." In *Women & Christian Origins*, edited by Ross Shepard Kraemer and Mary Rose D'Angelo, 129–49. New York: Oxford University Press, 1999.

Fehribach, Adeline. "The 'Birthing' Bridegroom: The Portrayal of Jesus in the Fourth Gospel." In *A Feminist Companion to John*, edited by Amy-Jill Levine and Marianne Blickenstaff, vol. 2, 104–29. London/ New York: Sheffield Academic Press, 2003. http://site.ebrary.com/id/10869591.

———. *The Women in the Life of the Bridegroom: A Feminist Historical-Literary Analysis of the Female Characters in the Fourth Gospel*. Collegeville: Liturgical Press, 1998.

Hauptman, Judith. "Feminist Perspectives on Rabbinic Texts." In *Feminist Perspectives on Jewish Studies*, edited by Shelly Tenenbaum and Lynn Davidman, 40–61. New Haven: Yale University Press, 1994.

Keith, Chris, and Anthony Le Donne. *Jesus, Criteria, and the Demise of Authenticity.* London/ New York: T&T Clark, 2012.

Köstenberger, Margaret Elizabeth. *Jesus and the Feminists: Who Do They Say That He Is?* Wheaton: Crossway Books, 2008.

Levine, Amy-Jill. *A Feminist Companion to John.* 2 vols. London/ New York: Sheffield Academic Press, 2003.

———. "Introduction." In *A Feminist Companion to John*, edited by Amy-Jill Levine and Marianne Blickenstaff, 1–14 in vol. 2. London/ New York: Sheffield Academic Press, 2003.

———. "Response." *Journal of Feminist Studies in Religion* 20.1 (2004): 125–32.

Levine, Amy-Jill, and Marianne Blickenstaff. *A Feminist Companion to John.* Vol. 2. London/ New York: Sheffield Academic Press, 2003.

Martyn, J. Louis. *History and Theology in the Fourth Gospel.* Louisville: Westminster John Knox Press, 2003.

McKnight, Scot. *A New Vision for Israel: The Teachings of Jesus in National Context.* Grand Rapids: William B. Eerdmans, 1999.

Meeks, Wayne A. "Man from Heaven in Johannine Sectarianism." *Journal of Biblical Literature* 91.1 (1972): 44–72.

Plaskow, Judith. "Feminist Anti-Judaism and the Christian God." *Journal of Feminist Studies in Religion* 7.2 (1991): 99–108.

Reinhartz, Adele. *Cast Out of the Covenant: Jews and Anti-Judaism in the Gospel of John.* Lanham: Lexington Books/Fortress Academic, 2018.

———. "To Love the Lord: An Intertextual Reading of John 20." In *The Labour of Reading: Essays in Honour of Robert C. Culley*, edited by Fiona Black, Roland Boer, Christian Kelm, and Erin Runions, 56–69. Atlanta: Scholars Press, 1999.

———. "Women in the Johannine Community: An Exercise in Historical Imagination." In *A Feminist Companion to John*, edited by Amy-Jill Levine and Marianne Blickenstaff, vol. 2, 14–33. London/ New York: Sheffield Academic Press, 2003.

Sawyer, Deborah. "John 19:34: From Crucifixion to Birth, or Creation?" In *A Feminist Companion to John*, edited by Amy-Jill Levine and Marianne Blickenstaff, vol. 2, 130–39. London/ New York: Sheffield Academic Press, 2003. http://site.ebrary.com/id/10869591.

Schneiders, Sandra M. "'Because of the Woman's Testimony . . .': Reexamining the Issue of Authorship in the Fourth Gospel." *NTS* 44 (1998): 513–35.

———. "Women in the Fourth Gospel and the Role of Women in the Contemporary Church." *Biblical Theology Bulletin* 12.2 (1982): 35–45.

Schüssler Fiorenza, Elisabeth. *In Memory of Her: A Feminist Theological Reconstruction of Christian Origins.* New York: Crossroad, 2002.

Scott, Martin. *Sophia and the Johannine Jesus.* Sheffield: JSOT Press, 2016.

Seim, Turid Karlsen. "Roles of Women in the Gospel of John." In *Aspects on the Johannine Literature: Papers Presented at a Conf of Scandinavian NT Exegetes at Uppsala, June 1986*, edited by Lars Hartman and Birger Olsson, 56–73. Uppsala: Almqvist & Wiksell, 1987.

Stegemann, Ekkehard, and Wolfgang Stegemann. *The Jesus Movement: A Social History of Its First Century.* Minneapolis: Fortress Press, 1999.

Wacker, Marie-Theres, and Eileen Schuller. *Early Jewish Writings*. Bible and Women 3.1. Atlanta: SBL Press, 2017.

Wilkinson, John. "Incident of the Blood and Water in John 19:34." *Scottish Journal of Theology* 28.2 (1975): 149–72.

Winsor, Ann Roberts. *A King Is Bound in the Tresses: Allusions to the Song of Songs in the Fourth Gospel*. New York: P. Lang, 1999.

Witherington, Ben. *Women in the Ministry of Jesus: A Study of Jesus' Attitudes to Women and Their Roles as Reflected in His Earthly Life*. Cambridge/New York: Cambridge University Press, 2001.

Chapter Eight

The Framing of Female Knowledge in the Prologue of the Sibylline Oracles

Francis Borchardt

A pair of manuscripts of the Sibylline Oracles introduce the anthology with a rather extensive prologue of 103 lines.[1] These are the fifteenth century manuscripts referred to as A and S, which are grouped along with manuscripts P, B, and D into a family denoted by the Greek letter Φ.[2] The prologue they transmit is usually dated to the late fifth or early sixth century due to two primary factors.[3] The first of these is that the prologue is apparently reliant upon the *Theosophy*, an epitome of an appendix to a non–extant treatise known by the title *On True Belief*.[4] Because the *Theosophy* contains a historical chronicle from Adam to Caesar Zenon, whose reign ended in 491 CE, the prologue cannot be older than this date.[5] The second reason for dating the prologue to the early sixth century is that the contents suggest that it is written to justify the anthology of books 1–8 of the Sibylline Oracles seen in the Φ manuscripts.[6]

After situating the Sibylline Oracles among Greek divine writings, the prologist takes credit for placing the previously scattered oracles in a unity so that the reading experience will be more beneficial and more diverse (Pr. 1–14). The prologue goes on to discuss the ways in which these oracles apparently testify to the trinity, the virgin birth of Christ, his miracles, his passion and resurrection, the coming judgment in the afterlife, and what is found in the writings of Moses and the prophets about the creation of the world, the formation of humanity, and the ejection from the garden (Pr. 15–25).[7] The prologue continues with an adapted form of a passage found in both the *Theosophy* and the *Divine Institutes* of Lactantius, both discussing the etymology of the name Sibyl, and enumerating and identifying the known sibyls in the world (Pr. 29–50).[8] Another passage adapted from the *Theosophy*, but also related in the *Divine Institutes* and Dionysius of Halicarnassus 4.62, concerns the exploits of the Cumean sibyl when she brought nine books of her oracles to the Roman king Tarquinius Priscus (Pr. 51–66).[9] There follows a brief account of how the oracles of the various sibyls have been preserved and transmitted in Rome and around the world (Prologue 66–74). The prologue continues with a defense of the quality of the preservation of the oracles (ostensibly by Firmianus Lactantius, but seemingly by Pseudo–Justin), which reaffirms their divine nature (Pr. 75–92).[10] The prologue ends with a quote attributed to a sibyl regarding the nature of God (Pr. 93–103).

This prologue is terribly understudied, and there is much of interest in it, despite Geffcken's claims to the contrary.[11] However, of particular interest is the gendered way in which this prologue frames the sibyls as legitimate performers of divine knowledge. In order to establish the oracles as authoritative specimens of divine wisdom the prologue presents the embodiment, transmission, and divine origins of those performances by suppressing feminine sibylline agency and simultaneously emphasizing the masculine mediation of that knowledge. This reveals an inherent skepticism in female divinatory performance with the result that its product is only legitimized through male curation. In the following, I shall demonstrate how the prologue communicates this underlying suspicion of female prophetic performance by analyzing its function within the context of other Greek prefatory writings.[12] I will further examine how the depictions of the embodiment of prophetic performance, oracular transmission through history, and ultimately divine origins erase the agency of the sibyls, and thereby endorse the quality of the oracles.

Despite its unusual length and heavy reliance upon earlier compositions, the prologue to the Sibylline Oracles conforms with a special class of prefatory writings that have been identified by classicist Markus Dubischar. These prologues are attached to a set of writings he terms auxiliary texts, which are works that provide vital help and render an important service to the text in trouble. Auxiliary texts allow, facilitate, or even assure that a primary text or primary corpus is read as, in the opinion of the auxiliary author, it deserves to be read.[13]

Dubischar identifies as "auxiliary" texts like summaries, epitomes, glossaries, commentaries, and compilations, which rearrange knowledge in order to preserve it in new settings.[14] These auxiliary texts respond to perceived shortcomings in earlier compositions which put at risk their ability to communicate knowledge well.[15] Dubischar comes to this realization by examining the prologues which are frequently attached to such "auxiliary" texts. In addition to a host of atypical components, these prefatory writings share three common elements which offer the motivation for the creation of such "auxiliary" texts and thereby provide insight into ancient measures of literary value. 1) They praise the texts, corpora, or traditions they are adapting, usually by focusing upon the knowledge content and/or its source. 2) They highlight perceived flaws in the earlier transmission that have become obstacles to reaping the true value offered by the earlier texts, corpora, or traditions. 3) They offer solutions to the problems they have pointed out, rendering the knowledge content of the previous texts, corpora, or traditions more accessible.[16] Dubischar finds that the problems pointed out in these prologues often correspond to the categories of conversational value theorized by Paul Grice: quantity, quality, relation, and manner.[17] Problems with quantity relate to whether a communication is too long or short for its particular use. Problems with quality relate to the perception of falsity, either inherent or due to lack of evidence for truth. Problems with relation have to do with whether all aspects perceived to be linked to the content are adequately covered. Problems with manner relate to a perceived lack of clarity in communication.[18] According to Dubischar, then, prologues to auxiliary texts praise the texts, corpora, or traditions that they enrich, point out specific types of problems in their presentation, and offer solutions to those problems. The overall effect is that the newly presented knowledge or content is justified by its attachment to something of value to the past and its re-crafting for present aesthetic and epistemic sensibilities. I would suggest that the prologue to the Sibylline Oracles contains the very elements I have just described and functions in the same way.

As the prologue opens, the first seven lines comprise an instance of implicational logic in which the axiomatic protasis is that reading the literature of the Greeks produces a great benefit in that it makes one erudite (Pr. 1–3). The conditional apodosis is that it is doubly good to read τὰς θείας γραφὰς (the divine writings) because they discuss God and the things related to spiritual benefit (ὠφέλειαν ψυχικὴν προξενούντων), and thereby reward both the reader and those with whom the reader comes into contact (Pr. 4–7). Some translations treat the phrase τὰς θείας γραφὰς as referring to holy scriptures, but this seems unlikely considering the rhetorical function of this passage.[19] Rather, the logic here seems to be that τὰς θείας γραφὰς are a special class of divine writings within Greek literature which produce both erudition and spiritual benefit in the reader, which then affects the reader's conduct in society.[20] Given the context in the following three lines which bring this discussion into direct connection with the Sibylline Oracles, it is clear that they are to be included among these divine writings. Therefore, these first seven lines function as one instance of praise for the Sibylline Oracles in the prologue. As Dubischar notes, the function of this type of praise is to assert the value of the knowledge that will be represented. After all, there would be no reason to recast that knowledge were it not valuable in the first place.[21]

A second point at which the prologue insists upon the value of the Sibylline Oracles comes in lines 15 through 28. Here, aside from the final line of the section, the oracles are praised not for the benefit they bring to readers, but for their interesting contents. The oracles are of special interest because they are perceived to plainly discuss the trinity (Pr. 15–17), Christ's life, death, and resurrection (Pr. 18–21), the judgment and penalty that will follow human life (Pr. 21–22), and everything found in Moses and the prophets (Pr. 23–25). In sum, they tell clearly of what has happened and accurately predict what will happen (Pr. 26–27). These lines may suggest that there is perceived value in these ostensibly non–Christian writings confirming the myths and stories considered central to Christian constructions of history. Such a sentiment is familiar in apologetic writings of late antiquity, such as those of Firmianus Lactantius with whom the prologist is apparently familiar.[22] It is also possible that the purported sibylline knowledge of Christ's life and what is communicated in the writings of Moses are merely or primarily understood as the proof that their predictions of the future will come true, following the logic of *ex–eventu* prophecy.[23] In either case, the oracles are here valued for their contents in addition to the benefits they might confer. Yet, a problem lurks, preventing readers from apprehending their true value.

In accordance with Dubischar's three common features of auxiliary prefaces, the flaw in this raw material is also underlined in the sibylline prologue. Line 9 of the prologue notes that the oracles are found scattered (σποράδην εὐρισκομένους) and their reading is confused (συγκεχυμένην τὴν τούτων ἀνάγνωσιν). This is the entire problem statement, but performs its function perfectly because it justifies the solution claimed by the prologist, which, as we shall soon see, is to make a compendium of sibylline oracles. The problem here does not appear to have to do with either the text quality or the contents of the oracles as they are preserved. Rather, it has to do with their preservation separated from one another, whether in fragments or individual works. This state of preservation leads to the oracles being read in a way that obscures their proper understanding. Although the point is not expanded upon, one can imagine two possible problems envisioned here. First, due to their scattered transmission, one never knows whether there are more oracles or more sibyls. Some valuable piece of knowledge might be missing. Moreover, because these texts are separated, it is difficult to read them in light of one another. Thus, any connections between oracles might be missed.

The solution offered in lines 8 and 10–14 appears to straighten out both of these problems. The prologue suggests the problems are solved by making public the oracles in one harmonious unity so that they can be easily perused by those reading and provide greater value to them. Placing them in a compendium essentially creates a library or canon of sibylline oracles which makes claims to a universal library of sibylline texts beyond which one need not search.[24] This universal library then not only allows, but insists on an interpretative connection between its contents. So, problem solved. The value of the oracles has reached its full potential through the creation of the anthology.

Thus far, it is obvious that the prologue is consistent with Dubischar's prologues to auxiliary texts. The Sibylline Oracles, as a compendium, is presented as an auxiliary to the separately preserved oracles that ostensibly preceded the collection. The prologue clearly spells out their inherent value, the problematic preservation as separate oracles or collections, and the intended solution. Yet, the prologue goes on for over seventy more lines and discusses a range of topics, largely building on material known from Dionysius of Halicarnassus, Lactantius, and the *Theosophy*. In the context of the prologue, this remaining material both offers explanations for the haphazard preservation referred to in the problem section and insists on the high value of the oracles despite this. It does so by embodying the oracular performances in history, depicting their paths of transmission, and ultimately asserting their status as authentic divine speech. This borrowed material is where the gendered aspect of the prologue becomes most evident.

One notable feature of this material is the way in which it situates the sibyls in relation to male figures from the past. Sambethe, the Chaldean or Persian sibyl, is said to be from Noah's line, to have predicted the career of Alexander the Great, and to have been mentioned by Nikanor, Alexander's biographer (Pr. 32–6).[25] Likewise, the Italian sibyl of Cimmeria is reported to have birthed Evander, who is known for establishing a shrine to Pan (Pr. 39–41).[26] The Cumean sibyl, too, is said to have been named Deiphobe by Vergil, and to be the daughter of Glaucus (Pr. 44–6).[27] Later in the prologue she is shown to have interacted with the Roman king Tarquinius Priscus (Pr. 51–67).[28] In fact, all but two of the ten enumerated sibyls are related to past figures, all of them noted men.[29] These last two are not mediated by any figure at all. They are merely presented as the Phrygian and Tiburian sibyls, the latter of whom is called Abounaia.[30]

Interestingly, this connection with men from the past does not, as one might expect with divinatory figures, concentrate on the accuracy of the prophecies of the sibyls.[31] The contents of their oracles are mentioned only three times in this latter part of the prologue: the Chaldean sibyl predicts the career of Alexander (Pr. 34–5), the Erythrean sibyl prophesies about the Trojan war (Pr. 41–2), and the Cumean sibyl prophesies about unspecified events in Italy (Pr. 70–1). All these examples are without any substance. Not one specific prediction is noted, suggesting that the reference to these male characters performs some other function. In some cases, they merely mention the sibyls, as with Euripides of the Libyan sibyl, and Eratosthenes of the Samian sibyl.[32] Even where these men are the source for additional information about the sibyl, it is banal geographic, temporal, onomastic, or genetic information, as is the case with Chrysippus of the Delphian sibyl, Vergil of the Cumean sibyl, and Heracleides Ponticus of the Hellespontian sibyl.[33] So, the function of these male figures cannot relate to the accuracy of the predictions. Rather, they appear to perform two related tasks: 1) they concretize the performance of the oracles by sibyls in history, and 2) thereby assert a canon of sibyls whose oracles have been properly identified and cultivated through history.[34]

As Jacqueline Vayntrub has demonstrated in poetic and torahic material in the Hebrew Bible, the construction of such performance contexts implies a chain of transmission for the material produced in those contexts, and thereby asserts its persistent value.[35] Though Vayntrub's work focuses primarily on instances of material depicted as speech, I would argue that the mere confirmation of the existence of the sibyls and their contexts through noted male figures performs much the same function. It implies that these men knew of each of these sibyls, and presumably associated with them oracles of some value. As mentioned already, this is explicit on three occasions, but is likely implied elsewhere. If this is the case, the longer the gap between those men who recognize a particular sibyl and the ostensible era of sibylline performance the better. This may be why only two of the men mentioning any of the sibyls are contemporary with them, disrupting modern expectations for confirmation.[36] The first occasion comes with the claim that Evander is the son of the Italian sibyl (Pr. 39–41). Here, I would suggest that relationship recalls tropes of idealized parent–child transmission of knowledge in both Jewish and Christian texts, as pointed out by Benjamin Wright, among others.[37] The second instance is when the Cumean sibyl unsuccessfully attempts to sell her oracles to Tarquinius Priscus, resulting in only one third of them being preserved due to the sibyl's destruction of the scrolls (Pr. 51–67). Other than these two cases all the male figures seem to be literary and at some remove from the sibyls themselves, implying generations of transmission between them, thus increasing the perceived value of the oracles. The implication may even be that the knowledge revealed in the oracles has not only stood the test of time, but that the oracles have been found continually relevant for the acquisition of knowledge through time. That is, it is possible that new meanings and new uses may have been found for the oracles through their transmission in the ways similar to what is observable among the Dead Sea scrolls.[38]

Returning to the significance of gender, we must question what this concretization of sibylline oracular performance through male mediation implies about the female sibyls as performers of divine knowledge and about their oracles. One might also investigate what this framing suggests about female figures as curators of knowledge. Not one of the figures relating or related to the sibyls could be identified as a woman. Not one of the sibyls is constructed as an idealized hearer, reader, or disciple of the knowledge they transmit. This suggests that not only is there a degree of distrust in female *performance* of prophetic oracles, but also female *curation* of this knowledge.[39] The female gender of the sibyls is constructed in various ways. It first occurs through the imagined etymology of the word sibyl (Pr. 29–30), which is argued to be the Latin word for prophetess. The female gender is then reasserted with the Italian sibyl's childbearing of Evander (Pr. 39–41), or the Cumean sibyl's primary identity as a daughter (Pr. 44–6). The maleness of referees is evident through these same constructions as well as the reference to Tarquinius Priscus as king. This presentation of the sibyls has the effect that the female divinatory speakers become real and are esteemed primarily because they have been mediated by male figures. Were it not for the male interaction with these women, none of them would even have individual names other than sibyl, as the prologue makes explicit in line 30, noting "therefore the female diviners are called by one name" (ὅθεν ἑνὶ ὀνόματι αἱ θήλειαι μάντιδες ὠνομάσθησαν). Nor would any of the sibyls' oracles be differentiated, as is made clear in lines 72–74:

> On the one hand, the records of the Erythrean have a second name by which she was called by that place. But, of the other it is not written down to whom they are attributed, but is recorded without distinction.
> ἀλλὰ τὰ μὲν τῆς Ἐρυθραίας προγεγραμμένα ἔχει τοῦτο ἀπὸ τοῦ χωρίου ἐπικεκλημένον
> αὐτῇ ὄνομα· τὰ δέ γε ἄλλα οὐκ ἐπιγράφονται ποῖα ποίας εἰσίν, ἀδιάκριτα δὲ καθέστηκε.

Even with this mediation, only four sibyls are named beyond a geographic identifier. Their embodiment in the prologue depends almost entirely on male curation.

By extension, the knowledge these women transmit would apparently be lost forever if not for men. This is made obvious in the aforementioned interaction between the Cumean sibyl and Tarquinius Priscus, the brief discussion of the collection and preservation of the oracles in Rome, and the reflection attributed to Firmianus and Plato on the relative accuracy of recording of the sibyl's ecstatic prophecies.

When the Cumean sibyl attempts to sell nine volumes of her prophecies to Tarquinius Priscus for 300 didrachms, she is twice turned away by the Roman king without him inquiring about their contents. In response she burns six of the nine volumes of her oracles. Finally, on the third attempt, the king reads the oracles and is amazed by their contents. He then takes responsibility for their preservation, paying 100 didrachms for them. In addition, Tarquinius asks the Cumean sibyl about the contents of the destroyed books. She replies that she is not able to reproduce them, because they are produced through inspiration. This passage highlights several highly gendered elements about the transmission process.[40] First, by showing Tarquinius twice rejecting the

Cumean sibyl without even considering her oracles, the story puts on explicit display the underlying doubts concerning female performers of divine knowledge. Women are apparently so devalued both as performers and curators of knowledge that they can be dismissed without consequence. This conforms with what Hanna Tervanotko and Rhiannon Graybill have each shown in separate work to be a typical reaction to the female prophetic voice. It is demonstrably problematic, doubted, and often silenced in early Jewish literature.[41] This also aligns with the polemics against Montanists, which show the prominence of public female prophets was the aspect of their praxis that drew most criticism from other Christians.[42] But beyond this, the passage also depicts the preservation of the oracles as the result of male curation. Not only does Tarquinius pay for the three remaining books of the Cumean sibyl's oracles, saving them from the same fate as the first six, but he then takes it upon himself to collect the scrolls of all the sibyls from various cities and lands and deposit them in the Capitol in Rome.[43] When this is contrasted with the Cumean sibyl's presentation as not only being unaware of the contents of her oracles, but actively engaged in destroying them, the construction could not be more obvious. The female sibyl here is both ignorant of the oracles and also their true worth. This once again constructs the female prophets as not only problematic performers, but perhaps more importantly, inept curators of knowledge. It is male agency that transmits these prophecies and recognizes, even assures, their value.

Even in the one passage of the prologue that might be construed as valuing sibylline oracular performance over and against the efforts of men who have transmitted the oracles in text, the agency of the sibyls is in question. In a passage attributed to Lactantius, but evidently borrowed from Pseudo–Justin's *Exhortatio ad Graecos* 37 the prologue defends the quality of the oracles against criticisms lobbed by those familiar with Greek culture. The most important of these criticisms is that not all the verses preserve the proper poetic meter. Since the sibyls were supposed to deliver their oracles in perfect hexameter, this was a serious accusation. It meant their prophecies might not be authentic. But this passage taken from Pseudo–Justin defends against this claim by ostensibly citing Plato in suggesting that this was the fault of the scribes, who were not able to keep up with the speed of the divine speech or were ignorant of the contents. The passage goes on to note that it was not the fault of the prophetess. This makes a fairly cogent argument against the men charged with transmitting the oracles and seemingly in favor of the sibyls. However, the the passage goes on to note that the reason it was not the fault of the sibyl is because they describe many things accurately *without knowing what was said*, in agreement with what the Cumean sibyl tells the king. While this does not distribute agency and responsibility for the oracles to male figures, it nonetheless robs the sibyls of agency once more. They are presented as merely empty vessels for the divine words. They do not interact with them in any conscious way at all. While this once again asserts the authenticity and quality of the oracles themselves, it accomplishes the task by removing agency from the sibyls.

This brief overview has shown that the extensive prologue to the sibylline oracles asserts the value of the prophecies by consistently removing female agency from the process. This happens in three spheres. 1) The divinatory performance is embodied through a male mediation of the sibyls. 2) The transmission and curation of the oracles themselves in text form is presented as the work of men. 3) The speech itself belongs not to the sibyls, but to divine entities. It is my argument that this rhetoric may be further evidence of the recurrent suspicion of female prophetic performance in antiquity.

NOTES

1. The best critical edition of the Sibylline Oracles, and the one used for this study is that of Johannes Geffcken, *Die Oracula Sibyllina* (Leipzig: J. C. Hinrichs'sche Buchhandlung, 1902).

2. Geffcken, *Oracula*, XXI–XXIII, does not know of manuscript D at all, and so does not group it together with P or B, which are also dated to the sixteenth century. Aloisius Rzach, "Sibyllinische Orakel," *PW*, 2.2:2103–83, esp. 2121–22, notes the existence of D, but does not sufficiently describe it so as to determine whether it contains all of the prologue, as in A and S, part of the prologue, as in P, or no prologue, as in B. Rieuwerd Buitenwerf, *Book III of the Sibylline Oracles and its Social Setting: With an Introduction, Translation, and Commentary* (Leiden: Brill, 2003), 66, n.3, reasons that because Rzach does not mention anything concerning the contents, that it must have contained the prologue.

3. On the sixth century date, see John Collins, "Sibylline Oracles: A New Translation and Introduction," in *Old Testament Pseudepigrapha, Volume I: Apocalyptic Literature and Testaments*, ed. James Charlesworth (Garden City, NY: Doubleday, 1983), 317–472, esp. 322; Rzach, "Sibyllinische," 2119–20, Buitenwerf, *Book III*, 86.

4. The most current edition of the *Theosophy*, which is preserved in two manuscripts, Tübingen Mb 27 (T) and Codex Ottobonensis gr.378, is to be found in Hartmut Erbse, *Theosophorum Graecorum Fragmenta*, (Stuttgart: Teubner, 1995). His edition is based on the so–called Tübingen *Theosophy* of Mb 27, which can be accessed digitally at: http://idb.ub.uni-tuebingen.de/diglit/Mb27/0175?sid=a489e376be3e9ca12d13a2571c70906c. Codex Ottobonensis gr. 378 can also be accessed digitally through the Vatican libraries at: https://digi.vatlib.it/view/MSS_Ott.gr.378. Pier Franco Beatrice, "Pagan Wisdom and Christian Theology according to the Tübingen Theosophy," *Journal of Early Christian Studies* 3 (1995): 403–18, esp. 403, identifies the text being epitomized. Geffcken, *Oracula*, 1, already notes the connection to the *Theosophy* in his treatment of the text.

5. Collins, "Sibylline," 322. Buitenwerf, *Book III*, 86.

6. Geffcken, *Oracula*, XIII, XXI notes that while Φ and Ψ (comprising manuscripts F, R, L, and T) transmit a collection consisting of books 1–8, a second collection is found in group Ω (containing manuscripts Q, M, V, H) includes book 9, which is book 6, 7.1, 8.218–428 of Φ, book 10, which is book 4 of Φ, and four different books labelled 11–14.

7. On the use of the sibyls for the purpose of bolstering Jewish and Christian claims in early apologetic literature, see H. W. Parke, *Sibyls and Sibylline Prophecy in Classical Antiquity*, ed. B. C. McGing (London: Routledge, 1988), 152–73, and John Bartlett, *Jews in the Hellenistic World: Josephus, Aristeas, the Sibylline Oracles, Eupolemus* (Cambridge: Cambridge University Press, 1985), 36.

8. Tübingen *Theosophy*, §75, 617–26. These lines can be found in Erbse, *Theosophorum*, 50–51. The relevant passage from Lactantius's *Divine Institutes* is found in L. Caelius Firmianus Lactantius, *Divinarum Institutionum*, 1.6.8–12. The place it can be found in the best current standard edition of this text is *L. Caelius Firmianus Lactantius Divinarum Institutionum Libri Septem: Fasc. 1. Libri I et II*, ed. Eberhard Heck and Antonie Wlosok (München: K. Saur, 2005), 24–25.

9. Tübingen *Theosophy*, §76, 627–51. These lines can be found in Erbse, *Theosophorum*, 51–52. The passage in Dionysius of Halicarnassus is found at *Roman Antiquities* 4.62.1–4.

10. This section is a very loose recasting of some material found in Pseudo–Justin, *Cohortatio ad Graecos*, 37. The critical edition of this text is *Ps.–Justin (Markell von Ankyra?) Ad Graecos de vera religione (bisher "Cohortatio ad Graecos"): Einleitung und Kommentar* (Basel: Friedrich Reinhardt, 1994).

11. Geffcken, *Oracula*, 1.

12. The classic study on such prefaces is of course that of Loveday Alexander, *The Preface to Luke's Gospel: Literary Convention and Social Context in Luke 1.1–4 and Acts 1.1* (Cambridge: Cambridge University Press, 1993). She, however, does not recognize in her analysis the class of prefaces I shall introduce.

13. The definition can be found in Markus Dubischar, "Survival of the Most Condensed? Auxiliary Texts, Communications Theory, and Condensation of Knowledge," in *Condensing Texts—Condensed Texts*, ed. Marietta Horster and Christiane Reitz (Stuttgart: Franz Steiner Verlag, 2010), 39–67, esp. 42. Other important works by Dubischar on this topic include, idem., "Typology of Ancient Philological Writings," in *Brill Companion to Ancient Scholarship*, ed. Stephanos Matthaios, Franco Montanari, and Antonios Rengakos (Leiden: Brill, 2015), 545–99; idem., "Preserved Knowledge: Summaries and Compilations," in *Wiley–Blackwell Companion to Greek Literature*, ed. Martin Hose and David Schenker (Chichester: Wiley-Blackwell, 2015), 427–40; idem., *Auxiliartexte: Praxis und Theorie einer Textfunktion im antiken literarischen Feld* (Berlin: De Gruyter, forthcoming).

14. Dubischar, "Survival," 43.

15. Dubischar, "Survival," 53–54.

16. Dubischar, "Survival," 46.

17. Paul Grice, *Studies in the Way of Words* (Cambridge: Harvard University Press, 1989), 27–28. Dubischar, "Survival," 51–56.

18. Grice, *Studies*, 26–27.

19. The phrase is used in the singular in the (probably Byzantine) pseudepigraphon known as "The Heartless Rich Man and the Precious Stone" to refer either to a collection of scriptures, or to Proverbs (or a particular verse thereof, which is under discussion in the text). The Greek text can be found in A.–M. Denis, ed., *Fragmenta pseudepigraphorum quae supersunt Graeca* (Leiden: Brill, 1970), 232–33. An English translation of the text can be found in William Adler, "The Heartless Rich Man and the Precious Stone," in *Old Testament Pseudepigrapha: More Noncanonical Scriptures. Volume One*, ed. Richard Bauckham, James Davila, Alexander Panayotov (Grand Rapids: Eerdmans, 2013), 360–67. The term is also used in the plural in the Early Christian Greek prologue to the Acts of Pilate to refer to a group of texts that apparently provide knowledge of Jesus Christ. This might be interpreted as a set of gospels, some set of Christian scriptures, or even a broader collection including a set of Hebrew scriptures as well. The Greek text with English translation can be found in Bart Ehrman, Zlatko Pleše, eds., *The Apocryphal Gospels: Texts and Translations* (Oxford: Oxford University Press, 2011), 419.

20. This appears to be the interpretation reflected in Collins, "Sibylline," 327.

21. Dubischar, "Survival," 47. See also Markus Mülke, "Die Epitome—das bessere Original?," in Horster and Reitz, *Condensing Texts-condensed texts*, 69–89, esp. 71–74.

22. On Lactantius's use of non–Christian oracles in his apologetic writing, see Stefan Freund, "Christian Use and Valuation of Theological Oracles: The Case of Lactantius's *Divine Institutes*," *Vigiliae Christianae* 60 (2006): 269–84, esp. 281–82. On the general trend to view the sibyls as valued prophetesses for early Christians, see Mischa Hooker, "The Use of Sibyls and Sibylline Oracles in Early Christian Writers" (PhD diss., University of Cincinnati, 2007), 139–84, and Beatrice, "Pagan," 403–4.

23. On the use of *ex-eventu* prophecy in the body of the sibylline oracles, see Buitenwerf, *Book III*, 63, and Matthew Neujahr, *Predicting the Past in the Ancient Near East: Mantic Historiography in Ancient Mesopotamia, Judah, and the Mediterranean World* (Providence: Brown University Press, 2012), 195–242.

24. On libraries and canons as claims to universal knowledge, see Gregory Nagy, "The Idea of the Library as a Classical Model for European Culture," [cited 17 April, 2018] Online: http://nrs.harvard.edu/urn-3:hlnc.essay:Nagy.The_Idea_of_the_Library_as_a_Classical_Model.1998, and also idem., "Homer as Model for the Ancient Library: Metaphors for Corpus and Cosmos," [cited 17 April, 2018] Online: http://nrs.harvard.edu/urn-3:hlnc.essay:Nagy.Homer_as_Model_for_the_Ancient_Library.2001.

25. Interestingly, in Lactantius, *Divine Institutes*, 1.6.8–12, which parallels this passage, the sibyl whom Nikanor mentions lacks a name, and is identified as Persian. The relationship to Noah is missing there as well. There is no Chaldean sibyl in his list. Further, Pausanias, *Description of Greece*, 10.12.9, identifies her name as Sabbe, and suggests she is either Babylonian or Egyptian. John Collins, *Seers, Sibyls and Sages in Hellenistic–Roman Judaism* (Leiden: Brill, 2001), 185, argues that the Jews were the only "eastern" people to compose sibylline oracles. The particular formulation

here is, however, found in Codex Ottobonensis gr. 378, 18r, which is the more extensive of the two *Theosophy* manuscripts at this point.

26. This identification is also different in Lactantius, *Divine Institutes*, 1.6.8–12 in that he identifies her only as Cimmerian, and mentions nothing about the relationship to Evander. The identification with Evander is also missing in the Tübingen manuscript of the *Theosophy*, Mb 27. The identification is only made in Codex Ottobonensis gr. 378, 18r, and in the Sibylline prologue. This Evander, incidentally, is almost certainly the figure known from Vergil's *Aeneid* 8.313 identified as the first king to build upon the Palatine hill.

27. Once again, Lactantius lacks any mention of Vergil in this context. However, the mediation by Vergil is found in both *Theosophy* manuscripts. Mb 27, 84v notes that Vergil calls her Deiphobe, while Ott. gr. 378, 18v has the additional detail that Vergil calls her the daughter of Glaucus. Vergil's identification of the Cumean sibyl as Deiphobe is found in *Aeneid* 6.36. The Cumean sibyl is also ostensibly cited in *Eclogue* 4.4.

28. Though Lactantius and both *Theosophy* manuscripts agree the king in question is Tarquinius Priscus, Dionysius of Halicarnassus *Roman Antiquities* 4.62.1–4 identifies the king as Tarquinius Superbus, the seventh and last Roman king. Tarquinius Priscus, according to Livy's *Ab Urbe Condita* 1.35.5–6 was the fifth Roman king. Interestingly, Livy also notes in *Ab Urbe Condita* 1.34.9, that he was gifted in interpreting divination. This might be a reason that he specifically is effective as the mediating figure in this story.

29. Collins, "Sibylline," 317–18, relies on the testimony in Lactantius's *Divine Institutes*, 1.6.8–12 to note that Varro is the source of the enumeration of ten sibyls.

30. The identification of these sibyls and their descriptions are the most significantly different in the various different lists. Lactantius and Ott. gr. 378, 18v label them Phryigian and Tiburian, though they differ on the name of the Tiburian. Mb 27, 84v calls them Phrygian and Egyptian, but agrees with Lactantius on the name of the Tiburian/Egyptian sibyl. However, none of these passages mediates these final two sibyls through male figures.

31. One need only think of the classic passages from the Hebrew Scriptures dealing with verification of divinatory figures: Deut 13:1–5 and 18:20–22. The first of these instructs the audience to evaluate the truth of prophecy by assessing its conformity with other divine teachings. The latter helpfully asserts that a prophecy is authentic if it comes true. Something different appears to be at play here.

32. Both Lactantius and Ott. gr. 378 contain the claims that the prologue to Euripides' *Lamia* mentions the Libyan sibyl and that Eratosthenes mentions the Samian sibyl, though the claims are missing in Mb 27. *Lamia* is only preserved in this one fragment, so it is not possible to verify the claim. However, Diodorus Siculus *Library of History* 20.41.6 places the mythical figure of Lamia in Libya. This at least explains the choice of a work with such a title as mediator for this sibyl. The fragment can be found in Augustus Nauck, Bruno Snell, eds., *Tragicorum Graecorum Fragmenta* (Hildesheim: Georg Olms Verlagsbuchhandlung, 1964), 506–7. Eratosthenes was a third-century BCE polymath and librarian of the Museion library in Alexandria. His works only survive in fragments, so this claim too cannot be checked for veracity.

A very brief recounting of Eratosthenes can be found in Ludolph Kuster, ed., *Suidae Lexicon Graece & Latine* (Cambridge: Typis Academicis, 1705), 805.

33. As is usual, Lactantius and Ott. gr. 378 contain the references to Chrysippus and Heracleides Ponticus, while Mb 27 lacks this. The writings of both figures survive only in fragments. Diogenes Laertius, *Lives of the Eminent Philosophers*, 7.179–85, describes Chrysippus as a Stoic philosopher and student of Cleanthes and Zeno, which would place him in the third century BCE. According to Diogenes Laertius, *Lives of the Eminent Philosophers*, 5.86, Heracleides Ponticus lived in the fourth century BCE and was a prolific writer in a large number of fields including astronomy, physics, biology, and literature.

34. On the importance of understanding the embodying function of constructed chains of transmission in ancient Jewish literature, see Jacqueline Vayntrub, "The Book of Proverbs and the Idea of Ancient Israelite Education," *ZAW* 128 (2016): 96–114. On the legitimating and curricular function of lists of figures in Jewish literature, see Burton Mack, *Wisdom and the Hebrew Epic: Ben Sira's Hymn in Praise of the Fathers* (Chicago: University of Chicago Press, 1985), 181–82.

35. Vayntrub, "Book of Proverbs," 108–9.

36. I refer here to the historical and source–critical theory developed/popularized by Leopold von Ranke which was influential for over a century, on which see Leonard Krieger, *Ranke: The Meaning of History* (Chicago: University of Chicago Press, 1977), 2.

37. Benjamin Wright, "From Generation to Generation: The Sage as Father in Early Jewish Literature," in *Biblical Traditions in Transmission: Essays in Honour of Michael A. Knibb*, eds. Charlotte Hempel and Judith Lieu (Leiden: Brill, 2006), 309–32.

38. On exegetical revelation in the Dead Sea scrolls and its relationship to Deuteronomy 29:28, see Naphtali Wieder, *The Judean Scrolls and Karaism* (London: East and West Library, 1962), 53–62, 78; Joseph Baumgarten, *Studies in Qumran Law* (Leiden: Brill, 1977), 29–35; Alex Jassen, *Mediating the Divine: Prophecy and Revelation in the Dead Sea Scrolls and Second Temple Judaism* (Leiden: Brill, 2007), 51, 332; Lawrence Schiffman, *The Halakah at Qumran* (Leiden: Brill, 1975), 22–32; Aharon Shemesh and Cana Werman, "Hidden Things and Their Revelation," *RevQ* 18 (1998): 409–27.

39. On the subversion of expectations for male curation of knowledge in Levantine literary texts, see Jacqueline Vayntrub, "Transmission and Mortal Anxiety in the Tale of Aqhat," in *"Like 'Ilu Are You Wise": Studies in Northwest Semitic Languages and Literature in Honor of Dennis G. Pardee*, ed. H.H. Hardy, Joseph Lam, Eric Reymond (Chicago: Oriental Institute Publications, forthcoming).

40. Parke, *Sibyls*, 190, correctly notes that this story, in its various versions is a highly constructed fiction. Though he argues the legend is created to explain why the Romans possessed and consulted these Greek oracular texts, the story here seems to function as a verification of the value of the new collection for the reader.

41. Hanna Tervanotko, "Unreliability and Gender? Untrusted Female Prophets in Ancient Greek and Jewish Texts," *JAJ* 6 (2016): 358–81. Rhiannon Graybill, *Are We*

Not Men? Unstable Masculinity in the Hebrew Prophets (Oxford: Oxford University Press, 2016), 128.

42. Antti Marjanen, "Female Prophets among Montanists," in *Prophets Male and Female: Gender and Prophecy in the Hebrew Bible, the Eastern Mediterranean, and the Ancient Near East,* ed. Jonathan Stökl and Corrine Carvalho (Atlanta: Society of Biblical Literature, 2013), 127–43. Christine Trevett, *Montanism: Gender, Authority, and the New Prophecy* (Cambridge: Cambridge University Press, 1996), 185–91.

43. In Aulus Gellius, *Noctes Atticae* 1.19.11, as well as in Lactantius, *Divine Institutes*, 1.6 the *quindecimviri sacris faciundis* are appointed to guard and curate the oracles. This part of the story is absent in the prologue and in Mb 27. It is vaguely alluded to in Ott. gr. 378.

BIBLIOGRAPHY

Adler, William. "The Heartless Rich Man and the Precious Stone." In *Old Testament Pseudepigrapha: More Noncanonical Scriptures. Volume One*, edited by Richard Bauckham, James Davila, Alexander Panayotov, 360–67. Grand Rapids: Eerdmans, 2013.

Alexander, Loveday. *The Preface to Luke's Gospel: Literary Convention and Social Context in Luke 1.1–4 and Acts 1.1.* Cambridge: Cambridge University Press, 1993.

Bartlett, John. *Jews in the Hellenistic World: Josephus, Aristeas, the Sibylline Oracles, Eupolemus.* Cambridge: Cambridge University Press, 1985.

Baumgarten, Joseph. *Studies in Qumran Law*. Leiden: Brill, 1977.

Beatrice, Pier Franco. "Pagan Wisdom and Christian Theology according to the Tübingen Theosophy." *Journal of Early Christian Studies* 3 (1995): 403–18.

Buitenwerf, Rieuwerd. *Book III of the Sibylline Oracles and its Social Setting: With an Introduction, Translation, and Commentary.* Leiden: Brill, 2003.

Collins, John. *Seers, Sibyls and Sages in Hellenistic–Roman Judaism*. Leiden: Brill, 2001.

———. "Sibylline Oracles: A New Translation and Introduction." In *Old Testament Pseudepigrapha, Volume I: Apocalyptic Literature and Testaments*, edited by James Charlesworth, 317–472. Garden City, NY: Doubleday, 1983.

Denis, A.–M. *Fragmenta pseudepigraphorum quae supersunt Graeca.* Leiden: Brill, 1970.

Dubischar, Markus. *Auxiliartexte: Praxis und Theorie einer Textfunktion im antiken literarischen Feld.* Berlin: De Gruyter, forthcoming.

———. "Preserved Knowledge: Summaries and Compilations." In *Wiley–Blackwell Companion to Greek Literature,* edited by Martin Hose and David Schenker, 427–40. Chichester: Wiley–Blackwell, 2015.

———. "Survival of the Most Condensed? Auxiliary Texts, Communications Theory, and Condensation of Knowledge." In *Condensing Texts—Condensed Texts*, edited by Marietta Horster and Christiane Reitz, 39–67. Stuttgart: Franz Steiner Verlag, 2010.

———. "Typology of Ancient Philological Writings." In *Brill Companion to Ancient Scholarship*, edited by Stephanos Matthaios, Franco Montanari, and Antonios Rengakos, 545–99. Leiden: Brill, 2015.

Ehrman, Bart, and Zlatko Pleše. *The Apocryphal Gospels: Texts and Translations*. Oxford: Oxford University Press, 2011.

Erbse, Hartmut. *Theosophorum Graecorum Fragmenta*. Stuttgart: Teubner, 1995.

Freund, Stefan. "Christian Use and Valuation of Theological Oracles: The Case of Lactantius' *Divine Institutes*." *Vigiliae Christianae* 60 (2006): 269–84.

Geffcken, Johannes. *Die Oracula Sibyllina*. Leipzig: J. C. Hinrichs'sche Buchhandlung, 1902.

Graybill, Rhiannon. *Are We Not Men? Unstable Masculinity in the Hebrew Prophets*. Oxford: Oxford University Press, 2016.

Grice, Paul. *Studies in the Way of Words*. Cambridge: Harvard University Press, 1989.

Heck, Eberhard, and Antonie Wlosok. *L. Caelius Firmianus Lactantius Divinarum Institutionum Libri Septem: Fasc. 1. Libri I et II*. München: K. Saur, 2005.

Hooker, Mischa. *The Use of Sibyls and Sibylline Oracles in Early Christian Writers*. PhD diss., University of Cincinnati, 2007.

Jassen, Alex. *Mediating the Divine: Prophecy and Revelation in the Dead Sea Scrolls and Second Temple Judaism*. Leiden: Brill, 2007.

Krieger, Leonard. *Ranke: The Meaning of History*. Chicago: University of Chicago Press, 1977.

Kuster, Ludolph. *Suidae Lexicon Graece & Latine*. Cambridge: Typis Academicis, 1705.

Mack, Burton. *Wisdom and the Hebrew Epic: Ben Sira's Hymn in Praise of the Fathers*. Chicago: University of Chicago Press, 1985.

Marjanen, Antti. "Female Prophets among Montanists." In *Prophets Male and Female: Gender and Prophecy in the Hebrew Bible, the Eastern Mediterranean, and the Ancient, Near East*, edited by Jonathan Stökl and Corrine Carvalho, 127–43. Atlanta: Society of Biblical Literature, 2013.

Mülke, Markus. "Die Epitome—das bessere Original?" In *Condensing Texts—condensed Texts*, edited by Marietta Horster and Christiane Reitz, 69–89. Stuttgart: Franz Steiner Verlag, 2010.

Nagy, Gregory. "Homer as Model for the Ancient Library: Metaphors for Corpus and Cosmos," (2001). http://nrs.harvard.edu/urn-3:hlnc.essay:Nagy.Homer_as_Model_for_the_Ancient_Library.2001.

———. "The Idea of the Library as a Classical Model for European Culture" (1998). http://nrs.harvard.edu/urn-3:hlnc.essay:Nagy.The_Idea_of_the_Library_as_a_Classical_Model.1998

Nauck, Augustus, and Bruno Snell. *Tragicorum Graecorum Fragmenta*. Hildesheim: Georg Olms Verlagsbuchhandlung, 1964.

Neujahr, Matthew. *Predicting the Past in the Ancient Near East: Mantic Historiography in Ancient Mesopotamia, Judah, and the Mediterranean World*. Providence: Brown University Press, 2012.

Parke, Herbert William. *Sibyls and Sibylline Prophecy in Classical Antiquity*, edited by B.C. McGing. London: Routledge, 1988.

Riedweg, Christoph. *Ps.–Justin (Markell von Ankyra?) Ad Graecos de vera religione (bisher "Cohortatio ad Graecos"): Einleitung und Kommentar*. Basel: Friedrich Reinhardt, 1994.

Rzach, Aloisius. "Sibyllinische Orakel." In *Paulys Real–Encyclopädie der classischen Altertumswissenschaft* 11A, 2073–2183. Stuttgart: Metzler and Druckenmüller, 1923.

Schiffman, Lawrence. *The Halakah at Qumran*. Leiden: Brill, 1975.

Shemesh, Aharon, and Cana Werman. "Cana, Hidden Things and Their Revelation." *RevQ* 18 (1998): 409–27.

Tervanotko, Hanna. "Unreliability and Gender? Untrusted Female Prophets in Ancient Greek and Jewish Texts." *JAJ* 6 (2016): 358–81.

Trevett, Christine. *Montanism: Gender, Authority, and the New Prophecy*. Cambridge: Cambridge University Press, 1996.

Vayntrub, Jacqueline. "The Book of Proverbs and the Idea of Ancient Israelite Education." *ZAW* 128 (2016): 96–114.

———. "Transmission and Mortal Anxiety in the Tale of Aqhat." In *"Like 'Ilu Are You Wise'": Studies in Northwest Semitic Languages and Literature in Honor of Dennis G. Pardee*, edited by H.H. Hardy, Joseph Lam, and Eric Reymond. Chicago: Oriental Institute Publications, forthcoming.

Wieder, Naphtali. *The Judean Scrolls and Karaism*. London: East and West Library, 1962.

Wright, Benjamin. "From Generation to Generation: The Sage as Father in Early Jewish Literature." In *Biblical Traditions in Transmission: Essays in Honour of Michael A. Knibb*, edited by Charlotte Hempel and Judith Lieu, 309–32. Leiden: Brill, 2006.

Chapter Nine

Female Authorship in Jewish Antiquity?

Gerbern S. Oegema

INTRODUCTION

This paper wants to 1) investigate the existence of female authorship in Jewish antiquity by looking at what constitutes authorship and whether this could apply to women, and 2) whether 2 Maccabees 7 could have been written by a female Jewish author. There are several aspects to look at when talking about authorship in antiquity. First of all, it was standard practice to use a secretary for the actual writing process (so Cicero, Claudius, Vespasian, Paul, and many others; cf. Rom 16:22 et al.), although the one dictating the letter and never the secretary was always seen as the original and responsible composer. On the other hand, it was also standard practice for religious texts to claim to be the Word of God, to be inspired by Christ or the Holy Spirit (see Moses, Isaiah, etc.) or by the Muses, the inspirational goddesses in art, literature, and science in Greek and Roman mythology (Hesiod, Homer, Herodotes, etc.). Then we also have to have a look at the audience for which a work was composed as well as the ruler, who could commission a specific work. Having said this, in Greek and Roman literature we do know of quite a few female authors (Perictione, Ptolemais of Cyrene, Anyte of Tegea, etc.),[1] and hence the question is permitted whether we can also find Jewish female authors in antiquity.

This paper will look in particular at one Jewish text: 2 Maccabees 7, and ask whether it could have been written by a woman according to the criteria formulated above. Obviously, using a secretary does not exclude female authorship behind the narrative of the mother and her seven sons dying the painful death of martyrdom under the reign of Antiochus IV. Epiphanes, on the contrary. Second, whether it was God himself or His Torah in the form of Lady Wisdom (see Prov 8:22), who inspired the author, the fact is that 2 Maccabees uses both Biblical and Hellenistic historiographies as models to compose its own interpretation of the history of the Maccabean Revolt. In this book from the Septuagint the mother and her seven sons stand in the very center: 2 Maccabees 7 is not only the exact middle of book, but also marks the very turning point in the fate of Jewish people. Third, 2 Maccabees was partly written to be recited in the court of the Hasmonean rulers in front of an audience consisting of middle- and upper-class educated and Greek-speaking Jewish people, men and women alike. And fourth, depending on the date of 2 Maccabees, it is not to be excluded that the Hasmonean queen Salome Alexandra herself had commissioned the work or at least had some influence on the final edition and publication of it, and that she may have insisted that chapter 7 be included in it or even placed in the center. Furthermore, when looking at the contents of 2 Maccabees 7, we see some very typical female concepts defining its quite novel theology: motherhood, birth, giving life and connected with it also the resurrection, possible even taken up similar imagery from Isaiah 66. And finally, the whole book of 2 Maccabees differs in many ways from 1 Maccabees, in that it is much less masculine, male- and power-centered in its depiction of Jewishness, and instead depicts softer topics such as God's miraculous working in history, angels and motherhood as crucial for the Jewish faith.[2] In short, it will be argued that all of this points to a female authorship of at least 2 Maccabees 7.

2 MACCABEES 7 AS PART OF THE BOOK OF 2 MACCABEES: GENRE, STRUCTURE, AND HISTORY

According to Ulrike Mittmann-Richert, the book of 2 Maccabees has the following structure:[3]

1,1–10a	1st Letter to the Egyptian Diaspora
1,10b–2,18	2nd Letter to the Egyptian Diaspora
2,19–32	Preface of the author
3,1–40	The divine salvation of the Temple from Heliodor
4,1–6,17	The successful attack of the Temple by the heathens as God's Punishment of the people's not abiding by the Law
6,18–31	The death of the first martyrs
7,1–42	*The death of the mother and her seven sons*
8,1–36	Judas' victory over Nicanor
9,1–29	The death of Antiochus Ivth
10,1–8	Purification of the Temple with Sukkoth

10,9–13,26	The unsuccessful attack of the heathes againt the purified Temple as the centre of the Tora abiding people
14,1–15,36	The divine salvation of the Temple from Nicanor; 2nd victory of Judas over Nicanor
15,37–39	Postscript of the author

Chapter 7 is therefore exactly in the center of the book of 2 Maccabees and also narrates the turning point in the fight of the Maccabees against their Syrian oppressors. Within the seventh chapter the mother of the seven sons clearly plays the key role, is the key dialogue partner with Antiochus IVth Epiphanes, and also reveals in her speeches many religious and educational truths, that are at the core of the theology of the Jewish resistance against the Syrian empire. In other words, the words coming out of the mouth of the mother of the seven sons form the very center of chapter 7 and its theology as well as of the whole book of 2 Maccabees.

THE WOMEN IN 1–2 MACCABEES AND THE MOTHER IN 2 MACCABEES 7

Unlike the portrayal of women in 1 Maccabees (cf. 1 Macc 1:26–27.32.60; 2:1–5; 8:10, and 16:11), which first of all are only depicted because of their Jewishness, for which very reason they—like their male brethren—had been persecuted, and second as women remain rather pale,[4] 2 Maccabees adds much more detail, color and character to its portrayal of women; this is especially so in 2 Maccabees 7 (but see also 2 Macc 3:10, and 6:10). The author of 2 Maccabees really seems to have cared to give women at least some character and identity, although they remain still—like the women in so many other Biblical and post-Biblical texts, without a name.[5] Before we move on to 2 Maccabees 7 it is worthwhile to recapture what the other two passages 2 Macc 3:10 and 6:10 are about, and here I quote myself from an earlier study:

> "As in 1 Maccabees, also in 2 Maccabees women and children are portrayed as weak and in need of protection, but this time not in order to portray them as victims of adversary powers. They are weak according to creation, and it is within God's order [of creation] that they are taken care of. The Mosaic Law prescribes that, when they have lost either their husband or their father, other members of the Jewish community should take care of them. In 2 Maccabees, the care for women and children forms one of the central pillars of Jewish social security in the Palestine of those days. Also in the Jewish communities of the Diaspora, where the author probably lived, such a social system was in practice.

Furthermore, the author juxtaposes a non-Jewish way of life, which is characterized by greediness, to a Jewish way of life, which is focused on loving one's neighbor. [. . .] Contrary to the description of the same events in 1 Macc 1:60, in 2 Macc 6:10 the women and their children are less anonymous. This is due to the fact that this passage does not deal with a number of unknown women, but with two exemplary women. Although their names are not mentioned, they are depicted in a detailed, vivid and passionate way, as if their identities were known to the author and his reader. The great concern of the author of 2 Maccabees for women and their fate can, therefore, be contrasted to the attitude of the author of 1 Maccabees, who portrays women rater as anonymous objects.[6]

As for the central text of 2 Maccabees 7, compared to all the other passages in both 1 and 2 Maccabees, the portrayal of women then completely changes. Not only is the chapter located in the very center of 2 Maccabees and is the lengthiest treatment of women in most of the other so-called Apocrypha, except for the book of Judith, but also its contents, thematic, focus, and theology are radically different from anything we have seen before. Crucial for our topic are the verses 20–23 in 2 Maccabees 7:

> [20] The mother was especially admirable and worthy of honorable memory. Although she saw her seven sons perish within a single day, she bore it with good courage because of her hope in the Lord. [21] She encouraged each of them in the language of their ancestors. Filled with a noble spirit, she reinforced her woman's reasoning with a man's courage, and said to them, [22] "I do not know how you came into being in my womb. It was not I who gave you life and breath, nor I who set in order the elements within each of you. [23] Therefore the Creator of the world, who shaped the beginning of humankind and devised the origin of all things, will in his mercy give life and breath back to you again, since you now forget yourselves for the sake of his laws."[7]

The passage describes both the mother's character and her words. Her character is described as follows: she was especially admirable, worthy of honorable memory, she bore the death of her seven sons with good courage, she hoped in the Lord, she encouraged them, was filled with a noble spirit, reinforced her woman's reasoning, and had a man's courage. Her words, "spoken in the language of their ancestors" are described as follows: "I do not know how you came into being in my womb. It was not I who gave you life and breath, nor I who set in order the elements within each of you.[23] Therefore the Creator of the world, who shaped the beginning of humankind and devised the origin of all things, will in his mercy give life and breath back to you again, since you now forget yourselves for the sake of his laws."

When we start with her character and leave the contents of her speech for later, a look into the commentaries immediately reveals a strong male bias in assessing her qualities. Most commentators agree that the mother cannot possess strong qualities as a woman, and if she has them they must be male qualities; thus the interpretation of the striking term of her having "a man's courage" (ἄρσενι θυμῷ) in 2 Macc 7:21. A selection of the commentaries, nicely listed up in Daniel Schwartz' Commentary on 2 Maccabees,[8] begins with a quote from Young, "'Woman,'" 70, clearly showing these prejudices: "By having the mother become masculine, the author inducts her into the same group as her sons, all of whom followed the manly model of Eleazar." The quote from Young then makes Schwartz himself wonder whether this is really the correct interpretation of the verse and the "male reasoning," which women apparently naturally do not possess. In order to find a more appropriate meaning, he then compares the text with passages in Polybius (2.4.8; 36.15; 2.56.9), Josephus (*Bell* 1.59), and Philo (*Leg* 319–20), which indeed confirm the dominant notion of those days that women were considered to be the weaker of both sexes (with further references to supporting secondary literature). In other words, by adding more evidence, Schwartz confirms the contemporaneous bias toward the mother as a woman who cannot possess strong qualities as they can only be male qualities.[9]

However, the Greek word for "male" as found in 2 Macc 7:21 is frequently used in the Septuagint (see also Mt 19:4; Mk 10:6; Lk 2:23; Rom 1:27; Gal 3:28; Rev 12:5.13), where it does not have this negative connotation. The first use of the term in the Septuagint is found in Gen 1:27 (καὶ ἐποίησεν ὁ θεὸς τὸν ἄνθρωπον κατ᾽ εἰκόνα θεοῦ ἐποίησεν αὐτόν ἄρσεν καὶ θῆλυ ἐποίησεν αὐτούς; see also Gen 5:2; cf. Josephus, *Ant* 1, 2 §§ 34f.). The words "male and female" are complimentary terms for the two sides of mankind. In 2 Macc 7:21 we then find both words from Gen 1:27 reoccuring, or should we say quoting?, when it reads: τὸν θῆλυν λογισμὸν ἄρσενι θυμῷ. It is obvious that the author of 2 Maccabees 7 refers to Gen 1:27 and the few other passages in the Hebrew Bible in Greek, where both terms appear together in reference to the creation of mankind (see also Gen 1:27 and 5:2 quoted in Mk 10:6 and Mt 19:4; in other passages like Gen 6:19; 7:16 and Num 7:16 both terms together refer to the creation of animals). The passage in the Septuagint translation of Gen 1:27 as well as the quotations in Mk 10:6 and Mt 19:4 show that Gen 1:27 and the combination of both terms were very well known and used in the Greco-Roman period of Judaism. And as the mother repeatedly refers to the creation in 2 Macc 7:22–23, the reference of male and female must have been taken from Gen 1:27. In conclusion, the mother in 2 Maccabees 7 represents mankind in its various male and female aspects and the description of the mother is a reference to God's creation. There is no way to interpret this as referring to a woman's inferiority.

In light of the broader context of the depiction of women in 2 Maccabees, two questions about the mother ask for our special attention: 1) what or who inspired her?, and 2) what role does her motherhood play in her being a woman? Concerning 1) two staple themes of Biblical theology during Second-Temple Period Judaism are a) the important role of Lady Wisdom in creation and in Jewish history, and b) the portrayal of Jerusalem as a woman, and often also as a woman weeping for her children. As for a), in Proverbs, Jesus Sirach and the Wisdom of Solomon, three Greek texts close to 1 and 2 Maccabees, the Torah as Lady Wisdom is the leading theme or red thread in the history of the Jewish people since the creation. As for b), starting in the book of Lamentations Jerusalem is portrayed as a wailing woman, who mourns the loss of her children during the destruction of Jerusalem and the Temple. This theme could be picked up in later times, when a similar destruction of Jerusalem as in 587 BCE triggered similar emotions, such as in 4 Ezra about the destruction of Jerusalem in 70 CE. But also the desecration caused by Antiochus IV in 167 BCE is no different from this; and although it was not a physical destruction of the Temple, it was a destruction of the Temple as a place of worship and hence it would lead to equally strong feelings and even an uprising. In other words, having a woman as the central character in 2 Maccabees, a book which narrates the desecration and imminent destruction of Jerusalem, has some strong examples in Biblical literature. With this as the historical and theological context of 2 Maccabees 7, we move on to the question who could have written it.

THE AUTHOR BEHIND 2 MACCABEES 7

In order to find out, who the author behind 2 Maccabees was and whether the author could have been a woman, there are several questions to be answered. Did the author write 2 Maccabees her- or himself or did she or he have a secretary? While it was standard practice to use a secretary for the actual writing process (so Cicero, Claudius, Vespasian, Paul, and many others; cf. Rom 16:22 et al.), the one dictating the letter—and not the secretary—was normally considered to be the original and responsible composer. We must therefore look for the creator of the texts and the ideas in it and not solely for the one in charge of writing down the words. In doing so, we need to look for clues whether the vocabulary and ideas found in our text would or could be associated with a woman or not. As for 2 Maccabees 7 we can differentiate between chapter 7 as being part of the whole book of 2 Maccabees—and as such therefore being subject to the standard authorial and editorial practices —and the seventh chapter per se. In terms of contents, chapter 7 clearly stands out among the other chapters, as it is not only central to the book, but also narrates and problematizes partly very different themes than the rest of the book. Whereas the theme of martyrdom had started in chapter 6 and continues into chapter 7, it is the theme of motherhood together with the theme of the resurrection that constitute the new topics in chapter 7; for the topic of the resurrection this is even true for the whole history of Biblical literature. The challenge now lies in connecting these themes with female authorship, a problem that needs to be solved on two levels. First, one needs to establish the possibility of female authorship as such in Jewish antiquity, and second it needs to be proven that chapter 7 was more likely written by a female than by a male author.

Furthermore, as it was standard practice for religious texts to claim to be the Word of God, to be inspired by Christ or the Holy Spirit (see Moses, Isaiah, etc.) or by the Muses, the inspirational goddesses in art, literature, and science in Greek and Roman mythology (Hesiod, Homer, Herodotes, etc.), we also need to look for a connection between the creator of the text, the origin of the ideas in the text and the identity of the inspiration behind it. The inspiration behind 2 Maccabees 7 is, according to the text, God and the mother's belief in God. In addition to this and possibly in the background of our text, we should also underline the importance of wisdom and its personification as Lady Wisdom in sapiential literature, as indicated above. This wisdom is often found in speculations about the creation, the universe and the ages, i.e., history and the eschaton. 2 Maccabees 7 clearly deals with these questions, especially when the mother asks the question, how her sons got into her womb in the first place, i.e., how conception and birth take place, which are clearly elements of the creation process, and then concludes that if God the Creator can create life like this, He (or She) can also re-create it or even create something new after death (vv. 22–23: "I do not know how you came into being in my womb. It was not I who gave you life and breath, nor I who set in order the elements within each of you.[23] Therefore the Creator of the world, who shaped the beginning of humankind and devised the origin of all things, will in his mercy give life and breath back to you again"). In other words, motherhood, giving birth, creation, and resurrection are here intrinsically interwoven with each other

Another question pertaining to authorship deals with the audience for which a book was composed and the ruler, who could have commissioned this specific work. As suggested, it may have been Salome Alexandra, who had commissioned the work of 2 Maccabees; at least it was written during her reign or shortly before it, so that she could have been aware of it. And here the final answer to the question depends on how much power she had to commission a work such as 2 Maccabees. From our sources it becomes clear that Salome Alexandra, despite being a woman and the first Jewish queen, was no different than the other Hasmonean rulers and had an equal amount of power and influence as them.[10] As the most powerful person in the Hasmonean kingdom, 2 Maccabees could never have been published or even composed without her consent. Even more so, she also had a reason to allow the composition and publication of 2 Maccabees or at least the inclusion of chapter 7. She was the one who would reorganize the Sanhedrin by giving more power to the Pharisees and limiting that of the Sadducees, two of the three main religious and political parties at the time, which among many other things had different views about the belief in the resurrection. With the Pharisees having now gained influence through the influence of Salome Alexandra, the way was also free for a growing importance in the belief in the resurrection, which from the second and first centuries BCE onward became central to the tradition of Second Temple Judaism. 2 Maccabees 7 promotes this belief in the resurrection and is the first text to explicitly do so in Second-Temple Judaism. In other words, Salome Alexandra could not only have had the power to commission a work like 2 Maccabees as a whole, but also an interest in supporting the influence of the Pharisees and with that in promoting the belief in the resurrection.[11]

This does not yet constitute an argument for a female authorship of either 2 Maccabees or of only chapter 7 per se, but it does narrow it significantly down to a female authorship of at least chapter 7 and the support this may have had from Queen Salome Alexandra, who most likely had commissioned the whole book of 2 Maccabees. In the following, we will only look at the possibility of a female authorship of chapter 7 as an inclusion of, or addition to, the whole book of 2 Maccabees. The main purpose of this inclusion may have been to add an example of a female martyr to the story of the male martyrdom of Eleazar in chapter 6 in order to provide the narrative with a more balanced account of the sacrifices both Jewish men and women had made for the Jewish cause. In addition to this, it is important to look at evidence for Queen Salome's supporting or commissioning of the publication of books in general and the inclusion of strong women or women's topics in particular and with it the possibility of supporting or even initiating female authorship. As for the former, Tal Ilan has given ample evidence of the possible evidence between the queen's reign and various contemporary compositions dealing with powerful women, such as Esther, Judith, and Susanna, as found in the texts with the same names.[12]

A key question is here what constitutes the characteristics and differences of male versus female authorship and how one can discern the differences. For this we will have a look at the wider context of female authorship in antiquity.

FEMALE WRITERS IN THE GRECO-ROMAN WORLD

If we were to be dealing with a female Jewish author in the case of 2 Maccabees 7, how would she compare to other female authors in Greek and Roman literature, like Perictione, Ptolemais of Cyrene, Anyte of Tegea, etc.? I. M. Plant lists in total 55 names of female authors in just over 200 pages, which means that about many female authors as such we know very little, other than that their number was considerable.[13] Important here is to acknowledge the existence of many female authors in Greco-Roman antiquity, the fact that throughout history they have mostly been forgotten, and that we can learn a lot from unearthing their existence and their works. A few examples will suffice here.

Perictione

Perictione (fifth century BCE) was the mother of the Greek philosopher Plato. Her fifth child, Antiphon appears in Plato's *Parmenides*. There are two works attributed to Perictione and they have survived in fragments, *On the Harmony of Women* and *On Wisdom*. They are though of later and different dates and are pseudonymous Pythagorean literature. *On the Harmony of Women*, written in Ionic Greek from the fourth or third centuries BCE, concerns the duties of a woman to her husband, her marriage, and to her parents. *On Wisdom*, written in Doric Greek from the third or second centuries BCE, offers a philosophical definition of wisdom.

Ptolemais of Cyrene

Ptolemais of Cyrene (third century BCE or later) is the author of *Pythagorean Principles of Music*. The work is only referred to in Porphyry's commentary on Ptolemy's *Harmonics*. According to I. M. Plante, she shares the same place of origin (Cyrene, Libya) as Arete of Cyrene (a female philosopher of the Cyrenaic school, whose doctrines included Pythagorean elements) and Eratosthenes (whose many interests also included music theory). She is one of several women writers associated with Pythagoreanism.[14]

Anyte of Tegea

Anyte of Tegea (early third century BCE) is one of the nine outstanding ancient women poets listed by Antipater of Thessalonica in the Palatine Anthology. He called her the female Homer because her poetry was so admired. Though little is known about Anyte's life, more of her poetry has survived than of any other ancient Greek woman, with the exception of Sappho. Twenty-four epigrams attributed to Anyte survive today. One of these is preserved by Julius Pollux; the remainder is part of either the *Palatine* or Planudean Anthology. Of these, Kathryn Gutzwiller considers that twenty of these were genuinely composed by Anyte. Anyte's poetry is often interested in women and children, and Gutzwiller argues "that it was deliberately composed in opposition to traditional epigrams, which were composed by an anonymous author from a masculine and urban perspective." Accordingly, of five epitaphs written by Anyte which survive, only one marks the death of a young man, as was traditional in the genre; the remaining four all commemorate women who died young. She is also known to have written epitaphs for animals and poetry celebrating war.[15]

In conclusion and in reference to our question about the authorship of 2 Maccabees (7), a few aspects of female Greek authors stand out: 1. there was a considerable number of female authors from the fifth century BCE onward; 2. they were very skilled in the various forms of literature; 3. though little has survived of what they have written; 4. not a few were influenced by the Greek philosophers, especially by Plato and Pythagoras; 5. among the topics covered by them were womanhood, wisdom and music, but also animals and death by war. The author of 2 Maccabees 7 clearly fits within these observations of a generally supportive and creative context of female authorship that in the later mostly male transmission history had a hard time to survive.

MOTHERHOOD AND RESURRECTION

Without being able to show any direct dependence of the author of 2 Maccabees 7 on any of the aforementioned or other Greek female authors, we can make a few general observations about our author of 2 Maccabees as a whole and/or of chapter 7: 1) she or he knew Greek, had been educated in Greek, and worked in Greek, and will have been familiar with at least some aspects Greek literature and philosophy, as since the third century BCE many educated Jews had been; 2) the author—like her or his Greek counterparts—lived in an age, in which creativity and new ideas were widely appreciated and strived for and authors experimented with new ideas, and 3) women had been accepted in politics, literature, and philosophy in a very visible way. Taking all together, to posit a female authorship of at least 2 Maccabees 7 is not only very plausible, but there is also nothing that speaks against it.

How likely is it, then, that the author was female and not male? According to me, the answer to this question also very much depends on the contents and theme of 2 Maccabees 7, and not only on the other criteria we have discussed above. When looking for a possible background and origin of the theological concepts found in chapter 7, we need to look at possible parallels in the Hebrew Bible, the Septuagint, and any Hebrew or Greek historiographic work, in which the author may have found examples and inspiration or by which she or he may have been influenced. Two main themes will need to be looked at in particular: the creation of mankind according to Genesis 1–3 (with possible interpretations of it like the New Creation in Isaiah 65–66), and the resurrection of the dead (with possible connections with the themes birth/rebirth). As a connection with Gen 1:27 had already been established in the use of "male and female He created them," a second text that comes to mind is Isaiah 66. As a matter of fact, all of the themes so prominent in 2 Maccabees 7 seem to meet in Isa 66:1–24 (with another text from Isaiah, namely Isa 42:5–12 being the possible haftarah reading to Genesis, namely to Gen 1:1–13, as a second possible background).

The sixty-sixth chapter of Isaiah is of particular interest for 2 Maccabees 7, as it implies a situation of grave iniquity, abomination, and Temple desecration, not the least caused by members of its own people, under which the pious among Israel suffer (vv. 2–5). Jerusalem and the Temple are then compared with a woman crying over her children, even more so a woman, who is in labor of giving birth to a son, a city, which is called Zion, and who has given birth to many children (vv. 6–11). Jerusalem and the mother, as well as the children of Israel and the mother's children, overlap to the extent that the meaning of the former is expressed in the image of the latter and the latter symbolizes the former. The image of a child-bearing and breast-feeding mother, central in 2 Macc 7:22, is most clearly present in the vv. 10–11 of Isaiah 66, where it reads:

> [10] Rejoice, O Jerusalem, and all ye that love her hold in her a general assembly: rejoice greatly with her, all that now mourn over her:[11] that ye may suck, and be satisfied with the breast of her consolation; that ye may milk out, and delight yourselves with the influx of her glory.

For this woman, God will do the same, and reward her for her suffering, a reward that even has a hint of the resurrection in it, as it reads in vv. 13–14:

> [13] As if his mother should comfort one, so will I also comfort you; and ye shall be comforted in Jerusalem.[14] And ye shall see, and your heart shall rejoice, and your bones shall thrive like grass: and the hand of the Lord shall be known to them that fear him, and he shall threaten the disobedient.

This hint to the resurrection is further elaborated in v. 22, where it reads:

²² For as the new heaven and the new earth, which I make, remain before me, saith the Lord, so shall your seed and your name continue.

This makes Isaiah 66 clearly a passage about a new life and a new heaven and earth as the reward for the righteous, who have suffered under the iniquities and abominations of the wicked.

To conclude, the imagery of the mother, who gives birth, breastfeeds, nurtures and raises her sons, is both present in 2 Maccabees and Isaiah 66. In both texts the mother and her sons overlap with Jerusalem and her pious children, the children of Israel. In both texts, a time of desecration and immanent destruction of Jerusalem and the Temple is the starting point of the expectation of a new beginning, a new heaven and a new earth, and even the resurrection. It is obvious that with so much overlap the older Biblical passage of Isaiah 66 stands in the background of or even has influenced the late second/early first century BCE text of 2 Maccabees 7.

CONCLUSION

The decisive question in this paper is, who could or would have been more sensitive and open to the very particular imagery of the wailing, breastfeeding, and nurturing mother, who loses her children in Isaiah 66 as an interpretative means of dealing with the events leading up to the Maccabean Revolt, when Antiochus IV desecrates the Temple and tortures to death the law abiding children of Israel: a male or a female author? As 2 Maccabees as a whole clearly describes the fate of women and children during the oppressive years of Antiochus IV and chapter 7 impressively thematizes this, furthermore because female authorship was a very accepted reality in the Greco-Roman world with female Greek authors having reflected on motherhood, death, and wisdom, with Jewish authors picking up models and themes both from Biblical and Greek literature, and finally because both audience and ruler were open to a female authorship and the promotion of new ideas, I am of the opinion that only our male bias stands in the way of assuming a female author behind 2 Maccabees 7.

Even more so, as only mothers fully understand the pain and new life that come with giving birth, and are existentially aware of what it means to lose the life of one's own child, only a woman could have written this text. It was in the end the wisdom of Salome Alexandra, a mother herself, who had sons of her own, who would recognize the importance of this and may have asked the central seventh chapter to be included in 2 Maccabees if not the whole book being written. By doing so, Queen Salome Alexandra, who had the reputation of being a very pious person, and was the sister of Rabbi Shimon ben Shetach, the head of the Sanhedrin reformed by her, could use this text to cement the position of her favorite party of the Pharisees. They who now for the first time in their history and in the history of Israel and Judaism had their belief in the resurrection written down in a book about a pious Jewish woman commissioned by the first Hasmonean queen.

NOTES

1. See, for details further below, as well as I. M. Plant (ed. and trans.), *Women Writers of Ancient Greece and Rome: an Anthology* (Norman: University of Oklahoma Press, 2004).

2. See further, in G. S. Oegema, "Portrayals of Women in 1 and 2 Maccabees," in *Transformative Encounters. Jesus and Women Re-Viewed*, ed. I. R. Kitzberger (Leiden: E. J. Brill 2000), 245–64.

3. Ulrike Mittmann-Richert, *Einführung zu den historischen und legendarischen Erzählungen* (Gütersloh: Gütersloher Verlagshaushaus, 2000), 40–64.

4. See, for the former Gerbern S. Oegema, "Portrayals of Women in 1 and 2 Maccabees," 245–64, esp. 250–55.

5. Ibid., 255–59.

6. Ibid., 255–56. See in more detail, Sara Parks, The Role of Women in 1 and 2 Maccabees, MA Thesis, McGill University, 2005.

7. 2 Macc 7:20–23 [20] ὑπεραγόντως δὲ ἡ μήτηρ θαυμαστὴ καὶ μνήμης ἀγαθῆς ἀξία ἥτις ἀπολλυμένους υἱοὺς ἑπτὰ συνορῶσα μιᾶς ὑπὸ καιρὸν ἡμέρας εὐψύχως ἔφερεν διὰ τὰς ἐπὶ κύριον ἐλπίδας [21] ἕκαστον δὲ αὐτῶν παρεκάλει τῇ πατρίῳ φωνῇ γενναίῳ πεπληρωμένη φρονήματι καὶ τὸν θῆλυν λογισμὸν ἄρσενι θυμῷ διεγείρασα λέγουσα πρὸς αὐτούς [22] οὐκ οἶδ᾽ ὅπως εἰς τὴν ἐμὴν ἐφάνητε κοιλίαν οὐδὲ ἐγὼ τὸ πνεῦμα καὶ τὴν ζωὴν ὑμῖν ἐχαρισάμην καὶ τὴν ἑκάστου στοιχείωσιν οὐκ ἐγὼ διερρύθμισα [23] τοιγαροῦν ὁ τοῦ κόσμου κτίστης ὁ πλάσας ἀνθρώπου γένεσιν καὶ πάντων ἐξευρὼν γένεσιν καὶ τὸ πνεῦμα καὶ τὴν ζωὴν ὑμῖν πάλιν ἀποδίδωσιν μετ᾽ ἐλέους ὡς νῦν ὑπερορᾶτε ἑαυτοὺς διὰ τοὺς αὐτοῦ νόμους.

8. Daniel Schwartz, Commentary on 2 Maccabees (CEJL) (Berlin-New York: De Gruyter, 2008), 308–09.

9. See also Tal Ilan, "Things Unbecoming a Woman," in *Integrating Women into Second Temple History* (Tübingen: Mohr, 1999), 86–125. Cf. Josephus, *Ant.* 13 §§ 430–32.

10. See Kenneth Atkinson, *Queen Salome: Jerusalem's Warrior Monarch of the First Century B.C.E.* (Jefferson: McFarland, 2012).

11. See Tal Ilan, "'Fear not the Pharisees' (BTSotah 22b): The Attraction of Aristocratic Women to Pharisaism," in *Integrating Women*, 11–42.

12. Tal Ilan, "'And Who Knows Whether You Have not Come to Dominion for a Time Like This?' (Esther 4:14): Esther, Judith and Susanna as Propaganda for Shelamzion's Queenship," in Ilan, *Integrating Women*, 127–153.

13. I. M. Plant, *Women Writers*.

14. I. M. Plant, *Women Writers*, 87–89.
15. Gutzwiller, "Book," 71–89.

BIBLIOGRAPHY

Atkinson, Kenneth. *Queen Salome: Jerusalem's Warrior Monarch of the First Century B.C.E.* Jefferson: McFarland, 2012.

Boyarin, Daniel. *Dying for God and the Making of Christianity and Judaism.* Stanford: Stanford University Press, 1999.

Darling Young, Robin. "The Woman with the Soul of Abraham. Traditions about the Mother of the Seven Martyrs." In *Women Like This: New Perspectives on Jewish Women in the Greco-Roman Period*, edited by Amy Jill-Levine, 67–81. Atlanta: Scholars Press, 1991.

Gutzwiller, Kathryn. *Poetic Garlands: Hellenistic Epigrams in Context.* Berkeley: University of California Press, 1998.

Gutzwiller, Kathryn. "Anyte's Epigram Book." *Syllecta Classica 4* (1993): 71–89.

Hemelrijk, Emily, and Matrona Docta. *Educated Women in the Roman Elite from Cornelia to Julia Domna.* London: Routledge, 1999.

Ilan, Tal. *Integrating Women into Second Temple History.* Tübingen: Mohr, 1999.

Moore, Stephen D., and Janice Capel Anderson. "Taking it Like a Man: Masculinity in 4 Maccabees." *JBL* 117.2 (1998): 249–73.

Mittmann-Richert, Ulrike. *Einführung zu den historischen und legendarischen Erzählungen* (Jüdische Schriften aus hellenistisch-römischer Zeit, Vol. VI.1.1). Gütersloh: Gütersloher Verlagshaushaus 2000.

Oegema, Gerbern S. "Portrayals of Women in 1 and 2 Maccabees." In *Transformative Encounters: Jesus and Women Re-Viewed*, edited by I.R. Kitzberger, 245–64. Leiden: Brill, 2000.

Plant, Ian Michael. *Women Writers of Ancient Greece and Rome: An Anthology.* Norman: University of Oklahoma Press, 2004.

Schwartz, Daniel. *2 Maccabees.* Berlin-New York: De Gruyter, 2008.

Skoie, Mathilde. *Reading Sulpicia: Commentaries 1475–1990.* Oxford: Oxford University Press, 2002.

Snyder, Jane. *The Woman and the Lyre: Women Writers in Classical Greece and Rome.* Carbondale: Southern Illinois University Press, 1991.

Stevenson, Jane. *Women Latin Poets: Language, Gender, and Authority from Antiquity to the Eighteenth Century.* Oxford: Oxford University Press, 2005.

van Henten, Jan Willem. *The Maccabean Martyrs as Saviors of the Jewish People. A Study of 2 and 4 Maccabees.* Leiden: Brill, 1997.

Chapter Ten

Pheroras' Wife
A Pharisee Woman
Tal Ilan

In the Mishnah, the Rabbis make the following statement:[1]

> [Rabbi Yehoshua] used to say: A pious fool (חסיד) and a sly villain and a *perushah* woman (אשה פרושה) and the injuries of the *perushim* (מכות פרושים), these wear out the world. (*mSotah* 3:4)

For those of us who have been instructed that the Rabbis are the Pharisees, and the closer chronologically to the Second-Temple Period they are (like the early Mishnah), the more likely that they are still voicing Pharisee sentiments, this statement is rather odd. Is it possible that the Mishnah denigrates its own? Thus, there have been scholars who suggested that the reference here is not to Pharisees, and the *perushah* woman is not a Pharisee—just an overly pious (or a hypocritically pious) one. Despite disagreements among scholars,[2] I am of the opinion, and have also argued in writing (and so will not repeat what I said), that the *perushim* here refer to members of the Pharisee sect.[3] *Perushim* is the term used in rabbinic literature to describe the Pharisees and thus, the injuries described here are those they inflict; the *perushah* woman mentioned next to them is a Pharisee woman. The text views neither the Pharisee woman nor the Pharisees in general favorably. The Pharisees can inflict injuries that wear out the world, and the Pharisee woman seems to be one of these injuries, since she too wears out the world. The pious fool and the sly villain at the beginning of this statement may be general categories, under which the Pharisee woman and the injuries of the Pharisees are subsumed—too much piety enacted foolishly and villains who take advantage of the pious are dangerous. Obviously, the rabbis of the Mishnah knew of Pharisee women and were not favorably disposed toward them.

Interestingly, Josephus (who was himself a self-professed Pharisee—see *Vita* 12) voices a similar sentiment regarding Pharisee women. He writes:

> There was also a group of Jews priding itself on its adherence to ancestral custom and claiming to observe the laws of which the Deity approves, and by these men, called Pharisees, the women were ruled. These men were able to help the king greatly because of their foresight, and yet they were obviously intent upon combating and injuring him. (*AJ* 17:41)

This text, like the mishnaic one just mentioned, is not particularly sympathetic to the Pharisees, and is not especially thrilled by the fact that they had a great influence on women. It does not doubt, however, that there were women Pharisees and that they were associated with the Pharisee sect.

This last text judges the Pharisees negatively, because "these men were able to help the king greatly because of their foresight, and yet they were obviously intent upon combating and injuring him." The king in question is Herod, who had a stormy relationship with the Pharisees. Pheroras, whose wife is the main subject of this article, was Herod's youngest brother. Pheroras' wife is, in consequence, Herod's sister-in-law. I do not name her because Josephus does not name her, and Josephus does not name her most likely because his source on the Herodian household, Herod's court historian Nicolaus of Damascus, does not name her.

Nicolaus of Damascus was Josephus' main source on the Herodian household. As I had argued in my previous study of Josephus and Nicolaus on women, the latter was more interested than most political historians of antiquity that I know, in court intrigue and in women's role in these machinations.[4] From the Hasmonean period, we hardly know the name of one royal woman. In the Herodian house we know many more than a dozen.[5] Some of them we only know because they were daughters or granddaughters of Herod, and nothing more. Obviously, Nicolaus is our source for these women and their names. Once Josephus' major source on the Herodian house dwindles and peters out, we are again left with a few nameless women. Yet Pheroras' wife is mentioned often in the writings of Josephus, and, as we shall see, was involved in many actions, but is never named.

I believe the failure to name the woman was a conscious decision made by Nicolaus, a sort of *damnatio memoriae* of one, whom he believed had been wicked to Herod and therefore deserved to have her name blotted out. Nicolaus probably believed that she deserved this first and foremost because she was a Pharisee woman. Immediately after describing the Pharisees as we just saw, Josephus adds the following description:

> At least when the whole Jewish people affirmed by an oath that it would be loyal to Caesar and to the king's government, these men, over six thousand in number, refused to take this oath, and when the king punished them with a fine, Pheroras' wife paid the fine for them. In return for her friendliness they foretold—for they were believed to have foreknowledge of things through God's appearances to them—that by God's decree Herod's throne would be taken from him, both from himself and his descendants, and the royal power would fall to her and to Pheroras and to any children they might have. (*Ant.* 17.42-43)

One can hardly describe a more loyal and at the same time subversive act a woman can undertake on behalf of the Pharisees. And of course, not just anyone can pay a fine on behalf of 6,000 people. She was not just devout to the cause of these people—she was also wealthy. Whether she paid the fine because, in return the Pharisees foretold that her children would become the rulers of the land has to be left open. Nicolaus, who is fond of explaining most political developments as ensuing from the ambition of one royal male to become the next king, could easily have invented this prophecy.[6] Pharisee women, on the other hand, and as we saw above, were also known from elsewhere. The last independent Hasmonean monarch (Queen Shelamzion Alexandra) had been a Pharisee woman.[7] Perhaps the Pharisees courted rich and powerful women.[8]

In the ensuing lines I will attempt to tell the story of Pheroras' wife. She is first mentioned in Josephus' first book, *The Jewish War* in the following manner:

> Herod had conferred upon Pheroras the further honor of marrying one of the royal family, by uniting him with the sister of his own wife. On her death he had pledged to him the eldest of his own daughters, with a dowry of three hundred talents; but Pheroras rejected the royal wedding to run after a slave-girl of whom he was enamored. (*BJ* 1.483-84)

The claim that Pheroras' wife was a slave is repeated twice in Josephus' *AJ* account of the same events (16.194, 197), but it is patently untrue. This and the ensuing similar statements are more a slur invented by Nicolaus than a historical fact. After all, Pheroras lived in a world in which fancying one's own slave does not require marrying her. As brother of the king, he could have practically any slave woman he desired, and a large number of freewomen to boot. If we begin speculating that he had an egalitarian, feminist ideology, which did not allow him to take advantage of a slave woman, we are imposing our values on a time and place in which they make no sense. Furthermore, if we believe Josephus that Pheroras' wife paid the Pharisees' fine, she must have been an extremely wealthy woman, and this rules out the possibility that she had been a slave. If we wish to suggest that she had used

Pheroras' funds to pay the fine, we are in such a case suggesting that Pheroras himself was the guilty party in this transaction, and Nicolaus would have lost no opportunity to accuse him, as he did in many other cases. Josephus, based on Nicolaus, never suggests this. Further arguments against the woman having been a slave will be brought presently, followed by a suggestion as to why Nicolaus chose to describe her as such.

In the *Jewish Antiquities* we are not told that Pheroras was a widower when he married his slave girl, or that he had previously also been a brother-in-law to the king; instead we are informed that on Herod's demand:

> Pheroras . . . put away the woman (i.e., his "unsuitable" wife T. I.), though he had already had a son by her. He also promised the king that he would marry his second daughter, and fixed the wedding for thirty days from then. In addition he took an oath that he would no longer consort with the woman who had been put away. But when the thirty days had passed, he was so enslaved to his love that he was unable to do any of the things he had promised but resumed relations with his former wife. (*AJ* 16.198–99)

In a modern novel, we would have sympathy for Pheroras, identify with his passion and love, and congratulate his courage to put away social conventions in favor of true love. I believe this was not in the least the intention of either Nicolaus or of Josephus, through whom this report has reached us, when inserting this description. Both would most probably like us to think that Pheroras' passion is ridiculous and that he deserved whatever consequences he suffered from this decision.

It is impossible to know when Pheroras married this nameless woman. In the Loeb edition of Josephus, H. St. J. Thackeray dates the event that follows this marriage (a plot to poison Herod) to 10 BCE,[9] when Pheroras was at least forty-five years old. It may however be a flashback. An independent report of the fine Herod imposed on the Pharisees is found in *Antiquities* 15 (368–70), and because of the association of this event with Augustus' well-dated visit to Herod's kingdom (*AJ* 15.354–64) in 20 BCE, the marriage took place ten years earlier, when Pheroras was only thirty-five years old. This means that the *Jewish War* got the chronology wrong. Alternatively, the woman could have paid the fine imposed on the Pharisees before she married Pheroras. This would absolutely rule out the claim that she was a slave.

The most dramatic event in which Pheroras' wife was implicated took place after the execution of Herod's two Hasmonean sons in 7 BCE and before Herod's own death in 4 BCE. According to the low-chronology of *BJ*, they would have been, at this time married between three and seven years. According to the higher chronology of *AJ*, they would now have been married perhaps even seventeen years. This period is covered in Josephus by a very complex description of court intrigue, instigated first and foremost by Herod's eldest son Antipater, whom Herod executed just before he died, but in which Pheroras and his wife also played a major role (and during which Pheroras himself died, allegedly of poisoning). The story begins with a statement that also contradicts the assertion that Pheroras' wife was a slave. In the *Jewish War* Josephus wrote:

> There was moreover a gang of women at court, who created new disturbances. The wife of Pheroras, in league with her mother and sister, and the mother of Antipater, displayed constant effrontery in the palace and even ventured to insult two young daughters of the king. She became in consequence the object of Herod's aversion; yet notwithstanding the king's hatred, these women domineered over the rest. (*BJ* 1.568)

A similar report is found in the *Jewish Antiquities* (17.33–36).[10] If these reports are anything to go by, they are probably the best proof that Pheroras' wife was not a slave, because had she been one, how could her mother and sister (who were either themselves slaves, or had come from such a poor family that they had to sell their daughter into slavery) been members of Herod's court. Thus, Pheroras' wife could not have been a slave because she came from a family who were important members of Herod's court.

The events that developed out of the intrigues woven by Antipater together with his mother, Pheroras, and the women around him is told in great excruciating detail by Josephus, twice. I bring part of the story in his words (mostly from the *Jewish Wars*, where he is mercifully brief), but sometimes I paraphrase. Josephus begins by stating that:

> Herod accordingly assembled a council of his friends and relations, and accused the wretched woman of numerous misdeeds, among others of insulting his own daughters, of subsidizing the Pharisees to oppose him, and of alienating his brother, by bewitching him with drugs. (*BJ* 1.571)

This text appears to describe a sort of trial; it does not end, however, with the woman's conviction, but rather Herod turns to Pheroras and demands of him to choose between his wife and his brother, to which Pheroras' replies that he would rather die than leave his wife. In light of this statement, Herod banishes Pheroras and his wife to Pheroras' territory beyond the Jordan. Josephus (or rather Nicolaus) now resorts to the literary device of comparison between the two brothers, to Pheroras' detriment. When Herod fell sick, his brother failed to visit him, although

> ... Herod believing that he was dying, desired to leave him certain instructions. Herod, however, unexpectedly recovered, and not long after Pheroras himself

fell sick; Herod thereupon displayed greater humanity, for he went to him, and affectionately tended him. But he could not cope with the malady, and a few days later Pheroras expired. (*BJ* 1.580; cf. *AJ* 17.58–59)

Once Pheroras died, all hell broke loose for his wife. First, some freedmen of the couple came and reported to Herod that Pheroras had been poisoned by his wife (*BJ* 1.582; *AJ* 17.61). This brought about a flurry of investigational activity. Herod had most of the domestics of Pheroras' household put to the torture, as well as "some ladies above that rank" (*BJ* 1.584), or as diplomatically put in *AJ* "some of their freedwomen" (17.64). This is important, because according to Roman law, torturing slaves to get information is more than legitimate. Information gotten from a slave not under torture was considered unreliable, because it was believed that slaves were, by nature, liars. On the other hand, torturing free persons was considered illegal, and was resorted to only in extreme cases.[11] Perhaps, if the woman tortured were only "freedwomen" this was not so bad. All this torture seems to have revealed to Herod that his brother Pheroras had indeed been a member of a conspiracy against the king, but that its ringleader was Antipater, his firstborn son. Moreover, the torture of the slave women revealed that the real female culprit in all this story was Antipater's mother—Doris—a woman Herod had married in his youth, put away when he married the Hasmonean Miriamme (*BJ* 1.241; 432), and retook after he executed the Hasmonean princess. At this point in the story he removes her once again and strips her of all her riches (*BJ* 1.590).[12]

Now Pheroras' wife again enters the scene. Twice Josephus tells of Herod's sudden goodwill toward her. In the *Antiquities* 17.69 he writes: "He also made peace with Pheroras' women." In the *Jewish War* 1.591, much more dramatically we are informed that "With the ladies of Pheroras' household he made his peace and showed them special attentions after their tortures." So now we know which ladies, who were more than mere slaves, were tortured. Since, as I said before, torture was the order of the day in the case of the involvement of slaves in a criminal investigation, obviously Herod tortured them. Perhaps the status "slave," which Nicolaus attached to Pheroras' wife, and the title "freedwomen" to the nonslaves tortured according to *AJ* 17.64 was intended to make her torture in the present investigation legal.

Up to this point we may gain the impression that Herod had investigated as far as he wished and found out that there was talk against him among his close family members, and that chief among them was his son Antipater, while the others were hangers-on who were not guilty, or only partially guilty. This is why he removed his first wife Doris, and befriended the women of Pheroras' household. Now, however, we hear that Herod is not done:

> Herod's attention was now directed toward Antipater the Samaritan, agent of his son Antipater. From him under torture, he learnt that Antipater procured from Egypt through Antiphilus, one of his companions, a deadly poison intended for the king; that from Antiphilus it had passed into the hands of Theudion, Antipater's uncle, who had delivered it to Pheroras, since it was he whom Antipater had commissioned to kill Herod, while he himself was at Rome, and out of the way of suspicion; and that Pheroras had entrusted the poison to his wife. (*BJ* 1.592; cf. *AJ* 17.69–70)[13]

This piece of information implies that although previously Herod had been convinced that Pheroras was not poisoned by his wife, and that his chief enemy was Antipater, he now learns that the woman is nevertheless implicated in a much more serious poisoning attempt—his own poisoning. Obviously, despite torture and other unsavory means, not all that the woman knew had been revealed to Herod. Josephus continues:

> The king sent for her, and ordered her instantly to produce what she had received. She went out, as though to fetch it with her, and then flung herself from the roof, in order to evade conviction and the king's rack. (*Jewish War* 1.593; cf. *AJ* 17.71)

From this text it is clear that Pheroras' wife knew she would now not escape torture, so she chose to commit suicide instead. Does this mean that she assumed this, or that she had been tortured before, and therefore understood what was coming? We do not know, but the latter seems more likely, because it makes sense that one chooses suicide, when one knows that something worse than death is in store for her.

The Babylonian Talmud seems to have known this story too, though he confused the woman who attempted this form of suicide with another—Miriamme the Hasmonean, Herod's wife, who was actually executed by Herod (*BJ* 1.443; cf. *AJ* 15.229–31; 236–37). When, according to the Babylonian Talmud, she understood that Herod planned to marry her, she committed suicide by jumping off the roof (*bBava Batra* 3b; cf. *bQiddushin* 70b).[14]

In any case, because this story is melodrama rather than drama, this is not the woman's end. Josephus continues:

> However, by the providence, it seems, of God, whose vengeance was pursuing Antipater, she fell not on her head, but on another parts of her body, and was not killed. She was carried to the king, who had restoratives applied, as she was stunned by the fall. He then asked her why she had thrown herself off the roof; and swore that if she told the truth, he would exempt her from punishment; but that if she prevaricated, he would tear her body to pieces with tortures, and leave not a limb for burial. (*BJ* 1.592–93)[15]

Note that here torture is expressly mentioned and Herod is the one who uses it to threaten the woman. At this point in the story, Pheroras' wife decides to attempt a defense of her actions and so opens her mouth and we hear her own words (or rather the words Nicolaus of Damascus put in her mouth) for the first time. This is the official version in her defense, in a case I fail to follow precisely and definitely fail to understand who is against whom, and what is at stake. This is what Josephus (or Nicolaus) claims that the woman said:

> After all, why should I longer guard these secrets, now that Pheroras is dead? Merely to save Antipater, who has been the ruin of us all? Listen to me, O king, and may God hear me too, a witness to the truth of my words who cannot be deceived. At the time when you were sitting weeping beside the dying Pheroras, he called me to him, and said: Much have I been mistaken, my wife, in my brother's feelings towards me; I hated him who loved me tenderly; I plotted to kill him who is overwhelmed with grief for me even before my death. I am but receiving the reward of my impiety; as for you, bring what poison which Antipater left us, and you are keeping for his destruction, and promptly destroy it before my eyes, lest I carry away with me an avenging demon to the world below. So I brought it as he bade me, and emptied most of it into the fire, but reserved a little for myself, against the uncertainties of the future, and my terror of you. (*BJ* 1.595–97; cf. *AJ* 17.73–75)

After this speech she produced the small portion of poison of which she spoke. We do not know, following Pheroras' wife's dramatic confession, whether telling her truth convinced Herod, and got her off the hook, or whether instead this was an admittance of murderous intent, which deserved execution. We do not know this because the entire purpose of the story up to this point was to pile up evidence which will convince anyone that Antipater, Herod's son, was guilty of plotting against his father and that he was consequently rightly executed. Thus, she is mentioned just one more time on the pages of Josephus, and this quite incidentally.[16] While the trial was going on, another portion of poison, sent also from Antipater, was delivered to the wife of Pheroras for safe-keeping. She was of course in custody and in no position to receive it. We do not know whether this additional incriminating evidence tightened the noose around her neck, because we know nothing more about her.

So to conclude, Nicolaus, followed by Josephus, described the politics of Herod's court as being mainly driven by intrigue, spun by hierarchically lower status members of the court—relatives of the king and the women surrounding them. The king is the object of the plotting and the people who plot are flat figures with transparent motives. They are all continually involved in plotting the removal of the present king in order to put some relative or other of his on the throne in his stead. Among these, Pheroras' wife stands out for the following reasons:

1. She has a very dramatic story which takes up many pages in Josephus' account; it is considerably longer and more eventful than the account of any other royal woman in her status.
2. She is nameless. This does not place her in the shadows, but rather brings her out of them, because, being nameless, she is unlike any of the other royal women of the time. Obviously, Nicolaus' decision not to name her was consciously taken. She was in his eyes so evil that he wanted her name erased.
3. This is because she had political and religious convictions that went beyond the intrigues in which she is implicated—she was a Pharisee woman.

I end this presentation with a thought. Perhaps the venomous presentation of this nameless woman on the pages of Josephus had to do with her support of the Pharisees, who were at some point Herod's enemies. We should remember that Nicolaus had said explicitly that though they could help the king, they worked constantly against him. Although the woman came from a wealthy background, Herod opposed her marriage to Pheroras, because she was already known as a Pharisee supporter (either because she had already paid the fine for them prior to her marriage, or because it was well known and further materialized when she paid it after she became Pheroras' wife). Why Pheroras married her in the first place is hard to tell, but that they had a relationship of trust and partnership emerges from the cracks in the negative account. He tried to divorce her but came back; he preferred exile to divorcing her. The one thing we cannot know from all the verbose references to her is whether she had plotted against Herod, and even whether she was executed in the end for her role in the plot. It is clear though that after Pheroras' death, the woman was left unprotected, and Herod took advantage of the situation to vent his anger against her. I believe this had to do with her previous (and perhaps continuous) support of the Pharisees. Pheroras' wife thus furnishes proof for the thesis that influential women supported the Pharisees (perhaps even in opposition to their husbands' positions).

NOTES

1. Pheroras' wife is one of many Herodian women, some of whom have been discussed by scholars, myself among them, see Ilan, "Josephus and Nicolaus on Women"; reprinted in Tal Ilan, *Integrating Women*, 85-125 and bibliography there. See, relatively recently, Bar Kochva, "Doris"; Schwartz, "Malthace." Much has been

written about Berenice, Herod's great-granddaughter, including my new upcoming biography of her: *Berenice: Princess of Judea* (provisional title). The woman discussed here has been almost fully ignored, even by myself (but see my *Integrating Women*, 15–17; 23 and also very recently, Ilan, "Josephus's Samias Source," 205–06), despite the fact that she had a very interesting biography, and was instrumental in many important events of her day.

2. Foremost among them, and most explicitly Rivkin, "Defining the Pharisees," 240–41.

3. Ilan, *Silencing the Queen,* 74–97, where I blame Rashi for obscuring the fact that the woman in question is a Pharisee.

4. Ilan, *Integrating Women*, 85–125.

5. (1) Herod's mother Cyprus e.g., *AJ* 15.184; (2) Herod's sister, Salome e.g. *AJ* 15.80; (3–10) Herod's wives: Miriam I e.g., *AJ* 15.23; Miriam II e.g., *AJ* 18.136; Doris e.g., *AJ* 17.68; Mathace e.g., *AJ* 17.250; Cleopatra e.g., *AJ* 17.21; Pallas e.g., *AJ* 17.21; Phaedra e.g., *AJ* 17.21; Elpis e.g., *AJ* 17.21; (11–15) Herod's daughters: Salampsio e.g., *AJ* 18.130; Cypros e.g., *AJ* 18.130; Roxane e.g., *AJ* 17.21; Salome e.g., *AJ* 17.21; Olympias e.g., *AJ* 17.21; (16) Herod's Niece, Berenice e.g., *AJ* 16.11 etc.

6. On another prophecy (to Herod himself) which did come true, told not by a Pharisee but by an Essene, see *AJ* 15.373–74.

7. See Josephus, *BJ* 1.110–111; *AJ* 13.399–406.

8. "The Attraction of Aristocratic Women to Pharisaism" is how I called the chapter on Pharisee women in my book *Integrating Women*, 11–42.

9. Thackeray, *Josephus*, 229–30.

10. I have chosen to quote the *BJ* account because the *AJ* account is longer, more confusing, and probably has one clear error in it, but these need not concern us here.

11. On torture in Greek and Roman law, see Peters, *Torture*, 11–32, and especially 18–19.

12. For a detailed discussion of this woman, see Bar Kochva "Doris," where he discusses the same events described here, but from the angle of another woman—Doris. Like this article, Bar-Kochva's article has the purpose of reading between the lines of Josephus (and Nicolaus) so as to show the woman's real position and power, of which she was stripped not so much by Herod (who probably loved this woman, and certainly respected her), but rather by his historian(s).

13. I have discussed this chain of transmission in Ilan, *Silencing the Queen*, 230, because except for the last link in the chain, all the persons involved in its preparation and transmission were men. Earlier it was insinuated that women had concocted it and transferred it (*BJ* 1.582–83; *AJ* 17.61–63).

14. The identification of the two was made by Schwartz, "Herod in Ancient Jewish Literature," 48. On the story of Miriam in rabbinic literature, see in Ilan and Noam, *Josephus and the Rabbis* I, 397–400.

15. Cf. *AJ* 17.72, where the words Herod said to her are: "he would crush her with extreme torture if she preferred to be defiant."

16. Bar-Kochva, "Doris," 16, although speaking of Doris and not of Pheroras' wife, claims that if nothing is said about further punishment, there was none, since Nicolaus was very meticulous about listing all punishments Herod meted out to his

enemies. Unlike other topics, however, this claim is not followed by a footnote detailing all such examples.

BIBLIOGRAPHY

Bar Kochva, Bezalel. "Doris, Herod's First Wife," *Cathedra* 110 (2003): 1–18 (in Hebrew).

Ilan, Tal. *Integrating Women into Second Temple History*. Tübingen: J. C. B. Mohr, 1999.

———. "Josephus and Nicolaus on Women," in *Geschichte-Tradition-Reflexion: Festschrift für Martin Hengel zum 70. Geburtstag*, edited by Hubert Cancik, Herman Lichtenberger and Peter Schaefer, 221–62. Tübingen: J.C.B. Mohr, 1996.

———. "Josephus's Samias Source." In *Strength to Strength: Essays in Appreciation of Shaye, J. D. Cohen*, edited by Michael L. Satlow, 197–217. Providence: Brown Judaic Studies, 2018.

———. *Silencing the Queen: The Literary Histories of Shelamzion and Other Jewish Women*. Tübingen: J.C.B. Mohr, 2006.

——— and Vered Noam, in collaboration with Meir Ben Shahar, Daphne Barat, and Yael Fisch. *Josephus and the Rabbis*. Jerusalem: Yad Ben-Zvi, 2017 (in Hebrew).

Peters, Edward. *Torture*. New York: Basil Blackwell Inc., 1985.

Rivkin, Elias. "Defining the Pharisees: The Tannaitic Sources." *Hebrew Union College Annual* 40–41 (1970): 205–49.

Schwartz, Daniel R. "Herod in Ancient Jewish Literature." In *The World of the Herods*, edited by N. Kokkinos, 45–53. Stuttgart: Franz Steiner Verlag, 2007.

———. "Malthace, Archelaus, and Herod Antipas: Between Genealogy and Typology." In *Sources and Interpretation in Ancient Judaism: Studies for Tal Ilan at Sixty*, edited by Meron M. Piotrkowski, Geoffrey Herman, and Saskia Dönitz, 32–40. Leiden: Brill, 2018.

Thackeray, H. St. J. *Josephus II: The Jewish War I–III* (translation and notes), LCL; Cambridge: Harvard University Press, 1927.

Chapter Eleven

Cross-dressing Zealots in Josephus's War Account

Gabriella Gelardini

A GENDER-CODED FIND

Any examination of Josephus's war report in relation to gender will encounter all sorts of features common to war situations:[1] descriptions of masculinity called for in military conflict (e.g., *B.J.* 6.34–53), examples of "effeminate" cowardice on the part of soldiers (e.g., *B.J.* 3.127–31), mentions of systematic violation of women by male warriors (e.g., *B.J.* 4.560), rare reports of military action by women (e.g., *B.J.* 3.289–306), and then the following rather curious anecdote:

[4.558] ἦν δὲ τῷ δήμῳ Σίμων μὲν ἔξωθεν Ῥωμαίων φοβερώτερος, οἱ ζηλωταὶ δ' ἔνδον ἑκατέρων χαλεπώτεροι, κἂν τούτοις ἐπινοίᾳ κακῶν καὶ τόλμῃ τὸ σύνταγμα τῶν Γαλιλαίων διέφερεν· [559] τόν τε γὰρ Ἰωάννην παρήγαγον εἰς ἰσχὺν οὗτοι, κἀκεῖνος αὐτοὺς ἐξ ἧς περιεποίησαν δυναστείας ἠμείβετο, πάντα ἐπιτρέπων δρᾶν ὧν ἕκαστος ἐπεθύμει. [560] πόθοι δ' ἦσαν ἁρπαγῆς ἀπλήρωτοι καὶ τῶν πλουσίων οἴκων ἔρευνα, φόνος τε ἀνδρῶν καὶ γυναικῶν ὕβρεις ἐπαίζοντο, [561] μεθ' αἵματός τε τὰ συληθέντα κατέπινον καὶ μετ' ἀδείας ἐνεθηλυπάθουν τῷ κόρῳ, κόμας συνθετιζόμενοι καὶ γυναικείας ἐσθῆτας ἀναλαμβάνοντες, καταντλούμενοι δὲ μύροις καὶ πρὸς εὐπρέπειαν ὑπογράφοντες ὀφθαλμούς. [562] οὐ μόνον δὲ κόσμον, ἀλλὰ καὶ πάθη γυναικῶν ἐμιμοῦντο καὶ δι' ὑπερβολὴν ἀσελγείας ἀθεμίτους ἐπενόησαν ἔρωτας· ἐνηλινδοῦντο δ' ὡς πορνείῳ τῇ πόλει καὶ πᾶσαν ἀκαθάρτοις ἐμίαναν ἔργοις. [563] γυναικιζόμενοι δὲ τὰς ὄψεις ἐφόνων ταῖς δεξιαῖς, θρυπτόμενοί τε τοῖς βαδίσμασιν ἐπιόντες ἐξαπίνης ἐγίνοντο πολεμισταί, τά τε ξίφη προφέροντες ἀπὸ τῶν βεβαμμένων χλανιδίων τὸν προστυχόντα διήλαυνον.

[4.558] The citizens thus found Simon without the walls a greater terror than the Romans, and the Zealots within more oppressive than either; while among the latter for mischievous ingenuity and audacity none surpassed the Galilaean contingent, [559] for it was they who had promoted John to power, and he from the position of authority which they had won for him requited them by allowing everyone to do whatever he desired. [560] With an insatiable lust for loot, they ransacked the houses of the wealthy; the murder of men and the violation of women were their sport; [561] they caroused on their spoils, with blood to wash them down, and from mere satiety unscrupulously indulged in effeminate practices, plaiting their hair and attiring themselves in women's apparel, drenching themselves with perfumes and painting their eyelids to enhance their beauty. [562] And not only did they imitate the dress, but also the passions of women, devising in their excess of lasciviousness unlawful pleasures and wallowing as in a brothel in the city, which they polluted from end to end with their foul deeds. [563] Yet, while they wore women's faces, their hands were murderous, and approaching with mincing steps they would suddenly become warriors and whipping out their swords from under their dyed mantles transfix whomsoever they met. (Josephus, *B.J.* 4.558–563 [Thackeray, LCL])

We are told some odd things here about the Galilean Zealots: because they helped their fellow citizen and leader John, one of the two Judean pretenders in the uprising against the Romans, to achieve a strong position, the latter in turn grants them what they crave. Their minds are at first set on prey. Regardless of human cost, they pursue it, then devour it without inhibitions, until finally and out of sheer tedium indulge in more reprehensible activities—or even perhaps *the* most despicable activity: the imitation of women. For not only would the Galilean Zealots dress like them, they would also imitate their sexual passions, and tarnish all Jerusalem with their mutual and forbidden revelry.

What on earth does Josephus aim to convey to his readership with this bizarre anecdote? How perverted the behavior of the Galilean Zealots is in the midst of the war crimes they have perpetrated? How their unrestrained violence couples up with infantile regression toward the weak? How in the midst of murder—for no apparent reason—they stoop to engage in transvestite war theater? Regrettably, in his works Josephus offers no real help with interpretation, as they contain no similar narrative. However, if we are to appreciate this anecdote as a luck find, in terms of gender-specifics, we need to view what has been said from different perspectives. Let's start with the vocabulary: Of what exactly are the Galilean Zealots supposedly guilty?

THE CHARGE: A LINGUISTIC ANALYSIS

Josephus describes the main charge in *B.J.* 4.561–63. In *B.J.* 4.561 it is said that the Galilean Zealots "indulged in effeminate practices" out of "satiety" (κόρος). The verb used is ἐνθηλυπαθέω, which, according to *The Complete*

Concordance to Flavius Josephus is unsurprisingly a *hapax legomenon* in Josephus. The *Concordance* renders its meaning in this specific context as "to act effeminately (as male)."[2] The Zealots had manifested this behavior, Josephus continues in the same verse, by having "artificially arranged or prepared their hair (συνθετίζομαι),"[3] and by donning women's clothes, perfuming themselves, and applying make-up to their eyelids.

Beside this external distortion of their sexual identity, *B.J.* 4.562 also says that the Galilean Zealots imitated the "passions" of women. In this specific context, the *Concordance* renders the ambiguous noun πάθος as imitation of the "sexual behavior[4] of women."[5] Josephus is more specific: in their excess of "lasciviousness or lechery (ἀσέλγεια),"[6] they invented "ways of making love (ἔρως)"[7]—the *Concordance* suggests at this point—and "rolled around (ἐναλινδέομαι)"[8] through the city as if it were a "brothel" (πορνεῖον).[9] With their "unclean" (ἀκάθαρτος) acts they had "stained" (μιαίνω)[10]—also in a cultic sense—the city.[11]

To the infringement of two boundaries imposed on natural sex, Josephus adds a further charge in *B.J.* 4.563: while outwardly in appearance as well as in their (sexual) behavior "the Galilean Zealots conducted themselves (or acted) like women (γυναικίζω)"—this verb too is a *hapax legomenon*[12]—they would nonetheless kill like men, like ruthless warriors, in fact, stabbing anyone they met (without cause). Ruthless, but cowardly, because this form of camouflage leaves those attacked no way of defending themselves.

So much is clear: the Galilean Zealots are accused not only of indiscriminate and insidious murder, but also of violating women, and furthermore of robbery, and finally of transvestism and homosexual practices associated with it.[13] All the charges are weighty, but this discussion will focus on the last two, transvestism and homosexual practices. When, consequently, Josephus castigates in *B.J.* 4.562 the manner of their love-making as "unlawful" (ἀθέμιτος), to what law is he referring? Probably the one he, as a Pharisaic descendant of a distinguished priestly-royal family of Jerusalem, claims to have been particularly knowledgeable about since his youth (*Vita* 1, 9, 12): the Mosaic law, the Torah. And this law clearly prohibits cross-dressing, for both sexes in fact. Likewise, it prohibits male homosexuality. So with regard to transvestism, we read in Deut 22:5:

> A woman shall not wear a man's apparel, nor shall a man put on a woman's garment; for whoever does such things is abhorrent to the LORD your God.[14]

The Torah condemns homosexuality even more strongly: it is an abomination that even deserves the death penalty:[15]

> You shall not lie with a male as with a woman; it is an abomination. (Lev 18:22)

If a man lies with a male as with a woman, both of them have committed an abomination; they shall be put to death; their blood is upon them. (Lev 20:13)

In two passages, Josephus himself comments on homosexuality. In accordance with Lev 20:13, he condemns it as worthy of death:

> What are our marriage laws? The Law relating to marriage recognizes no sexual connexions, except the natural union of man and wife, and that only for the procreation of children. Sodomy it abhors, and punishes any guilty of such assault with death. (*C. Ap.* 2.199 [Thackeray, LCL])

> The penalty for most offences against the Law is death: for adultery, for violating an unmarried woman, for outrage upon a male, for consent of one so tempted to such abuse. (*C. Ap.* 2.215 [Thackeray, LCL])

Philo of Alexandria also pillories homosexuality, especially in the form of pederasty—even more so when combined with castration in a cultic context. It is noticeable in Philo's statements how his transcription of homosexual practice is quite similar to that of Josephus. Did the younger perhaps borrow from his elder counterpart in his description of the Galilean Zealots?

> 3.37 Much graver than the above is another evil, which has ramped its way into the cities, namely pederasty. In former days the very mention of it was a great disgrace, but now it is a matter of boasting not only to the active but to the passive partners, who habituate themselves to endure the disease of *effemination*,[16] let both body and soul run to waste, and leave no ember of their male sex-nature to smoulder. Mark how conspicuously they braid and adorn the *hair* of their heads, and how they scrub and paint their *faces* with cosmetics and pigments and the like, and smother themselves with *fragrant* unguents. [. . .] In fact the transformation of the male nature to the female is practised by them as an art and does not raise a blush. 38 These persons are rightly judged worthy of death by those who obey the law, which ordains that the man-woman who debases the sterling coin of nature should perish unavenged, suffered not to live for a day or even an hour, as a disgrace to himself, his house, his native land and the whole human race. 39 And the lover of such may be assured that he is subject to the same penalty. He pursues an unnatural pleasure and does his best to render cities desolate and uninhabited by destroying the means of procreation. Furthermore he sees no harm in becoming a tutor and instructor in the grievous vices of unmanliness and effeminacy by prolonging the bloom of the young and emasculating the flower of their prime, which should rightly be trained to strength and robustness. Finally, like a bad husbandman he lets the deep-soiled and fruitful fields lie sterile, by taking steps to keep them from bearing, while he spends his labour night and day on soil from which no growth at all can be

expected.⁴⁰ The reason is, I think, to be found in the prizes awarded in many nations to licentiousness and effeminacy. Certainly you may see these hybrids of man and woman continually strutting about through the thick of the market, heading the processions at the feasts, appointed to serve as unholy ministers of holy things, leading the mysteries and initiations and celebrating the rites of Demeter. ⁴¹ Those of them who by way of heightening still further their youthful beauty have desired to be completely changed into women and gone on to mutilate their genital organs, are *clad in purple* like signal benefactors of their native lands, and march in front escorted by a bodyguard, attracting the attention of those who meet them. ⁴² But if such indignation as our lawgiver felt was directed against those who do not shrink from such conduct, if they were cut off without condonation as public enemies, each of them a curse and a *pollution* of his country, many others would be found to take the warning. For relentless punishment of criminals already condemned acts as a considerable check on those who are eager to practise the like. (*Spec*. 3.37–42 [Colson, LCL])¹⁷

Josephus's Pharisaic contemporary Paul also places homosexuality outside the law in his Letter to the Romans, stating in Rom 1:24–27, especially in verse 27:

> [A]lso the men, giving up natural intercourse with women, were consumed with passion for one another. Men committed shameless acts with men and received in their own persons the due penalty for their error.

Paul comes to the same verdict in 1 Cor 6:9:

> Do you not know that wrongdoers will not inherit the kingdom of God? Do not be deceived! Fornicators, idolaters, adulterers, male prostitutes (μαλακοὶ), sodomites (ἀρσενοκοῖται), . . .¹⁸

The Mosaic law, then, as well as two of its warrantors, Philo and Paul, support Josephus's view regarding the two charges of transvestism and homosexuality: like the ungodly denounced by Paul, the Galilean Zealots had therefore set themselves outside of the Torah. Accordingly, they were found by God to have fallen away, as unfaithful fornicators, as the term "brothel" (πορνεῖον) in *B.J.* 4.562 insinuates. Regardless of the collateral damage—other people's lives, for instance—they have become those who give their own lives up to material loot, just as they have given up their bodies to forbidden sexual gratification. Josephus's accusation in relation to the two charges, transvestism and homosexuality, seems thus to be proven, at least *prima facie*. Is it right then? Let us turn our attention to an analysis of the chronology of the content.

THE UNVERIFIABLE CHARGE:
A CONTENT-CHRONOLOGICAL ANALYSIS

Josephus is firmly convinced of the truth of his war report. He confidently writes:

> During that time no incident escaped my knowledge. I kept a careful record of all that went on under my eyes in the Roman camp, and was alone in a position to understand the information brought by deserters. (*C.A.* 1.49 [Thackeray, LCL])

Josephus thus claims to have been "present in person at all the events," as an eyewitness (*C.A.* 1.47), to have recorded everything in writing and also to have understood the language of both warring parties. So reliable and impartial is his wartime history, he boasts, that all truth-loving eyewitnesses —be they on the Roman or the Jewish side—have authenticated it. With this, Josephus distances himself markedly from those Greek historians who have only second-hand knowledge of the events and have allegedly embellished their coverage with "fabrications and flatteries" (*B.J.* 1.6; see also 1.1–3, 7–8, 13–16, 18, 30). In spite of all his truth claims, Josephus can certainly not have witnessed first-hand what he tells us about the Galilean Zealots, for when the events occur at the given time and place, he is certainly not in Jerusalem, nor close by, but rather in Caesarea Maritima as a prisoner of war! But let us take things in order.

The so-called First Jewish-Roman War breaks out in the twelfth year of Nero's rule, that is 66 CE (*B.J.* 1.20), after the Syrian legate, Gaius Cestius Gallus, has failed to suppress the Jewish revolt in the late autumn of the same year (*B.J.* 2.499–555). Thereupon Nero—who is on an artistic tour in Greece at this time (Suetonius, *Nero* 22.3)—commissions Vespasian with this task (*B.J.* 3.3–7). A short time later, the new commander-in-chief of the Syrian troops sets out with his army from Antioch, arriving in Galilee via Ptolomais, which is the first city he captures (*B.J.* 3.29–4.120). On this occasion, Vespasian holds Josephus in the well-secured, fiercely-contested, and finally-seized city of Jotopata (*B.J.* 3.392–98), in July of 67 CE (*B.J.* 3.339). What is the Jerusalemite doing in Galilee? Well, after the defeat of Cestius, the Jerusalem People's Assembly, anticipating that Nero would not simply accept the failure of his Syrian legate, had appointed generals for each part of the country, and Josephus was dispatched to Galilee (*B.J.* 2.562–68, esp. 2.568; see also *Vita* 28–29). Josephus's tenure was brief and ultimately unsuccessful, predictably so in view of the Roman army's superiority. Strengthened by this stage-one victory, Vespasian returns to Caesarea, the administrative city of the Romans in Judaea (*B.J.* 4.130). Meanwhile, in the entire country—and especially in the capital—civil war-like conflicts flare up between moderates and war hawks. While the former place reliance on negotiations with the Romans, the latter insist on freedom and on shaking off the Roman yoke (*B.J.* 4.131–365, 389–409). The hawks prevail, especially in Jerusalem. Vespasian now recognizes that for a Roman victory in Judea, the capital city must be taken. However, he opts strategically for a careful approach to prevent ambushes (*B.J.* 4.366–76, 413). In concrete terms, this means the prior subjugation of all remaining non-conquered areas and the complete encirclement of Jerusalem.

Vespasian proceeds speedily to the implementation of his plan, and by early summer 68 CE Perea, Judea, Idumea, and also Samaria are conquered (*B.J.* 4.410–50). Finally, when Jerusalem too is completely encircled, Vespasian again goes to Caesarea to prepare for the march on the capital (*B.J.* 4.489–90, 588). At this very moment, however, news of the death of Nero (*B.J.* 4.491) overtakes him. What is to be done if the supreme commander and principal of this war has turned his weapon on himself? Vespasian decides to suspend the campaign against Jerusalem for the time being, and in the winter of the same year sends his son Titus to Rome to receive instructions from the new emperor, Galba, on the further pursuit of this war. Titus immediately sets off not by ship but over land, it being winter. In Greece, however, news reaches him that Galba is dead, murdered, and Marcus Salvius Otho has taken over supreme command in Rome. Titus interrupts his journey and decides in January 69 CE to return to his father in Caesarea. Once there, father and son await developments in Rome, because there too, as in Jerusalem, a civil war is raging (*B.J.* 4.497–502). The war in Jerusalem escalates and rages more violently and brutally, sometimes on three fronts, sometimes on two (*B.J.* 4.566–84). It is at *this* time, while Vespasian and Titus in Caesarea anxiously await developments in Rome, that the depicted scene with the Galilean Zealots takes place in Jerusalem (*B.J.* 4.558–63). At this point, Josephus is scraping out an abject existence as a Roman prisoner not in, nor even near Jerusalem, as mentioned, but in the Roman administrative city of Caesarea.

The situation in the distant homeland does not ease; on the contrary, it comes to a head. After just three months, Otho too dies by suicide. Aulus Vitellius seizes power in his place. When Vespasian's commanding officers in Caesarea learn of Vitellius's assumption of power in April 69 CE, they consider staging a coup (*B.J.* 4.592–600). Since Vespasian deems it just as unworthy as they do "to own as master one who laid mad hands upon the empire as though it were forlorn" (*B.J.* 4.589), he accepts the acclamation of his troops and commits himself to service as state leader (*B.J.* 4.589–604). The so-called Four Emperors Year has found its winner. As the good news spreads like wildfire throughout the empire (*B.J.* 4.618) and the situation develops in his favor, Vespasian is said, according to Josephus, to have recognized divine providence in the events (*B.J.* 4.622), and recognized in him, the prisoner—who had predicted this honor for him when Nero was still alive—the "voice of God" (*B.J.* 4.626, see also 3.401). Hereupon, Josephus is freed from his shackles and has his freedom and allegedly all his civil rights returned to him (*B.J.* 4.629). After returning to his starting point in Antioch in Syria, Vespasian goes with Titus to Egypt (*B.J.* 4.656) to secure the support of this crucially important province for supplies to Rome (*B.J.* 4.605–6). When this succeeds, he prepares for the crossing to Rome, before his departure entrusting his son Titus with the siege and conquest of Jerusalem (*B.J.* 4.657–63). He commands Josephus to be at Titus's side as interpreter (*Vita* 416), so that around Passover of the year 70 CE he at last reaches the city wall of his home town, four years after leaving Jerusalem for Galilee as one of the appointed Judean generals (*B.J.* 5.51).

Our conclusion must be that Josephus did not and could not have witnessed in person the described episode with the Galilean Zealots in the winter of 69 CE, for at this time he is eking out an existence as a Roman prisoner in Caesarea Maritima. So is this nothing but rhetoric, fake news? No, not necessarily. Various (historical) scenarios are conceivable. The events Josephus reports, or similar events, may indeed have occurred in Jerusalem. But he did not witness them himself, receiving second-hand reports, from defectors perhaps, who did apparently flock to Caesarea at the time (e.g., *B.J.* 4.377–79, 397, 410–12). It is also conceivable that a report is made to Josephus a year later, again by defectors (e.g. *B.J.* 5.452–59), in 70 CE, as he stands with Titus before Jerusalem's city walls. It would, further, be possible that at this time Josephus himself witnessed such behavior by the Galilean Zealots as described, for example, in the course of one of his rides along the city wall (e.g. *B.J.* 5.258–61). However, what Josephus then would have witnessed can hardly have been observed in the manner described, for to be seen it would have had to happen *on* the city wall. What the Zealots then would have been displaying on the city walls would hardly have been behavior that undermined their own credibility, but rather a behavior and thus a message to the Romans designed to taunt, offend, or deceive the besieging opponent. As a matter of fact, Josephus constantly tells us of messages sent across the city walls, ridiculing and insulting (e.g., *B.J.* 6.129) or deceptive in nature (e.g., *B.J.* 5.109–19), addressed by the rebels to the Romans and occasionally Josephus himself, their interpreter (e.g., *B.J.* 6.98). Messages in the opposite direction occur too, offers of willingness to negotiate on the part of the Romans, presented by Josephus in person (e.g., *B.J.* 6.93–110), as well as intimidating (e.g., *B.J.* 5.348–55) or even threatening messages (e.g., *B.J.* 5.284–90). Finally, Josephus's report could also be fabricated, purely rhetorical in nature, but this version of events seems unlikely to me. Let us investigate possible historical contexts and interpretative approaches. I shall start with discussion of strategic aspects before moving on to biographical ones.

THE GENDER-CODED FIND IN STRATEGIC AND BIOGRAPHICAL LIGHT

Fighters disguising themselves in combat in order to defeat the enemy with less effort—and especially less loss of blood—is a classic strategy in warfare, then and now. Camouflage in this form was one of the standard strategies in antiquity and can be found repeatedly in the relevant collections of stratagems, such as those of Frontinus[19] and Polyaenus.[20] An occasional ploy is the wearing of women's clothing. We might give our attention to an illustrative anecdote from Greek history that Frontinus[21] records in his *Stratagems*, just a decade or two after[22] the events in Judea:

> When Epaminondas, the Theban, was campaigning in Arcadia, and on a certain holiday the women of the enemy strolled in large numbers outside the walls, he sent among them a number of his own troops dressed in women's attire. In consequence of this disguise, the men were admitted towards nightfall to the town, whereupon they seized it and threw it open to their companions. (Frontinus, *Strat*. 3.2.7 [Bennett, LCL])

The Galilean Zealots also wear women's clothing, which evidently affords them strategic advantages. However, what distinguishes Josephus's report from the anecdotes of other military historians is the combination of cross-dressing for a strategic purpose and homosexuality. To my knowledge at least, this is unique. Josephus accuses the Galilean Zealots not only of feminization, but also of ethical blemish. What is his intention here, does he mean to pursue a classical motive[23] and show the Roman public that they are weak in two respects, and thus an easily defeated enemy? I do not think so, as it is at odds with his historical-theoretical approach, which sets out in the introduction to his war history—and in contrast to other writers—as follows: "But I fail to see how the conquerors of a puny people deserve to be accounted great" (*B.J.* 1.8). Josephus, however, has no wish to depict Titus, and especially Vespasian, as feeble. That is not an option for him (see below). So he seems to associate the one with the other, casting aspersions on the Galilean Zealots in regard to their masculinity as well as their ethics, without denying that they remain dangerous. A clever move. On the notion that the insurgents in Jerusalem included women bearing weapons, Josephus remains silent. Cornelius Tacitus, at least, is interested in this in his *Histories*, published some twenty-five[24] years later (5.13.3).[25] Of course, this information from Tacitus, to depict the enemy as particularly dangerous, could, for the reasons just described, be rhetorical in nature—that is, fabricated. Be that as it may. At this point I would like to leave to one side the idea that Josephus allows himself so much freedom of interpretation as to turn the weapon-carrying women into men behaving effeminately.

Somehow, Josephus seems to heap attention on the group of Galilean Zealots, labelling them as the worst insurgents after the Romans, Simon ben Giora and his men, and the other Zealots (*B.J.* 4.558; see also 7.252–75). But why? Hardly because the Galileans as a whole are considered "from infancy inured to war" (*B.J.* 3.42). No, Josephus associates John and his men with an unpleasant, even traumatic background: for, when he goes there as the new commander of Galilee, freshly appointed by the Jerusalem People's Assembly, he soon finds an "intriguing opponent" in John of Giscala, whom he describes as "the most unscrupulous and crafty of all who have ever gained notoriety by such infamous means" (*B.J.* 2.585). Immediately John challenges him for the office of commander of Galilee, initially secretly and, as his position strengthens, quite openly (*B.J.* 2.590, 593). John has come into money and thus to influence by devious means (*B.J.* 2.590–632). Now like-minded people come running up to him, from whom he carefully selects only "good, strapping fellows, with stout hearts and military experience." They already number 400 (*B.J.* 2.588), and citizens of Giscala join him later (*B.J.* 4.84). John is well able to assert himself, even when Josephus has long since become a Roman prisoner. Giscala is then the last city in Galilee that Vespasian deals with (*B.J.* 4.120, see also 4.1). He does not take it in person, but sends his son Titus to do so. Saying he is tired of killing, he decides not to fight John and his men, but to negotiate with him (*B.J.* 4.92). However, by playing a trick, John succeeds in outsmarting Titus (*B.J.* 4.97–105) and escapes to Jerusalem with a portion of his men, where he finds admission and provisional protection (*B.J.* 4.106–21). The city does not have a single high command at this time (*B.J.* 4.136). John is able to exploit this thanks to his strategic skill, and is soon able to rise—alongside Simon ben Giora—as one of the two key warmongers of the embattled capital (*B.J.* 5.248–57).

However, the professional rivalry between Josephus and John does not end here; in fact, it intensifies and even affects the ideological and personal sphere. John of Giscala must have been the cause of much personal pain for Josephus. What is particularly appalling to Josephus, the Jerusalemite of priestly-royal descent, is that the Zealots under Eleazar and with them John, misuses, of all things, the holy temple precinct as a military camp (*B.J.* 4.151; 5.5–10), thereby desecrating holy objects (*B.J.* 5.36–38; 5.562–66) and worse still, defiling it in an irrevocable way. For blood is staining its holy ground, and corpses of fellow countrymen line the various courtyards (*B.J.* 4.305–13;

5.10–19). Hatred has ended the lives of those prepared to negotiate with the Romans, and hatred does not do them the honor of a statutory funeral (e.g., *B.J.* 4.317). Instead, their neglected bodies lie rotting where they fell, or even more cruelly, are thrown over the city wall naked to the dogs and wild beasts (e.g., *B.J.* 4.314–25). All this must have been dreadful for Josephus and others, bordering on the traumatic. To make matters worse for him as a Jerusalemite, he must fear a similarly brutal fate for his well-regarded family. Friends, relatives, brother, mother, in fact even his (first) wife are stuck in the capital (*B.J.* 5.419, 544; *Vita* 419–21), as are other Jerusalemites, together with hundreds of thousands of pilgrims (*B.J.* 6.420–21). All of them have fallen hostage to mindless rioters, defenseless against their whims, and to the increasingly devastating famine (e.g., *B.J.* 4.137; 6.421). Josephus claims to have repeatedly tried to negotiate with John over the city wall, persuading him to see reason and surrender (*B.J.* 5.362–419; 6.93–110), without success. Then the unthinkable occurs: suspension of the daily sacrifices in the temple under the pressure of the siege (*B.J.* 6.93). How can anyone think God is on their side under such conditions, Josephus complains. However, it seems that John is acting on exactly this assumption. Josephus's assessment is quite different, and theological: It is he, John, who has caused the defilement of the city. Such a temple can no longer be worthy of God's presence. But what God has forsaken is surrendered to the enemy, and so doomed to destruction (*B.J.* 6.93–110). Here, Josephus is concerned with nothing less than the interpretation of the war, with blame for the war as a whole, which he chiefly and unmistakably lays at the door of John and his Galilean Zealots, and not, as the Romans, at that of Simon ben Giora[26] (*B.J.* 1.10–12; 4.314–25, 386–88; 5.375–419).

So much is clear: the strategy of wearing women's clothing has a firm place in ancient warfare. But Josephus goes a step further with regard to the Galilean Zealots: for their purpose in disguising themselves was not only a military one, but also to behave outwardly and sexually like women. "So what?" we might reply to Josephus.[27] Not so a Roman audience of that time, however, where for which masculinity—and not femininity—was the measure of all things. The rhetorician Quintilian puts it as follows: "However (let me say this again) this Ornament must be manly, strong, and chaste. It must not favour effeminate smoothness or the false colouring of cosmetics."[28] But the Galilean Zealots are said to have transgressed precisely against this presupposition of masculinity, and that as warriors! Certainly, this "effeminate" behavior may have earned them even more contempt than was already prevalent toward Judaic insurgents in the aftermath of this war. But exactly this might have been fine with Josephus, for the theological and—above all—personal motives described. However, this possibly willful vilification of the

Galilean Zealots is not made by Josephus at the expense of their military ingenuity or their dangerousness. This is clever of him, because it is a way of flattering the first readers of his war report, no lesser figures than Vespasian and Titus (*C.A.* 1.50–51). And he has to do so, as a court historian of the new ruling house.

THE GENDER-CODED FIND IN A POLITICAL LIGHT: NERO AND THE CRISIS OF MASCULINITY

So Josephus seems interested in disavowing the Galilean Zealots. This is understandable from his point of view. But why, of all things, does he make use of the charge of cross-dressing in connection with homosexuality, as there is no context for such an accusation in Judea, nor anything like it in his entire text corpus? Perhaps we must turn our look to the Roman context, where[29] Josephus writes his war report around 75–79[30] and where it is not uncommon to smear one's opponents with accusations of sexual aberrations—even fictitious ones.[31] This insight brings us closer to the answer we seek, but still does not explain the charge of transvestism in association with homosexuality. But there is a concrete context for this in Rome, and it is a problem so huge that even in the most remote provinces it provokes outrage and, among other things, a desire to secede from Rome. This problem's name is Nero.[32]

According to Dio Cassius, Boudicca, the British queen and general under Nero, used the following speech[33] (60/61 CE) to rouse her people to secede from Rome.

> I thank thee, Andraste,[34] and call upon thee as woman speaking to woman; for I rule over no burden-bearing Egyptians as did Nitocris, nor over trafficking Assyrians as did Semiramis (for we have by now gained thus much learning from the Romans!), much less over the Romans themselves as did Messalina once and afterwards Agrippina and now Nero (who, though in name a man, is in fact a woman, as is proved by his singing, lyre-playing and beautification of his person[35]); nay, those over whom I rule are Britons, men that know not how to till the soil or ply a trade, but are thoroughly versed in the art of war and hold all things in common, even children and wives, so that the latter possess the same valour as the men. As the queen, then, of such men and of such women, I supplicate and pray thee for victory, preservation of life, and liberty against men insolent, unjust, insatiable, impious,—if, indeed, we ought to term those people men who bathe in warm water, eat artificial dainties, drink unmixed wine, anoint themselves with myrrh, sleep on soft couches with boys for bedfellows,—boys past their prime at that,—and are slaves to a lyre-player and a poor one too. Wherefore may this Mistress Domitia-Nero reign no longer over me or over you men; let the wench sing and lord it over Romans, for they surely

deserve to be the slaves of such a woman after having submitted to her so long. But for us, Mistress, be thou alone ever our leader. (Dio Cassius, *Hist*. 62.6.2–5 [Cary and Foster, LCL])

Nero is not a man, she rants, but a "wench" who plays music, sings, and beautifies her person. Furthermore, she "sleeps on soft couches with boys for bedfellows"! That sounds a little over the top, and it could be dismissed if Boudicca's voice were the only one.

But it is not. While her uprising was unsuccessful (Dio Cassius, *Hist*. 62.1–12), the following speech by Gaius Julius Vindex, addressing the Gauls, heralded the end of Nero. This was in 68 CE:

"[B]ecause," as he said, "he has despoiled the whole Roman world, because he has destroyed all the flower of their senate, because he debauched and then killed his mother, and does not preserve even the semblance of sovereignty. Many murders, robberies and outrages, it is true, have often been committed by others; but as for the other deeds committed by Nero, how could one find words fittingly to describe them? I have seen him, my friends and allies,—believe me,—I have seen that man (*if man he is* who has married Sporus and been given in marriage to Pythagoras), in the circle of the theatre, that is, in the orchestra, sometimes holding the lyre and dressed in loose tunic and buskins, and again wearing high-soled shoes and mask. I have often heard him sing, play the herald, and act[36] in tragedies. I have seen him in chains, hustled about as a miscreant, heavy with child, aye, in the travail of childbirth—in short, imitating all the situations of mythology by what he said and by what was said to him, by what he submitted to and by what he did. Will anyone, then, style such a person Caesar and emperor and Augustus? Never! Let no one abuse those sacred titles. They were held by Augustus and by Claudius, whereas this fellow might most properly be termed Thyestes, Oedipus, Alcmeon, or Orestes; for these are the characters that he represents on the stage and it is these titles that he has assumed in place of the others. Therefore rise now at length against him; succour yourselves and succour the Romans; liberate the entire world!" (Dio Cassius, *Hist*. 63.22.2–6 [Cary and Foster, LCL])

Nero, a "man," who is married to a Sporus and a Pythagoras? That would be homosexuality, nothing unusual at the imperial court.[37] But the way Nero stages it in 65 CE goes well beyond the bounds of good taste:

Sabina also perished at this time through an act of Nero's; either accidentally or intentionally he had leaped upon her with his feet while she was pregnant.... Nero missed her so greatly ... that ... later he caused a boy of the freedmen, whom he used to call Sporus, to be castrated, since he, too, resembled Sabina. (Dio Cassius, *Hist*. 62.28.1–2 [trans. Cary and Foster, LCL])

> ... and actually tried to make a woman of him; and he married him with all the usual ceremonies, including a dowry and a bridal veil, took him to his house attended by a great throng, and treated him as his wife. ... This Sporus, decked out with the finery of the empresses and riding in a litter, he took with him to the assizes and marts of Greece, and later at Rome through the Street of the Images, fondly kissing him from time to time. (Suetonius, *Nero* 28.1–2 [trans. Rolfe, LCL]

> [A]nd when he had sated his mad lust, [he] was finished off by his freedman Doryphorus [= Pythagoras]; for he was even married to this man in the same way that he himself had taken Sporus, going so far as to imitate the cries and lamentations of a maiden being deflowered. (Suetonius, *Nero*, 29.1 [trans. Rolfe, LCL]

> Nero had two bedfellows at once, Pythagoras to play the rôle of husband to him, and Sporus that of wife. (Dio Cassius, *Hist.* 63.13.2 [Cary and Foster, LCL])

Not surprisingly, Nero's behavior is assessed as "immoral," even by his close followers:

> While Nero had Sporus, the eunuch, as a wife, one of his associates in Rome, who had made a study of philosophy, on being asked whether the marriage and cohabitation in question met with his approval, replied: "You do well, Caesar, to seek the company of such wives. Would that your father had had the same ambition and had lived with a similar consort!"—indicating that if this had been the case, Nero would not have been born, and the state would now be free of great evils. (Dio Cassius, *Hist.* 62.28.3a)

So much is clear: Nero practices a form a transvestism[38] and homosexuality, which is blatantly condemned throughout the entire Empire. His behavior damaged the office of emperor and seems to have prompted a crisis of masculinity in the empire. Unsurprisingly, Quintilian, the famous teacher of rhetoric appointed by Nero's successor, virtually conjures manhood in his *Institutio*.

Nero violates, for example, a vestal virgin called Rubria (Suetonius, *Nero* 28.1);[39] others even say his mother (Suetonius, *Nero* 28.2). Nero murders nobles, or rather has them murdered (Dio Cassius, *Hist.* 63.17), as well as senators (Dio Cassius, *Hist.* 63.22.3); his closest advisors such as his teacher Lucius Annaeus Seneca (Tacitus, *Ann.* 14.52–58; 15.45.3, 60.2–64; Suetonius, *Nero* 35.5; Dio Cassius, *Hist.* 62.13.3; 62.25.1); relatives such as his younger stepbrother Britannicus (Tacitus, *Ann.* 15–17; Suetonius, *Nero* 33; 34.5; 35.4–5; Dio Cassius, *Hist.* 61.1.2; 61.7.4; 62.17.1); his wives[40] Claudia Octavia and Poppaea Sabina (Tacitus, *Ann.* 14.60–64; 16.6; Suetonius, Nero 35.1–3; Dio Cassius, *Hist.* 62.13.1–2; 62.28.1); and indeed even his mother

Agrippina, which is considered a particularly grave sin[41] (Tacitus, *Ann.* 14.2–13; Suetonius, *Nero* 34.1–4; Dio Cassius, *Hist.* 62.13–14, 16).

After the public purse is emptied because of his wastefulness, Nero plunders the possessions of other people, not even stopping in front of the temple (Suetonius, *Nero* 32; Dio Cassius, *Hist.* 61.5.3–6, 5; 62.18.5), robbing the provinces (Suetonius, *Nero* 38.3; Dio Cassius, *Hist.* 62.1–2; 62.3.2–5), particularly in the course of the fire of the century[42] in 64 CE, for which he may have been partly responsible (Suetonius, *Nero* 38; Dio Cassius, *Hist.* 62.16–18). To add insult to injury, this drives him to undertake an accelerated building spree, to which context his magnificent edifice, the *Domus Aurea* belongs (Suetonius, *Nero* 31.1–3).

Looking at Nero's sins[43] as a whole, it is striking that they are the same ones that Josephus notes of the Galilean Zealots (see section 1). Coincidental? Hardly. It seems, rather, that he makes this link so as to be able to say that the Zealots were just as "sick" as Nero (Josephus, *B.J.* 1.4–5), whom by the way Josephus had had the pleasure of meeting in Rome in the context of an embassy (*Vita* 13–16) (*B.J.* 4.376). And furthermore, to be able to say that just as Nero led the Roman state to ruin, thereby incurring the wrath of the gods (Dio Cassius, *Hist.* 62.15.1), so did the Zealots with Jerusalem, the Judean nation, and their God.

What does Josephus gain by this parallelization? Well, a double contrast: on the one hand a correspondingly brighter picture of Vespasian's virtues in contrast to Nero, as well as a shinier picture of himself as the rightful commander of Galilee in contrast to John of Giscala and his Zealot cronies. Josephus must draw a good picture of the new emperor, in whose service he now stands as court historian[44] and under whose protection[45] he came and remained (*Vita* 425). His war report has to serve the political objective and legitimize the new ruler, one who cannot boast of any Julian-Claudian and thus senatorial or divine descent (Sueton, *Vesp.* 4.5). This ruler is also responsible for the destruction of the Capitoline temple in the struggle for the throne (Sueton, *Vit.* 15.3; Cassius Dio, *Gesch.* 64.17.3). But still through his glorious victory he is shown to have fate on his side.

For in battle Vespasian incurred no blame, always behaving in an exemplary fashion, indeed behaving virtuously, which revealed his *auctoritas* and *maiestas* previously hidden (Tacitus, *Hist.* 4.81.1; Sueton, *Vesp.* 7.2). After fourteen[46] years of horrific rule under Nero, it is no effeminate emperor who puts himself forward, but rather just what the people wish for, a man called by a divine hand.

I come to my conclusion. Did what Josephus tells us in his account of the Galilean Zealots really happen? I have tried to show that this cannot really be the case. So is all this a pack of lies? No, that is not the case either.

An element of it might be true, such as that the Zealots engaged in cross-dressing. Perhaps not because they were as ruthless as Josephus draws them. For they had legitimate reasons for rebelling against Rome, just like the Britons and the Gauls, and later, the Spaniards. This is also evident from Josephus's comments on the last three procurators sent by Nero, Porcius Festus (60–62 CE; *B.J.* 2.271; *A.J.* 20,182), Lucceius Albinus (62–64 CE; *B.J.* 2.272; *Ant.* 20.197) and the warmonger Gessius Florus (64–66 CE; *B.J.* 2.277; *A.J.* 20.215).

No, the Galilean Zealots could indeed have put on a transvestite act from the city walls, this, in order to hold up to their besieger dispatched by Nero a mirror image of their abnormal commissioner. As a mockery strategy, so to speak, which, as mentioned, is what indeed occurred. If this interpretation is correct, then Josephus would have spoken the truth about the Galilean Zealots, but for strategic, personal, and political reasons, he interpreted it in a biased and incorrect way. It is fascinating how this gender-coded find teaches us how facts can become fake news.

NOTES

1. I am grateful to Dr. David E. Orton for proofreading this chapter.
2. Karl Heinrich Rengstorf, ed., in cooperation with Erwin Buck et al., *A Complete Concordance to Flavius Josephus: Study Edition*, 2 vols. (Leiden: Brill, 2002), 1:103.
3. This verb too is a *hapax legomenon* (Rengstorf, *Complete Concordance*, 2:124).
4. Rengstorf, *Complete Concordance*, 2:263.
5. The combination of γυνή and πάθος is found in the work of Josephus only in *A.J.* 2.53 again, namely in connection with Potiphar's wife, who had kept an eye on Joseph and had approached him in an inappropriate manner (Gen 38:1–18).
6. Rengstorf, *Complete Concordance*, 1:252.
7. Rengstorf, *Complete Concordance*, 1:214.
8. This verb too is a *hapax legomenon* (Rengstorf, *Complete Concordance*, 1:94).
9. The noun is otherwise found only in Josephus, *A.J.* 19.357.
10. Rengstorf, *Complete Concordance*, 2:111.
11. This adjective is otherwise found only in Josephus, *C. Ap.* 1.307 (Rengstorf, *Complete Concordance*, 1:47).
12. Rengstorf, *Complete Concordance*, 1:398.
13. It is also possible that the phrase μεθ' αἵματός in Josephus *B.J.* 4.561 hides an accusation of blood consumption. The Torah declares this crime to be worthy of death, especially if it is human blood (Gen 9:2–4; Lev 3:17; 7:26–27; 17:11–12; Deut 12:23–25). The New Testament too rejects it, even for believers from the nations (Acts 15:20).
14. Where not otherwise indicated, for biblical quotations I follow the New Revised Standard Version.

15. Cf. also Gen 19 and Judg 19. The prohibition of homosexuality also includes temple prostitution for both sexes: "None of the daughters of Israel shall be a temple prostitute; none of the sons of Israel shall be a temple prostitute" (Deut 23:17).

16. Italics mine.

17. Philo says something similar, albeit much more succinctly, in *Spec.* 1.325 (Colson, LCL): "Thus, knowing that in assemblies there are not a few worthless persons who steal their way in and remain unobserved in the large numbers which surround them, it guards against this danger by precluding all the unworthy from entering the holy congregation. It begins with the men who belie their sex and are affected with effemination, who debase the currency of nature and violate it by assuming the passions and the outward form of licentious women. For it expels those whose generative organs are fractured or mutilated, who husband the flower of their youthful bloom, lest it should quickly wither, and restamp the masculine cast into a feminine form."

Philo has little time, either, for idealized pederasty as propagated in Plato's Symposium. He states in *Contempl.* 59–62 (Colson, LCL): [59] "In Plato's banquet the talk is almost entirely concerned with love, not merely with the love-sickness of men for women, or women for men, passions recognized by the laws of nature, but of men for other males differing from them only in age. For, if we find some clever subtlety dealing apparently with the heavenly Love and Aphrodite, it is brought in to give a touch of humour. [60] The chief part is taken up by the common vulgar love which robs men of the courage which is the virtue most valuable for the life both of peace and war, sets up the disease of effeminacy in their souls and turns into a hybrid of man and woman those who should have been disciplined in all the practices which make for valour. [61] And having wrought havoc with the years of boyhood and reduced the boy to the grade and condition of a girl besieged by a lover it inflicts damage on the lovers also in three most essential respects, their bodies, their souls and their property. For the mind of the lover is necessarily set towards his darling and its sight is keen for him only, blind to all other interests, private and public; his body wastes away through desire, particularly if his suit is unsuccessful, while his property is diminished by two causes, neglect and expenditure on his beloved. [62] As a side growth we have another greater evil of national importance. Cities are desolated, the best kind of men become scarce, sterility and childlessness ensue through the devices of these who imitate men who have no knowledge of husbandry by sowing not in the deep soil of the lowland but in briny fields and stony and stubborn places, which not only give no possibility for anything to grow but even destroy the seed deposited within them."

18. The NET Bible renders μαλακοί with "passive homosexual partners" and ἀρσενοκοῖται with "practicing homosexuals."

19. See, e.g., Frontinus, *Strat.* 3.2.3–4, 8–9, 11.

20. See, e.g., Polyaenus, *Strat.* 1.34; 2.16; 3.9.52; 7.28.2; see also 8.64.

21. Polyaenus also records one, in *Strat.* 2.3.1; and so does Josephus, *A.J.* 19.30.

22. Frontinus, *Stratagems, Aqueducts of Rome*, ed. Mary B. McElwain, trans. C. E. Bennett, LCL 174 (Cambridge, MA: Harvard University Press, 1925), xiv.

23. Cf. Claudia D. Bergmann, "We Have Seen the Enemy, and He Is Only a 'She': The Portrayal of Warriors as Women," in *Writing and Reading War: Rhetoric,*

Gender, and Ethics in Biblical and Modern Contexts, ed. Brad E. Kelle and Frank Ritchel Ames (SBLSymS 42; Leiden: Brill, 2008), 129–142.

24. Tacitus, *Histories: Books 4–5. Annals: Books 1–3*, trans. Clifford H. Moore, John Jackson, LCL 249 (Cambridge, MA: Harvard University Press, 1931), front flap.

25. "We have heard that the total number of the besieged of every age and both sexes was six hundred thousand: there were arms for all who could use them, and the number ready to fight was larger than could have been anticipated from the total population. Both men and women showed the same determination; and if they were to be forced to change their home, they feared life more than death" (Tacitus, *Hist.* 5.13.3 [Moore and Jackson, LCL]).

26. Accordingly, in the context of their jointly celebrated triumphal procession in 71 CE, the victorious generals lead Simon ben Giora to his death. John, on the other hand, is sentenced to life imprisonment (*B.J.* 6.434; 7.36, 118, 154).

27. From today's point of view, of course, the converse, that femininity is viewed negatively, is regrettable. But discussion of this would be the task of another essay.

28. This quotation, recorded in Quintilian's *Institutio* (8.3.6 [Russell, LCL]), is but one of countless references in both Roman and ancient literature that propagate masculinity as the standard.

29. Josephus had come to the capital along with Titus (Josephus, *Vita* 422).

30. Flavius Josephus, *De bello Judaico—Der jüdische Krieg: Griechisch und Deutsch*, 3 vols. in 4 parts, edited, introduced and annotated by Otto Michel and Otto Bauernfeind (Darmstadt: WBG, 1963–1982), 1:XX.

31. See, e.g., the famous *Carmen* 16 of Catullus (see also Eckhard Meyer-Zwiffelhoffer, *Im Zeichen des Phallus: Die Ordnung des Geschlechtslebens im antiken Rom*, Historische Studien 15 [Frankfurt am Main: Campus, 1995]).

32. Anyone questioning the most important three sources on the life of Nero, Tacitus, Suetonius, and Dio Cassius, meets a predominantly negative description of his person as well as his rule. This negative image is questioned, to some extent, by current research, especially since there are also hints of its popularity, at least among the common people, as graffiti in Pompeii prove. At least three points should be kept in mind when dealing with these sources: all three authors write about Nero from a distance. Some forty years after Nero's death, Tacitus is the only one who could have seen him, albeit only as a child. His report is the most objective. Suetonius writes more than fifty years after his death; his style is anecdotal. And Dio Cassius is more than 160 years removed, and his style tends at times to the legendary. In addition, the Roman senate decided to give Nero, the last scion of the Julio-Claudian dynasty, the *Damnatio memoriae*. Even from the state's point of view, there was no interest in a fair remembrance, certainly not on the part of the new Flavian rulers. And finally, all three authors came either from the senatorial or knightly nobility, both of them groups of people whom Nero took on towards the end of his reign. (Marcus Rueter, "Wer war Nero? Versuch einer Annäherung," in *Nero: Kaiser, Künstler und Tyrann*, ed. Jürgen Merten, Schriftenreihe des Rheinischen Landesmuseums Trier 40 [Darmstadt: Konrad Theiss Verlag, 2016], 12–21).

33. It takes the form of a prayer, embedded in a longer commander's speech.

34. A goddess of the Britons.

35. This is also reflected in the fact that Nero infringed the usual emperor's clothing style, and he did not—as was customary for emperors from Augustus onward—wear his hair short, but long and cascading over the shoulders (Suetonius, *Nero* 51; Dio Cassius, *Hist.* 63.13.3; 63.9.1; Alexandra T. Croom, *Roman Clothing and Fashion* [Stroud: Tempus, 2002], esp. 66; cf. also 1 Cor 11:14–15a).

36. Vindex's indictment is understandable, especially as the choice of the acting and gladiatorial professions (and similar activities) for members of senatorial and aristocratic families had been banned in several legal decrees (Korana Deppmeyer, "Die Verfehlungen des Künstlers Nero," in *Nero: Kaiser, Künstler und Tyrann*, 210–16, esp. 212).

37. Generally, lovers and marriage-like relationships were tolerated, and also reputation-damaging actions with persons of lower rank (Annetta Alexandridis, "Frauen um Nero—Ehefrauen und Geliebte," in *Nero: Kaiser, Künstler und Tyrann*, 64–73, esp. 69; John R. Clarke, *Ars Erotica: Sexualität und ihre Bilder im antiken Rom*, trans. Jörg Fündling [Darmstadt: Primus Verlag, 2009], esp. 157).

38. Like Caligula (Suetonius, *Cal.* 52), Nero seems to have enjoyed dressing up, not only in his marriage to Pythagoras and in the theatre (e.g., Suetonius, *Nero* 21.3), but already in 56 CE, where he enjoys roaming through Rome at night dressed in slave's clothes while perpetrating his "rampant" mischief (Tacitus, *Ann.* 13.25.1).

39. Nero is also accused of being a regular brothel visitor (Tacitus, *Ann.* 13.25.1).

40. Nero was married three times. Only his third wife, Statilia Messalina, survived him (Alexandridis, "Frauen um Nero," 64–73, esp. 64).

41. The murder of one's own mother, a so-called *parricidium*, was considered one of the worst evils in Greco-Roman antiquity (Yvonne Schmuhl, "Neros Mord an seiner Mutter Agrippina," in *Nero: Kaiser, Künstler und Tyrann*, 228–34, esp. 233).

42. This fire was the worst in Rome, destructive and devastating, not least because Rome was the largest conurbation in antiquity (Clementina Panella, "Nero und der große Brand von Rom im Jahre 64," in *Nero: Kaiser, Künstler und Tyrann*, 241–49, esp. 241).

43. Suetonius (*Nero* 26–28) accuses him of five: petulance (*petulantia*), lust (*libido*), wastefulness (*luxuria*), greed (*avaritia*), and cruelty (*crudelitas*).

44. Josephus is given accommodation in Vespasian's house, which the latter lived in before becoming ruler. At the same time, he is given Roman civil rights as well as financial support (Josephus, *Vita* 423).

45. Josephus was later granted protection also by Titus and likewise Domitian (Josephus, *Vita* 428–29).

46. The first five of these fourteen years appear indeed to have been "golden" years, i.e., good ones. These were the years 54–59 CE, while the young Nero is still being guided by his mother and counselors, his educator and teacher Seneca, as well as his Pretorian prefect Afranius Burrus. The murder of his mother puts an end to this so-called *quinquennium Neronis*, for according to Tacitus it "disinhibited" him (*Ann.* 14.13.2; cf. also Katharina Ackenheil, "'Goldene Zeiten'—Neros Herrschaftsantritt und die ersten Regierungsjahre," in *Nero: Kaiser, Künstler und Tyrann*, 34–43; Alexander Bätz, "Nero—eine Bilanz," in *Nero: Kaiser, Künstler und Tyrann*, 390–99, esp. 394).

BIBLIOGRAPHY

Ackenheil, Katharina. "'Goldene Zeiten'—Neros Herrschaftsantritt und die ersten Regierungsjahre." In *Nero: Kaiser, Künstler und Tyrann*, edited by Jürgen Merten, 43–43. Darmstadt: Konrad Theiss Verlag, 2016.

Alexandridis, Annetta. "Frauen um Nero—Ehefrauen und Geliebte." In *Nero: Kaiser, Künstler und Tyrann*, edited by Jürgen Merten, 64–73. Darmstadt: Konrad Theiss Verlag, 2016.

Bätz, Alexander. "Nero—eine Bilanz." In *Nero: Kaiser, Künstler und Tyrann*, edited by Jürgen Merten, 390–99. Darmstadt: Konrad Theiss Verlag, 2016.

Bergmann, Claudia D. "We Have Seen the Enemy, and He Is Only a 'She': The Portrayal of Warriors as Women." In *Writing and Reading War: Rhetoric, Gender, and Ethics in Biblical and Modern Contexts*, edited by Brad E. Kelle and Frank Ritchel Ames, 129–42. Leiden: Brill, 2008.

Clarke, John R. *Ars Erotica: Sexualität und ihre Bilder im antiken Rom*. Translated by Jörg Fündling. Darmstadt: Primus Verlag, 2009.

Croom, Alexandra T. *Roman Clothing and Fashion*. Stroud: Tempus, 2002.

Deppmeyer, Korana. "Die Verfehlungen des Künstlers Nero." In *Nero: Kaiser, Künstler und Tyrann*, edited by Jürgen Merten, 210–16. Darmstadt: Konrad Theiss Verlag, 2016.

Dio Cassius. *Roman History, Volume VIII: Books 61–70*. Translated by Earnest Cary, Herbert B. Foster. Loeb Classical Library 176. Cambridge, MA: Harvard University Press, 1925.

Frontinus. *Stratagems. Aqueducts of Rome*. Edited by Mary B. McElwain. Translated by C. E. Bennett. Loeb Classical Library 174. Cambridge, MA: Harvard University Press, 1925.

Josephus. *De bello Judaico—Der jüdische Krieg: Griechisch und Deutsch*. 3 vols. in four parts. Edited, introduced, and provided with notes by Otto Michel and Otto Bauernfeind. Different editions. Darmstadt: WBG, 1963–1982.

———. *Jewish Antiquities, Volume I: Books 1–3*. Translated by H. St. J. Thackeray. Loeb Classical Library 242. Cambridge, MA: Harvard University Press, 1930.

———. *Jewish Antiquities, Volume VIII: Books 18–19*. Translated by Louis H. Feldman. Loeb Classical Library 433. Cambridge, MA: Harvard University Press, 1965.

———. *Jewish Antiquities, Volume IX: Book 20*. Translated by Louis H. Feldman. Loeb Classical Library 456. Cambridge, MA: Harvard University Press, 1965.

———. *The Jewish War, Volume I: Books 1–2*. Translated by H. St. J. Thackeray. Loeb Classical Library 203. Cambridge, MA: Harvard University Press, 1927.

———. *The Jewish War, Volume II: Books 3–4*. Translated by H. St. J. Thackeray. Loeb Classical Library 487. Cambridge, MA: Harvard University Press, 1927.

———. *The Jewish War, Volume III: Books 5–7*. Translated by H. St. J. Thackeray. Loeb Classical Library 210. Cambridge, MA: Harvard University Press, 1928.

———. *The Life. Against Apion*. Translated by H. St. J. Thackeray. Loeb Classical Library 186. Cambridge, MA: Harvard University Press, 1926.

Merten, Jürgen. *Nero: Kaiser, Künstler und Tyrann*. Darmstadt: Konrad Theiss Verlag, 2016.

Meyer-Zwiffelhoffer, Eckhard. *Im Zeichen des Phallus: Die Ordnung des Geschlechtslebens im antiken Rom*. Frankfurt a.M.: Campus Verlag, 1995.

New English Translation—Novum Testamentum Graece: New Testament. English text and notes: The NET Bible®. Text and notes edited by Michael H. Burer, W. Hall Harris III, and Daniel B. Wallace. Greek text and critical apparatus: Nestle-Aland, Novum Testamentum Graece, 27th edition. Stuttgart: Deutsche Bibelgesellschaft; Dallas: Net Bible Press, 2004.

The New Oxford Annotated Bible with the Apocryphal/Deuterocanonical Books: New Revised Standard Version. Edited by Bruce M. Metzger and Roland E. Murphy. New York: Oxford University Press, 1994.

Panella, Clementina. "Nero und der große Brand von Rom im Jahre 64." In *Nero: Kaiser, Künstler und Tyrann*, edited by Jürgen Merten, 241–49. Darmstadt: Konrad Theiss Verlag, 2016.

Philo. *Every Good Man is Free. On the Contemplative Life. On the Eternity of the World. Against Flaccus. Apology for the Jews. On Providence*. Translated by F. H. Colson. Loeb Classical Library 363. Cambridge, MA: Harvard University Press, 1941.

———. *On the Decalogue. On the Special Laws, Books 1–3*. Translated by F. H. Colson. Loeb Classical Library 320. Cambridge, MA: Harvard University Press, 1937.

Polyaenus. *Strategems of War*. 2 vols. Edited and translated by Peter Krentz and Everett L. Wheeler. Chicago: Ares, 1994.

Quintilian. *The Orator's Education, Volume III: Books 6–8*. Edited and translated by Donald A. Russell. Loeb Classical Library 126. Cambridge, MA: Harvard University Press, 2002.

Rengstorf, Karl Heinrich, ed., in cooperation with Erwin Buck, Eberhard Güting, Bernhard Justus, George W.E. Nickelsburg, Heinz Schreckenberg, Jürgen Schwark, and William L. Weiler. *A Complete Concordance to Flavius Josephus: Study Edition*. 2 vols. Leiden: Brill, 2002.

Rueter, Marcus. "Wer war Nero? Versuch einer Annäherung." In *Nero: Kaiser, Künstler und Tyrann*, edited by Jürgen Merten, 12–21. Darmstadt: Konrad Theiss Verlag, 2016.

Schmuhl, Yvonne. "Neros Mord an seiner Mutter Agrippina." In *Nero: Kaiser, Künstler und Tyrann*, edited by Jürgen Merten, 228–34. Darmstadt: Konrad Theiss Verlag, 2016.

Suetonius. *Lives of the Caesars, Volume II: Claudius. Nero. Galba, Otho, and Vitellius. Vespasian. Titus, Domitian. Lives of Illustrious Men: Grammarians and Rhetoricians. Poets (Terence. Virgil. Horace. Tibullus. Persius. Lucan). Lives of Pliny the Elder and Passienus Crispus*. Translated by J. C. Rolfe. Loeb Classical Library 38. Cambridge, MA: Harvard University Press, 1914.

Tacitus. *Histories: Books 4–5. Annals: Books 1–3*. Translated by Clifford H. Moore, John Jackson. Loeb Classical Library 249. Cambridge, MA: Harvard University Press, 1931.

Chapter Twelve

Female Officiants in Second-Temple Judaism[1]

Angela Standhartinger

In antiquity λειτουρία (from λαός, people and ἔργον, work) "signified a 'benefit/service for the people,' especially a benefit for the state or a part of the state, which was provided by rich citizens from their own means."[2] There is ample evidence for female liturgical officiants of this kind from Hellenistic and Roman times. They served their cities and groups by financing public buildings, military expense, games, and banquets.[3] Sometimes they also acted as priestesses, founding and renovating sanctuaries or covering the costs of festivals. The LXX adopts λειτουρία for the cult service at the Temple in Jerusalem.[4] In Byzantine Christianity the term designates "patterns of communal worship" celebrated in a given church.[5] This paper asks what we can learn about women serving publicly in cultic settings from Jewish texts. After an overview on woman's religious practices in the Greco-Roman and late antique Christian world I will turn to the Therapeutrides in *De vita contemplative* and Job's Daughters in the Testament of Job.

1. FEMALE OFFICIANTS IN GREEK AND ROMAN RELIGIONS

Women's religious activities in Greek and Roman antiquity have been almost ignored for many decades. With philosophers from Plato and Xenophon to the Church fathers, many interpreters took for granted that women in antiquity had been confined to their homes under the guardianship of their fathers, husbands, and masters. In silence they remained invisible to outsiders. Only recently some scholars notice that this is half of the story. The other half is religion. Euripides has the Melanippe say:

And in divine affairs—I think this is the first and importance—we have the greatest part. For at oracles of Phoebus women expound Apollo's will. And the holy seat of Dodona by the sacred oak the female race conveys the thoughts of Zeus to all Greeks who desire it. As for the holy rituals performed for the Fates and the nameless goddesses, these are not holy in men's hands, but among women they flourish, every one of them. Thus in holy service woman play the righteous role.[6]

Material evidence, artefacts, images, inscriptions, and alike, all document women serving their Gods in manifold ways.[7] They act as priestesses, lead processions, offer prayers, preside in sacrifices, pour out libations, decorate statues, preside over cultic meals, and perform many other religious activities. As Melanippe states in Euripides' play: to approach a given God successfully —not only a female deity but also male ones—women are indispensable. In fact, it is in the area of religion that at least some Greek and Roman women exercised agency in public life.

This obvious tension between moral discourse and religion lets us rethink the binary models private-public, male and female, that have guided scholarship for long. Cult practice not only affects women's agency on their own live but also require them to act for the salvation of their whole communities. This was also noticed not at least by the famous Jewish first-century author Philo of Alexandria. In his explanations of the Jewish laws, Philo claims: "The women are best suited to the indoor life which never strays from the house"[8] Yet religion is the exemption of this rule:

> A woman, then, should not be a busybody, meddling with matters outside her household concerns, but should seek a life of seclusion. . . . except when she has to go to the temple, . . . (to) make her oblations and offer her prayers to avert the evil and gain the good.[9]

The reference to a (Jewish?) temple (ἱερόν) at Alexandria and offering of sacrifices (θυσίας ἐπιτελεῖν) is striking. Either Philo uses cultic language metaphorically or he adopts "the language of Gentile communal worship."[10] In any case, he has to accept that women's religious agency affects the well-being of the given community and thereby public life.

Not only single women act as priestesses and liturgical officiants; groups of women also contribute to sacred rites. One example comes from the geographer Pausanias (115–180 CE) in his description of the cult of Eileithyias in Elis:

> At the foot of Mount Cronius, [. . .] is a sanctuary of Eileithyia, and in it Sosipolis, a native Elean deity, is worshipped. Now they surname Eileithyia Olympian, and choose a priestess for the goddess every year. The old woman who tends

Sosipolis herself too by an Elean custom lives in chastity, bringing water for the god's bath and setting before him barley cakes kneaded with honey. In the front part of the temple, for it is built in two parts, is an altar of Eileithyia and an entrance for the public; in the inner part Sosipolis is worshipped, and no one may enter it except the woman who tends the god, and she must wrap her head and face in a white veil. Maidens (παρθένοι) and matrons (γυναῖκες) wait in the sanctuary of Eileithyia chanting a hymn; they burn all manner of incense to the god, but it is not the custom to pour libations of wine. An oath is taken by Sosipolis on the most important occasions.[11]

At the sanctuary of the Olympian Eileithyia serves a professional priestess who alone is allowed to enter the inner cell with the cult statue of Sosipolis, "savior of the city." Pausanias has heard (λέγεται) the cult legend telling about a woman who was sent by a dream to save her city with her baby.[12] When the professional priest enters the inner cell, other women attract the gods by singing and burning incense. Pausanias does not give the hymns to Eileithyia and Sosipolis, perhaps because he was not allowed to listen to it. Plutarch cites a women's cultic song from the same region: "Come, O hero Dionysus, To thy Elean holy Temple, with the Graces, To thy temple with thy bull's foot hasting." As a refrain, the women chant twice "O worthy bull."[13] This hymn seems to represent a feature from the Dionysus myth. Yet when Plutarch tries to place this into his own knowledge of the myth, he puzzles with the song's meaning. Some divinities had ceremonies for women alone. This made them more mysterious to men.[14] While exclusion sometimes led to suspect and scandalization, Plutarch and Pausanias respect women's essential ritual work.[15] As Deborah Lyons puts it: "the recurring silence at the heart of these texts highlights the ritual knowledge and competence of women."[16]

The majority of priestesses in Greece, professionals as well as temporarily elected, came from the cities' elites.[17] In Rome, all "women were vital participants in the religious lives of their families and of their communities." However, whether a women was married or not, freeborn, freed, or slave, what family she came from and how she behaved privately "determined what religious offices were open to her . . . and what rites or cults she might attend."[18] One might therefore argue that the religious sphere reinforced societies' social distinctions. Yet this did not fully determine its meaning for its participants. In both Greek and Roman religious rituals, choral singing was sometimes acted out by virgins or younger girls (παρθένοι) and/or married women (γυναῖκες).[19] Some interpreters explained the segmentation of women into age- and/or marriage-status groups as age and class imitation for girls.[20] Others find the initiation paradigm imposed. For them ritual practice is "the primary arena" in which women stage "various negotiations between 'ideology' and agency.'"[21] And while groups of female singers might sometimes reinforce gender roles and ideology through the script and laws of the ritual, the performers have to stage their own identity through performance. First and foremost, singing and dancing in context of religious festivals aims to honor and delight a deity. Or, to say it with the words of Eva Stele:

> So far as the evidence goes, it indicates that women performing communal poetry combined the function of providing reflection and model with a staging of their own subordinate status in the community. Yet they did perform. Their self-presentation could not be wholly discredited without jeopardizing the communal function they filled, and they themselves could undermine their words by irony or mocking exaggeration. Dancing is a sensuous activity. Performers cannot in the nature of the event be inhibited from projecting their subjectivity through inflection and body language. The demand that women affirm in their own persons the dominant culture's self-contradictory meaning of the sign "female" gave women a psychological power that they could always try to reclaim.[22]

In the following, I will trace some Jewish religious practitioners, namely two female groups of hymn singers. But first, let's look briefly at the evidence from the emerging Christian movement.

2. FEMALE LITURGICAL OFFICIANTS IN EARLY CHRISTIANITY

While the majority of New Testament authors do not call themselves Christian, it is worth noting that most of their writings do not postulate gender segregation during worship services. Paul might argue for veiled and unveiled heads or a gender-specific hairstyle, yet there is no doubt that all genders pray and prophesy in Corinth according to 1 Cor 11:2–16. Therefore, most interpreters argue today that women and men contributed equally to the worship liturgy by "a hymn, a lesson, a revelation, a tongue, or an interpretation" (1 Cor 14:26).[23] Likewise, Nympha and the community at her house at Laodicea will "teach and admonish" one another "with psalms, hymns, and spiritual songs."[24]

Separate groups of female hymnodists and musicians appear in the writings of Clement of Alexandria. When he compares worship of his group to the festivals of the god Dionysus:

> The righteous form this company, and their song is a hymn in praise of the King of all. The maidens (αἱ κόραι) play the harp (ψάλλω), angels give glory, prophets speak, a noise of music rises; swiftly they pursue the sacred band (θίασος), those who have been called hasting with eager longing to receive the Father.[25]

This sacred *thiasos* is a gender-mixed group accompanied by angels, with special roles for unmarried girls and prophets. Similarly, Methodius of Olympus has one of the participants of his literary symposium, the virgin Agathe say: "I have become the torch-bearer of the unapproachable lights, and I join with their company in the new song of the archangels showing forth the new grace of the Church."[26] From third-century Antioch we hear of female psalm-singers (ψαλμῳδεῖν γυναῖκα) "in the middle of the church on the great day of the Pascha."[27] However, this notice is part of the indictment of Paul of Samosata. He might be rebuked for public female singing, or for training women to sing hymns to himself, or both. Indeed, women's public singing was banned in later centuries in some quarters of the emerging church.

In Syria, however, women's liturgical choirs became prominent from the fourth century onward. Their task was to perform metrical hymns called *madrashe* publicly during services in the churches.[28] The anonymous *Vita Ephraemi* describes this as follow:

> [Blessed Ephrem] established and arranged the Daughters of the covenant in opposition to the diversions and popular movements of the deceivers [the Bardaisanites]. He taught them metrical hymns (*madrashe*) and songs (*sblatha*) and antiphons (*'onitha*) [. . .]. Every day the Daughters of the Covenant gathered in the churches on feasts of the Lord and on Sundays and for the celebration of the martyrs.[29]

With *madrashe*, female voices present doctrinal instruction to the larger Christian community.[30] Their songs perform biblical stories in a lively, dramatic way, for instance, expanding them with imagined speeches and dialogues between Sarah and Abraham, Mary and the archangel Gabriel, or the so-called Sinful Women with Satan.[31] According to Jakob of Seruq, Ephraem introduced these women's choirs to counter seductive hymns of the heretics.[32] This theses sounds apologetic.[33] It is a reaction, as Susan Ashbrook Harvey has shown, to the emerging critic to public female singing elsewhere.[34]

3. FEMALE LITURGICAL OFFICIANTS IN JEWISH TEXTS

The Bible does not exclude women from the temple. Hannah prays at the temple at Shiloh and her New Testament counterpart, the widowed prophetess Hannah, stays at the Temple in Jerusalem.[35] First Chronicles mentions among the temple singers three daughters of Heman who play "cymbals, harps, and lyres for the service of the house of God."[36] Twice mentioned are women who serve at the entrance to the tent of meeting.[37] A special women's court at the Jerusalem temple is mentioned for the first time by Josephus and therefore might belong to Herodes' rebuilding of Second Temple in the first century CE.[38]

The Bible also alludes to women dancing choral dances outside the city wall.[39] From a Greek perspective one is reminded of the maenads in the *thiasos* of Dionysus. And indeed, women perform choral dances with olive crowns on their head and the *thyros* in their hands in the book of Judith.[40] Another group of female cultic dancers are the Therapeutrides to whom I will turn now.

3.1 The Therapeutrides

In *De vita contemplativa* Philo of Alexandria portrays a community of male and female philosophers called *Therapeutae* and *Therapeutrides*.[41] In the first part of this writing he describes their settlement, their ascetic life with allegorical studies, and their noticeable gender segregation community meeting on the seventh day.[42] The second part presents a detailed description of their festal meal and subsequent an all-night vigil at every fiftieth day. When the celebration reaches its climax, the gender segregation is completely reversed.

At the outset, the festival starts as typical Greco-Roman symposium. Yet, the Therapeutae's and Therapeutrides' banquet surpasses all other symposia ever held among Greeks and Romans by modesty and the cultivation of its participants.[43] The followers of the "the truly sacred instruction of the prophet Moses" gather in white robes to recline, after their initial praying, on plank beds without any luxury.[44] Women recline beside men, yet among themselves on the left side of the room.[45] The ascetic meal consists of water, bread, salt, and—at least for some—hyssop.[46] The banqueters are entertained by the president's lecture on questions arising from Holy Scriptures and allegorical interpretation to which they listen silently.

With the libation between eating and drinking, all formal banquets contain some religious rites as well as many religious festivals include festive meals.[47] The Therapeutrae's and Therapeutrides' symposium reveals its religious character gradually. The president's talk resembles Philo's own accounts of Jewish synagogue worship elsewhere in his writings. Here as there, people come together to listen "quietly"[48] to the lecture by one of special experience who instructs them in the philosophy of their fathers.[49] Moreover, food and participants are compared to cultic practice elsewhere. The female participants "have kept their chastity not under compulsion, like some of the Greek priestesses, but of their own free will in their ardent yearning for wisdom."[50] "Abstinence from wine is enjoined by right reason as for the priest when sacrificing."[51] And the table is filled with "the truly purified meal of leavened bread seasoned with salt mixed with hyssop, out of reverence for the holy table enshrined in the sacred vestibule of the temple."[52] On the table in the Jerusalem temple, of course, lie unleavened loaves and salt without condiments.[53] The Therapeutrides and their male companions surpass other priesthoods and, at the same time, remodel them and finally respect at a certain distance to an alluded cult in the Jerusalem temple.

As in many ancient symposia the banqueters chant and listen to hymns.[54] Philo highlights the religious character of the Therapeutae's singing.

> Then the President rises and sings a hymn composed as an address to God, either a new one of his own composition or an old one by poets of an earlier day who have left behind them hymns in many measures and melodies, hexameters (ἔπος) and iambics (τρίμετρος), lyrics suitable for processions (προσόδιον ὕμνος) or in libations (παρασπόνδειος) and at the altars (παραβώμιος), or for the chorus whilst standing (στάσιμος) or dancing (χορικός), with careful metrical arrangements to fit the various evolutions (στροφαῖς πολυστρόφοις εὖ διαμεμετρημένος). After him all the others take their turn as they are arranged and in the proper order while all the rest listen in complete silence except when they have to chant the closing lines or refrains (ἀκροτελεύτια καὶ ἐφύμνια), for then they all lift up their voices, men and women alike.[55]

As Peter Jeffery has shown, three of the names are suggestive of pagan rituals. A προσόδιον ὕμνος is a processional hymn sung while approaching an altar for sacrifice.[56] A παρασπόνδειος is a song at or for a libation. A παραβώμιος is a hymn sung at the altar. The other genres are reminiscent of the Greek drama. Iambic lines or τρίμετρος are "often used in Greek drama for the dialogue or recitative between the solo and choral songs."[57] The στάσιμος was sung by the chorus in Greek while dancing. Dancing is also implied by the terms χορικός, "for a choral dance," and στροφή, the turning of a chorus. Yet, at least in classical time, Greek dramas were themselves cult occasions and, as recent interpreters have shown, there is "a specific intersection of drama with women's rituals."[58] Philo, who proofs competence on the theoretical and cultural aspects of music elsewhere, would not have chosen the various musical genres without intention.[59] Here, however, women and men participate alike in active roles by chanting one after the other their hymns and closing lines refrains.

Finally, the symposium of the Therapeutae and Therapeutrides culminates in "honorable drunkenness" and bacchantic enthusiasm[60]—and indeed, in the "sacred vigil," which, as the word παννυχίς suggests, has orgiastic features.[61]

> They rise up all together and standing in the middle of the refectory form themselves first into two choirs, one of men and one of women, the leader and precentor chosen for each being the most honored amongst them and also the most musical. Then they sing hymns to God composed of many measures and

set to many melodies, sometimes chanting together, sometimes taking up the harmony antiphonally, hands and feet keeping time in accompaniment, and rapt with enthusiasm reproduce sometimes the lyrics of the procession (προσόδια) sometimes of the halt (στάσιμα) and of the wheeling and counter-wheeling of a choric dance (στροφάς τε τὰς ἐν χορείᾳ καὶ ἀντιστροφὰς ποιούμενοι). Then when each choir has separately done its own part in the feast, having drunk as in the Bacchic rites of the strong wine of God's love they mix and both together become a single choir, a copy of the choir set up of old beside the Red Sea in honor of the wonders there wrought.[62]

In a musical dimension, this "rapt enthusiasm" is reflected by the reversed order of *strophe, anastrophe*, and *stasimon* of the classical Greek drama.[63] Yet, the myth staged at the Therapeutic all-night-vigil is Israel's exodus from Egypt. As a cultic drama the festival becomes an imitation (μίμημα) of this decisive moment in Israel's history with God. With their singing and dancing, the Therapeutae and Therapeutrides "represent" (ἀπεικονίζειν) the choir with Moses and Miriam at the Red Sea.[64] A women's chorus lead by Miriam is already included in the Exodus account (Eoxd 15:20–21). The mixing of the two choirs at the Red Sea is an exegetical tradition mentioned by Philo several times.[65] The Dead Sea Scrolls preserved an extended version of Miriam's song.[66] This raises the question as to how far Philo's depiction of the Therapeutrides reflect an actual cultic practice among Jewish women in the first century.[67]

Philo places the most important settlement of the group at Lake Mareotis not far away from Alexandria.[68] However, at times Philo's imaginal description of the group's ascetic practice sounds throughout idealized and strikingly resemble a group of Egyptian priests represented by the contemporary Stoic philosopher Chaeremon.[69] Therefore, some scholars doubt the existence of the group while other reconstruct a sect of Jewish philosophers.[70] In my view, *De vita contemplative* is an ethnography of Judaism in the guise of an Egyptian sect.[71] Indeed, this "race" (γένος) that "exists in many places in the inhabited world" reveals itself only progressively as Jewish.[72] Yet, while its members remain as citizens of Heaven beyond this world, they nonetheless reflect some actual Jewish religious practice. Therefore, the Therapeutrides' religious practice of dramatic reenactment of Israel's deliverance from Egypt as well as women's choirs chanting with Miriam at the Red Sea are, in my view, hardly only a fictive imagination.

3.2 Job's Daughters

My second example for Jewish female liturgical officiants comes from the Testament of Job, Job's farewell at the end of his life before his sons and daughters. T.Job is preserved in four Greek, one Coptic, and at least nine Slavonic manuscripts.[73] Dating ranges between first century BCE and second century CE. As it is typical in this testament genre, Job recapitulates his life and gives some advice to his children.[74] In addition to the biblical *Vorlage*, Job is informed by an inaugural vision that after destroying the temple of the idols, he will fight against Satan, but if he manages to resist, all he loses will be restored. The voice from the light says: "[Y]ou will be like a sparring athlete, both enduring pains and winning the crown."[75] One theme of the book is endurance and patience in the attacks of Satan, who appears throughout the story as a quick-change artist.[76] In the role of a beggar, he fools Job's doormaid (T.Job 6–7); in the guise of a bread seller he disguises Job's wife Sitis/sidotis (24–25) until he finally unmasks himself as Job's last friend Elihu (41–42).[77] These are not the only humoristic features of the story.[78] Job's philanthropic benefactions to strangers, widows, orphans, and slaves are extraordinary.[79] After the daily feeding of the widows, he reminds them to glorify God and accompanies their chanting by playing the lyre.[80] Many passages of T.Job are given in exalted prose and, like the chorus in the classical drama, summarize information or add comments.[81] Exactly at this passage manuscripts and translations differ. Presumably T.Job was actually performed by some of its readers.[82]

The most important part for our question follows at the end. In contradiction to the biblical *Vorlage*, Job distributes his recovered estate among his sons alone.[83] His daughters, named in common with the LXX Hemera (Day), Kasia (Cinnamon), and Amaltheias-Keras (horn of plenty)[84] complain: "(A) re we not also your children" (T.Job 46:2). Job, however, promises to them a better inheritance, hidden in three golden boxes.

> [7]And he (Job) opened them and brought out three multicolored cords (χορδή) whose appearance was such[8] as no one could describe, since they were not from earth but from heaven, shimmering with fiery sparks like the rays of the sun. [9]And he gave each one (of his daughters) a cord, saying: "Place these about your breast, so it may go well with you all the days of your life." (T.Job 46:7–9)

The daughters' inherence consists of three cords of obviously heavenly origin which they are going to wrap around their breast. Similar girds, or belts, are worn by angles and heavenly messengers elsewhere.[85] However, the Greek word for this cord, or belt, χορδή is unique. Its normal meaning would be "that which is make from guts," for instance, strings of a harp or a lyre. This detail might be a first hint to the cord's function as a musical instrument. But the cords are multifunctional, fulfilling at least five tasks.[86] Job explains: "Not only shall you gain a living from these, but these cords will lead you into a better world, to live in the heavens." (T.Job 47:3). Additionally, the cords or, as they were called sometimes, bands (σπάρτη), are an efficacious remedy to cure equally body and soul. Job recalls that they had been given to him, as God said "gird your loins like a man" (Job 38:3; 40:2). Suddenly, worms and plagues disappeared from Job's body and he forgot the pains of his heart (T.Job 47:6). Furthermore, the cords are a protective amulet, or *phylacterion* (φυλακτήριον).[87] With these cords, Hemera, Kasia, and Amaltheias-Keras will no longer face the enemy nor have to worry of him in their mind (47:10–11). Finally, the cords mediate visions of the heavenly reality (47:11; cf. 52:1–10).

The cords actually have transformative power. When the first daughter girds herself:

> ²She took another heart—no longer minded toward earthly things—³but she spoke ecstatically in the angelic dialect, sending up a hymn to God in accord with the hymnic style of the angles (κατὰ τὴν τῶν ἀγγέλων ὑμνολογίαν). ⁴And she spoke ecstatically, she allowed "the Spirit" to be inscribed on her garment.[88]

Similarly, when Kasia girded herself, she

> ¹. . . had her heart changed so that she no longer regarded worldly things. ²And her mouth took on the dialect of the archons and she praises God for the creation of the heights. ³So, if anyone wishes to know "the Creation of the Heavens" she or he will be able to find it in "The Hymns of Kasia."[89]

At last, Amaltheias Keras girds hersel, and her

> mouth spoke ecstatically in the dialect of those of high ² since her heart also was changed, keeping aloof from worldy from worldly things. For she spoke in the dialect of the cherubim, glorfying the Master of virtues by exhibiting their splendor. And finally whoever wishes to grasp a trace of "The Paternal Splendor" will find it written down in the "Prayers of Amaltheia's Horn."

The three girded daughters guide us through classes of angels, their languages, and the transmission of heavenly knowledge.[90] It remains open if the narrator envisions the daughters in the middle of the angelic worship in Heaven, as mediators between earthly devotees and Heaven, or if the daughter's hymns mirror the heavenly worship on earth. Either way, in the Greek and Coptic version there is also an interest to keep their songs in writing form in order to transmit them to posterity. Indeed, the daughters act as theologians, are guided by the spirit, praise the creation, and glorify the master of the virtues. Transmission of the songs by writing is, however, eradicated from the Slavonic version. Mysterious hymns authored or transmitted by women became increasingly suspect and provocative in some quarters of the later church.

In the last scene of the book, the three daughters escort Job's soul into heaven with their music. This time Herma plays the lyre (κιθάρα), Kasia holds the censer (θυμιατήριον), and Amaltheia Kera beats the kettle drum (τύμπανον).[91] Unseen by bystanders they welcome the heavenly chariot that came down to carry Job's soul back home into Heaven. Lyre and censer belong to the temple cult.[92] The kettle drum is an instrument played by women in the Bible.[93] Later, they lead the funeral procession for Job's body.

Equipped with their cords, the three daughters Herma, Kasia, and Amaltheia Kera are transformed into liturgical officiants. Such as in many other ancient religions, their cultic practice leads to ecstatic transformation. As religious professionals they enact knowledge of the heavenly hosts and their dialects, theological expertise, hymns, and cultic music that helps welcome heavenly beings among their worshipers, and they lead processions into heaven and on earth alike.

Caused by the strikingly different images of the five women represented in T.Job, feminist evaluation of T.Job has led to diverging conclusions.[94] Most scholars detect two negative characters, the disobedient doormaid and the betrayed wife Sitidos and the positive group of the three daughters. Some ascribe this opposing characterisation to two authors.[95] Others argue that while the writing uses enslaved and married female characters only as a foil to enhance through negative contrast Job's virtue and spiritual knowledge, it values virginity in high esteem because it transforms women into nonsexual transgendered men.[96] However, nowhere in T.Job does the marriage status of Hemera, Kasia, and Amaltheias-Keras becomes explicit. Moreover, Nancy Klancher has argued that all five female characters reflect Job's challenges and conflicts on his spiritual path.[97] The kind-hearted doormaid who offers bread to the beggar accords perfectly with Job's action in other passages. Likewise, Sitidos's selling of her hair to feed Job is an act of remarkable generosity. Both characters "mirror the former Job, Job before his enlightenment by the angel" in his initial vision.[98] Yet, Sitidos' character develops and she is finally rewarded by an eternal memorial with the Lord (T.Job 40:3–4). The daughters represent the healed and transformed Job. "However, the state into which they are ushered is not manhood as opposed to womenhood, but monotheistic inheritance, protection from Satan, prophetic ecstasy, and praise and glorification of the creator God, and "Master of Virtues.""[99]

Literary readings deny any possibility to draw conclusions from literature to realities behind a given text. Rightly so, since direct mirror readings from texts to groups in which texts might have originated and transmitted tend to become circular.[100] However, texts exist not beyond a social reality experienced by their authors and readers. As I have shown above, in all ancient religions women act as spiritual leaders in manifold ways. Therefore, it is not coincidental when Hermera, Kasia, and Amaltheia-Kera likewise lead processions, welcome heavenly guests, and channel prayers between this world and another. It is not extraordinary when they act vicariously on behalf of men and women, nor that parts of their ritual acts remain unseen and unheard by outsiders. They just act, as many of their Greek and Roman sisters, in a cultic setting that demands women's religious performance. Job's daughters should therefore no longer be seen as extraordinary nor merely as purely fiction. They are just to be placed within the context of women's religious leadership in antiquity.[101]

4. CONCLUSION

I hope to have made the existence of Jewish liturgical officiant plausible. While Philo's Therapeutrides and Job's Daughters remain literary figures, their cultic roles are by no means exceptional nor historically implausible in antiquity. Hymn singers and dancers who reenact parts of the central myth of a given religion are many among their Greek and Roman sisters. Likewise, women as actors of the exodus story, as participants and witnesses to the heavenly cult, and as leaders of religious processions must have existed also in ancient Judaism. Some of their religious rites might have found their way to some quarters of the later Christian church, while at the same time become re-dramatized by readers of *Contempl.* and T.Job among Jews and Christians alike. "Performers cannot in the nature of the event be inhibited from projecting their subjectivity through inflection and body language."[102] That is, some Jewish women throughout history acted as liturgical officiants in some ways or others, yet either way claimed publicly their agency to worship of their God.

NOTES

1. Parts of this paper are also published in my article "Performing Salvation: The Therapeutrides and Job's Daughters in Context" in *Remaking the World: Christianity and Categories, Essays in Honor of Karen L. King,* WUNT 434, ed. Taylor G. Petrey, 173–96 (Tübingen: Mohr Siebeck, 2019).

2. Peter J. Rhodes, "Liturgy I Political," *Brill's New Pauly online* http://dx.doi.org/10.1163/1574-9347_bnp_e707770 (18. February 2018). Cf. Karl Leo Noethlichs, "Liturgie I," *RAC* 23: 208–90.

3. Anne Bielman, "Female Patronage in the Greek Hellenistic and Roman Republican Periods" in *A Companion to Women in the Ancient World,* eds. Sharon L. James and Sheila Dillon (Chichester: Blackwell Publishing Ltd, 2012), 238–48.

4. Exod 37:17; Num 8:22; 16:9; 2 Chron 31:2 et al., Cf: Lk 1:23; Hebr 9:21. Diodorus Siculus, *Bibliotheca* 1.21.7 proves that λειτουργία is connected to θεραπεία τῶν θεῶν (worship of the Gods) also in the pagan world.

5. Alexander Lingas, "Liturgy, Byzantine," in *The Encyclopedia of Ancient History* VIII: 4116.

6. Euripides, *The Captive Melanippe* Fragment 494 (P. Berlin 2772). Translation Helen Foley, see: Joan B. Connelly, "Priestesses—Women in Cult. In Divne Affairs—the Greatest Part: Women and Priesthoods in Classical Athens" in *Worshiping Women. Ritual and Reality in Classical Athens*, eds. Nikolaos Kaltsas and Alan Shapiro (New York: Alexander S. Onassis Public Benefit Foundation, 2008), 186.

7. For Greece: Eva M. Stehle, "Women and Religion in Greece," in *A Companion to Women in the Ancient World*, eds. Sharon L. James and Sheila Dillon (Chichester: Blackwell Publishing, 2012), 191–203. Connelly, *Portrait of a Priestess. Women and Ritual in Ancient Greece* (Princeton: Princeton University Press, 2007). Barbara Goff, *Citizen Bacchae: Women's Ritual Practice in Ancient Greece* (Berkeley: University of California Press, 2004); Matthew Dillon, *Girls and Women in Classical Greek Religion* (London: Routledge, 2002). For Rome: Lora L. Holland, "Women and Roman Religion," in *A Companion to Women in the Ancient World*, eds. Sharon L. James and Sheila Dillon (Chichester: Blackwell, 2012), 204–14.

8. Philo, *Spec.* 3.169. Translation: F. H. Colson, LCL.

9. Philo, *Spec.* 3.171.

10. Shelly Matthews, *First Converts. Rich Pagan Women and the Rhetoric of Mission in Early Judaism and Christianity* (Stanford: Stanford University Press, 2001), 85. Cf. F.H. Colson, *Philo in Ten Volumes VII* (Cambridge: Harvard University Press, 1984), 640. He might also refer to a popular handbook of common morality as it is documented by the tractate of the Phintys who likewise states: "Women of importance leave the house to sacrifice (θυηπολεῖν) to the leading divinity of the community on behalf of themselves and their husbands and their households." (Thesleff 154,1f.).

11. Pausanias, *Descr.* 6.20,3. Translation Wiliam Jones, LCL.

12. Pausanias reports also an etiology for the cult. Informed by a dream a woman placed her baby in front of the army that tried to defend her hometown. When the enemies approached the baby turned into a snake and put them to flight (*Descr.* 6.20,4–5).

13. Plutarch, *Quest. Rom.* 36 (*mor.* 299A/B).

14. Rules of participation and gender politics differ from cult to cult. Cf. Susan G. Cole, *Landscapes, Gender, and Ritual Space: The Ancient Greek Experience* (Berkeley: California University Press, 2004), 92–104.

15. Others look for scandals, see: Deborah J. Lyons, "The Scandal of Women's Ritual," in *Finding Persephone: Women's Rituals in the Ancient Mediterranean*, eds. Maryline Parca and Angeliki Tzanetou (Bloomington: Indiana University Press, 2007), 28–51.

16. Lyons, "What the Women Know," in *Women's Ritual Competence in the Greco-Roman Mediterranean*, eds. Matthew Dillon, Esther Eidinow, and Lisa Maurizio (London: Routledge, 2016), 236.

17. In Greece, some priesthoods were held by inheritance, others were sold among the elite families. Cf. Connelly, "Priestesses," 189–90; *Portrait*, 44–55. Connelly compares Greek and Helleistic priestesses with women leaders of ancient synagogues as well as with Christian female officeholder, two groups that are mostly documented through inscriptions (cf. *Portrait*, 259–73). For female priesthood in Rome, cf. Emily A. Hemelrijk, "Women and Sacrifice in the Roman Empire," in *Ritual Dynamics and Religious Change in the Roman Empire*, eds. Olivier Hekster, Sebastian Schmidt-Hofner, and Christian Witschel (Leiden: Brill, 2009), 253–68.

18. Celia E. Schultz, *Women's Religious Activity in the Roman Republic* (Chapel Hill: University of North Carolina Press, 2006) 149. Eadem "Sanctissima Femina: Social Categorization and Women's Religious Experience in the Roman Republic" in *Finding Persephone. Women's Rituals in the Ancient Mediterranean*, eds. Maryline Parca and Angeliki Tzanetou (Bloomington: Indiana University Press, 2007), 92–113.

19. Cf. Livius 27.37.11–14; Macrobius, *Saturnalia* 1.6.14.

20. Claude Calame, *Choruses of Young Women in Ancient Greece. Their Morphology, Religious Role, and Social Function* (Lanham: Rowman & Littlefield 1997) [French original 1977].

21. Goff, *Citizen Bacchae*, 14.

22. Eva Stehle, *Performance and Gender in Ancient Greece. Nondramatic Poetry in its Setting* (Princeton: University of Princeton Press, 1997), 113.

23. 1 Cor 14:33b–35(6) is a later gloss. Cf- Plutarch, *Conj. praec.* 142C–D.

24. Col 3:16; 4:15. The dancing song in Acts John 95–96 is led by the female personification of *Charis*.

25. Clement of Alexandria, *Protr.* 12,119.2–3. Translation: Georg Butterworth, LCL.

26. Methodius von Olympus, *Symp.* 6,5. Translation: Wiliam A. Clark, ANF.

27. Cf. Eusebius, *Hist. eccl.* 7.30.10.

28. Susan Ashbrook Harvey, "Singing Women's Stories in Syriac Tradition," *IKZ* 100 (2010), 171–89. Eadem, *Song and Memory. Biblical Women in Syriac Tradition* (Milwaukee: Marquette University Press, 2010). Eadem, "Performance as Exegesis. Women's Liturgical Choirs in Syriac Tradition," in *Inquiries into Eastern Christian Worship. Acts of the Second International Congress of the Society of Oriental Liturgy*, eds. Bert J. Groen, Stefanos Alexopoulos and Steven Hawkes-Teeples, Eastern Christian Studies 12 (Leuven: Peeters, 2012), 47–64. The choirs are called "Daughters of the covenant."

29. Quoted from Harvey, "Performance," 49. Ephraem himself refers to these women's choirs in his *Hymnos on Easter* 2.8–9.

30. Cf. from the same *vita*: "[Blessed Ephrem] put in the metrical hymns (*madrashe*) words with subtle connotation and spiritual understanding concerning the birth and baptism and fasting and the entire plan of Christ: the passion and resurrection and ascension, and concerning the martyrs." (Harvey, "Performance," 54).

31. Cf. Harvey, "Singing," 157–88; *Song*, 39–92. Cf. Eadem., "Bearing Witness: New Testament Women in Early Byzantine Hymnography," in *The New Testament in Byzantium*, eds. Derek Krueger and Robert Nelson (Cambridge: Harvard University Press, 2016), 205–19.

32. Harvey, "Singing," 175; *Song*, 35 and 45–46.

33. Harvey, "Performance," 59–60. Kathleen McVey, "Ephrem the Kitharode and Proponent of Women. Jacob of Serug's Portrait of a Fourth-Century Churchman for the Sixth-Century Viewer and its Significance for the Twenty-First Century Ecumenist," in *Orthodox and Wesleyan Ecclesiology*, ed. S. T. Kimbrough (Crestwood: St Vladimirs Seminary, 2007), 229–53.

34. Critic to hymn singing by women is raised by Cyrill von Jerusalem, *Procatechesis* 14 and Isidore of Pelusium (third–fourth century CE), *ep.* 90 (PG 78.224–25). Johannes Quasten, *Musik und Gesang in den Kulten der heidnischen Antike und christlichen Frühzeit*, LQF 25 (Münster: Aschendorff, 1930), 121, argues that women's singing was generally repressed by the so-called mainline Church. However, the evidence is more ambivalent, as Harvey, "Performance" 51–52 proves.

35. 1 Sam 2; Lk 2:26–38.

36. 1 Chr 25:6. The מְצִלְתַּיִם / κύμβαλον, cymbal, is a metal percussion instrument, the כִּנּוֹר/κινύρα is a stringed instrument and the נֶבֶל / νάβλα is musical instrument of ten or twelve strings. All three instruments are mentions several times in the context of the Jerusalem temple cult in Persian and Hellenistic times. See: 1 Chr 13:8; 15:19–21.28; 16:5; 25:1; 2 Chr 5:12; 29:25; Neh 12:27; (inauguration of the city wall); 1 Macc 4:45.

37. Exod 38:8; 1 Sam 2:22.

38. Josephus, *B.J.* 5:198–200; *C. Ap.* 2.102-104. Cf. Susan Grossman, "Women and the Jerusalem Temple," in *Daughters of the King. Women and the Synagogue*, ed. by Rivka Haut (Philadelphia: Jewish Publication Society, 1992), 19–20.

39. Judg 21:21: הָלְחֹם bzw. χορεύειν ἐν τοῖς χοροῖς; cf. Judg 11:34.

40. Jdt 15:12–13.

41. Philo *Contempl.* 1–2. Philo explains their name θεραπευταὶ καὶ θεραπευτρίδες by the double meaning of the word "healer of the soul" and "worshipers of God." The feminine θεραπευτρίς seems to be Philo's own invention, used also in *Somn.* 1.332; 2.273 and *Post.* 184.

42. At the worship meeting on the seventh day in a κοινὸν σεμνεῖον, common sanctuary, women are seated within hearing distance behind a wall, so that "the modesty becoming to the female sex is preserved" (*Contempl.* 33). The lecture room thus described, similar to a synagogue, is the sole example in antiquity of a segregation of the sexes in a synagogue. See Bernadette Brooten, *Women Leaders in the Ancient Synagogue: Inscriptional Evidence and Background Issues*, BJS 36 (Chico: Scholars Press, 1982), 133–34.

43. *Contempl.* 40–63 contains a satirical description of all kinds of deviant meals, including the symposium of Xenophon and Plato. See Standhartinger, "The School of Moses at Table: Sympotic Teaching in Philo's *De vita contemplativa*," *LTQy* 47 (2017): 67–84.

44. *Contempl.* 63.

45. Lucian shows a similar seating arrangement for a wedding feast (*Symp.* 8).

46. The food is mentioned twice with some difference in *Contempl.* 73. 82. Hyssop is called a luxury taken only by some in the first place. For *Contempl.* 82 see below.

47. Cf. Dennis E. Smith, *From Symposium to Eucharist. The Banquet in the Early Christian World* (Minneapolis: Fortress Press 2003).
48. *Spec.* 2.62.
49. *Mos.* 2.215–6; *Spec.* 2.62.
50. *Contempl.* 68.
51. *Contempl.* 74.
52. *Contempl.* 81.
53. Philo does not name the temple in Jerusalem here, however, one is reminded to the table with the Bread of the Presence according to Ex 25:30. Lev 24:7LXX mentions also salt on this table. Cf. *Mos.* 2.104.
54. Cf. Plato, *Symp.* 176a; 181a; 214b; Xenophon, *Symp.* 3.1; 7.1. Plutarch, *Sept. sap. conv.* 157e; *quaest. conv.* 704c–706e etc.; Athenaeus, *Deipn.* 14.8–43 (617f–639a).
55. *Contempl.* 80. All Translations are taken from F. H. Colson, LCL.
56. Peter Jeffery, "Philo's Impact on Christian Psalmody," in *Psalms in Community: Jewish and Christian Textual, Liturgical, and Artistic Traditions*, SBLSS 25, eds. Harold W. Attridge and Margot E. Fassler (Atlanta: Society of Biblical Literature, 2003), 147–87.
57. Ibid 166.
58. Goff, *Citizen Bacchae*, 289–370, quotation at 290.
59. Everett Ferguson, "The Art of Praise: Philo and Philodemus on Music," in *Early Christianity and Classical Culture: Comparative Studies in Honor of Abraham J. Malherbe*, eds. John T. Fitzgerald et al., NovTSup 110 (Leiden: Brill, 2003), 391–426. Philo calls the composer of biblical psalms ὑμνογράφος (*Gig.* 17; *Agr.* 50) and ὑμνῳδός (Philo, *Det.* 74; *Plant.* 39; *Conf.* 59), but only here he states that the psalms are acutely composed "in all sorts of meters and melodies," hexameter and trimeter (*Contempl.* 29; 80).
60. *Contempl.* 89; cf. 11. In *Contempl.* 87, Philo explicitly states that both women and men are equally possessed by God (ἐνθουσιῶντές τε ἄνδρες ὁμοῦ καὶ γυναῖκες). Cf. Matthews, *First Converts*, 83–85.
61. Cf. Euripides, *Bacch.* 882; Athenaeus, *Deipn.* 6.55 (250a); 14.6 (647c); 15.7 (668d).
62. *Contempl.* 84–85.
63. Siegmund Levarie, "Philo on Music," *The Journal of Musicology* 9 (1991), 129.
64. *Contempl.* 88.
65. Philo, *Agr.* 82: "The same hymn is sung by both choirs, and it has a most noteworthy refrain, the recurrence of which is strikingly beautiful. It is this: 'Let us sing unto the Lord, for gloriously hath He been glorified; horse and rider He threw into the sea.'" Cf. *Mos.* 2.256. That the men's and the women's choir sing together is already stated in Wis 10:20. See Peter Enns, "A Retelling of the Song at the Sea in Wis 10,10–21," *Bib* 76 (1995): 1–24.
66. Cf. 4Q365 6aII 1–7. Cf. Sidnie White Crawford, "Traditions about Miriam in the Qumran Scrolls," *Studies in Jewish Civilization* 14 (2003): 33–44, 36–37; and H. Tervanotko, "'The Hope of the Enemy Has Perished': The Figure of Miriam in the Qumran Library," in *From Qumran to Aleppo: A Discussion with Emanuel Tov*

about the Textual History of Jewish Scriptures in Honor of his 65th Birthday, eds. A. Lange and M. Weigold, FRLANT 230 (Göttingen: Vandenhoeck & Ruprecht, 2009), 156–75. Cf. Tervanotko, *Denying Her Voice: The Figure of Miriam in Ancient Jewish Literature* (Göttingen: Vandenhoeck, & Ruprecht, 2016), 147–62.

67. For Judith Newman, Philo "provides a picture of what ritual life might be like at some distance from the Temple." Cf. Newman, "The Composition of Prayers and Songs in Philo's *De Vita Contemplativa*," in *Empsychoi Logoi—Religious Innovations in Antiquity: Studies in Honour of Pieter Willem van der Horst*, eds. Alberdina Houtman, Albert de Jong, and Magda Misset-van de Weg, AJEC 73 (Leiden: Brill, 2008), 468.

68. *Contempl.* 22.

69. The link was first noted by Paul Wendland, "Geschichte des hellenistischen Judentums," *Jahrbücher für klassische Philologie, Supplement* 22 (1896), 693–772, 755.

70. See: Ross S. Kraemer, *Unreliable Witnesses: Religion, Gender, and History in the Greco-Roman Mediterranean* (Oxford: Oxford University Press, 2011), 57–115, versus Joan E. Taylor, *Jewish Women Philosophers of First-Century Alexandria. Philo's "Therapeutae" reconsidered* (Oxford: Oxford University Press, 2003).

71. Angela Standhartinger, "Best practice. Religious reformation in Philo's representation of the Therapeutae and Therapeutrides," in *Beyond Priesthood. Religious Entrepreneurs and Innovators in the Roman Empire*, RVV 66, eds. Richard L. Gordon, Georgia Petridou and Jörg Rüpke (Berlin: De Gruyter, 2017), 129–56.

72. Philo presents us with a group of people who live in temple-like houses by a lakeside just south of Alexandria in Egypt, abstain from wine-like sacrificing priests *(Contempl.* 84), share food in reverence to a holy table enshrined in the vestibule of an unnamed temple (*Contempl.* 81), and have ecstatic experiences like bacchanals or corybants (*Contempl.* 12; 85). Only in the last third of the text does Philo mention that the members of the group "have dedicated their own life and themselves to knowledge and the contemplation of the verities of nature, following the truly sacred instructions of the prophet Moses" (*Contempl.* 64). Cf. Standhartinger, "Best practice," 147–49.

73. The Greek text of P, preserved in two manuscripts from the eleventh and sixteenth centuries, is edited by Sebastian P. Brock, *Testamentum Jobi*, PVTG 2 (Leiden: Brill, 1967). A second edition on the basis of manuscript S (1307 CE) and V (thirteenth century) is edited by Robert A. Kraft, *The Testament of Job according to the SV Text*, SBLTT 4 (Missoula: SBL Press, 1974). The Coptic papyrus is edited by Gesa Schenke, *Der koptische Kölner Papyruskodex 3221, Teil I: Das Testament des Iob* (Paderborn: Schöningh, 2009) and Schenke, "Neue Fragmente des Kölner Kodex 3221. Textzuwachs am koptischen Testament des Iob," *ZPE* 188 (2014): 87–105. The Coptic papyrus proves that the text must have existed in the fourth century CE. It elaborates on some hymns in T.Job 32–33, 43. Cf. Schenke, *Kölner Papyruscodex*, 21–31. One can speculate how these hymns might have been performed when the text was read aloud. For the Slavonic tradition, see Maria Haralambakis, *The Testament of Job: Text, Narrative and Reception History* (London: Bloomsbury, 2012), 185–212.

74. For the genre, see John J. Collins, "Structure and Meaning in the Testament of Job," *SBLSP* 1 (1974): 37–39. More recently, Robin Waugh ("The Testament of Job as an Example of Profeminine Patience Literature," *JBL* 133 [2014]: 777–92) identifies T.Job as patience literature in the context of ancient discourse on martyrdom, which includes also feminization and admiration of women's patience and endurance.

75. T.Job 4:11. Translation if not indicated, otherwise, R. P. Spittler, OTP. In T.Job 27:1–6 Job challenges Satan to fight openly against him.

76. ὑπομονή κτλ. T.Job 1:5; 4:6; 5:1: μακροθυμία κτλ.: T.Job 11:10; 21:4; 26:5; 27:7; 28:5; 34:4.

77. The name is given as Sitis or Sitidos, the former does not exist elsewhere, that latter would be "giver of bread," a role Job's wife take (cf. Hi 2,9LXX and T.Job 21–25. For the evidence, see: Pieter W. van der Horst, "The Role of Women in the Testament of Job," *NedTT* 40 (1986), 273–89, 275–76.

78. For humor in T.Job, see: Haralambakis, *Testament,* 174.

79. Cf. T.Job 9–15: 53,1–6.

80. T.Job 14:1–2.

81. See, e.g., the lament for Sitidos in T.Job 25.

82. Schenke and Schenke Robinson, *Papyruskodex*, 21–31.

83. Some read T.Job as a midrash to biblical inherence law in the light of Job 42:15. Cf. Peter Machinist, "Job's Daughters and their Inheritance in the Testament of Job and its Biblical Congeners," in *The Echoes of Many Texts. Reflections on Jewish and Christian Traditions Essays in Honor of Lou H. Silberman*, ed. William G. Dever and J. Edward Wright, BJS 313. (Atlanta: Scholars,1997), 67–80.

84. In Greek mythology, Amaltheias is the name of the goat that suckled Zeus. In Roman, the cornucopia stands for nourishment and abundance.

85. Dan 10:5; Ezek 9:2, 10; Rev 1:13; 15:6; Apoc. Zeph. 6:12; Acts Pet. 12 Apos. (NHC VI 1) 2. Cf. Heike Omerzu, "Das bessere Erbe. Die privilegierte Stellung der Töchter Hiobs im Testament Hiobs," in *Körper und Kommunikation. Beiträge aus der theologischen Genderforschung*, eds. Katharina Greschat and Heike Omerzu (Leipzig: Eva, 2003), 80–85.

86. Cf. Rebecca Lesses, "Amulets and Angels: Visionary Experience in the Testament of Job and the Hekhalot Literature," in *Heavenly Tablets: Interpretation, Identity and Tradition in Ancient Judaism*, ed. Lynn LiDonnici and Andrea Lieber, JSJSup 119 (Leiden: Brill, 2007), 49–74.

87. T.Job 47:11.

88. T.Job 48:2–4. The Coptic papyrus reads the Greek loanword στήλη (monument) instead of στολή (garment). The Slavonic version reads: "When she completed the angelic song, she rejoiced and stopped."

89. T.Job 49:1–3.Again the Slavonic tradition skips the last verse. 49:3 reads: "She sang praise to the highest, as no single human can say, songs say Kasia."

90. It is not obvious whether T.Job thinks of one or many angelic languages by referring to ἀγγελική διάλεκτος (48:3), διάλεκτος τῶν ἀρχῶν (49:2), διάλεκτος τῶν ἐν ὕψει (50:1), and διάλεκτος τῶν Χερουβιμ. Zephania and Abraham are also taught angelic languages (Apoc. Zeph. 8:4; Apoc. Ab. 17).

91. T.Job 52:1–10.

92. 2 Chr 9:11; ψ 42:4; 80:3 (LXX). As an instrument of the heavenly worship service, see Rev 5:8; 14:2; 15:2.
93. Exod 15:20; Judg 11:34; 1 Sam 18:6; Jer 38:4 (LXX); Jdt 16:1
94. For an overview, see Maria Haralambakis, "'I Am Not Afraid of Anybody, I Am the Ruler of This Land': Job as Man in Charge in the Testament of Job," in *Men and Masculinity in the Hebrew Bible and Beyond*, ed. Ovodopi Creangă (Sheffield: Sheffield Phoenix, 2010), 127–28; and Nancy Klancher, "Female Soul in Drag: Women-as-Job in the 'Testament of Job,'" *JSP* 19 (2010): 228–31.
95. van der Horst, "Role," 281–89.
96. Susan R. Garrett, "The 'Weaker Sex' in the Testament of Job," *JBL* 112 (1993): 55–70; Robert A. Kugler and Richard L. Rohrbaugh, "On Women and Honor in the Testament of Job," *JSP* 14 (2004): 43–62.
97. Klancher, "The Male Soul," 225–45. Cf. Emily O. Gravett, "Biblical Responses: Past and Present Retellings of the Enigmatic Mrs. Job," *BibInt* 20 (2012): 97–125.
98. Klancher, "Male," 236.
99. Ibid. 237.
100. Already Kaufman Kohler placed the writing among the writings of Philo's Therapeutae. Cf. "The Testament of Job: An Essene Midrasch on the Book of Job Reedited and Translated with Introductory and Exegetical Notes," in *Semitic Studies in Memory of Rev. Dr. Alexander Kohut*, ed. Georg A. Kohut [Berlin: Calvery 1897], 264–338. Others look for mystic groups in Hekhalot literature. See, e.g., Rebecca Lesses, "The Daughters of Job," in *Searching the Scriptures II: A Feminist Commentary*, ed. Elisabeth Schüssler Fiorenza (New York: Crossroad, 1994), 144–45.
101. Cf. Lesses, "Daughters," 144, who thinks of women who held synagogue offices.
102. Stehle, *Performance*, 113.

BIBLIOGRAPHY

Bielman, Anne. "Female Patronage in the Greek Hellenistic and Roman Republican Periods." In *A Companion to Women in the Ancient World*, edited by Sharon L. James and Sheila Dillon, 238–48. Chichester: Blackwell Publishing Ltd, 2012.
Brock, Sebastian P. *Testamentum Jobi*. PVTG 2. Leiden: Brill, 1967.
Brooten, Bernadette. *Women Leaders in the Ancient Synagogue: Inscriptional Evidence and Background Issues*, BJS 36. Chico: Scholars Press, 1982.
Calame, Claude. *Choruses of Young Women in Ancient Greece. Their Morphology, Religious Role, and Social Function*. Lanham: Rowman & Littlefield 1997. [French original 1977].
Cole, Susan G. *Landscapes, Gender, and Ritual Space. The Ancient Greek Experience*. Berkeley et. al.: California University Press, 2004.
Collins, John J. "Structure and Meaning in the Testament of Job." *SBLSP* 1 (1974): 36–52.
Colson, H. *Philo in Ten Volumes VII*. Cambridge: Harvard University Press, 1984.

Connelly, Joan B. "Priestesses—Women in Cult. In Divine Affairs—the Greatest Part: Women and Priesthoods in Classical Athens." In *Worshiping Women. Ritual and Reality in Classical Athens*, edited by Nikolaos Kaltsas and Alan Shapiro, 186–241. New York: Alexander S. Onassis Public Benefit Foundation, 2008.

———. *Portrait of a Priestess. Women and Ritual in Ancient Greece*. Princeton: Princeton University Press, 2007.

Crawford, Sidnie White. "Traditions about Miriam in the Qumran Scrolls." *Studies in Jewish Civilization* 14 (2003): 33–44.

Dillon, Matthew. *Girls and Women in Classical Greek Religion*. London: Routledge, 2002.

Enns, Peter. "A Retelling of the Song at the Sea in Wis 10,10–21." *Bib* 76 (1995): 1–24.

Ferguson, Everett. "The Art of Praise. Philo and Philodemus on Music." In *Early Christianity and Classical Culture. Comparative Studies in honor of Abraham J. Malherbe*, edited by John T. Fitzgerald et al., 391–426. Leiden: Brill, 2003.

Garrett, Susan R. "The 'Weaker Sex' in the Testament of Job." *JBL* 112 (1993): 55–70.

Goff, Barbara. *Citizen Bacchae: Women's Ritual Practice in Ancient Greece*. Berkeley: University of California Press, 2004.

Gravett, Emily O. "Biblical Responses: Past and Present Retellings of the Enigmatic Mrs. Job." *BibInt* 20 (2012): 97–125.

Grossman, Susan. "Women and the Jerusalem Temple." In *Daughters of the King. Women and the Synagogue*, edited by Rivka Haut, 15–37. Philadelphia: Jewish Publication Society, 1992.

Haralambakis, Maria. "'I Am Not Afraid of Anybody, I Am the Ruler of This Land': Job as Man in Charge in the Testament of Job." In *Men and Masculinity in the Hebrew Bible and Beyond*, edited by Ovodopi Creangă, 127–44. Sheffield: Sheffield Phoenix, 2010.

———. *The Testament of Job. Text, Narrative and Reception History*. London: Bloomsbury, 2012.

Harvey, Susan Ashbrook. "Bearing Witness: New Testament Women in Early Byzantine Hymnography." In *The New Testament in Byzantium*, edited by Derek Krueger and Robert Nelson, 205–19. Cambridge: Harvard University Press, 2016.

———. "Performance as Exegesis. Women's Liturgical Choirs in Syriac Tradition," In *Inquiries into Eastern Christian Worship. Acts of the Second International Congress of the Society of Oriental Liturgy*, edited by Bert J. Groen, Stefanos Alexopoulos and Steven Hawkes-Teeples, 47–64. Leuven: Peeters, 2012.

———. "Singing Women's Stories in Syriac Tradition." *IKZ* 100 (2010): 171–89.

———. *Song and Memory. Biblical Women in Syriac Tradition*. Milwaukee: Marquette University Press, 2010.

Hemelrijk, Emily A. "Women and Sacrifice in the Roman Empire." In *Ritual Dynamics and Religious Change in the Roman Empire*, edited by Olivier Hekster, Sebastian Schmidt-Hofner, and Christian Witschel, 253–68. Leiden: Brill, 2009.

Holland, Lora L. "Women and Roman Religion." In *A Companion to Women in the Ancient World*, edited by Sharon L. James and Sheila Dillon, 204–14. Chichester: Blackwell, 2012.

Klancher, Nancy. "The Male Soul in Drag: Women-as-Job in the 'Testament of Job.'" *JSP* 19 (2010): 225–45.

Kohler, Kaufman. "The Testament of Job: An Essene Midrash on the Book of Job Reedited and Translated with Introductory and Exegetical Notes." In *Semitic Studies in Memory of Rev. Dr. Alexander Kohut*, edited by Georg A. Kohut, 264–338. Berlin: Calvery, 1897.

Kraemer, Ross S. *Unreliable Witnesses: Religion, Gender, and History in the Greco-Roman Mediterranean.* Oxford: Oxford University Press, 2011.

Kraft, Robert A. *The Testament of Job according to the SV Text.* SBLTT 4. Missoula: SBL Press, 1974.

Kugler, Robert A., and Richard L. Rohrbaugh."On Women and Honor in the Testament of Job." *JSP* 14 (2004): 43–62.

Jeffrey, Peter. "Philo's Impact on Christian Psalmody." In *Psalms in Community. Jewish and Christian Textual, Liturgical, and Artistic Traditions*, edited by Harold W. Attridge and Magot E. Fassler, 147–88. Atlanta: SBL Press, 2004.

Lesses, Rebecca. "Amulets and Angels: Visionary Experience in the Testament of Job and the Hekhalot Literature," In *Heavenly Tablets: Interpretation, Identity and Tradition in Ancient Judaism*, edited by Lynn LiDonnici and Andrea Lieber, 49–74. Leiden: Brill, 2007.

———. "The Daughters of Job." In *Searching the Scriptures II: A Feminist Commentary*, edited by Elisabeth Schüssler Fiorenza, 139–49. New York: Crossroad, 1994.

Levarie, Siegmund. "Philo on Music," *The Journal of Musicology* 9 (1991): 124–30.

Lingas, Alexander. "Liturgy, Byzantine." *The Encyclopedia of Ancient History* 8: 4116.

Lyons, Deborah J. "The Scandal of Women's Ritual." In *Finding Persephone. Women's Rituals in the Ancient Mediterranean*, edited by Maryline Parca and Angeliki Tzanetou, 29–51. Bloomington: Indiana University Press, 2007.

———. "What the Women Know": In *Women's Ritual Competence in the Greco-Roman Mediterranean*, edited by Matthew Dillon, Esther Eidinow, and Lisa Maurizio, 229–40. London/ New York: Routledge, 2016.

McVey, Kathleen, "Ephrem the Kitharode and Proponent of Women. Jacob of Serug's Portrait of a Fourth-Century Churchman for the Sixth-Century Viewer and its Significance for the Twenty-First Century Ecumenist." In *Orthodox and Wesleyan Ecclesiology*, edited by S. T. Kimbrough, 229–53. Crestwood: St Vladimirs Seminary, 2007.

Matthews, Shelly. *First Converts: Rich Pagan Women and the Rhetoric of Mission in Early Judaism and Christianity.* Stanford: Stanford University Press, 2001.

Newman, Judith. "The Composition of Prayers and Songs in Philo's *De Vita Contemplativa*," in *Empsychoi Logoi—Religious Innovations in Antiquity: Studies in Honour of Pieter Willem van der Horst*, edited by Alberdina Houtman, Albert de Jong, and Magda Misset-van de Weg, 457–68. Leiden: Brill, 2008.

Noethlichs, Karl Leo. "Liturgie I." *RAC* 23: 208–90.

Omerzu, Heike. "Das bessere Erbe. Die privilegierte Stellung der Töchter Hiobs im Testament Hiobs." In *Körper und Kommunikation. Beiträge aus der theologischen*

Genderforschung, edited by Katharina Greschat and Heike Omerzu, 57–93. Leipzig: Eva, 2003.

Quasten, Johannes. *Musik und Gesang in den Kulten der heidnischen Antike und christlichen Frühzeit.* Münster: Aschendorff, 1930.

Rhodes, Peter J. "Liturgy I Political." *Brill's New Pauly online* http://dx.doi.org/10.1163/1574-9347_bnp_e707770 (18th of February, 2018).

Schenke, Gesa. "Neue Fragmente des Kölner Kodex 3221. Textzuwachs am koptischen Testament des Iob." *ZPE* 188 (2014): 87–105.

Schenke, Gesa, and Gesine Schenke Robinson. *Der koptische Kölner Papyruskodex 3221, Teil I: Das Testament des Iob.* Paderborn: Schöningh, 2009.

Schultz, Celia E. "Sanctissima Femina: Social Categorization and Women's Religious Experience in the Roman Republic" In *Finding Persephone. Women's Rituals in the Ancient Mediterranean*, edited by Maryline Parca and Angeliki Tzanetou, 92–113. Bloomington: Indiana University Press, 2007.

———. *Women's Religious Activity in the Roman Republic.* Chapel Hill: University of North Carolina Press, 2006.

Smith, Dennis E. *From Symposium to Eucharist. The Banquet in the Early Christian World.* Minneapolis: Fortress Press, 2003.

Standhartinger, Angela."Best Practice. Religious Reformation in Philo's Representation of the Therapeutae and Therapeutrides." In *Beyond Priesthood. Religious Entrepreneurs and Innovators in the Roman Empire*, edited by Richard L. Gordon, Georgia Petridou and Jörg Rüpke, 129–56. Berlin: De Gruyter, 2017.

———. "The School of Moses at Table: Sympotic Teaching in Philo's *De vita contemplative.*" *LTQy* 47 (2017): 67–84.

Stehle, Eva M. *Performance and Gender in Ancient Greece. Nondramatic Poetry in its Setting.* Princeton: University of Princeton Press, 1997.

———. "Women and Religion in Greece." In *A Companion to Women in the Ancient World*, edited by Sharon L. James and Sheila Dillon, 191–203. Chichester: Blackwell Publishing, 2012.

Taylor, Joan E. *Jewish Women Philosophers of First-Century Alexandria. Philo's "Therapeutae" reconsidered.* Oxford: Oxford University Press, 2003.

Tervanotko, Hanna. *Denying Her Voice: The Figure of Miriam in Ancient Jewish Literature.* Göttingen: Vandenhoeck, & Ruprecht, 2016.

———. "The Hope of the Enemy Has Perished': The Figure of Miriam in the Qumran Library." In *From Qumran to Aleppo: A Discussion with Emanuel Tov about the Textual History of Jewish Scriptures in Honor of his 65th Birthday*, edited by Armin Lange and Matthias Weigold, 156–75. Göttingen: Vandenhoek & Ruprecht, 2009.

van der Horst, Pieter W. "The Role of Women in the Testament of Job." *NedTT* 40 (1986): 273–89.

Waugh, Robin. "The Testament of Job as an Example of Profeminine Patience Literature." *JBL* 133 (2014): 777–92.

Wendland, Paul. "Geschichte des hellenistischen Judentums." *Jahrbücher für klassische Philologie*, Supplement 22 (1896): 693–772.

Index

Achtemeier, Elizabeth, 41n8
Ackenheil, Katharina, 215n46
Adler, William, 165n19
Alexander, Loveday, 164n12
Alexandridis, Annetta, 215n37
Alston, Richard, 81n21
Alter, Robert, 94n10
Anderson, Benedict, 151n49
Anderson, Janice Capel, 132n13
Anderson, Matthew, 15n1
Arnal, William, 41n12, 60n9
Ashbrook Harvey, Susan, 223, 232n28, 232nn30–34
Aslan, Reza, 45, 46
Atkinson, Kenneth, 183n10

Bachmann-Medick, Doris, 82n42
Baden, Joel S., 60n23
Baker, Cynthia M., 4, 17n16, 57, 61n39, 62nn40–41
Barker, James, 50, 61n27
Baron, Solo Wittmayer, 26
Bartchy, Scott S., 80n18
Bartlett, John, 164n7
Barton, Carlin, 70, 80n17, 81nn23–24
Baskin, Judith, 90–91, 96n38
Bassler, Jouette M., 98n49, 98n60
Batnitzky, Leora, 17n16
Batten, Alicia, 31

Bätz, Alexander, 215n46
Bauernfeind, Otto, 214n30
Baumgarten, Albert, 78, 83n50
Baumgarten, Joseph, 167n38
Beatrice, Pier Franco, 163n4, 165n22
Becker, Adam H., 88, 95n24
Bergmann, Claudia D., 213n23
Bernstein, Moshe J., 111, 113n43
Bielman, Anne, 230n3
Bird, Phyllis, 112n12
Blickenstaff, Marianne, 137, 148n5
Boccaccini, Gabriele, 81n39, 148n2
Borchardt, Francis, 14, 18n27, 155–170
Boxel, Piet van, 107, 112n2, 113n42
Boyarin, Daniel, 16n9, 16n15, 80n10
Brant, Jo-Ann A., 150n37
Brawley, Robert, 80n8
Brock, Sebastian P., 235n73
Brooten, Bernadette, 14, 17n22, 23–30, 38, 233n42
Brown, Raymond E., 95n26, 137, 139, 143–145, 148n3, 149nn9–12, 150n40
Buitenwerk, Rieuwerd, 163nn2–3, 165n23
Burrus, Virginia, 15n4, 39
Butler, Judith, 15n3, 101, 112nn3–4

Calame, Claude, 232n20
Camp, Claudia V., 132n12

Carlos, Segovia, 81n39
Chesnutt, Randall, 114n67
Christensen, Joel, 94n14
Clarke, John R., 215n37
Cohen, Shaye J.D., 16n15
Cole, Susan G., 231n14
Collins, John J., 114n63, 163n3, 164n5, 165n20, 165n25, 166n29, 236n74
Colson, Francis Henry, 230n10
Connell, Raewyn, 102, 112nn5–6, 112n9
Connelly, Joan B., 230nn6–7, 232n17
Conway, Colleen, 143, 150n36
Conzelmann, Hans, 96n27, 97n41
Corley, Jeremy, 89, 96n32
Corley, Kathleen E., 60n19
Cotter, Wendy, 33
Crenshaw, Kimberlé, 16n8
Croom, Alexandra T., 215n35
Crossan, John Dominic, 48, 60n18
Culpepper, R. Alan, 151n48
Curley, Christine, 94n18

D'Angelo, Mary Rose, 139, 149n13
Degele, Nina, 132n13, 133n17
Deleuze, Gilles, 82n51
Denis, Albert-Marie, 165n19
Deppmeyer, Korana, 215n36
Derrida, Jacques, 18n35
Destro, Adriana, 57, 62nn42–43
Dibelius, Martin, 96n27, 97n41
Dillon, Matthew, 230n7
Dillon, Sheila, 27
Dimant, Devorah, 114n64
Dohrmann, Nathalie B., 79nn3–4
Dowell, Thomas M., 35
Dubischar, Markus, 156–159, 164nn13–17, 165n21
Duby, Georges, 40n4
Duncan, Carrie, 25

Ehrensperger, Kathy, 1, 14, 18n34, 65–84
Ehrman, Bart, 165n19
Eisen, Ute E., 40n4

Endres, John, 106, 112n2, 113n34, 113n36, 134nn36–37
Enns, Peter, 234n65
Erbse, Hartmut, 163n4, 164nn8–9

Fehribach, Adeline, 144, 148n6, 150n38
Fein, Sarah E.G., 14, 85–100, 114n60
Ferguson, Everett, 234n59
Fiore, Benjamin, 18n29
Foley, Helen, 230n6
Fowl, Steven, 82n41
Foxhall, Lin, 79n5, 80n14
Franke, Edith, 133n16
Fredriksen, Paula, 60n22, 81n39
Freund, Stefan, 165n22
Frey, Jörg, 88, 95n25
Freyne, Sean, 58, 62n44, 62n46
Fricker, Denis, 41n12
Fuchs, Esther, 104, 108, 112nn15–16, 112n18, 113n22, 113nn28–29, 114nn52–53

Garrett, Susan R., 237n96
Geffcken, Johannes, 156, 163n2, 163n4, 164n6, 164n11
Gelardini, Gabriella, 15, 196–217
Gildemeister, Regine, 132n4, 132n13, 133n18
Gillingham, Susan, 132n14
Gilmore, David, 80n15
Glancy, Jennifer A., 18n31, 80n19, 81n27
Glass, Gillian, 114n60
Gleason, Maud W., 80n14
Goff, Barbara, 230n7, 232n21, 234n58
Goodacre, Mark, 61n26
Goulder, Michael, 95n22
Gravett, Emily O., 237n97
Graybill, Rhiannon, 162, 167n41
Grice, Paul, 157, 164nn17–18
Grossman, Susan, 27, 233n38
Guattari, Félix, 82n51
Gunderson, Erik, 81n31
Gurtner, Daniel M., 98n51
Gutzwiller, Kathryn, 180, 184n15

Haddox, Susan, 112n7, 113n24
Halpern-Amaru, Betsy, 109, 112n2, 113n39, 113n45, 114n57, 114n68, 120, 129, 133n18, 133n31, 134nn34–36, 134nn39–40, 134nn43–46, 134nn49–51
Haralambakis, Maria, 235n73, 236n78, 237n94
Harrington, Daniel, 18n29
Harrison, James R., 79n7, 80n9, 80n13
Hartin, Patrick John, 33
Hauptman, Judith, 96n36, 142, 149n30
Hemelrijk, Emily A., 232n17
Henten, Jan W. van, 81n35
Hericks, Katja, 132n4, 132n13, 133n18
Hezser, Catherine, 82n47
Ho, Sin-Pan Daniel, 81n33
Hoffmann, Paul, 34
Holland, Lola L., 230n7
Holmes, Brook, 79n5
Hooker, Mischa, 165n22
Horst, Pieter W. van der, 236n77, 237n95
Howes, Llewellyn, 33
Hubbard, Moyer, 97n40
Humphrey, Edith McEwan, 17n24
Hutson, Christopher, 88, 96n28, 96n35, 98n59

Ilan, Tal, 15, 30, 56, 61n36, 62n46, 183n9, 183nn11–12, 185–195

James, Sharon, 27
Jassen, Alex, 167n38
Jeansonne, Sharon Pace, 113n20
Jeffery, Peter, 225, 234nn56–57
Jeremias, Joachim, 41n11
Johnson Hodge, Caroline, 10, 18n33
Johnson, Timothy, 96n27, 98n54

Kalantzis, George, 95n22
Kautzsch, Emil, 94nn6–7
Keith, Chris, 38, 150n31
Klancher, Nancy, 229, 237n94, 237nn97–99

Kloppenborg, John S., 33, 34, 41n13
Knight, George W., 97n40
Kobel, Esther, 82n52
Kohler, Kaufman, 237n100
Köstenberger, Margaret Elizabeth, 143, 150n32
Koukouli-Chrysanthaki, Chaido, 79n2
Kraemer, Ross, 12, 18n38, 27, 235n70
Kraft, Robert A., 235n73
Krauss, Samuel, 26
Krieger, Leonard, 167n36
Krone, Kerstin von der, 17n17
Kugler, Robert A., 237n96
Küster, Ludolph, 167n32
Kvam, Kristen E., 93n2

Le Donne, Anthony, 150n31
Lefkovitz, Lori Hope, 113n27
Lesses, Rebecca, 236n86, 237nn100–101
Levarie, Siegmund, 234n63
Levine, Amy-Jill, 14, 18n32, 28, 31, 40n3, 45–64, 137, 142–143, 145, 148n5, 149n27, 150n33
Levine, Lee I., 27, 29
Lingas, Alexander, 231n5
Link, Hannelore, 132n14
Lipis, Mimi Levy, 61n38
Lipka, Hilary, 105, 113n23
Lipton, Diana, 133n26
Livneh, Atar, 133n15, 134n32, 134nn47–48
Loader, William, 110, 115n69
Lock, Walter, 97n40
Lopez, Davina C., 12, 19n39, 19n40, 80n19
Lyons, Deborah, 221, 231nn15–16

Machinist, Peter, 236n83
Mack, Burton, 33, 167n34
Malherbe, Abraham J., 92, 98n55
Marjanen, Antti, 168n42
Martyn, J. Louis, 145, 150n43
Maske, Verena, 133n16
Matthews, Shelly, 230n10, 234n60

McDonald, Lee Martin, 17n18
McDonnell, Myles, 80n11, 80n20, 81n22
McDowell, Markus, 114nn58–59
McKnight, Scot, 142, 150n31
McVey, Kathleen, 233n33
Meeks, Wayne, 146, 151n46
Meier, John P., 46–51, 53, 54, 57, 59n1, 59n7, 60nn15–17, 60nn20–21, 60n24, 61n28, 61nn31–33
Merz, Annette, 45
Metzger, Bruce, 36
Meyer-Zwiffelhoffer, Eckhard, 214n31
Meyers, Carol, 40n4, 94n8, 95n18, 119, 132nn2–4, 132n7, 132n9, 132n13, 133n17
Meyers, Eric, 62n44
Michel, Otto, 214n30
Mittmann-Richert, Ulrike, 172, 183n3
Moloney, Francis J., 41n16
Moore, Carey A., 18n30
Mor, Menagem, 16n12
Moss, Candida R., 60n23
Mroczek, Eva, 17n20, 40n6
Mülke, Markus, 165n21
Murphy, Cullen, 40n4

Nagy, Gregory, 165n24
Najman, Hindy, 16n12
Nanos, Mark D., 81n39
Nauck, Augustus, 166n32
Navarro Puerto, Mercedes, 54, 61n29
Neujahr, Matthew, 165n23
Neusner, Jacob, 98n51
Neutel, Karin B., 15n7
Newman, Judith, 235n67
Niditch, Susan, 112n17
Nissinen, Martti, 102, 112n8, 112n11
Noethlichs, Karl Leo, 230n2

Oakes, Peter, 79n2, 80n8
Oegema, Gerbern, 15, 16n10, 41n10, 171–184
Olson, Dennis T., 75, 82n46

Omerzu, Heike, 236n85
Or, Tamara, 61n39
Orton, David E., 212n1
Osiek, Caroline, 62n43

Panella, Clementina, 215n42
Parke, Herbert William, 164n7, 167n40
Parks, Sara, 14, 15n2, 15n7, 23–44, 183n6
Penny, Laurie, 132n2, 132n8
Perrin, Nick, 61n26
Perrot, Michelle, 40n4
Pesce, Mauro, 57, 62nn42–43
Peters, Edward, 194n11
Peterson, Brian, 94n18
Pilhofer, Peter, 80n11
Piper, Ronald A., 33, 41n14, 41n15
Plant, Ian Michael, 179, 183n1, 183nn13–14
Plaskow, Judith, 31, 142, 149n27
Pleše, Zlatko, 165n19
Poirier, John C., 61n26
Porter, Stanley E., 97n40, 97n46, 98n48, 98n58

Quasten, Johannes, 233n34

Rajak, Tessa, 74, 81nn37–38, 81n40
Reed, Annette Yoshiko, 79nn3–4, 88, 95n24
Reinach, Salomon, 25
Reinhartz, Adele, 14, 137–153
Roberts Winsor, Ann, 149n25
Rengstorf, Karl Heinrich, 212nn2–4, 212nn6–8, 212nn10–12
Reynolds, Benjamin E., 17n23, 148n2
Rhodes, Peter J., 230n2
Ricci, Carla, 47, 60n13
Rivkin, Elias, 194n2
Robinson, James, 34
Rohrbaugh, Richard L., 237n96
Romney Wegner, Judith, 90, 96n37
Rooke, Deborah W., 131n2, 132nn10–11

Rosa, Hartmut, 82n43
Rubenstein, Jeffrey L., 16n13
Rudd, Niall, 17n26
Rueter, Marcus, 214n32
Ruiten, Jacques van, 94n15, 134n41
Rzach, Aloisius, 163nn2–3

Sanders, Ed Parish, 98n53
Sanders, James A., 17n18
Sarna, Nahum M., 113n19, 113n25
Sawyer, Deborah, 148n6
Schearing, Linda S., 93n2
Scheinfeld, Shayna, 1–21
Schenke, Gesa, 235n73, 236n83
Schiffman, Lawrence, 167n38
Schmuhl, Yvonne, 215n41
Schneider, Tammi J., 113n21
Schneiders, Sandra, 137, 139–141, 143–145, 148n4, 149nn14–20, 150n39
Schnelle, Udo, 38
Schottroff, Luise, 45, 47, 55, 59n4, 60n14, 61nn34–35
Schubert, Friedemann, 134n32
Schuller, Eileen, 148n1
Schulz, Siegfried, 33, 41n13
Schulzu, Celia E., 232n18
Schürer, Emil, 26
Schüssler Fiorenza, Elisabeth, 11, 15n5, 17n22, 18n27, 18n35, 23, 29–31, 40n4, 137, 139–142, 144–145, 148n4, 149nn21–23, 149nn28–29, 150nn41–42
Schwartz, Daniel R., 16n15, 17n16, 81n35, 175, 183n8
Scott, Martin, 149n24
Seeman, Chris, 59n2
Segal, Michael, 134n33
Seim, Turid, 143, 150n34
Shellard, Barbar, 36
Shemesh, Aharon, 167n38
Sim, David C., 61n30
Simkovich, Malka Z., 16n11
Smend, Rudolf, 96n31
Smith, Dennis E., 234n47

Smith, Roland R.R., 81n25
Snell, Bruno, 166n32
Solevåg, Anna, 92, 95n19, 97nn44–47, 98n56
Standhartinger, Angela, 15, 40n4, 81n32, 219–240
Stegemann, Ekkehard, 143, 146, 150n35
Stegemann, Wolfgang, 143, 146, 150n35
Stehle, Eva M., 230n7, 232n22, 237n102
Steinberg, Naomi, 112n13, 113n26
Stele, Eva, 222
Stuckenbruck, Loren T., 17n24
Sumney, Jerry L., 95n22
Syfox, Chontel, 14, 18n32, 101–117

Taylor, Joan E., 18n35, 235n70
Tervanotko, Hanna, 110, 115n70, 162, 167n41, 234n66
Testuz, Michel, 109, 114n54
Thackeray, Henry St. J., 188, 194n9, 200
Theissen, Gerd, 45
Trebilco, Paul, 87, 95n20, 95nn22–23
Trebolle Barrera, Julio C., 17n19
Trenchard, Warren, 96n31
Trevett, Christine, 168n42
Trible, Phyllis, 94n12

Vaage, Lief, 33
VanderKam, James, 106, 109, 112nn1–2, 113n30, 113nn37–38, 113nn40–41, 113n44, 114nn47–48, 114nn55–56, 114nn61–62, 134n42
Vayntrub, Jacqueline, 160, 167nn34–35, 167n39
Vorpahl, Daniel, 14, 119–136

Wacker, Marie-Theres, 148n1
Wagner, Brigitte, 82n42
Wainwright, Elaine, 62n46
Warren, Meredith J.C., 16n10
Watson, Wilfred G.E., 94n11

Waugh, Robin, 236n74
Weinberg, Magnus, 25
Weitzman, Steven, 17n16
Wendland, Paul, 235n69
Werman, Cana, 167n38
White Crawford, Sidnie, 40n4, 113n43, 234n66
Wieder, Naphtali, 167n38
Wilkinson, John, 148n6
Windisch, Hans, 35

Witherington, Ben, 97n40, 142, 149n26
Wright, Benjamin, 160, 167n37

Yarbro Collins, Adela, 40n4

Zemanek, Evi, 132n14
Zetterholm, Magnus, 81n39
Ziegler, Valarie H., 93n2
Zlotnick, Helena, 114n49, 114n51, 134n32, 134n52

About the Contributors

Francis Borchardt is an associate professor of Hebrew Bible and Jewish Studies at Lutheran Theological Seminary, Hong Kong. He has written broadly on a number of topics relevant to Second-Temple Judaism. His recent research focuses on the production and transmission of knowledge among Jews and non–Jews in the ancient Mediterranean world.

Kathy Ehrensperger is a research professor of New Testament in Jewish Perspective at the Abraham Geiger Kolleg, University of Potsdam, Germany; she previously was reader in New Testament Studies at the School of Theology, Religious Studies and Islamic Studies, University of Wales, Trinity Saint David, UK. Among her publications are: *That We May Be Mutually Encouraged: Feminism and the New Perspective on Paul* (2004); *Paul and the Dynamics of Power: Communication and Interaction in the Early Christ Movement* (2008); *Paul at the Crossroads of Cultures: Theologizing in the Space-Between* (2013); and *Searching Paul: Conversations with the Jewish Apostle to the Nations* (2019). She is the executive editor of the Encyclopedia of Jewish-Christian Relations.

Sarah E. G. Fein is a PhD candidate in the Near Eastern and Judaic Studies Department at Brandeis University in Waltham, MA. Her areas of interest include Hebrew Bible, Judaism and Christianity in late antiquity, and women and gender studies. Sarah's dissertation is on the reception history of biblical mothers in early Jewish art and literature. She lives in Newton, MA with her husband and daughter.

Gabriella Gelardini is a professor of Christianity, Religion, Worldview, and Ethics at Nord University, Norway. Her numerous publications on New

Testament topics—among them gender—and beyond include *Christus militans: Studien zur politisch-militärischen Semantik im Markusevangelium vor dem Hintergrund des ersten jüdisch-römischen Krieges* (NovTSup 165, Brill 2016) and *"Verhärtet eure Herzen nicht": Der Hebräer, eine Synagogenhomilie zu Tischa be-Aw* (BINS 83, Brill 2007). She is also the editor of *Hebrews in Contexts* (together with Harold W. Attridge, AJEC 91, Brill 2016) and *Hebrews: Contemporary Methods—New Insights* (BINS 75, Brill 2005).

Tal Ilan was born in Israel (1956) and has been a professor for Jewish studies at the Freie Universität Berlin since 2003. She has published extensively on gender and Jewish women in late Antiquity. She heads the series *A Feminist Commentary on the Babylonian Talmud*, in which eight commentaries and two introductory volumes have appeared. She herself wrote the commentaries on Tractates Taanit and Hullin. She is also coauthor of the double volume *Josephus and the Rabbis* (that appeared in Hebrew) which gathers and analyzes all parallel narratives found both in Josephus and in rabbinic literature.

Amy-Jill Levine is the university professor of New Testament and Jewish Studies and Mary Jane Werthan Professor of Jewish Studies at Vanderbilt Divinity School and Program in Jewish Studies. Her thirty books include: *The Misunderstood Jew: The Church and the Scandal of the Jewish Jesus*; *Short Stories by Jesus: The Enigmatic Parables of a Controversial Rabbi*; four children's books (with Sandy Sasso); *The Gospel of Luke* (with Ben Witherington III); the thirteen-volume edited *Feminist Companions to the New Testament and Early Christian Literature*; and *The Jewish Annotated New Testament* (coedited with Marc Z. Brettler). In 2019 she became the first Jew to teach New Testament at Rome's Pontifical Biblical Institute.

Gerbern S. Oegema studied Biblical Studies, Jewish Studies, and Religious Studies at the Vrije Universiteit in Amsterdam, the Hebrew University of Jerusalem, and the Freie Universität Berlin. He has been an assistant professor and Privatdozent at the Universität Tübingen and a scholar-in-residence at the Center for Theological Inquiry in Princeton. Since 2002 he is professor of Biblical Studies in the School of Religious Studies at McGill University in Montreal. In his research and teaching he focuses on Second-Temple Judaism and Christian origins. He is the author and coeditor of more than twenty books, editor of the *Oxford Handbook of the Apocrypha*, as well as the coeditor of several book series.

Sara Parks, PhD (McGill University, 2017) is an assistant professor in New Testament Studies at the University of Nottingham. She works on women and gender in the Second-Temple period. She recently published the monograph *Gender in the Rhetoric of Jesus: Women in Q* (2019), and has written on Biblical Studies in the classroom and Harry Potter in the Bible. Her current projects include a textbook on Women in Ancient Judaism and Christianity (coauthored, Routledge) and research on anti-Judaism in feminist New Testament scholarship.

Adele Reinhartz, PhD (McMaster University, 1983) is a professor in the Department of Classics and Religious Studies at the University of Ottawa in Canada. She is the author of numerous books and articles, including: *Befriending the Beloved Disciple: A Jewish Reading of the Gospel of John* (2001); *Jesus of Hollywood* (2007); and *Bible and Cinema: An Introduction* (2013). Her most recent book is *Cast Out of the Covenant: Jews and Anti-Judaism in the Gospel of John*. Adele was the general editor of *The Journal of Biblical Literature* from 2010–2018 and currently serves as vice-president and president-elect (2019–2020) of the Society of Biblical Literature. She was elected to the Royal Society of Canada in 2005 and to the American Academy of Jewish Research in 2014.

Shayna Sheinfeld, PhD (McGill University, 2015) is Honorary Research Scholar at the Sheffield Institute of Interdisciplinary Biblical Studies (SIIBS), University of Sheffield. She has published extensively on ancient Judaism in the first and second centuries CE. Her current projects include a monograph on Leadership in Ancient Judaism and the textbook *Jewish and Christian Women in the Ancient Mediterranean* with Routledge Press (coedited). Dr. Sheinfeld also works with biblical afterlives in popular culture and is currently coediting collections on *Theology and Westworld* (Lexington/Fortress) and *Good Omens and the Bible* (Sheffield Phoenix).

Angela Standhartinger studied Protestant Theology at Frankfurt/Main, Munich and Heidelberg and was a visiting professor at Union Theological Seminary in New York. She has written more than a hundred articles and is author of *Das Frauenbild im Judentum der hellenistischen Zeit. Ein Beitrag anhand von 'Joseph und Aseneth'* (AGJU 26; Leiden et al.: Brill, 1995) and *Studien zur Entstehungsgeschichte und Intention des Kolosserbriefs* (NovTSup 94; Leiden et. al: Brill, 1999). With Ute Eva Eisen and Christine Gerber she edited Doing *Gender—Doing Religion. Fallstudien zur Intersektionalität im frühen Judentum, Christentum und Islam* (WUNT 302; Tübingen: Mohr Siebeck, 2013). Her research interests focus on Jewish Hellenistic Literature, Philo of Alexandria, Paul and deuteropauline literature, and gender studies.

Dr. Chontel Syfox is an assistant professor in the Department of Classical and Ancient Near Eastern Studies at the University of Wisconsin Madison. She received her PhD from the University of Notre Dame, where she subsequently served as a Mellon Postdoctoral Teaching Fellow. Dr. Syfox also holds an MTS from Emory University, where she was a Robert T. Jones Graduate Fellow, and a First Class Honours MTheol from the University of St Andrews. She has published peer-reviewed articles on the Book of Jubilees in both the English and Chinese languages. Dr. Syfox was named a national winner of the 2018 Society of Biblical Literature Regional Scholar Award.

Daniel Vorpahl is currently a research assistant for Hebrew Bible and Jewish Exegesis at the School of Jewish Theology/University of Potsdam. His main fields of research are literary gender construction, digitalized text analysis, discourse analytical reception study, and biblical motifs in narrative literature. Daniel Vorpahl studied Jewish Studies, Religious Studies and Comparative Literature at the University of Potsdam. In 2019 he did his PhD in Judaistic at the University of Bamberg on *A Discourse Analytical Study of the Early Jewish and Rabbinic Reception of the Book of Jonah.*

www.ingramcontent.com/pod-product-compliance
Lightning Source LLC
Chambersburg PA
CBHW050901300426
44111CB00010B/1337